Build Your Own
LOG HOME FROM SCRATCH
SECOND EDITION

Build Your Own
LOG HOME FROM SCRATCH

SECOND EDITION

S. BLACKWELL DUNCAN

TAB **TAB BOOKS Inc.**
Blue Ridge Summit, PA

SECOND EDITION
SECOND PRINTING

Copyright © 1988 by TAB BOOKS Inc.
First Edition copyright © 1978 by TAB BOOKS Inc.
Printed in the United States of America

Library of Congress Cataloging in Publication Data

Duncan, S. Blackwell.
    Build your own log home from scratch / by S. Blackwell Duncan. —
2nd ed.
        p. cm.
    Rev. ed. of: How to build your own log home & cabin from scratch.
1st ed. c1978.
    Includes index.
    ISBN 0-8306-9481-1   ISBN 0-8306-9081-6 (pbk.)
    1. Log cabins—Design and construction. I. Duncan, S. Blackwell.
How to build your own log home & cabin from scratch. II. Title.
TH4840.D85   1988
694'.2—dc19   88-17063
                              CIP

TAB BOOKS Inc. offers software for sale. For information and a catalog, please contact TAB Software Department, Blue Ridge Summit, PA 17294-0850.

Questions regarding the content of this book
should be addressed to:

    Reader Inquiry Branch
    TAB BOOKS Inc.
    Blue Ridge Summit, PA 17294-0214

Front and back cover photographs courtesy of Real Log Homes, P.O. Box 202, Hartland, VT 05028. Telephone toll-free 1-800-732-5564 or 436-2123 from within Vermont.

Contents

Introduction

LOG CABINS HAVE BEEN AROUND FOR CENTURIES. Over the decades, while log cabins continued as temporary dwellings, hunting lodges, and vacation retreats, they slowly evolved into full-blown primary residences as well, many of them of no mean proportions and comfort. Today there is a growing popularity for many reasons, of log houses as permanent dwelling places—homes in the true sense of the word.

Some of these log houses are professionally designed and built by a contractor, but many are bought in predesigned, pre-engineered kit form. A surprising number of log houses—some of them very large—are also being owner-built from scratch, beginning even as early in the construction sequence as selecting the trees in a woodlot. This book is for, and is dedicated to, those ambitious do-it-yourselfers who want to build their own log cabins or houses, or at least take an active part in the process.

In this revised and updated second edition of *Building Your Own Log Home From Scratch*, there is an entire chapter about log houses and cabins in general, their pros and cons, and the economics involved. There is also a wealth of information on such crucial matters as house design and planning, site selection, and site work. The real meat of the book, however, lies in the subsequent chapters, which explore the many design options and construction techniques involved in putting a log structure together, regardless of its size, shape, or purpose.

There is information on felling, curing, shaping, and preserving logs. The various types of foundations and how to make them are covered. You will learn how to set sills, build floor frames, construct log walls, and fashion corners and endwork. Second-story construction details are also considered, along with several methods of making roof frames and finishing the roof itself. There is a whole chapter on doors and windows, another on insulation, and a third on some of the more important aspects of interior construction. All of the latter information emphasizes those points that are peculiar to log construction.

There are, of course, other designs, styles, techniques, decorative effects, constructions and construction techniques, materials, ideas, and general practices and procedures than those mentioned in this book. After all, log construction is a hugely diverse field and subject to a lot of personal interpretation, ingenuity, inventiveness, and expression, especially when viewed on a worldwide basis. That is one of its great fascinations. However, the basics of what you need to know about log construction to be able to successfully design, build, supervise the building of, or just intelligently select a new log cabin or house for yourself is between these covers.

About Log Houses

MENTION OF A LOG CABIN IMMEDIATELY BRINGS to mine a rustic structure, sometimes painstakingly constructed of hand-hewn and fitted logs capped with a roof of riven shingles—a dwelling nestled comfortably in splendid isolation among great whispering pines. The simple but stout plank door and single window with the firelight flickering behind face forward into a small clearing, the fruits of months of hard labor. This is Home, a bulwark against the cold hard world, a symbol of the eternal struggles of man against nature.

A farfetched picture? Not really. The log cabin is an integral part of our culture. More than 150 years ago, the log cabin was indicative of the American pioneering spirit, of the solid, down-to-earth philosophy and wisdom of the countryman. This feeling was so genuine and for decades so deeply ingrained in our national consciousness that anyone without a log cabin background, especially in the West, was immediately a bit suspect and thought perhaps not to be a true homespun American. This was a false and baseless notion, but nonetheless a common one.

HISTORY

Despite the part it plays in our culture, the log cabin was by no means an American invention. Log cabins and other log structures had been used for shelter and storage in other parts of the world for centuries before the discovery of America. They were common in the sixteenth and seventeenth centuries in the Scandinavian countries, particularly in Sweden, and in Germany and other parts of Europe.

Contrary to common belief, log cabins were not among the first structures erected when this country was colonized early in the 1600s. In the first place, most of the early settlers were not all that familiar with log construction; they were attuned to entirely different types of buildings and surroundings.

1

In the second place, tools and equipment were in short supply, and so was time and manpower for the amount of work that had to be done just for the sake of survival. The first homes were mere shelters, pitched up from anything that would offer the most protection with the least amount of work. Tents were common and so were huts, and many of the more enterprising folks opted for wigwams patterned after the native Indian dwellings. When time, energy, tools, and materials finally did permit, the more permanent structures copied the familiar English cottages and similar European styles that the settlers had known from childhood. In the early colonies, the log cabin was a late arrival.

As near as can be determined, the first log structures (other than occasional log palisades or stockades erected for protection against native Indians and wildlife) appeared in the Delaware Bay area around 1638. These were built by Swedish and German immigrants and consisted mainly of fully round, saddle-notched logs chinked with wattle (a mixture of twigs and clay) and equipped with stone fireplaces topped with mud-and-stick chimneys. From that location, the log cabin spread in all directions with the increasing influx of settlers, and in a relatively short time log cabins were to be found wherever the white man took up residence.

Log cabins became particularly common all through the South, where they served both as permanent dwellings and as quarters for slaves. These cabins were also made with saddle-notched round logs, but frequently were left unchinked and with substantial gaps between the logs. Most New England cabins were of somewhat later origin. Because of the far more inclement winter weather, they were carefully and tightly made from square-hewn logs thoroughly chinked up and plastered over at the joints, and often with intricate compound-dovetail notching at the corners. Small, rugged cabins were introduced early on in the Northwest by Russian fur trappers, long

before the territory was really opened up. Meanwhile, as the East marched West in the pioneer movement, more cabins were built, first by the trappers, hunters, and miners, then by the farmers and ranchers. As the land became more settled, the small and often crude log cabin gave way to much larger, more comfortable, and more impressive ranch houses, many of which are occupied to this day.

Log construction was not confined only to homes. A great many of the early forts were of log, primarily because of their strength and impenetrability. Many trading posts (which often doubled as forts) were built from logs, as were farm and ranch outbuildings, taverns, stage stops or roadhouses, hotels, saloons, and other commercial buildings.

Although many log homes, especially the smaller and more austere cabins, were meant to be only temporary until something more stylish and commodious could be built, others were designed as permanent residences, carefully made and well appointed. Many, in fact, were so well put together that they still stand, forgotten and forlorn some 100 years after last having been occupied. Some are still sound enough that they have been resurrected and refurbished over the past decade or so.

There are many reasons for the building of log homes and their widespread popularity in the earlier years of this country. Chief among them was a desire for immediate and substantial shelter that could be quickly and readily, even though laboriously, put together. Second was the widespread availability of the raw material, usually free for the taking—pioneers and settlers often found themselves completely surrounded by the tremendous virgin forests that covered a large part of this country. A third reason was that sufficient land had to be cleared so crops could be raised for food. Because the trees had to be cut anyway, logic demanded that the logs be put to some useful purpose. Because in the early days there were few, if any, sawmills, and boards and planks were difficult to fashion and either expensive or impossible to buy, the logs were used whole. This procedure was aided by the facts that good logging equipment and sharp cutting tools were scarce; time and labor had to be put to the most effective use; and the fasteners necessary for plank construction were expensive, difficult to obtain, and heavy to transport.

As the years went by, all of these reasons diminished in importance, and fewer log homes were constructed. Yet they never died out completely. Even in the dark days of the Depression in the 1930s, some log buildings were being erected, primarily because both logs and labor were terribly cheap in some regions of the country.

Today the historic reasons for building log structures have almost disappeared, but the log home has not. Instead, there has been a recent surprisingly large resurgence of interest, involving not only small one- and two-room cabins for hunting camps, but also vacation homes and modern, year-round residences. Most of the year-round residences are substantial in size and contain all the latest conveniences, and some can only be described as palatial. The early log cabin architecture has been modified and upgraded to produce some remarkably handsome homes in which their owners rightfully take an immense amount of pride. What is the reason for this turnabout?

Part of the answer lies in the current and fairly widespread partial rejection of lifestyles that are entirely conventional. There is a restlessness, a sense of being at least partly unable or unwilling to cope with the awesome technological, sociopolitical, and economic complexities of our society, that has led to a yearning for the simpler and more bucolic life of years past. Many people have formed a desire for a more quiet and less stressful existence that most of us must contend with these days. This has prompted the "back to the land" movement of the past several years. It is a fact that at least a small part of the population is returning to rural and even rustic living. For some, a log cabin or home symbolizes this lifestyle.

There is also a marked desire on the part of many for increased self-reliance and the opportunity to do for oneself as much as possible. Self-dependence and a significant renewed interest in handicrafts (albeit often machine-assisted), have made the log cabin or house a natural choice.

However, the number of persons pursuing this lifestyle doesn't account for the great number of large and complex log homes that have been erected over the past few years, often at a considerable cost and entirely by contract labor, sometimes on speculation by a commercial builder, and frequently in suburban or even urban settings. There are even entire subdivisions today that allow log homes only, with the homes being built by a developer and placed on the open market with great success. So other factors are at work as well.

One factor is cost, because under certain conditions and with certain designs and construction methods a log home can be had for less cost than a comparable home of standard frame construction. Note, however, that the reverse is often true as well. Another factor is the desire to own a home that is somewhat different in appearance—at least outwardly and perhaps inwardly as well—than the much more conventional styles. Or, the owners might desire to live in a home that is a modern-day symbol of our log-cabin culture and heritage, evocative again of the yearnings for the days of our pioneer ancestors.

Perhaps the most obvious factor, however, is that the log cabin or log home has its own definite, unique charm, and character, and beauty that are fully brought out when the home is correctly built and tastefully furnished. The natural beauty of solid wood as a building material—honest and straightforward and without the synthetic aspects of plastic and chrome—also appeals to many. The fact that the very nature of log buildings allows for a wide variety of both interior and exterior decorating styles is another drawing card, as is great flexibility of design.

So for these and many other reasons—

strength, solidity, and practicality, for example—the log home is alive and well these days, and is unquestionably a viable and worthwhile building type that deserves serious consideration by any persons interested in owning their own homes.

Despite all the attractive features, the log home is not for everyone. There are some concrete advantages and disadvantages, many of which depend upon exactly how, where, and under what circumstances the prospective log home is to be designed and built.

ADVANTAGES

Perhaps the most immediately apparent characteristic of a log structure is the impression it gives of heavy, bulky strength. This is more than just an impression; it is a fact, providing that the structure is properly built. The bulk is plain to see, the great weight can be readily imagined. Because of the thickness of the logs, their considerable individual weight, and the manner in which the structural components are locked together, a log home is very strong and sturdy. Even a small cabin is massively hefty for its actual floor area.

In most log home designs, there is a certain amount of overkill in the construction; there is really more material, more strength, and more ruggedness than called for by present-day building standards, or for the job the structure is called upon to do. However, that is the nature of the beast. Consequently, a log home is exceptionally resistant to lateral pressures, external mechanical damage, storm violence, and general wear and tear. A good log structure is windproof and weatherproof, and because of its massiveness gives a fine sense of security against the outside world. It is also relatively vibration-free and soundproof, and the logs themselves provide a reasonable degree of thermal insulation. Also, well-built log structures can be exceptionally long-lived. Some of those in use in Europe today were built before the founding of America.

An aspect important to many is the unique charm and flavor that only a log structure can present. The rustic appearance harmonizes beautifully with country settings, and can do so with plain simplicity or dignified elegance. It also blends in well in more urban settings if properly done. The log house probably has a less adverse impact upon its surroundings than any other kind of house.

Another advantage—one that is variable depending upon the specific design of the structure—is the possibility of integrating the exterior and interior of the building. In most log structures, when the perimeter walls are built and finished, so are the interior walls, and no further additions need to be made. There is no necessity for putting up drywall, plaster, or paneling, and in many cases no need for store-bought thermal insulation (although all of these materials and more can be, and often are, installed).

Interior walls can be built in the conventional manner with studs and drywall or paneling, but in many designs they are also constructed from logs. In some instances, the interior surfaces of the perimeter walls are furred out and finished with wallboard in the usual manner. Wherever interior surfaces remain natural log, however, the amount of material and labor needed to complete the structure is greatly reduced. Once the log walls are in place, about the only additional work necessary is a few bits of trim around doors and windows and the application of a finish. Even the floors and ceiling can be built so that they too need only an application of sealer or other finish. In contrast with the conventional platform frame home, the amount of work required to finish the job and make a livable house once the shell is erected is certainly minimal.

Because of the interior/exterior integration, a log house shell can be put together with surprising speed, especially by a crew of several experienced workers. Once all the materials are at hand and the job is properly laid out, erection of even a large building can take place within a matter of days, rather than weeks. Installation of the electrical system, heating and cooling equipment, and plumbing frequently goes on as the walls are raised and the roof set. Thus, by the time the shell is complete the entire job is virtually done, and about all that is left is to clean up an assortment of minor details and then proceed with the finish work.

This short construction time can be helpful for a number of reasons. There is less pressure involved in climates where the building season is short. When the time factor is reduced, so are labor costs. The owner can move into a log home much sooner than for most other types of construction (except for modular or prefabricated), especially if moving into an unfinished shell and completing the finish work afterward is part of the program. This can be an important factor if the owner's present quarters must be vacated on short notice.

There are a number of advantages in log construction that specifically appeal to the do-it-yourselfer. For instance, experience in the building trades, although helpful, is not necessary. Those skills that are needed in the bulk of log construction are simple and readily learned by anyone with a modicum of dexterity. Once the project is started, most of the work is repetitive and requires only a normal amount of diligence in putting things together carefully and properly.

As far as building the shell is concerned, only simple hand tools are needed for the most part. Even all the cutting can be done by hand, although using power tools is of course much easier and faster. If the interior of the house is simple, again only a few of the more common hand tools are needed. The more complex the interior design becomes (fancy trimwork, parquetry, or extensive cabinetry, for example), the more sophisticated the equipment needed and the higher the skill level required for construction excellence. Even under these circumstances, however, an advanced do-it-yourselfer can build with little difficulty.

For the do-it-yourselfer working alone or with one or two helpers, when the shell is complete the interior is also nearly done. This can be of considerable consequence. In short, there is simply a whole lot less work to be done in order to make the structure livable. The total amount of time spent on the job by comparison with other types of construction is markedly less, and an owner/builder can accomplish more with somewhat less effort and help over a given time span. This is because of, at least in part, the simplicity of design and simplicity of construction procedures.

There is another factor that the do-it-yourselfer will want to consider: cost. Cost per square foot of living space varies greatly, not only with design complexity and the quality of the material used, but also with the amount of "sweat equity" the owner/builder is willing to invest in the construction of the home. There is a potential with log home construction for starting absolutely from scratch, and in this situation cost will be the lowest for a given design. The cost will be astonishingly low if the builder owns a woodlot and can fell and yard the logs; construct a foundation; fashion the logs; erect the log shell without the aid of hired help; install the electrical, plumbing, and heating systems; and then complete all the finish work. If the building site is already owned too, the total investment would seem almost ridiculous by comparison with today's average home prices. But this procedure is certainly not outside the realm of possibility. Many log home owners have built in just that way.

The less you do yourself, the higher the expenses become. Buying the building site, purchasing cut logs from a mill, hiring a work crew, subcontracting the installation of utilities, or ordering one of the various semicomplete or complete log house kits all serve to boost the price greatly. So for most do-it-yourselfers who want to build their own houses, a certain amount of compromise is necessary between sweat equity and capital outlay. Keep in mind that the outlay need not always be cash. Trading services—something you can do for someone who can do something else roughly comparable in terms of time and effort for you—is always a good possibility.

DISADVANTAGES

Despite all the favorable points involved in log home construction, there are also some disadvantages that must be considered. Some of them are dependent upon the kind of log home you would like to have, just how you plan to go about building it, and the exact design of the structure itself. Often, even these disadvantages can be worked around or at least minimized by making compromises. If you are only marginally inclined toward owning a log home, however, some of the disadvantages might turn you to another style altogether.

Perhaps one of the most dismaying problems, especially to a person dead-set on building a log home, is the fact that in many places a log structure cannot be built. This has nothing to do with economics, availability, or feasibility, but is simply a regulatory matter. You can't build a log home because you can't get a building permit because the zoning laws won't allow that kind of construction. Absurd, maybe, but true, and there is really no recourse unless you get fired up enough to seek a variance or attempt to get the restrictive law changed. And that's a struggle. Before you get your plans all set, then, thoroughly investigate not only the zoning situation but also any local building codes that apply. You also might find more regulations that, while not prohibiting log construction, could serve to make it much more difficult or perhaps even prohibitively expensive. Check also for any covenants that might apply in a housing subdivision, and investigate any rules that might have been laid down by an architectural control committee. Such rulings are often little publicized, can be arbitrary and capricious, and frequently have little to do with building codes or zoning laws. But they are enforceable, and sometimes can knock a builder's plans completely askew.

Another potential disadvantage of a log house, one that is most often subjective in nature, is the fact that you can't plunk one down any which way on just any old building site and expect it to look good. Just what looks good and what doesn't is always a matter of considerable discussion and is always open to question. For most people, a proper log house site is one with a natural setting, even though that site might not be out in the country. If such a building site is unavailable to you or is marginal, you might want to change your plans or perhaps alter them from a thoroughly rustic type of log house to a somewhat more sophisticated and formal log style (of which there are many) that blends in better with the given surroundings. It is good to keep in mind, though, that the log house is undoubtedly the most honest, most forgiving, and most adaptable of all building styles, and if properly designed and landscaped can be nicely established in virtually any location.

As mentioned earlier, the cost of a log house can be remarkably low. But it can also be remarkably high. If you are planning a turnkey design finished down to the last little detail by a building contractor, be prepared to pay well for it. The chances are good that such a structure will actually cost more than a comparable conventional style. But it will usually cost more because you're getting more.

Another problem that arises in some parts of the country, especially for the do-it-yourselfer who wants to build a log house from scratch, is a lack of materials. Not all the country is forested, and although ordinary building materials are readily available everywhere, logs are not. Furthermore, the logs that are available must be suitable for the job at hand and preferably obtainable within a short distance. Otherwise, building problems and freight charges escalate rapidly.

In places where there are no trees for the taking, there are some alternatives. You can contact a log supplier and arrange to have a suitable kind and number of raw logs either delivered to you, or stockpiled for pickup with your own (or a rented) truck. This option works nicely if the distances involved are not too great. The other possibility is to purchase a precut log house kit from one of the many manufacturers scattered about the country.

Another possible disadvantage of log construction, again depending upon the house design and the personnel involved, is the great amount of physical effort needed to erect the structure. It just isn't a physically easy job. In conventional platform-framing construction, the many components of the structure are comparatively lightweight and for the most part easy to handle. There seldom is much need for any great amount of physical exertion, except in instances where a few heavy girders or beams must be set or a few fairly heavy and awkward sheets of plywood or plasterboard maneuvered into difficult spots.

With logs, the story is considerably different. There are fewer individual components involved than in a frame building, but they are a lot chunkier. Only in the smaller homes can they be readily handled by one person. Larger log structures, and especially those that use 20-foot or longer pieces of 8- to 12-inch or more diameter, often pose some ticklish construction problems that cannot be solved by brute strength alone. Such logs are very heavy and awkward.

One type of wood occasionally used for log walls—though not a particularly good choice—is quaking aspen. It weighs about 26 pounds per cubic foot. That means a 20-foot log of an average 10-inch diameter will weigh in at somewhere around 280 pounds.

Aspen is a relative lightweight; many woods are far heavier (maple, 44 pounds per cubic foot; white oak, 47 pounds per cubic foot). These figures are for woods with only a 12 percent moisture content. Green or partly cured logs, depending upon the species and the length of time they have been off the stump, can easily be twice as heavy, possibly more.

All this means that erecting log walls is not the simplest chore in the world. Physical effort is required, and a considerable amount of caution must be employed. Logs are bulky and awkward to handle. Those that are fully round move as they please and they are often slippery. The butt ends are heavier and roll at a different rate than the lighter tip ends, which just makes matters more difficult. A certain amount of rigging and lashing and the use of leverage-gaining devices is essential, and that requires thought, preparation, and proper execution.

For the do-it-yourselfer who wants to begin from scratch by selecting and felling the trees, the lengthy time span between felling and the completion of a log home shell might be a drawback. Felling is better accomplished at certain times during the year, and if the trees are live and not standing deadwood, the logs must be allowed to cure. Following this step are some rather tedious operations in preparing the logs for construction, and the actual building process itself. Because most of this work is usually done by hand and often with only one or two people providing the labor, the time lapse can be substantial and must be reckoned with. A total period of 3 years from stump to shell for a good-sized dwelling is not at all unusual. So if the need for housing is immediate, an interim solution must be found, or a different type of house chosen.

A number of details in log house construction requires careful attention as the work progresses. Although a log building is forgiving in many ways, if the structure is not put together correctly, a good many difficulties are likely to arise later. This can be a disadvantage if the builder is not willing to pay attention to these details and treat them with due respect. If the object is to bang together a ticky-tacky box with slapdash methods and maximum corner-cutting, log construction is not the route to follow.

In many areas, insect damage is a major consideration, particularly from termites, carpenter ants, and similar creatures that thrive on solid wood. Decay fungi also can wreak havoc upon logs by rotting them away. The severity of these problems depends upon the geographic location of the structure. The wetter the climate or the greater the prevalence of certain kinds of insects, the greater the susceptibility.

Much also depends upon the type of wood used and the excellence of construction. Poor construction methods, like badly fitted joints that allow the entrance of moisture, lack of proper preservatives, improper caulking and sealing, or foundations incorrectly set, just invite difficulties. The wood itself plays a part because some species are much more naturally resistant than others. Hemlock, for instance, has a low resistance to decay and rot, while sugar maple has a high resistance. Some woods, like northern white cedar, are practically impervious to insect attacks.

There is one further characteristic of log houses that can be disadvantageous in those parts of the country with extremely long and cold winters, and advantageous in more temperate locales. This is the thermal insulating value of the log wall. In comparison with an uninsulated ordinary frame and stud wall, a solid log wall is a superior insulator, depending upon the specific species of wood and assuming that both types of walls are properly built. Compared to the usual frame wall construction of a decade or so ago—2- × -4 studs, sheathing, exterior siding, interior plasterboard, and 3½ inches of fiberglass insulation—a solid log wall holds its own and is somewhat better if thick enough.

However, yesterday's standard of thermal insulation in dwelling walls is rapidly being replaced in the colder climates by far more stringent requirements in local building codes. The result is that many log wall constructions are no longer considered thermally effective enough to be allowable. This in turn means that the interior surface of outside log walls sometimes must be buried behind a second, insulation-filled interior stud wall in order to achieve the necessary insulating value. This step raises costs markedly, causes extra work, and eliminates some of the reasons for choosing log construction in the first place.

With most types of log construction, compliance with the new regulations, many of which specify R-19 as a thermal rating, would result in a wall thickness of 13½ inches for even the most thermally efficient woods. Obviously this makes single-log wall construction impractical in most cases, although it can be done. To combat this situation, the kit manufacturers have devised methods of log wall construction using two separated subwalls, one interior and the other exterior, with an airspace between filled with additional insulating material. Thus the problem can be solved, but only at increased expense. This same basic system can be duplicated by the builder who works from scratch, but again at the expense of greater time and effort, as well as added material. The net result, however, is tremendously energy conserving, and the added cost will be recovered over time in lower heating cost.

BUILDING FROM SCRATCH

The log house is one of very few styles that can be built almost entirely from native materials and by one or two workers. When it is done entirely in this manner, the only cash outlay absolutely necessary is for small amounts of hardware, glass, and materials for the utilities systems. It is also possible for the builder to single-handedly, or with the aid of one or two helpers, construct the entire house, including foundation, heating and lighting, and plumbing. If desirable, no work need be let to subcontractors. Admittedly this is no easy chore, but it has been and is being done.

The first step in building from scratch is to work up a complete set of detailed drawings and diagrams showing the entire structure as it will appear in its final state. Accurate dimensions are important, as is correct engineering. For a successful job you should work out as many details as possible ahead of time. Make up auxiliary plans at the same time to show all necessary specifics, such as door and window installation details, treatments of soffits, lay-out of floor joists or roof beams or trusses, and methods of installing partitions. Also lay out electrical, heating, and plumbing systems completely. Work up material takeoff sheets that are as complete as possible, and run cost estimates if necessary.

The next step is locating and selecting logs. The least expensive route, of course, is to use logs from your own lot. This is also the most satisfactory situation because you have complete control over the selection process and can choose exactly what you need and want. If you do not own a lot, perhaps you can purchase suitable logs "on the stump" from someone who does. Then you can fell and limb the trees, buck them up as necessary, yard them, and crib them for curing. After a time you must peel the logs (usually) and treat them with preservatives. Meanwhile, you can build the foundation.

If you don't have a handy tree supply, you can still build almost from scratch. After working out your plans, determine exactly what you need in the way of logs. Contact a local mill or a commercial log supplier (the closer to hand the better) and purchase the logs. The cost may or may not include delivery to the site, depending on the supplier's facilities and the arrangements that you can work out. You might be able to purchase the logs either by the board foot, cubic foot, or linear foot. They might also be available either in the round and with the bark still on, or sawn flat on one or more sides. A few suppliers also offer milled logs. You might not be able to make the selection of individual logs yourself, but if you can talk the supplier into it, so much the better. If not, explain to the supplier exactly how the logs are to be used and hope for the best. Try also to work out an arrangement whereby you can return or trade in logs that simply are unusable.

Once the logs are on hand and the foundation is complete, you can begin the actual construction work. There are a number of ways to proceed, all of which will be explained in later chapters. The basic procedure is to first build a floor frame on the foundation and nail down the subfloor to make a working platform. Walls go up next, and windows and doors (sometimes just the empty frames, or bucks) are installed at the same time. Ceiling joists or a floor frame for the second level come next, then subflooring if required, and then the gable ends or second-story walls as necessary. The roof frame and roofing is the last major step to complete the shell of the structure properly.

Porches, decks, dormers, and such are added or included as the house takes shape. In many cases, the electrical, heating, and plumbing essentials are roughed in as construction proceeds, and the finish work is done after the shell has been completed, all "dried in" or "tight to the weather." Interior partitions are sometimes built during shell construction, sometimes not. Often it is easier and more convenient to let such things wait until the shell is closed up.

Obviously, during construction you can farm out some of the work or hire a number of hands to make the job go easier and faster. Obviously, too, the more work others do, the less you will be building from scratch yourself and the higher your costs will be. Be aware, too, that the work you subcontract might not be done to your liking or come up to your standards—although the reverse also can be true.

BASIC CONSIDERATIONS

The ideal situation from a number of standpoints is for the owner to build the log house entirely, start to finish, and this is exactly what a great many prospective log home owners would like to do. However, there are many reasons why this choice is not always practical, or even feasible. The ramifications of doing the entire job yourself versus contracting out part or even all of the job deserve careful scrutiny before you undertake such a large task.

Can you do it all yourself? Maybe, but probably not. The first step is to thoroughly investigate any applicable zoning laws and building regulations, including those that might be highly localized restrictions stemming from a set of subdivision covenants or architectural control committee regulations. In some areas, urban for the most part, no one can build a house unless he is a qualified and licensed building contractor. It makes no difference if the house is for the owner-builder, or for someone else. Other instances arise where either the plumbing, sewage, heating, or electrical system (or perhaps all of them) can be installed only by licensed tradespeople. This could mean that you must figure on subcontracting certain portions of the work whether you want to or not. However, it might also mean that you can make an arrangement with a licensed master professional who will, for a fee, oversee and direct the installations that you yourself make.

Other problems might arise with regard to time. Many areas impose a time limit on the construction of new homes, often requiring that the exterior be fully completed within 1 year. If you don't feel that you can finish your home within the allotted time working by yourself, obviously you will need to arrange for help of one sort or another. There is also your own time, or lack thereof, to consider. One man working alone or with an occasional part-time helper can easily spend 2 years working full-time to complete a good-sized house, inside and out. Or, you might spend 8 to 12 months getting the house to a point where it can be occupied, and then do the finish work and odds and ends as time permits. There might be a stumbling block here, too: in many areas the house must be inspected by a local authority and a certificate of occupancy issued before the house can be permanently occupied. The degree of completion required before the certificate can be issued varies from place to place.

Be aware that do-it-yourselfers who opt for moving into an unfinished house almost invariably find that completion of the house down to the last detail takes far longer than originally anticipated. Because golf is more fun than pounding nails and taking the kids skiing wins over painting trimwork almost every time, 5 or 6 years or more might go by before the job is done. Building a home is a huge project that eats up hundreds and hundreds of hours of labor, much of it tedious, even if the home is only a small one. The amount of that time you can afford or want to put in yourself only you can decide. Whatever is left over will have to be hired out.

Another excellent reason for hiring out some of the work is simply a matter of know-how, skills, and competence. Do-it-yourselfers as a breed are generally confident, competent, and willing to tackle just about anything. However, recognizing your limitations is important when undertaking a task this big. Not all do-it-yourselfers have experience, skills, or interest in all of the various trades that go into the building of a complete house. It is by far preferable to work in those areas that you know and like best, and leave other jobs to someone else. A lack of knowledge, confidence, and interest can result in poorly done work, especially if you are pressed for time, and a project as substantial and as costly as the building of a house is probably not the best one with which to experiment.

The most common situation, and probably the most practical for a lot of do-it-yourselfers, is a fairly even split of working alone or with the help of friends and family, and subcontracting. The owner/builder takes care of site preparation, for example, by hiring an excavator if necessary. Do-it-yourself construction of the foundation might be feasible, especially if it happens to be one of the simpler varieties. Shell erection also might be done by the owner/builder. Meantime, qualified electricians, plumbers, and other tradespeople can be busy installing the utilities systems, all according to applicable building code regulations.

The owner/builder then could take care of the finish roofing, exterior trim, doors, windows, exterior finishes, decks, and so on. If a freestanding stove or fireplace is part of the plan, the owner/builder might also install this. Complicated masonry fireplaces and chimneys, as well as other masonry or stonework, might best be subcontracted to a mason. Most of the interior finish work, including the building of the interior partitions, is often handled by the owner/builder, and there is little need to hire anything out except perhaps for carpet installation, tile setting, or some other type of specialized work.

Most would-be log home builders will indeed find it necessary to subcontract certain portions of the job. Other jobs can be done simply by rousting out the rest of the family or gathering some friends and putting them to work, or by hiring one or two part-time laborers as necessary.

When subcontracting, by all means get two or three bids for each job. Then you will have some basis for reasonable comparison. Note, though, that the lowest bid is not necessarily the best one. Check all the specifications and figures carefully, and also the reputation and qualifications of the bidders, before you make a final decision. Beware of the bid that comes in far lower than the others. You also can use the reasonable alternative of hiring subcontractors whom you already know and trust and who have good reputations for giving fair value and good work. In this case, the job can be done on a contract basis at a certain set fee, or on a time-and-materials basis where you pay the going rate for parts and materials plus a specified hourly charge for the amount of time actually spent on the job.

Whichever approach you take, the principal point to remember is that the more you do yourself, the the lower will be your overall cost. But try to recognize your limitations so you don't fall into that dismal trap so common to doing it yourself: biting off more than you can chew.

ECONOMICS

There seems to be a common misconception that log homes are cheaper to build than other kinds. Under some circumstances, a log home can run to considerably more money per square foot of living area than conventional platform-framed homes. To be sure, a simple one-room log hunting camp with no electricity or plumbing can be knocked together for little more than the cash price of a few panes of glass and a boxful of hardware, under the right circumstances. However, not many buildings of that sort are constructed these days. Most modern log houses contain the normal conveniences and amenities found in any house, even though they might only be small vacation retreats. We do like our luxuries!

Trying to pin down the average or potential costs of log houses in general is an impossibility. Comparisons with houses built by other construction methods is likewise difficult. As noted earlier, the potential for extremely low cost exists with log houses, but that potential is seldom realized. Everything depends not only upon the complexity of design and the quality of the materials and appointments, but also how much sweat equity the owner/builder invests, as well as how adept he is at buying materials on sale, scrounging up second-hand windows and doors, splitting roofing shakes by hand, and conning friends into lending a hand for a weekend or two in return for a cooler of cold drinks and a barbecue.

Each case is different, and each situation must be calculated separately. Comparisons between log construction and other types must be carried out among the specific houses in which the prospective owner/builder is interested.

To arrive at the total cost for a scratch-built log house, start with the cost of the building site, including all closing costs and allied expenses. Work up your plans and specifications as nearly complete as possible (though they can be in rough form), run off a material takeoff sheet, gather all the individual prices, and add them all up to arrive at a total for all the materials that will go into the house. Then add any applicable survey expenses, permit costs, building fees, and tap fees (to allow you to hook onto existing sewer and water lines). If sewer and/or water lines are not available, figure in the cost of a complete septic system and/or a drilled well or other water supply. Check with the local power company to see if there will be any charges for bringing electrical service to your building site. Figure out how much, if any, additional labor you must hire, and get bids or estimates for those phases of the construction that will be subcontracted. Put all of these costs together, along with any special expenses that might pertain to your situation (travel, meals out, freight charges, soil test fees, or engineering, for example), and you'll have the total cost of the house. Then add about 10 percent for contingencies and overlooked items.

For a quick, ballpark estimate that does not include land costs but only the house itself, and in circumstances where you will hire some labor to help in the erection of the shell and subcontract the utilities and the excavating, figure that the total cost will probably be somewhere around double the cost of materials. *Note:* this can be a very inaccurate assessment, good only for purposes of off-the-cuff comparisons.

To look at the picture from a different angle, a finished turn-key job by a building contractor might run to $45 per square foot of living area in a locale where building costs are low, to $100 or more in some areas. For complex designs and large houses, these costs would likely be higher. The costs would total anywhere from $67,500 to $150,000 for a finished 1500-square-foot house—which is not very large. By doing everything yourself that you are capable of doing and have the time for—such as building the foundation, doing the exterior and interior trimwork, putting on the roof, and doing all the finishing—you can

probably save about 25 percent of the total cost. By providing a great deal of the labor yourself and with the (free) help of friends and family, and perhaps including the installation of the electrical and plumbing systems as well, you might reduce your costs to about 55 to 60 percent of the total finished value, but probably not much more than that. Halving the completed value is difficult in most cases, unless the structure is small and simple and you are starting at square one in the woodlot.

It is worth noting, though, that some exceptional cases where the owner/builder is capable, energetic, and determined, and also has the time to invest—and assuming the construction is taking place in an area of rising property values—it is possible to construct a log home with a total capital outlay amounting to perhaps 25 percent of the final property value. In the case of a totally scratch-built house, this outlay could be even less—a very tough job, but one that makes your net-worth figure look mighty fine.

FINANCING

First, a word of advice concerning home financing: don't. If there is any possibility whatsoever to avoid borrowing mortgage money, pursue it with determination. Exhaust all other possibilities first. If you want freedom of action, independence, a minimum of paperwork, and bother, and a lack of major monetary worries, plus security, don't get tangled up with a construction loan and/or a mortgage. There are excellent reasons for doing so, despite all the ballyhoo about how helpful, advantageous, and socially acceptable a mortgage is.

First, a mortgage often means that from start to finish of the building project you are hemmed in by various regulations governing the construction that have nothing to do with building codes or good workmanship. Everything that goes into the project, everything that is done, might have to be specifically acceptable to the moneylender, and he calls the tune, always. You can even be assured, most likely, of finding a clause buried in the fine print that gives the lender the right to cancel the loan at any time if he spots anything in the construction that he doesn't like or any deviation from the plans. Furthermore, at any time in the future if you want to change something around, add to the structure, or take out a second mortgage, for example, every detail will need to be cleared with the lender and you could well be denied. Doing it yourself has very little place in the banking world, today less than ever before.

Once you sign the papers—this process alone will take about 3 months, sometimes longer—you are in bondage from another standpoint, too. The terms of the loan might be as short as 5 years or as long as 40, but probably would be either 15 or 30 years. Whatever the case, you are absolutely committed, month after month, to coming up with the prescribed amount of cash.

But you needn't philosophize to find a prime argument against borrowing mortgage money. Just look at the cost. First there are the *closing costs*, which are the charges levied against you for such matters as the application fee (nonrefundable), appraisal fee, improvement survey, title insurance, tax certificate, document recording fees, property inspections, credit report fee, and revenue stamps. Then there are the *points*, or a loan origination fee, which is a percentage of the total amount borrowed that must be paid as a lump sum to the lender at the time the mortgage goes into effect. Points might be as few as one (meaning 1 percent of the amount to be borrowed) but could be as high as nine or ten. Thus, five points on a $50,000 mortgage would amount to $2,500. So you borrow $50,000 but only get $47,500. Or, in some cases, you get $50,000 but have to pay off a principal of $52,500.

There is also the interest charge, which is tacked on faithfully every month. This charge varies among lenders and at different times, but 10 to 12 percent is not at all unusual; rates have been both higher and lower than this in recent years. For example, 10 percent doesn't sound like a lot for the opportunity of borrowing a substantial sum, and it's a common enough commission rate among salespeople and agents, so we are fairly well used to dealing with this number. But see what it does to your pocketbook. Let's use a 15-year fixed-rate or conventional mortgage for $40,000 at the 10 percent rate as an example. The monthly payments are $429.84 per month and the total of the payments over the full term is $77,372. Thus, it will cost you $37,372 to rent out someone else's $40,000. Now look at a 30-year mortgage, all other details the same. The monthly payment is only $351.03, which looks pretty good, doesn't it? But look out—the total payments come to $126,370.80. There is a slight fee of some $86,000 for the privilege of borrowing less than half that amount. A 40-year mortgage is even worse, with a total commitment of $163,036 involved.

This gets even better. Be aware that the *principal* of your mortgage (that is, the original amount you borrow), is not paid down on a straight-line basis. Every payment you make includes a portion for interest (which the lender keeps) and another for principal (which accrues to your credit against the amount you borrowed and becomes your equity). Many lenders also require that the payment include a small sum to be put toward insurance on the property, and another against taxes, but that is apart from the loan itself; they then pay those bills for you. These portions are fixed sums based on the estimated yearly tax and insurance costs, and are adjusted annually as required. The amounts that go toward principal and interest, though, are not fixed, although the combination of the two is. The amount that goes toward the principal starts at a very small figure and slowly escalates over the years, while the portion that goes toward interest starts at a very high figure and diminishes slowly. The first payment of a 10-percent, 30-year, $40,000 note, for example, includes $333.33 for interest and a mere $17.70 for principal.

As though this were not bad enough, the figures do not change at a steady rate. You might logically think that at the halfway point of the mortgage term—180 payments—you would be paying toward interest and principal in equal amounts, and half the loan would be paid off. Wrong! Payment 180 includes $277.86 for interest, but still only $78.16 toward the principal; about $32,665 remains for you to pay off, not $20,000. You are still building equity only slowly, and don't pick up speed until the last few remaining years of the contract. The lenders make sure to get theirs first, you see.

Having said all this, it is now time to enter the realm of reality. At first glance and especially in view of the disadvantages of having a mortgage, shelling out $126,000 for a $40,000 house, or expecting a person to faithfully make 360 monthly payments in order to do so, might seem a bit unreasonable. In years past, when neither costs nor charges were so high, a mortgage was a workable method for families to gradually reach the point where they owned their home free and clear. Today, though, the situation has changed and lenders recognize this fact. They are aware that people are using mortgages less and less, so they look upon the whole business as a sort of revolving-door arrangement. Mortgages nowadays are seldom held for 30 years, or even 15. The average length of time that a mortgage is paid down is around 7 to 8 years or so, whereupon the property is conveyed to another owner and remortgaged, and the revolving door spins once more. All the homeowner can do is hope to build up a small amount of equity at a substantial cost to get a roof overhead, but which even so is often better than a rental arrangement. The fact is that most people find there is simply no other way for them to own a house than to take out a mortgage.

Now, let's take a look at the mortgage picture with regard to log houses. The easiest mortgage to obtain is one on an existing house,

either newly built or previously lived in. This type of mortgage is available through a local bank, a savings and loan company, or a mortgage broker. The situation is straightforward, and if your earnings are high enough and stable, if you can come up with the down payment (for a primary residence this is usually 20 percent of the purchase price or the appraised value, whichever is lower), and if your credit rating and your financial outlook is good, you probably can put the deal together. This, however, has little to do with the prospective owner/builder who wants to be at least in part involved in the construction of a new home.

To follow that path, first you need a building site upon which to put your proposed home. However, savings and loan institutions cannot lend money for unimproved land, commercial banks seldom will, and mortgage brokers won't. (There might be exceptions, but they would be unusual.) In fact, borrowing money from any of the normal sources for the purposes of buying raw land or a building site is practically impossible.

You might well be able to finance the purchase of a building site in a housing development through the developer; this is a fairly common circumstance. Sometimes, too, it is possible to work out a financing arrangement with the current owner of a property, especially if the owner is desperate to sell; this is called an *owner carryback*. Failing these, you either will have to borrow from private sources or use your own resources to buy a piece of property for cash outright.

The next step is to seek a *construction loan*, which is a temporary loan that lasts only for the duration of the house construction process, and is then transmuted into a long-term mortgage loan of the usual sort. Basically, you pay an agreed-upon amount of monthly interest, and the lender, usually a commercial bank, pays off the construction bills. The mortgage, when it comes about, might be held by the original lender but is likely to be placed with a mortgage brokerage firm, which might

14

then sell it to a secondary market. Eventually the borrower ends up with a payment booklet and an address to send the payments to. The details of the ultimate mortgage contract are usually settled upon and committed to at the same time as the construction loan is granted.

Today, getting a construction loan and a mortgage is not a simple chore. Lenders are wary, interest rates rise and fall like a yo-yo, and numerous restrictions have been put into effect by both the primary and secondary mortgage markets. Money is available, however, if you can meet the requirements. If possible, shop around for the best interest rate—they do vary at any given time among lenders. For example, if you could shave one-half percentage point off a 10-percent, 30-year mortgage on $40,000, you would save almost $15 a month on the payment. That doesn't sound like much, but it amounts to almost $5,300 over the term of the mortgage, and that is a worthwhile savings.

At the same time, investigate the types of mortgage contracts available and their terms; these details vary, too. Study the possibilities to see what might be best for you, and don't be afraid to get legal or other professional advice from disinterested parties.

Your main choices will be between fixed-rate (conventional) mortgages and adjustable-rate mortgages (ARMs). The interest rate on the former remains the same throughout the life of the loan period, which customarily is 15 to 30 years, although other arrangements sometimes can be made. They are straightforward and you always know just what your payments, equity, and remaining principal balance are, or will be at any future point.

ARMs are much more complex, and you should study them before you commit yourself to one. The initial interest rate is always considerably lower than that of a conventional mortgage, but the lender can raise (or lower) the rate at certain times. The rate on a 1-year ARM can be adjusted after 1 year, a 3-year after 3 years, and so on. When the rate goes up, so

do the monthly payments, and the increase can be substantial. There might be a cap, which means that the total increase or decrease cannot exceed a certain amount: a 5-percent cap can only go up or down five percentage points from the starting point over the life of the loan. Time periods vary, but 10, 15, and 20 years are common. Other ARM details vary greatly, as well.

Balloon mortgages are also common, and can be very dangerous. Such a mortgage, which can be either a conventional or an ARM type, may be amortized over 30 years, for example, but carry a 5-year balloon. To translate: the loan payments are calculated as though there would be 360 payments, but after the first 60 payments the entire remaining balance (which usually is almost the whole loan amount) becomes due and payable at once, in one lump sum. If you cannot pay or refinance the loan, you lose everything. Although a useful financing tool under the proper circumstances, a balloon mortgage must be handled with great care.

If you plan to pursue the mortgage route, allow yourself plenty of lead time. You probably will need a month to investigate the possibilities, maybe more if a number of them are available to you. Once you make an application for a mortgage loan, you can figure on 3 months or more for processing—again, this could stretch out even further, depending upon the lender and the state of the market. You also must be ready to fill out innumerable forms and supply an immense amount of personal and financial information, including copies of past federal income tax returns. Be prepared for hours of paperwork, delays, telephone calls, and frustrations; this is not an easy job. The lender will make many demands of you, and he sits in the catbird's seat. A normal process might call for, believe it or not, as many as 200 signatures just from you.

What are your chances of obtaining a mortgage for your new log home? That depends. First assume that you have the required cash down payment, your credit is good, your net worth and general financial standing is substantial, you are an upstanding pillar of the community, and all else is in good order from the lender's standpoint. As the degree to which you want the builder to complete the home diminishes, so do your chances for getting the construction loan. If you would like only to do some of the interior finish work and decorating yourself or maybe build your own foundation or garage or porch, you might still be in the running. Incidentally, you stand the best chance of obtaining a loan if you already own the building site free and clear—this is one of the first questions you will be asked.

If you contemplate building a home, perhaps of your own design, from native logs, and your building contractor is a good one and known to be capable of doing such a job and will build the entire structure, you also might be able to obtain a construction loan. Again, the more you are personally involved in the construction and the less the contractor is involved, the slimmer your chances become.

Finally, down at the bottom of the heap are the poor, lonely do-it-all-yourselfers. To put it bluntly, they don't stand a chance of getting any financing whatsoever from normal commercial sources. This is true whether or not the land is owned, the trees or logs are on hand, the plan is to use a kit home as a basis, or part of the work will be subcontracted. Even if the owner/builder intends to only act as the general contractor to supervise all the construction, the chances of obtaining financing run anywhere between slim and zero.

Are there any alternatives to this grim picture? Probably, but only in isolated circumstances. For example, if you own a piece of land free and clear, you might bring the utilities in and build a foundation. Then you might be able to borrow enough, on the strength of these improvements and on your own creditworthy signature, to purchase a small log shell kit. Then, if you select an expandable design, you can erect and finish the building and use

that to borrow enough to put up an addition, and so on until the house has grown to completion. There are also various kinds of personal loans, including family, that might be sufficient to get going with, so that initial small improvements can be used to parlay your way up to a large house and fully established grounds and outbuildings. Cosigning of notes is another possibility, as is trading of services and bartering for materials.

There is also a ray of hope on the commercial lending horizon for log home owners and builders in general. For example, the Justice Mortgage Company of Plano, Texas, has developed a Log Home Division exclusively for log home owners. Justice probably knows more about the ins and outs of log house building and financing than any other lender in the country, and the company is developing a national lending operation for log houses, working by mail and telephone.

Still, much boils down to the fact that if you're planning to do it yourself, you might have to do to all yourself, money (or the scrounging up thereof) included. This is a discouraging picture indeed, but one that is best faced up to at the outset. But sometimes the determined do-it-yourselfer is able to do some finagling and in one way or another pull together enough cash to get the project well under way. Ingenuity is important in this aspect of do-it-yourselfing, too.

ECOLOGICS

Whether or not the building of a log home is an ecologically sound operation is open to some conjecture. This is an extremely complicated subject, and much depends upon your viewpoint. Unfortunately, there seem to be no hard and fast rules as to what constitutes an ecologically sound home. We all need shelter of one sort or another, so considering the building of a new single-family home as a poor use of natural resources is nonsense. We've gotten past the stage of living in caves (although we might yet get back to that). This leaves us, then, with the often-raised question of whether or not whole logs should properly be used to build a house, and comparisons with other types of houses and other uses of the wood.

There is little question that there are more cubic feet of lumber tied up in most log houses than in many other styles. That which is used, however, is put to a relatively permanent good purpose, by providing a shelter that should last at least a century and, with good care, might survive in usable fashion for two or more. Bear in mind, too, that a log house can be built from a number of species of wood, some of which are not currently employed to any great extent for other purposes and/or are of marginal value from a commercial standpoint. Thus, a resource that is in many instances renewable at a fairly rapid rate is being put to good use. There is not much waste involved in a log home. Slash is left behind for additional wildlife habitats and enrichment of forest soils; scraps are converted to fuel, various wood products, or other purposes; by-products of the whole process can further be transformed in some useful fashion. Virtually everything is used up through the construction of a log house, and mostly in a positive way.

The logs that go into a log house might well be those felled in a forest or woodlot thinning operation, or they might be relatively small and spindly, unsuitable for lumber or other commercial purposes. They could well be standing deadwood, killed earlier by disease or fire. Even short chunks, commercially useless, can be used in a log house. Defective wood can also be put to use. Because log house building from scratch is a labor-intensive endeavor, log materials that cannot be economically processed commercially can be used.

Direct comparisons between log and other kinds of houses are difficult to make, as far as ecological impacts are concerned. However, log houses are conservative of both manufactured energy and processed materials. A frame house, for example, is built with materials that are highly processed, involving much machinery, great quantities of energy, valuable petroleum, and other resources—sawn and resawn lumber, plywood, steel, plastics, fiberboard, and asphalt products. Some of these materials find their way into log houses, too, but usually to a lesser degree. Also, in some respects a log house, especially if owner-built, is likely to be more conservative of materials than other types of houses. Often an effort is made to use recycled or commercially useless materials, and to depend more upon labor and craftsmanship for an excellent structure than machinery and manufactured energy or processed technological innovations.

Admittedly these points can be argued to a degree. However, considering the fact that trees are a renewable resource, it seems reasonable to say that the log dwelling is one of the more ecologically sound options. Compared to the miles of newsprint, the bales of toilet and facial tissue, the mountains of paper cups, the acres of throwaway containers, and the hundreds of other questionable woodproduct consumables our manufacturing plants crank out every month, not to mention the millions of board feet of lumber that get shipped to Japan and other faraway points, the log house seems little short of a noble endeavor.

PERSONAL REQUIREMENTS

Would-be log house builders who want to start from scratch, or at least contribute substantially to the construction, often ask what personal requirements are needed to bring such a job to a successful conclusion. This is a valid concern. Someone who plans to be little involved, or perhaps will have a contractor take care of the whole job, needs only to decide what to have built, then sign the contracts and the checks. For the do-it-yourselfer, there is much more involved.

The first thing to recognize is that, even if the house is only a relatively small one, the project—taken from start to finish—is a huge one. In fact, it is the largest undertaking most do-it-yourselfers will ever become involved in. The job is not only complicated, it is immensely time-consuming. This being so, perhaps the two most important attributes a log house owner/builder can have are patience and perseverance. Both are required in large measure to see you through a long year or two or three (or maybe more) of work that sometimes becomes drudgery. An ability to hold an even temper and keep your chin up in the face of assorted foul-ups, frustrations, and setbacks helps a lot, too.

As to the physical requirements, they are of less importance than most prospective builders suppose. Great strength is not needed, despite the size and weight of the components of a log house. A working knowledge of physics is of much more help. Heavy logs and other materials should be handled either by several people to make the work easy, or by means of tools and equipment, rigging, and leverage—not by individual brute force. Building a house is indeed a hard job, but only normal strength, agility, and dexterity are needed.

The skills required depend upon what you plan to do yourself. There are a number of areas of expertise involved: rough carpentry, finish carpentry, cabinetmaking, electricity, plumb-ing, roofing, masonry, concrete work, and so on. There are two possible courses to follow. The first is to hire out any phase of the job that you feel incapable of doing competently (or simply are not interested in or cannot do because of local regulations). The second is to study and learn, perhaps by doing, those things that you are not presently familiar with. In practice, both courses are usually followed to a greater or lesser extent. If you have some experience in some phases of house construction, you will have little difficulty in learning about and undertaking others. Even if you don't, you probably can still quickly learn enough to do a fair share of the work, especially with some on-the-spot guidance.

In short, you need not feel that you must be a master builder, an Olympic athlete, and a walking encyclopedia of building techniques at the outset in order to undertake a log house project. No one is. Many a successful log home has been built, both from scratch and from a kit, by many a person who had little idea in the beginning what it was all about. Much more important is an ability to recognize your lack of knowledge or skill, a realization of your limitations, a willingness to learn, and the good sense to call for help just a little bit before it becomes necessary.

2

The Beginnings

ONCE YOU CONVINCE YOURSELF THAT A LOG home is exactly what you've always wanted and you successfully get past the first hurdle of financing, or lack thereof, you can actually begin the project. The first steps consist of designing the house, planning the house (two different matters), selecting the property, and integrating the house with the chosen site. All these operations are extremely important, because they form the basis for not only the house, but also the completed, improved property in its final state. Mistakes, deficiencies, and problems that occur in these early stages are difficult, expensive, and sometimes even impossible to correct later. Give all the steps all the time they need, plus a little extra. The last step before construction—preparation of the building site and immediate surroundings—also deserves considerable thought, though this aspect is unfortunately often short-changed and just attacked hastily at the last moment.

Although each item will be considered separately here, in practice all but the site preparation (and sometimes even that) frequently overlap or even coincide.

DESIGNING AND PLANNING

Designing the house is as much concerned with architectural detail, colors, general layout, and overall construction as it is with planning a home in which you can live comfortably and pleasurably with a maximum of convenience and a minimum of bother. This is an immense subject, one about which many volumes have been written and which we can only touch upon lightly here. But at the outset, you need to determine your basic design parameters. You have already chosen a log house style, so that is one major decision behind you.

The next step is to analyze yourself and your family, to see exactly how you live now, and how you would like to live in your new home. All your planning should revolve around the needs and desires of you and your family. Forget about how other houses are designed, except insofar as you might be able to use certain facets that you particularly admire or feel would be useful to you. After all, this house is for you, not somebody else. Draw up your plans the way you want them, not the way a developer or a real estate peddler or your brother-in-law would like to have them. If you build well and design for maximum convenience and comfort, the chances are pretty good that some family later on will feel the same way about the house as you do, if and when you decide to sell.

While you are considering your lifestyle and habits, work up a list of your basic requirements. You will want a certain number of bedrooms, a certain number of baths, a kitchen, and so forth. You might also want a specialized room or two not included in most houses, such as a full-fledged workshop, a library, a billiard room, a working pantry or a summer kitchen, a canning room, a root cellar, a separate room for a model railroad, or whatever. You need to determine whether or not you want a full basement, what you require in the way of storage areas and what type, the size of the garage if you want one, and also such auxiliary items as pool, greenhouse, decks and porches, hot tub, corral or paddock, or whatever else your interests and style of living suggest.

This is a good time, too, to consider the pros and cons of a two-story versus a single-story house. Many feel that a log house looks best in a low-posted, ground-hugging design that integrates closely with its surroundings. A two house-story, on the other hand, must be well designed if it is not to stick up on the horizon like the proverbial sore thumb. Compromises can be made via the split- and multi-level designs, or by building into a hillside so that the top floor is at grade level on one side and much of both ends, with the remaining side at two full levels.

There are advantages and disadvantages to both single-story and two-story designs. For example, when levels are stacked, there is less roof and sidewall exposure for a given floor area of living space, especially if the bottom level is at least partly below grade. Less wall, roof, floor, and foundation material is required, and usually there are fewer hallways and partitions needed. Also, the building is more compact and requires less ground space, is easier to heat/cool and ventilate, and solar exposure can often be better developed. Because of the compactness, less piping and wiring is usually needed. A single-floor house, on the the other hand, can be built on a lighter foundation, including piers, and there are no stairs to take up valuable space, to build, or to clamber up and down. Emergency evacuation is usually easier. The structure is not a wind and weather catcher, as is a tall building. Design and floor layout tends to be easier, and also more interesting. Construction is easier because materials do not have to be juggled as high. Soundproofing and sound isolation is easier, and the one-level arrangement is ideal for elderly, ill, or infirm occupants; it is the only alternative for wheelchair occupants or others unable to climb stairs, unless an elevator is installed. Exterior shading is easier, and smaller roof overhangs can be used for sun and weather protection of windows and sidewalls. The structure tends to be more stable with less bracing, masonry work is simpler, and chimneys are much shorter.

As you develop your broad requirements, you might want to work with both single- and multiple-level designs at the outset, to see which seems most satisfactory. If you already have your building site, the topography will probably influence your thinking. In any case, work out the rough sizes that the various rooms should ideally be. Most people have some fairly definite ideas along these lines, and this is the best time to figure out just what you like and what you don't. For instance, you might now have a tiny U-type kitchen that you abhor. Obviously you will want to change this situation, perhaps to a much larger L-type kitchen, maybe with a work island or two. Maybe you detest tiny bathrooms, or perhaps you prefer them for their efficiency. You might want a separate dining room, or maybe a combined living/dining area.

Whatever the specifics, work out some minimum dimensions for all your required rooms, taking into account the furnishings and built-ins that you would eventually like to have in them. You can arrive at appropriate size estimates simply by making a series of comparisons. Use the rooms that you now occupy as guidelines, and enlarge or reduce the sizes as necessary on your list or sketches. Compare with various rooms and room arrangements in

friends' houses, and visit model homes that are open to public viewing. Eventually you'll arrive at a set of reasonable figures.

With these basics worked out, the next step is to sketch a series of floor plans. Simple pencil drawings, not even to scale, work fine during these preliminary phases. Probably you will do a good many of them, so there's little point in turning out artistic renderings suitable for framing. A floor plan is just a layout of room arrangements as viewed from directly above, one for each level or floor of the house (Fig. 2-1). While you are doing these sketches, you can probably get some valuable ideas on room arrangements and overall house layouts by studying some of the published plans found in magazines and house plan books. Lay the

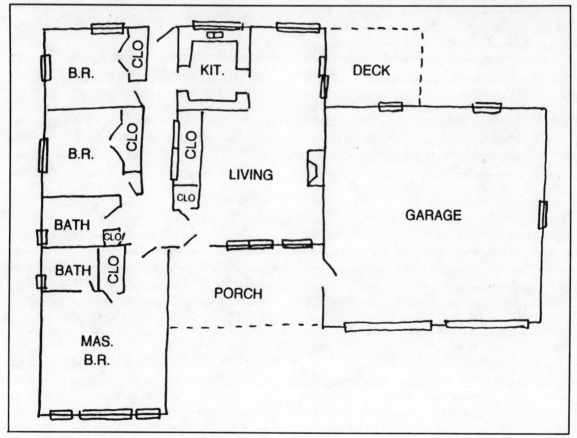

Fig. 2-1. Typical rough-sketch floor plan.

rooms out in rough proportions as a series of blocks, or other suitable shapes if your design concept is geometrically irregular. Add in the windows and doorways at points you think appropriate, and include major architectural elements like fireplaces or stairways. Shuffle these components around as you will, trying them first one way and then another.

What you are striving for right now is a workable relationship of rooms (or areas), halls, stairways, and access points, all blending together to provide the greatest amount of convenience and flexibility of living. Construction details, decorating schemes, final sizes, kinds of materials, and similar details are of little consequence yet—you are still working with concepts.

Analyze the traffic patterns so that all are logical and there is free and easy access to all points. For instance, the dining area should be handy to the kitchen and probably the living room as well, not in some remote location. Access to the only bath on a particular level should not be through a bedroom, nor should entrance to one bedroom be gained by going through another. Hallways should be kept to an absolute minimum because this kind of space is not well utilized and is therefore expensive. On the other hand, when hallways must be included, try to make them of decent size, not dark and narrow, and see if they might serve some other purpose than just traffic flow. For instance, perhaps one wall could be used as a little art gallery, or contain a large storage shelf section. Arrange rooms, storage areas, and access points so that as little space as possible is wasted or only marginally usable. Some compromise in room arrangement is almost always required, but with enough chewing on the end of your pencil you'll be able to work out a suitable preliminary plan.

As you make these initial sketches, there are a few important points to keep in mind that have to do with log house construction characteristics. The first is that the strongest log structure always consists of squares or rectangles.

They can be single or multiple, but 90-degree corners are the secret of strength. This is because all of the outside corners are jointed and locked together at each exterior wall corner, whether an inside or an outside corner. The 90-degree joints are the most effective; joints made at lesser angles hold together with less effectiveness because the angle either diminishes or increases. Also, 90-degree joints are the easiest to cut and fit. The second point bears on the first. Because the strength of a log structure lies in large measure in the corner construction, all window and exterior door openings should be kept as far as possible from either inside or outside corners. In addition, the fewer the openings of any sort in exterior walls, and the smaller they are, the stronger the structure will be.

After you have the preliminary room arrangement laid out, check the locations of interior doors to make sure they don't interfere with one another, can be fully opened, and are at the best possible location in relation to furnishings (or even the potential future location of furniture) and the traffic pattern. Place the exterior doors at the most convenient points, allowing ready access at the front of the house, at the rear, onto porches and decks, and to areas of major use such as a service yard or garage. Two exterior doors is an absolute minimum even in a small house, while large ones might have eight or ten.

Spot windows in the perimeter walls where they will do the most good. Some probably will be used only to admit light and to see out of; others will play a part in warm-weather ventilation. Still others may be placed because of a view. Keep cross-ventilation in mind; it should be available in every habitable room. In moderate climates large expanses of glass will do no harm, but in hot or cold climates the heat gain or loss can be terrific, adding greatly to the cooling or heating load of the building. Note, though, that some of the new types of glass can minimize these difficulties. In some cold-climate locales there are building code restrictions on the amount of glass that can be installed in a home—for instance, a maximum of 20 percent of the total exterior wall area. On the other hand, in areas where any of the model building codes apply, there are minimum glass areas that must be installed in all habitable rooms, typically 10 percent of the floor area of each room but no less than 10 square feet. Regardless of the possible regulations that might apply, if you live in an area of temperature extremes, keep the total glass area as low as seems reasonable in order to ease your heating/cooling burden.

As you locate windows, make a list of general specifications for them. Figure the approximate sizes you would like to have, note whether they will be fixed or openable, how high or low in the wall they will be positioned, whether framed with wood or some other material, and details of this nature. For openable windows, choose the types you want, such as double-hung, casement, awning, slider, patio door. Reference to a window manufacturer's catalog will help you out with standard sizes, styles, and types that are available.

When you have the room arrangements and the door and windows shuffled around into a floor plan that appears to be practical so far, add in the last of the principal elements of the house. These include the major plumbing fixtures such as shower stalls, bathtubs, toilets, and sinks. Locate places for the laundry equipment, hot water tanks, and furnace or individual heating units. You might need space for air conditioning equipment, well pump and water storage tank, or similar items. Include also any major built-in units that take up room space, like kitchen cabinets, storage walls, window seats, sewing center, permanent work benches, and built-in bunk beds. Items of this sort become part of the house and should be planned for from the beginning even if they will not immediately be installed.

Now take a few moments out and dream about the future. Do you anticipate the need for a nursery later on, or a guest bedroom? Perhaps you might need an office at home. If you're planning a large family you might need more bedrooms than you presently have in your plans. Maybe you'd like an attached greenhouse or sunspace sometime. Will you want a larger family room eventually? Is the plan you now have expandable anywhere, without major reconstruction, or are you locked in to what you have? Maybe your future needs will be no greater or no different than they are now, or they might be even less demanding.

Many families outgrow their new homes after only a few years. Ideas change, lifestyles change, living patterns change, and new needs and desires crop up. The time to make provision for future expansion is in the present, before that potential need becomes a reality. Many homes simply are not expandable without a major reconstruction job, but nearly any house can be expanded if the original design is made up with that possibility in mind, even if no specific, detailed plans are made.

The last part of the initial design stage involves a double check of everything that has been sketched out so far, along with an in-depth consideration of the whole arrangement. As a starting point, work up a ballpark estimate of how much it will cost to build the house you have designed. This is not an easy chore, but try to develop a reasonably true approximation. If the resulting figure appears to fit within your budget, fine. If not, you will have to redesign, perhaps making all the rooms a little smaller, chopping out a room or two, leaving off the decks or garage, setting aside a portion of the house to be built later (but staying with the original design), or whatever is necessary to bring the estimated cost into line with what you can presently afford.

After redesigning and re-estimating as necessary, further reconsideration is in order. This is not something that should be done in an hour or two after dinner, but rather is a lengthy process of mulling the plans over and letting them come together. If you can, think it over for several weeks or more, making such changes as might be desirable, until you are thoroughly satisfied with the plans you have drawn up so far.

CODES AND PERMITS

There are few places left in the country where at least some building code regulations do not apply or permits are not required. The time to investigate what dictates you might have to follow is during the very early planning stages, because many regulations exist that have definite consequence in the cost, the design, and even the placement of a house.

Zoning Laws

The first thing to check is the local zoning laws. There might not be any, in which case you can build what you want where you want (subject to other kinds of regulations that might apply). If there are laws in effect, make sure that you can comply. You might find, for instance, that a log house is not allowed in a particular location. Or you might be wary of building in a presently vacant zone that actually is meant for eventual commercial or light industrial use. Check also to see if changes in zones are being contemplated that might suddenly shift your proposed building site from an agricultural zone, for example, to a commercial or maybe a multiple-family building, subdivision use. You might also find minimum square-footage living space restrictions, height restrictions, property line setback requirements, and similar "do nots."

Covenants

Covenants consist of a variable-length list of do's and don'ts, and can be very restrictive. They are common in formal housing subdivisions, and are used along with, and sometimes in lieu of, zoning laws. They might specify such things as height of fences, no visible clotheslines, no above-ground fuel tanks, specific house colors or siding and roofing materials, and the particular spot on the build-

ing lot where the house must be set—the "building envelope." Often they are a legal part of the deed and title to the pieces of property that they cover. The owner of such property is legally bound to follow them even if unaware of their existence, which sometimes is not made known during property conveyance. Covenants must, however, be recorded with local government officials. You can find out at the local county clerk's or building assessor's office whether or not any covenants are in effect on you prospective property.

Building Codes

There are four principal model building codes that are widely used in various parts of the country: the Uniform Building Code (UBC), the National Building Code (NBC), the Basic Building Code (BBC), and the Southern Standard Building Code (SSBC). There are also several auxiliary codes that might be used in conjunction with or separately from the model building codes, such as the Basic Mechanical Code, the Standard Plumbing Code, and the Uniform Fire Code. In addition, there are several other codes that you might run into. The most widely known and used of these is the National Electrical Code, but there are others, such as the Chimneys, Fireplaces, and Vents Code and the Household Fire Warning Equipment Code, that are well recognized.

Some of these codes, or perhaps only sections of them, are in use in various areas, but not all, of the country and they are legally enforceable; their provisions must be followed. The degree of enforcement, as well as the exact provisions that are followed in any given place, are highly variable. You can get further details, as well as copies of applicable codes, from your local building department or city/county government offices.

For the most part, the provisions of these codes have been formulated through field experience and for valid reasons of safety and good construction practices, and following them whether you have to or not is a good idea.

Building Permit

In most places a building permit is required before actual construction—even ground breaking—can start. A general building permit covers all phases of the construction process. A usual requirement before the permit is issued is the submission of a full set of plans and specifications for the structure (often they need not be formal blueprints). The plans are checked for code violations and engineering problems, and any required adjustments are made and difficulties ironed out in consultation with the applicant. Then a fee is assessed and the permit issued. Part of the permit process involves inspections by a local authority, usually at the completion of certain phases of the construction. The next phase cannot be completed until each inspection has been made and the work approved. Spot inspections might also be made, and if the inspector finds code violations the job is "red-tagged"—stopped cold until corrections have been made.

You can get all the details on required building permits from your local building or government offices.

Variances

In situations where zoning laws and building codes are in force and your plans do not comply with regulations because the building is too high, or the wrong type or use for the area, or is too close to a lot line, or whatever, you might be able to take advantage of a variance. This involves taking your plans before a review board of some sort and presenting your case as to why you think you should be issued a building permit. You might win and you might not, but if you feel strongly that you have been wrongly turned down and you have a good case for issuance of the permit, the effort could be worthwhile. If you win, you build. If you do not, you will be forced to change your plans.

There is often a fee for this process.

Electrical Permit

An electrical permit might be required even if a local building permit is not; these are often controlled at the state level. It can be applied for at local building or government offices, and usually there is a fee. In most places you do not have to be a licensed electrician in order to obtain one if you are working on your own house; in a few, you must be whether the house is yours or not.

Plumbing Permit

A plumbing permit might be required under much the same circumstances as the electrical permit. This covers the installation of the domestic hot and cold water systems and the drain-waste-vent (DWV) system. Check with your local building department or government officials.

Soil Inspection

A soil inspection is sometimes part of the overall building permit process, sometimes not, and sometimes might be needed even if a formal building permit is not. In fact, if you are unsure about the soil conditions at your building site, you might want to have tests made whether officially required or not. This has nothing to do with whether you can grow corn in your soil, but rather how much weight it can bear per square foot of surface area without shifting or subsiding. These details are important to the health of your foundation, and consequently the structure. Depending upon the results, the foundation specifications might have to be changed; a few soils cannot be practically built upon.

Septic System Permit

A permit for the installation of a septic system must be obtained in almost all parts of the country where you cannot tap into a munici-

pal sewer system. This entails having a percolation test made to see how much moisture the
soil at the leach field site will absorb before becoming saturated, working out a suitable and
acceptable design for the system, and having
the installation inspected for proper installation. This process is usually governed at the
state level but administered by local county or
city officials, and there will be an attendant fee.

Well Permit

If you cannot tap onto a municipal or water district supply system, you will probably want to
have a well drilled. In many parts of the country you must have a permit and pay a fee to do
so, and often the usage will be specified as
domestic, not agricultural or irrigation. Again,
this is controlled at state level but locally administered. You must first file an application;
the waiting period before approval might be
fairly long, so this matter should be checked
into early on.

Water Tap

If your building site is within reasonable reach
of a municipal or water district supply line you
must tap onto it. This involves some paperwork
and a fee, often substantial. You will pay for
installation of the service line to the water
main, which must be done according to their
specifications, and they will make the actual
tap onto the water main. You can obtain details
at your local city water department or water
district offices.

Sewer Tap

As with the water tap, if your site is handy to
a municipal or a sanitation district sewer line,
you must tap onto it; you cannot use a septic
system. Again, paperwork and a fee are involved. You will have the main drain installed,
and they will make the tap. Check with local
officials for details.

Improvement Survey

An improvement survey is a formal land survey made of your property, which is translated
into a plot plan and certified by a registered or
licensed professional surveyor of your choice.
You pay the surveyor for services rendered.
Such a survey is often required by a lender if
the property and/or the house is being
financed. It might also be required for the issuance of a building permit. If required in both
circumstances, and if the time period between
the two needs is short (usually six months or
less), one survey will serve both purposes.

Fireplace Permit

As a pollution control measure, a number of
municipalities have cracked down severely on
fireplace and woodstove installations. In some
places fireplaces can no longer be installed in
new buildings, and in others that can only be
done in certain circumstances and under certain specifications. In several states only approved and certified models of woodstoves
may be installed, and they might be limited to
one per occupancy unit. In the future, some
towns and cities might ban them altogether.
Permits, fees, and inspections are required.
You can get the necessary information from
local building or health department officials.

Certificate of Occupancy

A certificate of occupancy, or CO, is usually
part and parcel of a building permit, though not
always. It is mentioned here because it is sometimes misunderstood or ignored, to the chagrin
of the would-be house occupants. In locales
where a CO is used, a new house (or other
building) must not be occupied until a formal
CO is issued to the owner or the prospective
occupants. Otherwise, all sorts of strife and
consternation, not to mention fines and legal
problems, can occur. Issuance is made only
after the structure has had its final inspection

and is deemed by the inspector to be safely and healthfully habitable. This situation is worth checking into, as you might find that you cannot move into your partly completed new house at as early a stage in the construction as you would like to.

In addition to these codes and permits, you might also come up against a few other, more minor ones that will impact your plans. These are likely to be regional regulations, such as a locally written fire code, ordinances against building in a designated floodplain, potential earth-slip area, or wetlands. You might have to consult with Fish and Game or Department of Wildlife officials about the potential impact of building in or near a winter deer grazing range or an elk migration route, or check with local officials on land use ordinances.

PLANS AND SPECIFICATIONS

The next stage in the planning is to boil down all those design sketches into working drawings, and all your ideas into a set of specifications. The extent to which this is done depends upon individual circumstances. If you plan to do all the work yourself and have a good grasp of log construction as well as general residential construction practices, and if the local building department does not require formal blueprints, you might need little more than a rudimentary set of sketches with the major dimensions. Specifications might not be necessary at all, if you already know what you want and can wing it as you go along. A few notes might help, though, so you don't forget what you had planned on.

If you are not intimately familiar with residential construction practices and materials, especially those applicable to log houses, you cannot now go ahead with this step in the planning. This is because many of the details and available construction options will have a direct bearing upon your refined plans and are essential to the specification sheet. You have two choices, The first is to seek the help of a professional—an architect or engineer, or a log house kit manufacturer. Using your basic sketches and doing a lot of consulting, you can end up with a full set of plans, for a fee. The second choice is to study the subject in depth and gain the knowledge you need, using this book and others. You might also attend a course in log building and/or residential construction, or even go to log-building school; such opportunities are available throughout the country, often as adult education classes. You might also hire on as a helper on a residential builder's crew for a while; the practical experience is irreplaceable.

If a subcontractor is to do part of the work, those jobs should be covered by complete, accurate working drawings and specification sheets so that there is little chance for error or misinterpretation. If most or all of the work is to be done by a builder, you will need a full set of working drawings, completely dimensioned and detailed, and a complete set of specifications. Rare indeed are the occasions where an owner/designer and a builder communicate so well that only a few sketches on an old shopping bag are needed. If there is any financing involved, the lender will also probably require a similar set of plans and specs. Sometimes these need not be formal architect's blueprints but can be design sketches neatly done to approximate scale and with full dimensioning and detailing.

Probably the most valuable set of working drawings you can devise is a series of scaled floor plans (Fig. 2-2). Copy your original floor plan sketches, but make them as large as you reasonably can. In these drawings include the thickness of the walls, and draw in to scale all the details that you did previously, even the direction the doors swing. Draw in all of the built-ins, too. As you do so, you might discover some difficulties that were not apparent earlier. Perhaps a room is a bit too small, a window is

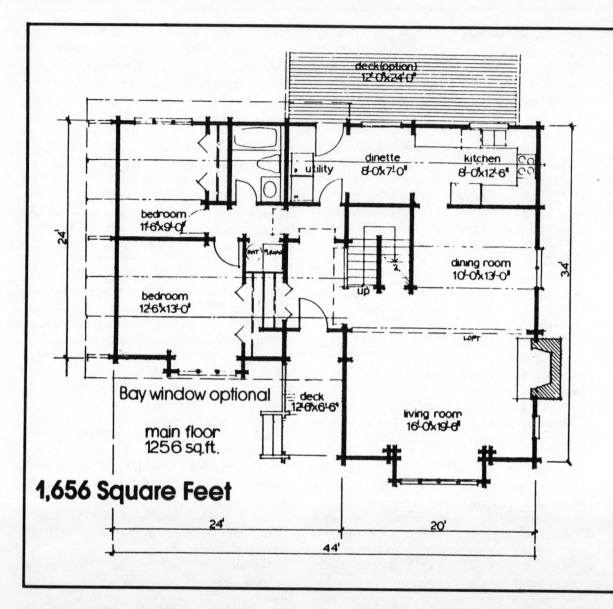

deck (option)
12'-0"x24'-0"

dinette
8'-0"x7'-0"

kitchen
8'-0"x12'-6"

utility

bedroom
11'-6"x9'-0"

dining room
10'-0"x13'-0"

up

bedroom
12'-6"x13'-0"

LOFT

Bay window optional

deck
12'-0"x6'-6"

living room
16'-0"x19'-6"

main floor
1256 sq. ft.

1,656 Square Feet

24'

34'

24'

20'

44'

in the wrong spot, a stairway doesn't fit quite right, or some elements are out of proportion. This is the time to straighten out all these details and to make sure you have ample space everywhere.

With this satisfactorily out of the way, scale in all the major pieces of furniture, both present and contemplated. An easy way to do this is to draw out the furnishings on a piece of stiff paper or light cardboard, then label them and cut them out. Then you can shuffle them around to suit. When you find a suitable spot, outline the cutouts lightly. Use actual dimensions where you can, and chase down approximate sizes in books and catalogs where you cannot.

The purpose of this exercise is to make sure that your furniture will fit comfortably into place with no crowding, that there is ample room to move around them, that they do not

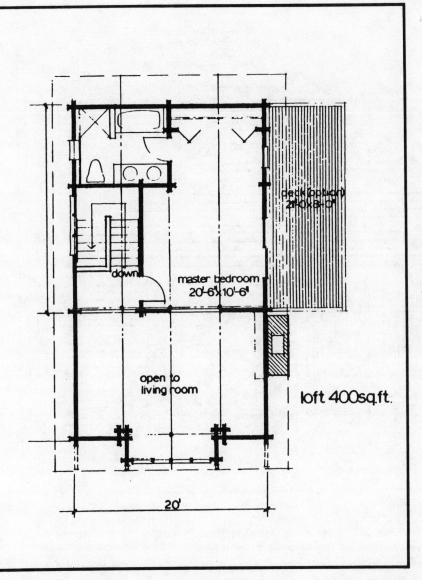

deck (option)
21'-0"x8'-0"

master bedroom
20'-6"x10'-6"

down

open to
living room

loft 400 sq. ft.

20'

Fig. 2-2. Typical scaled and dimensioned formal floor plan. A working blueprint floor plan would be much larger and include even more detail. (Courtesy of Pan Abode Cedar homes.)

interfere with built-ins, windows, or doors, and that the traffic patterns remain free. Here again, you might run into some problems that will require moving a door or window, changing the swing of a door, setting a partition back a bit, or even changing an entire section around. Be sure, too, that all your doorways are sufficiently wide; 2 feet 8 inches is the most common width, but making all passageway and entry doors 3 feet wide is the best arrangement.

Doorways should also be handily placed, allowing you to move furnishings and appliances in and around with a minimum of difficulty.

Next come the elevations, your second most important drawings. An elevation is a view of one exterior plane of a building, as though you were looking at it straight on (Fig. 2-3). In a simple design there are four elevations: front, back, and two sides or ends. These plans should also be done to scale and include

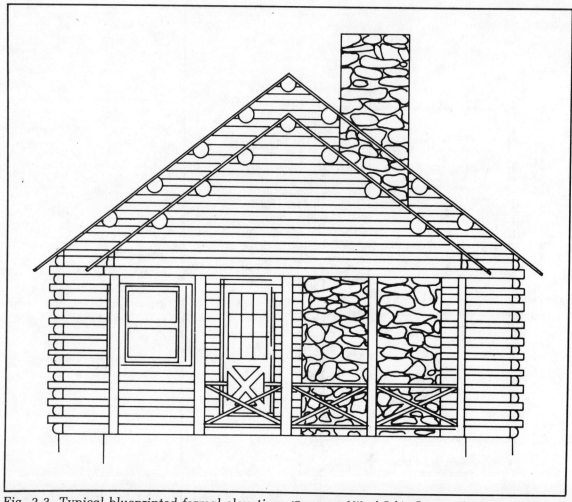

Fig. 2-3. Typical blueprinted formal elevation. (Courtesy of Ward Cabin Company.)

all exterior detail. Position windows and doors accurately, include whatever portion of the foundation is visible, draw the roof in perspective if it is visible in that elevation, and add any trim or other architectural details that might be present. The finished drawing is a picture of just what that particular face of the house will look like when completed. Once again you might discover some problems. Perhaps the window placement is not symmetrical but should be, or you don't like the way the front entrance shapes up, or the trim you have chosen seems out of proportion. Make whatever changes are indicated, and at the same time coordinate those changes as necessary with your floor plans.

That completes the most fundamental of the working drawings, but there is yet more work to be done. You need to draw a foundation plan. Also, there are some peculiarities in log construction that must be accounted for at the outset or you will encounter a lot of difficulties later on. Many of these details depend upon exactly how the house will be constructed, and whether or not and where conventional framing methods will be used in combination with log construction. These details will be considered at the appropriate points throughout the rest of this book, so unless you are already familiar with both log and frame construction you will need to digest this information—and perhaps do some further study as well—before you can adequately go ahead with final drawings, detailing, and specifications.

There are two particular points concerning log construction to keep in mind. The first is that all log houses settle to some degree, usually far more than conventional structures. There are a lot of specifics involved here, but you can usually anticipate anywhere from ½ inch to 5 inches or more of settling to take place in the walls. This means that certain methods must be used to attach things to these walls, because everything solidly anchored will be carried downward. This can lead to interesting problems like buckling pipes, bowing partitions, and support posts being driven through the floor.

The second point to remember is that the utilities cannot be installed in a log house with the same ease as in a framed house. Water pipes, wires, heat ducts, and vent pipes must be routed around the logs, and all points of conflict must be eliminated before construction. Spaces, chases, and pathways for utilities materials have to be planned for ahead of time. Many pipes and wires must be installed as the construction proceeds, rather than afterward, because there are no spaces or paths (or those become blocked in) into which they can be placed later.

This in turn means that the electrical, heating, and plumbing systems, as well as auxiliary systems like door chimes, stereo speakers, telephones, and security systems, should be located on additional plan sheets so each pipe and wire can be routed with the least number of problems. If this is not done, you might discover too late that you have a toilet sitting squarely atop a 12-inch girder, or a doorbell system that cannot be installed because you can't get the wires through, or a heat duct that sticks clear out into the room because no provision was made for recessing it.

These auxiliary plans, then, should be drawn up before construction begins, and coordinated with the floor plan and other plans and/or detail drawings that show the layout of the floor framing, foundation, rafters, etc. Installation details for doors, windows, fireplaces, chimneys, interior walls, cabinets, and built-ins can also be spelled out in auxiliary drawings (the details themselves will be discussed in later chapters). Admittedly this is a good deal of work, but if done now will save considerable time and probably a few headaches later on, and result in a more satisfactory job.

SITE SELECTION

If you are going to build a new house, the first thing needed is a piece of ground to put it on. The selection of a home site is a highly personal matter that needs to be addressed with great care. Every bit as much care, in fact, as you exercise in the designing and planning of the house itself. For in truth, the two go hand in hand and must form a happy marriage, as will become evident as we go along.

The site should be the biggest and best one that you can afford and reasonably take care of, even if the initial cost seems a bit high. There must be something about it that draws you, entices you, makes you feel that this, rather than somewhere else, is where you want to be. That something might be a a gurgling brook, an expansive view, a stand of old oak trees, a desert at one side or a mountain at the other, or perhaps a combination of factors. When you see the perfect place you'll know it, but only you can decide what elements go into the final decision to settle here or to move on.

As far as general locales where a log house might fit in, there is no right or wrong even though some spots will obviously be better than others. A log house will stand proudly in just about any surroundings you can name. It also fares as well in urban settings as in rural, though from a property-value standpoint it should be in keeping with the general tone of the neighborhood.

There are some practicalities involved in choosing a piece of land, and you will probably have to make a few further analyses of your lifestyle and your likes and dislikes as you go about making your selection. Cost is a prominent factor, because it's entirely possible to tie yourself up so tightly with land that you can no longer afford to build the house. The tax burden is another important item—not so much the taxes that are imposed upon the bare ground as you buy it, but those that will come into effect once the house is finished and the property is improved. You'll also have to decide upon the general type of land you want, depending upon your interests. You might like ground suitable for a garden, pasture land for horses or cows, a mixed hardwood and softwood woodlot for cutting your own firewood or the logs to build your house with, or perhaps just enough land around the house to admit a postage-stamp lawn and a few flower borders.

You'll also have to figure out how urban or rural you would like to be. These decisions revolve around such factors as proximity to one's work, the presence of children and their ages and activities, whether you prefer the readily available cultural, social, and shopping opportunities of the city or the peace and solitude of the country, and how much travelling you are willing to do for shopping and assorted errands.

There are other important considerations, too. For instance, how close do you need to be to medical and hospital facilities? Or a fire station? Or a police station? Evaluate the pros and cons of tapping onto a municipal sewage system and water supply as opposed to having and maintaining your own well and septic system. How about noise from highways, airports, schoolyards, or cattle feedlots? Do you want neighbors close by, or would you prefer no one around at all? How about a view, shade trees, maximum sunshine, irrigation water, a nearby

creek? All these questions need to be answered as you sort through pieces of land offered up by the real estate folks.

As you narrow your choices down to two or three spots, your questions about whether or not this one or that one is the right spot should become more and more pointed. Spend some time at these locations, during different parts of the day, different seasons if you can, and in varying weather. Note sun directions, shade possibilities, the prevailing wind directions. A spot high on a hilltop might have a fine view, but is open to the weather, and sound might travel upward to it. A spot low in the valley might be well protected, but damp and chilly. Are there trees and vegetation that can become part of the eventual landscaping plan? What about swampy spots, or a high water table, or runoff that might come through in the spring or during heavy rainstorms? Are there rock ledges that might have to be blasted out in order to build, or is there a lot or earthmoving or excavating to do? Can you build a driveway or access road without much trouble? The property should have as many natural assets that you can put to work for you, and as few drawbacks that will work against you, as possible.

Then come the final practicalities. Make sure the title to the property is clear and that there are no liens or other encumbrances that might cause future problems. Be sure you have free access to the property, and don't have to cross other private property to reach yours. Many an unwary landowner has ended up locked in (or out) with absolutely no access legally available.

If a septic system is required, be certain that the soil will pass the necessary percolation tests for soil/water absorption. If it can't, you won't be able to install a septic system and might not be able to build your house. If a water supply is needed, make certain the water rights don't belong to somebody else, and that a permit can be obtained if that regulation pertains. Also try to determine whether or not there is any underground water at a reasonable level to be had in that area. Drilling a dry hole is an expensive proposition.

Don't forget to get all the information on utilities, such as telephone service, fuel oil delivery, electrical service, natural gas hookup, television reception or cable, water and sewer tap fees if applicable, and any other matters that might be important to your building program and your future way of life. Be sure to check on all codes and regulations that might affect you, too. If all are acceptable, abide by them cheerfully and your building chores will proceed with a remarkable lack of bureaucratic hassle.

SITING THE HOUSE

Once the piece of property has been selected, the next step is to determine the best spot to locate the house. On a city or town lot this is usually a simple matter, because the house can only be shifted a few feet in any direction. On a large parcel of land, you could have several choices which must be worked down to a final location by the process of elimination. This spot should have as many advantages going for you as you can muster, and there are plenty of possibilities. Most of them come at no extra charge, so you might just as well extract as much benefit from them as you can.

Perhaps the greatest gift any homeowner can receive, especially when high energy costs are prevalent, is ample sunshine. The more the better (except in extra-hot locales), because if you don't have it on the site there is no way you can get it, but if you do, you can control and use it to provide whatever degree of light/shade and heat/coolness you want—within reason. Full sun the day long beaming directly upon the building site is usually a great plus. That sunshine will provide plenty of good light inside the house. It will also provide free heat during the cool months, but can be adequately blocked out when desirable during the warm months. And of course if your design includes solar heating/cooling of any kind (an ex-

cellent idea), day-long sunlight is a primary requirement. Solar heating systems, incidentally, can be incorporated very nicely into log structures.

A corollary of sunshine is shade, which can be another plus factor in proper house siting. If you know where the sun strikes at the site, and for how long, and at what angles and directions it falls in during the various seasons, you can determine where the shade will be and to what extent throughout the year. This includes not only the shadows cast by existing trees and shrubbery, but also that of the house itself. With this knowledge you can figure out the most effective compromise in the lie of the house to provide both sun and shade at various points simultaneously, and at different times of year. For instance, you might plan for a series of decks around the house that would be suitable for either sunbathing or relaxing in the shade at any given time. The same information might affect the placement of windows, greenhouse, gardens, various species of flowers or shrubs, or a swimming pool.

Another point to consider in siting the house is the weather. In most locations there will be one prevailing wind direction, as well as a secondary one from which the wind will blow less often and usually less forcefully. Major storms will generally follow the principal track, with minor ones coming in along the secondary track once in a while. There might also be a primary fair-weather wind direction and a somewhat different primary storm-track direction. By figuring out just where these tracks lie you can turn them to your advantage. Position the house so that the impact of the prevailing winds and the principal storms is minimized. This usually involves setting the narrowest portion of the building, that which has the least exposure of wall and roof, into the wind/storm flow so that the current has relatively less to slam into and moves on around the structure. This has the effect of reducing wind pressures and thus the possibility of structural damage, of reducing the overall weathering of the house exterior, and of reducing the total heat loss of the house during cold and windy weather.

Knowing the wind/weather patterns at your building site can also give you some clues as to window and door placement. For instance, as little glass as possible should be placed in walls that face the track, in order to conserve heat and minimize damage possibilities. Exterior doors, whether located in a vestibule-type air lock or in an exterior house wall proper, can also be placed out of the weather track, and can be positioned so that they swing open against the wind. This cuts down the amount of air (and debris as well) that enters when the door is opened. Also, as it is opened the door forms a shield for the user, and doesn't stand as much chance of being ripped off its hinges by a gust. By determining both the bad-weather wind track and the fair-weather track, you can arrange windows for the maximum of cross ventilation and a minimum of storm impact. Casement windows, for instance, can be installed so they open outward into the fair-weather breezes to act as scoops that direct fresh air into the house.

There might be other advantages in your building site, ones that can be all too easily overlooked. Before you barge ahead with a bulldozer, do a little looking around. See where you can make the lay of the land work for you, perhaps by providing a natural drainage watershed away from the house. Place both house and any proposed outbuildings so as to destroy as few trees and shrubs as possible. All these growing things can be easily worked into an overall landscaping plan, thereby saving you an immense amount of labor and dollars. If need be, you can always cull some or all of them out later on.

Make full use of any natural features like a big boulder, a meandering rivulet, a natural terrace, or whatever. Incorporate such features into the overall landscaping design and let them complement the house rather than going to the expense and difficulty of removing or re-

engineering them. Choose the easiest and most natural path for the driveway or access road. The results are usually much more pleasing and a good deal less expensive than blasting a road through all manner of obstacles. In short, many of the natural features of the homesite and its immediate surroundings can be used in your favor in one way or another if you take the time and exercise the imagination to coordinate them into a master estate plan.

Then there is the matter of a view. No matter where or how your house is located there is always a view, actually several of them. They may be short range—20 feet into a forest, or long range—40 miles toward a mountain backdrop. Whatever the case, situate the house, the windows, and the decks or porches so as to take the greatest advantage of them. And while you're performing this chore, plug in a few other factors as well. You'll want to see the sunrise from the breakfast nook, the sunset from the deck, the moon from your master bedroom window...

Does all this seem impossible? It isn't really. Compromise is necessary, and there will inevitably be some elements that will have to be either disregarded or completely eliminated. Nonetheless, list all the advantages in order of priority, shuffle them about, and squeeze all the good out of them that you can. The result is worth the effort.

But how do you begin? About the best way to tackle the problem of siting is to gather up all your information, arm yourself with a bundle of survey stakes, a hammer, a big ball of string, and go to the building site. With a compass, orient yourself so you know just where the cardinal directions lie, and then work out the sun and wind/weather tracks. Next, lay out one axis of the house so that it faces exactly in the direction you have selected as the most desirable (for solar designs, or for maximum solar input into nonsolar designs, the major collecting elements should face due south, plus or minus about 15 degrees to the east or west).

The next step is to locate all the corners

of the house, measuring out the proper distances with a 50- or 100-foot tape, keeping the whole outline as square and proportionate as you can. You'll probably have to do a bit of restaking and adjusting here and there, but with a little care you can make a surprisingly accurate layout. Run string from stake to stake to make an outline of the house. With a few more stakes you can include the first-floor rooms as well. You'll just have to imagine any upper or lower levels, but now you should be able to visualize the appearance of the house after construction, and you can see approximately how well the structure will fit in with its surroundings. You can also see if you have goofed anywhere.

For instance, by relating your sketches and plans to the full-size outline you have just made, you might discover that some of your window placements are not as good as they could be. Or perhaps there isn't quite enough room for the garage, the deck hangs out over a ledge or runs into a big tree that you want to save, or the driveway really shouldn't go where you had planned to put it. With the house in place, maybe there is no longer enough room at the immediate site to readily truck in, maneuver, and yard the logs for the structure—which is a must. You could even find that the overall orientation is not quite right, and the entire house should be moved a few feet this way or that in order to take full advantage of some natural features. You might also discover some new advantages or different possibilities in the siting, or that you even want to resite.

This kind of siting work is about the last chance you have to make any substantial changes and to reconsider your overall design. The final decisions should be made now, so that the paperwork can be finished, the final plans or working drawings made, and the business of site preparation begun. Therefore, there is no valid reason to rush at this stage. Take all the time you need, wander around the building site pondering and muttering to yourself. Shove all your questions back and forth until you get satisfactory answers; remember that you'll have to live with them, probably for quite a while. Curb your impatience to get on with the project. When you have covered everything you can think of and are satisfied and content with what you have wrought, quit. Set the stakes and strings in their final approximate locations and leave them for future reference. Pack up your gear and go home to make a plot plan.

The plot plan is the last one of the entire series. It shows in outline form the piece of property and the house, plus any outbuildings, in dimensional relationship to the property boundaries (Fig. 2-4). The building and the plot should be oriented to the proper compass direction. This plan will also show the driveway, power line route, septic tank layout or sewer line, well or water line, and any other pertinent details including some of the major dimensions and distances. Depending upon the scale and the actual size of the plan itself, you can also include any of the principal topographical features immediately surrounding the house, such as gardens, shrubbery, and shade trees. Such a plan can often be drawn up using a property improvement (or other) survey map as a basis.

A similar large plan can be drawn of just the house and its immediate surroundings, that shows all the plantings and natural features. This is called a landscaping plan and is not usually a part of the standard blueprint package of a residence, but rather is for the convenience of the owner or for a professional landscaper's use. Sometimes these plans are drawn up in minute detail by a professional landscape architect, even spelling out exactly what plants are to go where.

SITE PREPARATION

Site preparation is exactly what the term implies, getting the building site and the immediate vicinity ready for the construction process. To many builders this means hauling in a bull-

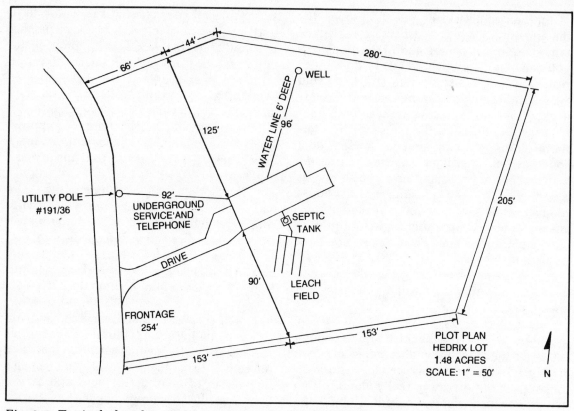

Fig. 2-4. *Typical plot plan. A large version also might include grade elevations, topographical features, sun and weather track, and other site features.*

dozer and a backhoe, hacking out an access road, scrubbing the site clean and flat, gouging out a big hole for foundations, and carving a series of trenches for water lines, power lines, and waste disposal system. This could as easily be called "site ruination," for the result looks like something left over from a bombing raid. Speed and convenience, which translates into dollars saved, are the demons that drive such builders. And to be sure, construction is a bit easier when there is nothing at all in the way and the site is as level as a pool table. However, the ultimate loss to the homeowner is sizable, because site restoration then must follow—at a huge outlay of both labor and expense and a lot of elapsed time. And the natural assets of the setting are virtually destroyed.

This is one aspect in particular of the building process where the homeowner is well advised to take an active part. The exact approach depends to some degree upon the type of foundation to be built, the kind and extent of the utilities systems, and the characteristics of the site. The goal to shoot for is an absolute minimum of disturbance to anything on or around the site that has not previously been earmarked as being fair game. This means careful consideration ahead of time about what must be moved or removed and what must not. Earth-moving and excavating machinery can be worked to great advantage if the operators are experienced, capable, and told exactly what they are to do, and have the benefit of constant supervision by someone who knows exactly what should be done. The homeowner usually best fulfills that role.

It is possible for the homeowner to prepare the site almost entirely alone, and by hand. Don't scoff; this has been done many times and will be again in the future. Not all of the following elements are necessary at every site, of course, but this is the general routine.

To begin, clear a route for the driveway, if necessary, by cutting out brush and trees with axe and/or saw. Buck up the trees and stack them to cure for firewood. Pile the brush and slash for removal, or burning it if that is convenient and permissible. Have the driveway rough-graded with a small machine. (Even though the job takes a bit longer, a small machine is more maneuverable and potentially causes less damage than a big one.) Determine ahead of time where any excess dirt will be placed. In some cases spoil dirt is best removed entirely from the site.

Perform the same tasks in the area where the construction materials will be placed and where the foundation will be built. If the foundation consists of piers, dig the pier holes with a post-hole shovel and a bar, or a power auger. Save the topsoil for use elsewhere, and pile the subsoil where it is handy for backfilling the piers; after the piers are set the little remaining subsoil can be scattered about.

A trench for underground power and telephone lines need only be 2 feet deep or less, and can be dug with a pick and shovel, or a power trencher that makes only a narrow slit. Water lines can be laid in the same way in warm areas, but in cold climates will have to be dug down 4 or 5 feet or more by machine, preferably a small, narrow-bucket backhoe. Choose a path that will disturb the least amount of vegetation and at the same time involve the least amount of digging. The hole and trenches for a septic tank and leach field can be dug by hand, but that's a big job; a machine is faster, easier, and damage can be minimized with care. However, all backfilling can be done by hand.

Most other kinds of foundations require a certain amount of excavation, and the only practical means is by machine. Again, opt for the smaller ones, and have a spot already picked out for disposal of spoil dirt. Exception: if a large full basement must be dug back into a hillside and a great deal of spoil removed, a big bucket-loader will do the job better, faster, and cheaper. Some of the spoil will be needed later for backfill, so this should be kept close at hand but out of the way of the construction work. Use the remaining spoil advantageously for fill or contouring, if possible; otherwise, have it trucked away. Topsoil should be scraped off first and set aside for later use in revegetating.

Investigate the relative difficulties of revegetating your particular area. In some places a cut made even deep into the subsoil will quickly re-cover itself and take on a natural appearance in short order. In semi-arid or arid areas, however, the natural process can take years. Forced restoration of vegetation is also difficult and costly, and can take a lot of time and attention before presenting a decent appearance.

In many cases a driveway comes directly to the house, so the parking pad, turnaround spot, or the area on which the garage will eventually sit are good possibilities for material storage and vehicle parking during the first stages of construction. Try to avoid indiscriminate piling of materials here and there around the site. Also avoid random driving around the building, especially when the ground is moist. The resulting damage is very difficult to repair. Sometimes the driveway and garage or parking pad are separated from the residence proper by a considerable distance. If so, the excavating equipment must make a track from driveway to house site, but you should only have to use it a few times. If you keep supply trucks and workers' vehicles off this track, your subsequent job of restoration will be much easier. Though more effort is involved at the time, store materials in the driveway and pack them to the construction site by hand. There might be a lot of complaining about this, but the al-

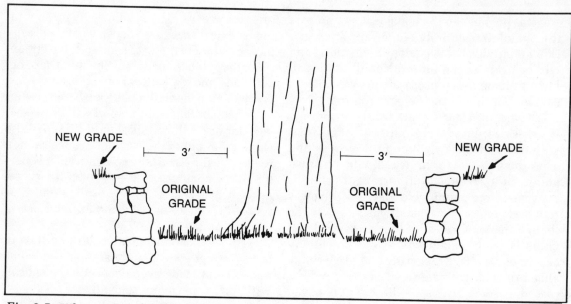

Fig. 2-5. When a new, higher grade level is established around a tree, create a large well around it with rock, railroad ties, or concrete landscaping block and leave the original grade undisturbed.

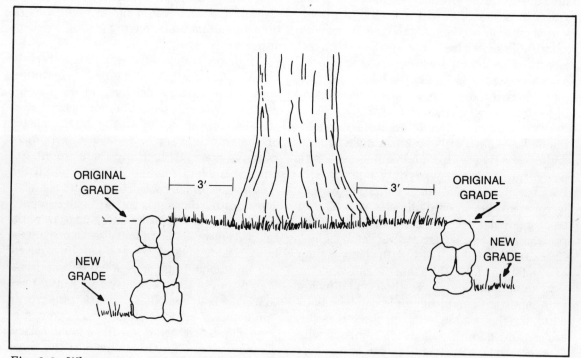

Fig. 2-6. When a new, lower grade level is established, maintain the original grade level for 3 feet or more around a tree by cribbing the soil with rock, railroad ties, or concrete landscaping block.

ternative for you is a considerable amount of cost and labor later on in repairing the damage to thoroughly torn up premises.

You'll be accused of doing everything the hard way, but if you make a conscious, determined effort to preserve every shrub, bush, tree, patch of natural wild grass, and clump of flowers, within a year after construction your new home will look as though it has always been right there.

One last point. Of all the natural elements to be found on your building site, by far the most valuable are the trees. Try to preserve every single tree possible around the site that hasn't been used for building. It takes a long time to grow a tree, but only a few minutes to destroy one. Trees that are damaged during house construction might well die within a season or two. Protect any trees that are close to the building site and might suffer mechanical damage by wrapping the trunks with burlap sacking or standing a row of boards or a ring of old auto tires in a cylinder around the trunks, wired or tied in place. If the bark of a tree gets gashed or skinned off, trim the bark carefully and then paint the wound with a commercial tree paint.

Recontouring the land also presents difficulties. If you push fill dirt around the trunk of a tree any deeper than just a few inches above the original grade, the tree is likely to die. Likewise, if you strip the soil away from around a tree, even if you don't lop off any major roots, it is also likely to die. When the grade level must be raised around a tree, build up a masonry or stone wall in a cylinder around the trunk first. This creates a well that should allow at least a foot of free space around the tree trunk; 2 or 3 feet is better. Base the wall on the original grade, then fill around the outside of it to the new grade level (Fig. 2-5). When you lower the grade level around a tree, reverse the situation, leaving a circle of original earth around the tree several feet in diameter. Build up a retaining wall from the new grade to the old, or higher (Fig. 2-6). Even at that, the tree might die if you have to cut away much of the root system. But both of these methods work fairly well in preserving trees that otherwise would be lost. The same methods, incidentally, serve equally well to preserve large shrubs and clumps of bushes.

3

Working With Logs

WHEN IT COMES TO WORKING WITH THE LOGS, most of us know little about it and have to start at the beginning. And because logs are the basis for log houses, it seems reasonable to investigate further. In fact, there are a good many things to discuss. This chapter will be of particular interest to do-it-yourselfers who want to start their log building projects at the point of origin, with the trees themselves. However, much of the information will also be needed by anyone planning to purchase raw or partly milled logs from a dealer.

WOOD CHARACTERISTICS

There are somewhere around 865 species of trees that are native to the portion of North America that lies north of Mexico. In addition, there are a number of other species that were imported from other countries years ago and have become naturalized, and there are many ornamental varieties. Obviously not all these species are suitable for log house building, or for that matter, any kind of log construction. There are many reasons for this. Some never grow tall enough, or big enough around to cut into a "log" much bigger than a walking stick. Many other species are in too short supply, or appear as widely scattered individual trees which would be difficult to gather in any quantity. Some grow gnarled and crooked and can't be cut into straight logs, while others consist mostly of branches. But even after all these species are eliminated from the running, that still leaves several dozen others that can potentially be used for log construction. Of these, about two dozen are widely used. Most of them, fortunately, are common varieties in forest regions throughout the country, and have names familiar to those who work with wood. These species have differing characteristics.

Of the many characteristics, there are several of particular interest to the log builder.

The species, as well as each individual tree used, must be of sufficient stature so that fairly long lengths of log of suitable diameter can be cut. Relative uniformity in length and roundness is important, as is a fairly gradual taper along the length of the log. The typical number of branches, their size, and the manner in which they branch is a factor. The trunk must be relatively straight, though minor imperfections, surface irregularities, and a slight degree of crookedness usually present no problems. In fact, these often add to the character of the prepared log, and thus the building itself.

Besides the physical traits that are readily apparent, there are other qualities not visible to the eye that must be considered. *Strength*, the resistance to applied stress and strain, is one such factor. Wood is an elastic material; once the limits of elasticity are reached, the wood will fail in one way or another. The elasticity of various species can be determined by test, leading to a value of relative stiffness called the *modulus of elasticity*.

Further testing gives rise to strength values against the three principal forms of stress: *compression*, *tensile*, and *shear*. All these strengths are variable depending upon the particular species, and may be measured across or with the grain of the wood. Compression strength parallel to the grain is an important consideration for structural members like support columns. Perpendicular to the grain, it reflects resistance to crushing and deformation under load. Tension strength perpendicular to the grain indicates, for example, resistance to splitting and checking. Shear strength parallel to the grain reflects the resistance of the wood fibers to separate in a plane, as in a glue joint. A fourth property is the bending behavior of wood, and is crucial to structural design; this is usually denoted as the *allowable bending stress* value. These values allow calculation of deflection of a structural member under load-carrying capacity, stiffness, allowable spans, and various assessments of the mechanical performance of structural members.

Assessment and calculation of these strength properties of woods is a complex engineering subject well beyond the scope of this book, and there is much yet to be discovered in this field. The point here for the would-be log house builder is that such factors must be taken into consideration in the design of the house.

If you are going to design your own house, you have two choices; the empirical approach, or the engineered approach. The first makes use of past experience in log building. Materials, techniques, procedures, beam spans and sizes, general designs, and construction details that have been successfully used for decades will continue to be successfully used in the future. All you have to do is find out what has worked before, and follow suit.

To use the engineered approach, you have four possibilities. First, study the subject thoroughly and do your own engineering—a difficult and lengthy process, and chancy. Second, make up your sketches and list your design ideas, then consult with a qualified architect or engineer and have them translated into a functional design. Third, make up the complete structural design yourself, then take it to a qualified architect or engineer and have all of the details checked for accuracy and modified as necessary. And last, have all of the engineering, and perhaps the design as well, done for you.

Why must all this engineering be done? So the completed structure will be safe, sturdy, and long-lived without a lot of problems, and also so that it will conform to building code regulations. For example, floor joists must be of a certain size, number, and unsupported length to hold up the weight imposed upon the floor. Roof members must withstand certain snow, wind, and dead-weight loads. Trusses must be properly designed if they are to hold up properly. Tie beams must be correctly figured and placed to withstand various stresses. The list could go on, but you get the idea.

Workability of a wood species is another significant factor, especially for a do-it-yourselfer. Some woods work easily with cutting tools, other do not. Furthermore, some woods react well to certain kinds of cutting or shaping, and not to others. The greater the workability of the particular species of wood, the more easily the logs can be shaped and fitted to construct a house.

Different species also have different *shrinkage* characteristics. Some logs will shrink rapidly and to a considerable extent, while others might shrink slowly and to only a slight extent. For example, the volumetric shrinkage of most softwoods runs around 10 to 12 percent, from fully green to oven-dry (no moisture at all). Proper allowances usually have to be made for this factor during construction.

Logs also have a certain insulating value, and this varies from species to species (although not markedly). Usually the thermal insulating value of wood is measured in terms of the R-factor or R-value per inch of thickness. Generally speaking, the lighter in weight the wood is, the greater its insulating value. The moisture content of the wood has a definite effect on insulating value, and the greater the moisture content the lower the value. Northern white cedar, for instance, is one of the lightest woods used for log construction, and at a 12 percent moisture content has an insulating R-factor of 1.41 per inch of thickness. Hickory, on the other hand, has an R-factor of only 0.71 per inch of thickness.

Some logs are more fireproof than others, though that might sound strange. In general, woods that have the best R-values because of a relatively low thermal conductivity rate also are more reluctant to burn and have a slow char penetration, and thus can resist fire penetration for a relatively longer time. Tests have shown that a 5 ½-inch-thick wall of northern white cedar will resist fire penetration for better than four hours. Most other species will not do as well.

The weight per cubic foot of the wood is important from a couple of standpoints. First and most obvious is that the heavier the logs are, the harder they will be to maneuver around and to erect into a log structure. For instance, the weight of western red cedar runs only about 23 pounds per cubic foot at a 12 percent moisture content. Beech, however, weighs about 45 pounds per cubic foot. It is apparent that the cedar will be easier to handle than the beech. In any case, if the logs have a high moisture content or are still green, right off the stump, the weight is far greater than the figures noted. Again, this varies according to the species, but the weight can easily be double or even more. The weight of the logs also is a factor in designing the foundation, which must hold up the entire weight of the structure without buckling, cracking, or settling.

Resistance to decay and insect attack is another factor to consider. Some species naturally have a high resistance; decay cannot get a foothold and insects are repelled because of the natural constituency of the wood. Redwood and cypress have an extremely high resistance, while birch and maple are at the opposite end of the scale. White birch left on the ground will rot away in one season. Redwood heartwood can be buried in the ground for years with few ill effects.

How does one decide, then, what should be used in log construction? Regardless of the final choice, a considerable amount of compromise is usually necessary. Any of the various woods used by commercial log home manufacturers are satisfactory—some are better in some ways than others. Another possibility is to check around your own area to see what readily available species have been used in the construction of log buildings. Whatever has been used in the past and has held up well can be used again to the same purpose.

If you plan to cut your own logs, you might find only one or two species locally available that fulfill the physical requirements appropriate for log construction. In fact, you can mix two or more species if you wish, and with proper care you can build a log house from virtually any species that will provide you with logs sizable enough to be suitable and workable. With one construction method, which will be discussed in Chapter 6, you can even use short chunks. A point for scratch-builders to keep in mind is that you might be able to get some good, solid information and advice on selection, cutting, tree thinning, reforestation, and like matters from the nearest U.S. Soil Conservation Service office and/or your state forestry department. Note too that permits for cutting cull trees on National Forest lands can sometimes be obtained through local Forest Service offices.

The conifers, or softwoods, are in greatest favor for log house construction at the present time. This is because they are the most readily available, usually the least expensive, and their uniformity, lightness, roundness, workability, and substantial size makes them easier to work with than most hardwoods. The inherent weakness of softwoods can be overcome by proper sizing, spacing, bracing, and other common construction practices.

Specifically, northern white cedar is perhaps one of the best woods for log house construction. Western red cedar is also an excellent choice, and Douglas fir is strong and durable. Lodgepole pine is durable and easy to work and tamarack is also fine, though less workable. Englemann spruce is a reasonable choice but not as weatherable and workable as the others. Western hemlock can be used and so can eastern hemlock, though both are susceptible to decay and the latter is difficult to work. Balsam is a fine wood to work with but decays easily and doesn't weather well, so is best used for interior work. White pine and red pine have built many a house. Among the deciduous trees, quaking aspen and yellow poplar (tuliptree) are about the easiest to work with, but the former has low decay resistance. Many other species, like locust, beech, yellow pine, red oak, and jack pine prove satisfactory. Table 3-1

Table 3-1. Wood Characteristics.

Species	Weight lbs/cu ft 12% Moisture	R-Factor Per Inch Thickness	Shrinkage	Decay Resistance	Workability
No. White Cedar	22	1.41	Very low	High	Excellent
East. Red Cedar	33	1.03	Very low	High	Excellent
West. Red Cedar	23	1.09	Very low	High	Excellent
Redwood	28	1.00	Very low	High	Excellent
Hemlock	28	1.16	Low	Low	Fair
White Pine	25	1.32	Low	Medium	Excellent
Ponderosa Pine	28	1.16	Low	Medium	Excellent
Douglas Fir	34	0.99	Medium	Medium	Fair
Tamarack	36	0.93	Medium	Medium	Fair
Red Pine	34	1.04	Low	Low	Excellent
Yellow Pine	38	0.91	Low	Medium	Hard
Aspen	26	1.22	Low	Low	Fair
Cottonwood	26	1.23	Medium	Low	Fair
White Birch	34	0.90	High	Very low	Hard
White Oak	47	0.75	Very high	High	Hard
Sugar Maple	44	0.80	High	Low	Hard
Beech	45	0.79	Very high	Low	Hard

shows the characteristics of several of the more commonly used species.

LOG SELECTION

The first step in selecting logs is to figure out exactly what you are going to need to build the house with. The average log diameter is the first question. Log size is often, but not necessarily, scaled to building size; small logs for small structures, large logs for large buildings. The possible range is anywhere from about 6 inches to 20 inches or better, but 8 to 10 inches seems to be the most common choice, probably because this size range is most readily available, and also a good compromise for weight, ease of handling, and visual impact. The average log diameter for the house relates to the mean diameter of each log. A log of 10-inch diameter at the butt and 8-inch at the tip would have a mean diameter of 9 inches. If all the logs in the house were kept about to this size, the average would thus be 9 inches. Whatever the diameter chosen, all of the logs used for each different structural purpose should be about the same. There is an exception: occasionally a log house design calls for large wall logs at the bottom, gradually becoming smaller toward the top.

Next, if you've not already done so, decide whether you will lay up the walls of the house first and then cut in the window and door openings, or set the window and door bucks first and piece the logs to them (this is the way most kit houses are built). For scratch-building, the former method is usually considered the best, using as many full-length, wall-to-wall logs as possible (all of them, preferably). This results in a strong structure that goes up nicely, without a lot of fooling around with shorts, bracing, and props. But, a case can be made for the other method, too, especially if long logs are in short supply.

Figure out how many logs high the walls will be, according to the average diameter. If your plans call for 8-foot walls and you have decided on 8-inch-diameter logs, the stack will be 12 logs high. It is best to stay with an even number, by the way, because in most constructions this is the easiest way to obtain a level top row; the even-numbered rows level out the odd-numbered ones and there is no need for split-log fillers. You will also need to determine what other structural members will be fashioned from logs rather than dimension stock, such as partitions, floor joists, tie beams, support posts, girders, trusses, purlins, or rafters. The diameters and required lengths of these pieces must also be established.

Now you can make up your grocery list, a complete schedule of each and every log section you will need to put the whole house together, keyed and numbered (Table 3-2). For example, the first log on the east wall might be EW-1, the second EW-2, a floor joist FJ-1, a purlin P-1, and so on. You will have to make up your own code, depending upon exactly what members are needed. Note the length of each log, allowing about 2 feet or more on each end for wall logs, and noting the diameters needed if different from the wall logs. Floor joists, for instance, need not necessarily be as thick as the wall logs, and can be spaced close or wide depending upon the diameter you finally settle upon. Other logs, such as the ridge pole, purlins, rafters, collar ties, and brace poles will be of various diameters. They can be just thick and long enough to fulfill their structural functions, or, as in the case of a visible ridge log and rafters, greatly oversized for dramatic impact.

Talley up the total number of logs needed for each different diameter. Make note of any logs that perhaps should have special characteristics, like an extra-massive and straight ridge log or particularly good sill or plate logs. If you will be using short lengths—as between a pair of windows set in as the walls are laid up—note the approximate diameter each piece should be at each end. Reference them against their position in the wall relative to the full-length logs below them so that you will have an approximate diameter match and a consistent taper.

Table 3-2. Typical Log Materials Keying List.

Walls—8″ Diameter	
EW-1 to 3—18′	Main Floor Joists-8″
EW-4A to 9A—6′	MJ-1 to 22—12′
EW-4B to 9B—3′	MJ-23 and 24—8′
EW-4C to 9C—4′	Ell Floor Joists—7″
EW-10 to 12—18′	EJ-1 to 8—8′
SW-1 to 12—12′	Main Roof Purlins—8″
SWW-1 to 12—7′	MP 1-8—24′
WW-1 to 3—18′	Ell Roof Purlins 6″
	EP-1 to 8—10′

There are two more items to add to your list. First, tally up the number of pieces you will need of each different diameter, and make a rough estimate of the number of trees you will need to fell of each diameter to fill your needs. You can base this on an estimate of the length of the full-length logs that can be obtained from your woodlot. And second, determine a maximum and a minimum butt-end circumference for each log diameter category, and make a note of it.

As an example, if your wall logs are to average 8 inches in diameter and you want a maximum taper of 3 inches for the full-length logs, the average butt diameter would be 9½ inches. Add to this an allowance for bark thickness, which depends upon the species of tree you will be cutting. If the bark happens to run about ¼ inch thick (all you can do is make an educated estimate), add ½ inch for the bark. Clearly, not all the trees that you select will be exactly 10 inches in diameter at the butt, so it is best to settle upon a diameter range that will be workable, say, plus or minus 1 inch. Then translate these maximum and minimum diameters, including bark, into the tree trunk circumference sizes that you will need to look for. Multiply 9 and 11 inches (to follow this example) by 3.1416. Thus, you would select trees between about 28¼ inches and 34½ inches in diameter. The measurement should always be taken at about waist height, not down near the ground where you will likely be cutting, or where the trunk flares outward as it reaches the root system.

Once you have made up a complete list of all your requirements you can take tape measure in hand and amble out into the woods to begin searching. Select the straightest, truest trees of your chosen species that you can find, and be picky about it. The less taper the better—strive for about 2 inches from butt to tip of the longest lengths you need. Not 2 inches for an entire log, necessarily, because while some trees might only yield one working log, others can be cut into two or more. The fewer branches the better, because this reduces felling problems, limbing labor, and peeling time.

Check each tree for straightness by standing well away—100 feet if you can manage it—and eyeballing the trunk, then move off to a 90-degree angle and do it again. If the tree looks good, move up to it and sight directly up the bole into the branches. If the tree is indeed straight, that fact will be apparent. Check also for obvious defect: splits, lightning damage, growths, or anything that might affect usefulness. Avoid trees with spiral grain (an obvious barber-pole effect) at all costs, because they are nothing but trouble.

As you search, bypass problem trees and select only those that can be felled with a minimum of difficulty. You can always come back to them later if you run short of prime choices. Trees that lean beyond just two or three degrees from the vertical can be troublesome, for example. Avoid any that do not have a relatively clear felling path and might get hung up in the branches of other trees while falling. Trees that grow out of the ground at an angle and curve upward contain reaction wood and will be very difficult to cut and to work. Those that grow out of ledges or rockpiles, or are located on steep slopes, are more trouble to fell than they are usually worth. In short, pick only the easy ones, unless forced to do otherwise by a short supply.

As you find each tree that seems suitable, measure its diameter at about waist height. If it falls within your diameter range, wrap a length of brightly colored plastic survey tape (available at any lumberyard) around it and go on to the next possibility. Work your way through your list of requirements, keeping track of the numbers and ticking off each category when you feel you have just about filled it. It is a good idea to write on the survey tape with an idelible marker what purpose you had in mind for the tree. When your initial selection is pretty much complete, you can come back and start felling them. After the trees have been felled, the process of selection continues. The logs have to be cut into lengths and keyed to your materials list. This will be discussed later in this chapter.

If you will not be cutting your own logs but instead buying them from a log supplier or directly from a mill, you will still need your list of requirements. In fact, you might want to refine it even more so that everything is clearly spelled out in the way of sizes. If possible, get permission to make the selection of logs yourself, with the help of the supplier. Failing that, request that you be allowed to inspect all the logs chosen for you before or as they are loaded at the shipping point, with the right of refusal for any inferior or incorrect pieces. The criteria to apply in selecting or inspecting purchased logs are just the same as for those you would cut yourself. In addition, though, you will need to look carefully for cracks, splits, checks,

mechanical damage, structural defects or weaknesses in each log. There's no point in paying for logs that you can't or won't use. But it is also a good idea to include a few extra logs in your order, against whatever circumstances might arise later on.

FELLING TREES

If you think that hacking down trees is an easy job, think again. It requires care, caution, physical exertion, and, above all, thought. Expert tree felling is a craft that requires the development of skill and judgement. A good woodsman or a professional logger can make everything look easy, but that comes from experience. A beginner who has never taken a tree down is well advised to start in on something besides those trees that have been singled out for use in the log house. (In fact, you could hire a professional to do all the felling, if you are wary of it.) Select a few small trees around the place that need to be culled out. Practice on these and trim them for later use as fence posts or deck railings, or buck them up and stack them to cure for firewood.

There are three ways you can cut down a tree. The traditional method is with an axe, and exactly which type you use of the several available is mostly a matter of personal preference. There are various combinations of head styles, weights, and handle configurations from which to choose. Select a single-bitted axe in the interest of safety and convenience, and leave the big double-bitted jobs to the loggers. For felling, a substantial head weight of 4 pounds or perhaps a bit more is good. The handle should be straight-grained and clear hickory with no knots or blemishes, no paint or varnish, and no warps or crookedness. A length of from 26 to 30 inches is about right, depending upon your reach. The same axe can be used for limbing, though many prefer a somewhat lighter model, around a 3-pound head with the same handle length.

The second method of felling uses an axe

in combination with a saw. For working alone, choose a pulp saw or a one-man timber saw. The two-man timber saw, which is available in several lengths and blade widths, is easier and faster to use—provided you can talk someone into manning the opposite handle. A narrow blade is best for felling, a wide one for bucking. Saws of this sort can often be bought used if you happen to live in timbering country, or can be purchased new through various tool supply houses. Either way, they are not terribly expensive.

The third and most favored method of felling is by chainsaw. There are many brands currently available, and choosing one is not a difficult matter. Price is a consideration, of course, and so is readily available service. Stay away from the production and gear-driven types, which are heavy and intended primarily for constant-duty, commercial production work. Choose a name brand, direct-drive saw of relatively light weight.

The power of a chainsaw is dependent in large measure on the engine displacement in cubic inches. A small saw has a displacement of about 1.5 cubic inches, ranging up to 9 cubic inches or more for the monsters. For general all-around work a displacement of about 3 or 4 inches is usually sufficient, and a saw of this size is fairly easy to handle.

The size of the guide bar, around which the cutting chain runs, can be matched to the size of the timber you plan to cut. Choose a bar that is a few inches longer than the greatest diameter, at cutting height, of the trees you plan to tackle. Thus, a 16-inch bar is more than adequate for taking down 12-inch trees. And although a 16-inch bar will cut through a 32-inch-diameter or even larger log on the ground by making two or more cuts, felling is best done with one continuous cut. Incidentally, most chainsaw dealers are willing to give you a demonstration plus a couple of quick lessons in proper saw care and handling, which is well worth the time spent.

About the only other tools you will need

for felling trees, besides sharpening equipment for your saw and axe (which should be kept very sharp at all times) are a couple of wedges. These are used in two ways: to help control the direction of the fall of a tree, and to keep the saw blade from binding in the cut. Wedges are mighty handy to have around, even if you are doing the whole job with an axe. The most common variety of wedge is steel. These are fine for use with axes or handsaws, but they should never be set in the same cut as a chainsaw, because of the possibility of the chain touching the wedge and being ruined in a fraction of a second. And chains are expensive. Plastic or hardwood wedges are best used with a chainsaw, and they are also available in aluminum and magnesium. The usual practice in setting wedges is to tap them into place with the back of an axe head, but you can use a small hand sledge if you wish.

There has always been some argument about the best time of year for cutting house logs. From some standpoints the best time is winter. This is the easiest time on both logs and loggers. Tree felling is hot, hard work in the best of circumstances, so working when the temperature is down is more pleasant. Also, you won't have to fight with black flies, mosquitoes, and other bothersome critters. More to the point is that there is little sap up in the trees, which makes for better curing when the logs are cribbed. Also, a snow cover acts as a protective cushion for the logs when they fall. Skidding the logs out is often easier on a frozen track, and the logs handle better and stay cleaner. On the other hand, there is the difficulty of getting around in deep snow, the possibility of too much cold, and the dangers presented by ice on logs or underfoot. Also, felling frozen trees can sometimes be tricky.

Late fall is a good time for felling. There is little sap activity at this time, though more than in the winter, so the logs will cure nicely and the cutting presents no problems out of the ordinary. This makes for a good time schedule, too, because the logs have time to cure fairly well in the 6 or 7 months before they are needed for summer construction.

Late summer or early fall works out reasonably well, too. Spring and early summer cutting is the best as far as the logs are concerned if you plan to peel them. This is when the job is most easily done, but only if they are peeled almost immediately after cutting. Otherwise the bark dries and shrinks, adhering tightly to the wood and making it more difficult to remove. And, immediate bark removal is itself an arguable proposition; some builders prefer to leave it on for slower curing and protection of the wood. For the logger, spring cutting tends to be miserable. There might be rotten snow, rain, soft ground or mud, and insects to contend with. Skidding, as well as general working conditions, might be difficult. In addition, spring-cut logs, depending upon the species, have a higher susceptibility to insect and fungus attack, and might be more likely to split, check, and crack as they dry.

Now, how does one actually go about the business of felling a tree? The first thing to do is check the lie of the tree. A tree is extremely heavy, often with a large percentage of the weight toward the top (depending upon the species and the season of the year). Many trees are impressively top-heavy, in fact, and invariably a tree leans in one direction or another, even if only slightly. By checking the lean and noting the conformation of the treetop to get an idea of about where the top-heavy weight lies, you can get a good indication of the direction in which the tree should naturally fall. Note that some trees also tend to be side-heavy, which can add to the fun.

Next, check the path of the fall and the area where the tree will land. The felling pathway and drop area should be clear, with no other trees or branches to interfere seriously, and no great boulders or a tangle of deadfall that might hinder the fall, hang the tree up, or smash the trunk when it hits the ground. Remember that these logs will be used for both structural and architectural purposes, so you don't want them gouged and bashed and beat up. It is very easy to break a tree's back or weaken the log with splits by felling it across another log or a big rock.

The natural fall line of a tree might be ideally clear, in which case you can go right to work. But more often than not there are other trees or ground obstructions in the way. Sometimes obstructions can be cleared away and interfering trees limbed or trimmed out completely to make a clear path. If this can't be done, the felling chore becomes trickier, because you have to redirect the natural lean of the tree so that it will drop in a more suitable direction.

Redirecting is not a job for a beginner, and often as not the best course is to leave the tree and select another. The possibilities of a "hanger," a tree that gets tangled up and comes to a halt halfway through its descent, is to be avoided. They're difficult and dangerous to work with, and should be left alone or taken down by a professional.

Another factor to keep in mind as you are making your felling calculations is the wind. The branches of a tree act as a sail to catch wind currents, and the pressure exerted in total from even a light breeze, even if there are no leaves on the tree, is amazing. It can create foul-ups that can be extremely dangerous. Moral: Don't try to fell trees on a breezy, much less windy, day.

Once you have settled upon what you feel is the proper fall line, clear away the area where you will be working. Lop off any brush, kick dead branches out of the way, and make sure you have good, solid footing and a stumble-free working spot. Then choose your own path of retreat. This is extremely important, because when the tree starts to topple, you will want to get out of the way quickly, and you'll need to know ahead of time exactly where to head.

Never pick a route toward the fall line direction, nor directly opposite and away from the fall line. Always move to left or right of the fall line and somewhat back and away. Pick a clear path that will move you out at least several feet, with no obstacles to trip over. Remember, the tree might go straight forward and fall just as planned, but it might also twist to one side or the other, or the butt could spring off the stump and be driven several feet back toward you. A falling tree is as unpredictable as a grumpy brown bear, so don't take any chances. And keep an eye peeled for widow-makers, those loose dead branches balanced in the limbs above just waiting to come crashing down at the slightest vibration.

If you are felling standing deadwood, either for use or just to clear out a felling path, all the foregoing applies, plus some additional points. Deadwood in good condition can be very hard. This makes cutting with an axe difficult, so beware of glancing blows and keep the axe as sharp as you can get it. On the other hand, deadwood often saws more easily than

green. Deadwood might also be weak, punky, or pithy, and so react peculiarly when being felled. There is a constant danger of weak or rotted limbs, or even a whole tip, crashing down on you. Also, deadwood can be brittle and prone to splitting or cracking, even breaking in half, when felled. A clean, clear bed must be made for the tree to fall onto.

With all these details sorted out, you can begin work. The first cut in the tree is called the undercut and is made on the side of the tree toward the fall line, and at a right angle to the fall line. Start the cut at a comfortable working height above the ground, below your marking tape. Make a flat-bottomed and wide-mouthed notch that extends approximately a third of the way through the bole (Fig. 3-1).

The second cut is called the *backcut*, and

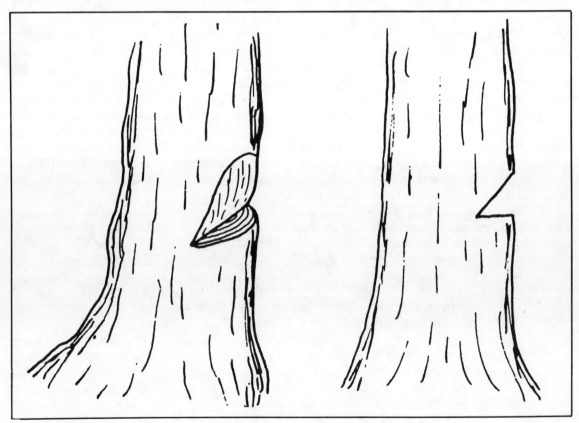

Fig. 3-1. The first step in felling a tree is making the undercut.

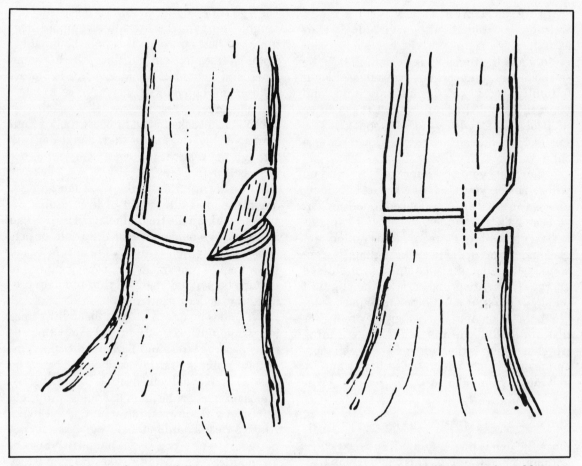

Fig. 3-2. The second step in felling a tree is making the backcut, leaving the hinge (dotted lines).

is made on the opposite side of the tree and parallel with the undercut, but from 1 to 2 inches higher (Fig. 3-2). Some loggers choose to start a bit higher and slant the cut slightly downward. Continue this cut until you get within about an inch or so of the undercut, or a couple of inches or more if you are working a big tree that leans. It never hurts, too, to stop before you get to this point and listen to the tree talking to you (shut off your chainsaw if necessary). A lot of creaks and groans and pops might mean she'll keel over sooner than you expected, or could be heralding a twister or a kicker: beware.

In any event, the narrow strip of wood left between the two cuts is called the *hinge*. It should be about the same thickness all across the bole, and theoretically should help guide the tree in its fall until it finally breaks apart. If, some way into the cut, the saw blade begins to bog down and bind, tap a wedge into place with the saw still resting in the cut. Drive the wedge just far enough to free up the blade, no more. On many trees, especially if you have correctly assessed the lean and the natural fall line, this will not be necessary because the saw cut will open of itself.

As you approach the point of making the hinge, slow the cutting down and watch the width of the saw cut, meanwhile keeping alert for any movement and/or splitting, cracking sounds. Continue cutting slowly, keeping a sharp eye and keen ear. The tree might give you warning, but it might also just suddenly start to fall. The instant the cut begins to open rapidly and the tree begins to lean, snatch the sawblade out. Forget about the wedges, they'll fall out. If the sawblade suddenly binds and you can't jerk it free on the first tug, you've probably got a twister—forget about the saw too. *Just get yourself clear away, down your escape route.*

If, despite your best intentions, you end up with a hanger, your best bet is to just let it hang unless you are well experienced in felling. Or, you can have a pro finish the job, if it happens to be a choice log. A tree that has gotten tangled and bound up halfway through its descent contains a tremendous amount of unreleased energy. It might spring loose at the slightest touch, or it might not. Somewhere in the tangle there probably will be a few key branches that are holding up the works. Determining which is which is difficult and always chancy, and many a logger has gotten seriously hurt by making a wrong choice.

LIMBING TREES

Once the tree is on the ground, the next chore is limbing and topping. This can be done with either an axe or a saw; you can use a chainsaw, too, but this leaves a ragged cut that you will probably want to hew smooth and flush later. Trim the branches close to the trunk so that no protruding stubs are left, and work carefully so as not to gouge the trunk. When using an axe, cut with the lie of the branch, from the bottom through to the top. Beware of glancing blows that can catch you in the legs. Saw cuts can be made in either direction. Large branches are often best cut from side to side, with an undercut made on one side followed by a topcut on the opposite side (Fig. 3-3).

Start at the butt end of the log and trim off all the branches that are free and accessible. Trim the log clear to the point where the diameter is down to 3 or 4 inches or so. Cut the remaining tip off and drag it out of the way.

Then go back and tackle the branches that are caught up under the log and are under pressure. The best approach is to roll the log until a branch frees up, cut it off, roll the log some more, and so on, but sometimes this is impossible or not convenient. If you have to cut a branch under pressure, watch out that it doesn't snap back at you or release the log onto your foot. Make a topcut first, about halfway through the branch, followed by an undercut from below (Fig. 3-4).

Finish trimming to the tip, then go back down the log to the point of least usable diameter, and lop the tip off the log. The tips can eventually be bucked up for firewood, or perhaps used in porch railings or furniture. Stack the branches into small windrow slashpiles to provide habitat for small wildlife and help promote forest floor growth.

There is no question at all that felling trees is a dangerous occupation, and safety precautions deserve stressing. Perhaps the most important point is to think safety and always be on the defensive. Plan ahead, be alert, observe the basic safety rules, and use the appropriate safety gear when working with cutting tools. Always wear a hard hat. Safety goggles are not necessary when you use a handsaw, but are a good idea when using an axe and mandatory with a chainsaw. Hearing protectors should be worn when you use a chainsaw, too, to lessen the constant drone of the saw and to minimize the very real potential damage to your hearing. Heavy leather gauntlet gloves are a good idea, and so are steel-toed work boots. Watch out for dangling scarves, unbuttoned shirt sleeves or jackets, and baggy clothing that might get caught up.

Axes must be kept as sharp as you can get them with file and stone; there are few hand implements more dangerous than a dull axe. Chainsaw chains must also be kept sharp and frequently touched up, so that they will not bind and kick back. Check the chain tension often, too, to minimize the danger of throwing a chain off the bar, and discard any chain that is worn way down or doesn't cut properly.

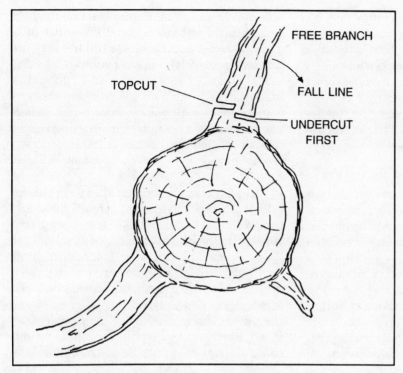

FREE BRANCH

TOPCUT

FALL LINE

UNDERCUT
FIRST

Fig. 3-3. A method of trimming a tree and unobstructed limb from a felled tree.

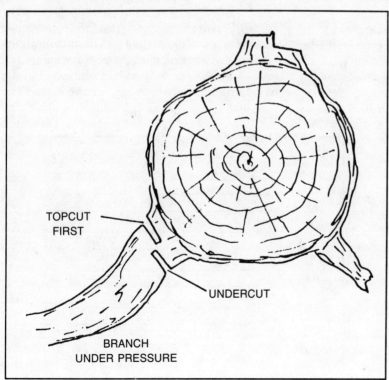

TOPCUT
FIRST

UNDERCUT

BRANCH
UNDER PRESSURE

Fig. 3-4. Use this method to trim a limb under pressure from the felled tree.

Handle fuel safely; shut the chainsaw off when not in use. When using an axe, always check behind you to see that there is nothing there to interfere with your backswing. Keep axes sheathed and all cutting tools set well aside when not being used, where they can't be bumped against or fallen upon. And finally, never go felling alone. Always have a companion with you, even if only for the company.

BUCKING LOGS

With the trees felled and limbed, you have a choice to make. You can cut the logs—buck them—into the required lengths where they lie, before skidding and yarding them, or you can haul the full-length logs into the yarding area and buck them there. The former course is easier in that the logs to be skidded are shorter and lighter, and the possibility of damage during skidding is lessened. On the other hand, the bucking operation might be easier on a cleared, level spot in the yarding area where you can easily set up some props to hold the logs steady and give you a clear cutting line.

If you buck on the felling site, take your materials list along with you and coordinate the notes you made on the log survey tape with the list. Cut each log into appropriate lengths according to your needs for each kind of component—wall, joist, rafter, purlin, and so on. As you buck each piece, write on the butt end with a lumber crayon the key for each (EW-1, J-1, R-1) and check it off your list. Make sure you have matching logs for opposite walls; East Wall l, for example, should be about the same size as West Wall l. If you run short of logs before you fill your requirements, search out a few more trees to fell; having an extra or two is not a bad idea, either, in case one or two get damaged later or show some hidden defects.

The process for bucking after you skid the full-length logs into the yard is much the same. However, first transfer your notes from the survey tape to the butt of each log before you skid them, so you'll know what you had in mind for it. Then make your selections for the individual pieces and buck the logs up. Whichever system you choose, the piece selection should be done with thought, so that you make maximum use of the logs and at the same time come up with good, usable pieces of the right diameters at both ends and the taper you want. Most likely, the pieces cut from each log will have different purposes; a girder plus a wall log from one, a wall log and a rafter from another, a rafter and a porch support post from a third, and so on. There will be bits and pieces left over, which will serve nicely for stovewood for the next winter or so.

Fig. 3-5. A log schedule and bucking chart like this one helps get the most out of the logs.

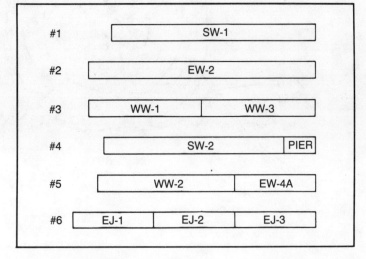

Fig. 3-6. Bucking logs is most easily done when there are four supports for the log.

One approach to this process is to make up a bucking chart. Inventory all your logs first, noting the usable butt and tip diameters and length of each. Then, before doing any cutting, balance the inventory against your materials list, inspect the logs as necessary, and decide for which purposes each can best be cut. As they are, note each on a log schedule like the one in Fig. 3-5. As you buck each piece, write the key on it with a lumber crayon.

Bucking the logs can sometimes be tricky, especially if done at the felling site where the log will probably have uneven support. The best bet is to move the log around if you can, so that you have a clear cutting line and proper support under the log so that the saw won't bind or the pieces jump apart or splinter off at the bottom of the cut. If some binding does occur, just tap a wedge into the bottom of the cut.

Ideally, there should be equal support under the log immediately to each side of the cut and toward each end of each section (Fig. 3-6), but this is not always possible. If the log is held up at one end, undercut about a third of the way through and then finish with a top-cut (Fig. 3-7). If the log is supported at both ends, topcut to about one-third the diameter of the log and finish off with an undercut (Fig. 3-8). Always stand on the uphill side of the log, and expect the cut pieces to do the unexpected. They might grab the saw, or roll, jump, or snap back at you. Be ready. You can avoid all this by bucking in the yard, by rolling the logs onto chunks of scrap log or dimension timber placed to support the pieces evenly and give you good ground clearance beneath the cut line. Then you can buzz right down through the log, top to bottom, in one pass.

YARDING LOGS

Whether you buck in the field or at the storage

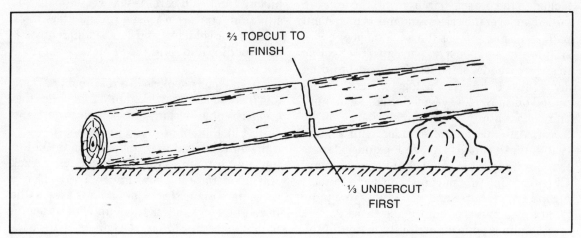

Fig. 3-7. Use this bucking method when the log is propped up at only one end.

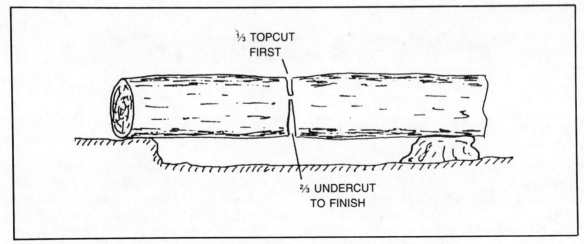

1/3 TOPCUT
FIRST

2/3 UNDERCUT
TO FINISH

Fig. 3-8. Cutting sequence for bucking a log supported only at the ends.

area, the logs must be yarded. Or if you prefer, twitched. Or hauled. No matter the term, the idea is to transport the logs out of the woods and to a storage area, which is best located directly adjacent to the building site. The closer the better, because this reduces the amount of handling necessary.

There are a number of ways to tackle this chore. One is to skid the logs out one by one with a horse providing the pulling power. This is the traditional method called twitching, and even in this mechanized age it is still used quite a bit. The logs are grabbed with a stout rope or chain, or grapple hooks or log tongs are attached to the horse's harness, and the logs are pulled out over the easiest and most convenient path. This method has the advantage of being simple and inexpensive, particularly effective in snowy woods, and doesn't require building any roads. It is easy on logs when they are pulled on snow, low vegetation, or even mud, and causes a minimum of disturbance to the forest. An experienced skidder with a good twitch horse can also snake logs out of spots that are impossible to reach with machinery. Of course, for this purpose you have to have a good twitch horse and know how to handle it, not a common circumstance these days.

A more practical possibility is to pull the logs out singly with a small machine. If the logs

are not too large, even a big garden tractor, or a three- or four-wheel all-terrain vehicle can often do the job.

Yet another alternative is to pull them out in twos or threes on a skidding pan or a yarding sled. The butt ends of the logs are secured to the sled or pan with chains or ropes, while the tip ends drag on the ground. Motive power can be provided by a horse, but for most operations a tractor, pickup truck, or fairly heavy four-wheel-drive vehicle of any sort is more practical.

After the large logs are yarded, small logs or short lengths can simply be muscled into a pickup truck and carted away. Obviously this situation requires at least a rudimentary track suitable for vehicles, and can be tough on both the woodlot floor and the vehicle if not done with care.

If the logs are close to a reasonably decent tote road, or can be worked into a few piles that are accessible by large truck, the fastest and easiest method of bringing in logs—especially if the felling location is remote from the building site—is to hire a self-loading logging truck and an operator for a few hours. The truck can drive right to the stacks, or perhaps even to the individual logs, pluck them up with its boom-mounted loading tongs, stack them on the back of the truck, and be gone in a matter of minutes.

When the logs are unloaded, they can be set down with no fuss and no strain exactly in the desired positions for curing.

CRIBBING AND CURING LOGS

There are two schools of thought regarding the proper curing of logs for house construction. One maintains that logs should be cured for a minimum of 6 months before they are used, the other that logs are best put to work right off the stump while they are still green. There's something to be said for both sides; both methods work if done just right.

When a tree is cut the wood will eventually season, regardless. There's no way to keep a log green. But the object is to assist the seasoning process so that the end result is most beneficial to the builder. In the cure-before-using method, the logs must be cribbed to allow them to season properly. Choose some fairly level patches of ground and lay out a series of skids, which could be small logs, chunks of old beams, or anything else that happens to be handy. Arrange your logs on these skids, butts at one end and tips at the other, and spaced at least 3 or 4 inches apart (Fig. 3-9).

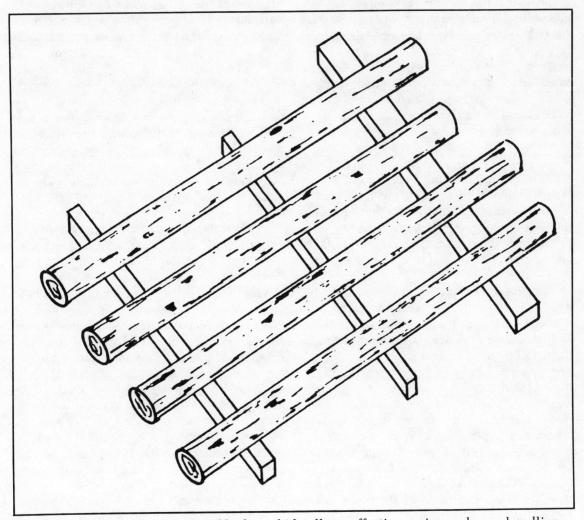

Fig. 3-9. *A single layer of logs cribbed on skids allows effective curing and easy handling.*

The entire row of logs should rest at least 6 inches above the ground, with no brush or debris below them. The idea is to allow full air circulation completely around all the logs except where they rest directly on the skids. There should also be enough skids beneath the logs so that the spans are quite short and the logs will not sag.

If space is short in the yard, you can arrange another layer of logs parallel to the first and set upon stickers (cross-sticks), a third layer on top of that, and so forth. Cover the top layer of logs with a screen of evergreen branches or brush to break the sunlight. Or, you can build a temporary shed roof on poles over the cribs. Plastic sheeting or a tarpaulin should be suspended well above the top layer of logs and never draped directly over them, so as to maintain a good air flow and eliminate condensation. Leave the logs cribbed up for at least 6 months and preferably longer before putting them to work.

If you have room, there is a better arrangement. Lay all the logs out on skids in a single layer, rather than cribbing them. Cover the logs in some protective fashion, allowing for plenty of air movement. About once a week turn all the logs 90 degrees from their previous position. This will minimize the possibility of their taking a set and warping unduly in one direction or another.

In either case, the rapidity of seasoning depends to some extent upon the weather, and the average relative humidity at the curing site. Curing proceeds relatively slowly during cold, damp winter months, much faster during hot, dry weather. Most of the drying takes place during the first two or three months of storage, depending upon air temperature and movement, humidity, the species of wood, and whether or not the logs have been peeled before cribbing. Until the wood reaches a level of approximately 28-percent moisture content—the average fiber saturation point for most woods—no shrinking takes place. After two or three months the free water contained within the cell cavities in the wood will have largely disappeared, and moisture absorbed in the cell walls begins to evaporate. Then shrinkage begins and can theoretically continue down to zero-percent moisture content (but this level can only be reached by forced oven-drying, done only for testing and research purposes).

A further curing period beyond three months or so will usually bring the moisture content down to around 15 percent, and the level will eventually go lower than that in hot, arid climates. Thus, if the logs are properly air cured for a fairly lengthy period, most or perhaps all of the initial shrinkage will already have taken place by the time construction begins. They will never, however, dry out completely. Regardless of how it is dried, any wood will eventually reach and maintain an *equilibrium moisture content* (EMC), a condition where a certain amount of bound moisture within the wood stays at a variable level in balance with the surrounding air temperature and relative humidity. As those factors change, so does the EMC. Thus, the wood never reaches complete dimensional stability; there is always some degree of shrinking and swelling going on.

Advocates of building with green logs have one argument in particular against cribbing logs and letting them season for a long time. They contend that this allows the logs a chance to take a firm set, depending upon how and where they were stacked in the crib, how often they were turned if at all, how much weight rested on them and so on. It's a valid point. Also, green logs are somewhat more limber, so slight curves can be pulled straight or a particular log can be more easily aligned with its neighbors despite some slight deformities. Cured logs, on the other hand, do take a set and are less easily aligned, especially if they happen to be short and thick. Hence the reason for not stacking them high and turning them frequently.

There are some other advantages to green log building, too, Peeling is easier, notching and cutting is easier, spiking is easier, the likelihood of splitting is reduced. Also, when the joints are cut and the logs fitted green, they will shrink and lock into place with one another, if properly managed. And, of course, there is no waiting period for curing before construction can begin.

To build with green logs the method is to cut and fit them in the usual manner. Some builders do not compensate for the shrinkage factor, but spike everything together thoroughly. Other builders do compensate, using techniques that will be explained in later chapters of this book. Most builders, including nearly all kit log house manufacturers, feel that shrinkage compensation techniques should be used at least to some degree in any log structure.

One method that is often used in green-log building is to assemble only the walls and the framing members. The whole affair, minus doors, windows, flooring, roofing, and all other appurtenances, is left to stand as is and open to the weather for several months for seasoning. By then, most of the shrinkage has taken place, and the remainder of the construction can go ahead. Even at that, there is likely to be further shrinkage and settling by the time the job is finished.

One further note: There is good reason to believe that the optimum seasoning of logs takes a minimum of two years, depending upon species and conditions. Many professional woodworkers believe that proper curing should be done over a period of three years, longer if possible. You will probably want to compromise.

PEELING LOGS

Log houses can be made from peeled logs— that is, with most or all of the bark removed— or with unpeeled logs. Peeled logs are usually preferred for several reasons. First, the bark is the least durable and weather-resistant part of the log. Bark simply does not stand up well, especially under continued exposure to the ele-

ments. Second, bark is particularly susceptible to retaining moisture and harboring insects, both of which can lead to structural damage of the wood from fungus, decay, and insect attack. Third, bark left on a log eventually separates from the wood, usually in a patchwork of chunks and strips, and most of it will eventually fall off anyway. This might take several years, but in the meantime the logs take on a shabby and scruffy appearance. There is no adequate way, even on interior log faces, to seal or otherwise treat the bark of most species so that it will remain on the logs, or present a decent, finished appearance. Also, effective chinking and sealing off between the wall logs is almost impossible. Last, peeled logs are generally easier to handle and to work with, especially when it comes to marking and scribing them for measurements and saw cuts.

On the other hand, logs with the bark left on do have a more natural appearance, at least for a while. Also, a great deal of time and labor is saved by not bothering with peeling. It's reasonable to decide that, because the bark is probably going to fall off anyway, there isn't much point in bothering—Reasonable, that is, if you don't mind the shabby appearance for a while, and provided you don't mind running the risk of fungus, rot, insect attack, and wind whistling through the loose chinking. Of course, all of these conditions are of less consequence in hot, arid climates than cold, damp ones. Unpeeled logs are employed only on log houses built from scratch, and often with logs that have been sawn flat on two or three faces (bark outside, or outside and inside).

Spring-cut logs are easiest to peel, especially if they are tackled right after cutting. However, as noted earlier, there are some drawbacks to spring cutting that can outweigh the advantage of easy peeling. Logs cut in other seasons will peel harder, but season better. All things considered, the best combination seems to be early-winter cutting and spring peeling, but that's a matter of opinion. and often opportunity as well.

If the logs are to be seasoned for a considerable length of time, don't peel them until just before they will be used. As long as the logs are well protected from the weather, are checked occasionally for excessive moisture (condensation, storms) and for rampant insect attack or fungus growth, and are turned regularly, the bark provides excellent protection for the seasoning wood. This helps to eliminate mildew, weathering, darkening of the wood, and mechanical damage. Some staining might occur or a few bark beetles take up residence, but by and large this causes no problems and could even add a bit of extra character to the wood. Peeling is no more difficult because of the time lapse, and in fact might be somewhat easier depending upon the tree species (the bark tightens at first, but then begins to separate from the wood).

The peeling process involves a combination of two tools: a peeling spud and a drawknife. Peeling spuds come in a number of forms, and can be bought from a logging supply house, or sometimes picked up at an auction or in secondhand shops. You can also cobble one up yourself by sharpening one end of an old car spring leaf; by cutting down, reshaping, and sharpening the end of a curved garden spade; or by attaching an oversized handle to a large (2-inch or bigger) carpenter's slick or wood chisel. Drawknives are readily available through woodworking tool supply houses, and are also common second-hand.

To peel a log, first secure it in a position where you can work on it comfortably. Prop one end up well off the ground on a short, notched chunk of log so that it is firmly set. A *log dog*, which is just a length of heavy steel bar turned down at each end into a pointed hook (Fig. 3-10) can be driven into the log and the chunk to further stabilize it. Or better, roll the log up onto a pair of narrow, very stout sawhorses and lock it in place at stand-up working height. Attack the bark with the peeling spud, paring off large chunks, but take care to gouge the wood as little as possible. After taking off most of the bark, finish up by shaving with a drawknife. (With some species, the bark is thin enough that the whole job can be just as easily done with the knife alone).

You can leave traces of the cambium and inner bark if you wish, for visual effect, and the overall result is a characteristic hand-finished appearance. Place the peeled logs in stacks or back in the crib, and protect them from damage or dirt and mud. Stains of any sort are difficult and time-consuming to remove later on, and they always seem to end up in the most visible places.

PRESERVATIVE TREATMENTS
Despite the fact that some woods, like the cedars, redwood, cypress, and black locust, have a natural resistance to fungus, rot, and insect attack, all logs used in house construction are

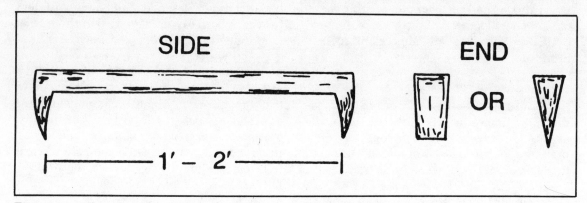

Fig. 3-10. A log dog like this can be easily made from steel bar stock.

best treated with a preservative. The naturally resistant woods only remain so for 20 years or so, far less than the expected life of a well-built house. True, probably far more log structures have been built without the benefit of preservatives than with, but that doesn't alter the fact that preservatives add measurably to the longevity of a structure, as well as reducing repair and maintenance work. Even though this is an added step that involves some problems and extra work, it should be considered necessary.

The biggest problem with preservatives lies in adequately penetrating through the surface of the log and deep into the wood fibers. Treatment under great pressure is the system used commercially, but is obviously out of the reach of the do-it-yourselfer. Alternate hot and cold baths in conjunction with steam heating are effective, but also unavailable to do-it-yourselfers.

The next best method is a cold soak in preservative, and this can be done on-site and with a minimum of equipment. All that is needed is a tank or trough of sufficient size to hold the largest logs on hand. A soak tank can be made from old 55-gallon drums. Cut them in half lengthwise and weld them together end to end. Or split a length of culvert lengthwise, weld end to end, and cap at the open ends,

with legs or cradles welded here and there to keep the trough stable (Fig. 3-11).

An alternative is to build a rectangular trough from heavy plywood, with seams sealed with silicone caulk. The outside frames must be well braced so the seams cannot spring apart, and closely spaced so there is plenty of strength to hold the weight of both the preservative and the log. With either type of trough, the log is rolled up a pair of short ramps and then lowered gently into the trough partly full of preservative. If the log cannot be completely covered, it can be turned from time to time. A soaking time of 5 minutes or so is adequate, but longer is better. For trough application you probably will have to have 100 gallons or more of preservative on hand. Some of this will be left over, but can be stored for later use.

Another possibility—not quite as effective, but a whole lot more convenient for the do-it-yourselfer—is preservative applied with either a brush or a spraygun. You can use an ordinary garden sprayer, but a small, inexpensive paint sprayer, either compressor or vibrator type, is easier and faster. When spraying, wear gloves, buttoned-up old clothing, a hat, and above all, an approved respirator. Wash up thoroughly when you are done.

Whatever method you use, apply preser-

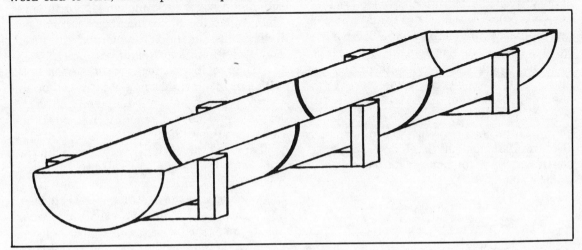

Fig. 3-11. *A preservative trough made out of old steel drums cut in half lengthwise and welded together end to end.*

vative to the whole logs before they are finally put in place. Ideally, the logs should be cut and fitted and all cutting or notching done before treatment. This is often not possible or practical, so any cuts in the treated wood of whatever sort—even light planing or trimming—should be liberally dosed with a brush before the log is finally installed. Penetration by either method, especially brushing, is not very great, so the exterior of the completed structure should be completely resprayed or rebrushed soon after the building is complete, and about every two years thereafter for maximum protection in humid climates. In very dry climates this can be extended to every four or five years.

No materials that are treated by dipping or coating should be direct-buried in the ground. Use only commercially pressure-treated woods for structural purposes. Redwood and cypress can be used for some purposes, though, like deck or fence posts. Also, do not use any preservative of potentially toxic nature on interior surfaces after the initial treating has been done. By the time the house is occupied, the initial toxicity will have disappeared.

Until recently, preservatives based on pentachlorophenol were the choice for do-it-yourself application. However, this material has been found to be very toxic, and is now virtually unavailable. Other more benign products have taken their place. Those containing copper napthenate are popular and effective, but leave a green tinge that remains a long time. Clear preservatives that work well are zinc napthenates (Cuprinol Clear #20), clear TBTO (bis[tributyltin]oxide) such as Sherwin Williams Clear Wood Finish, and copper-8-quinolinolate such as Woodguard, which is also a termite repellant. In all cases, apply according to the manufacturer's directions, and use caution.

SHAPING LOGS

As construction of the log house proceeds there is a substantial amount of shaping that must be done to the logs. A number of procedures are used, requiring different tools. Knots and stubs that were not cleanly trimmed off with an axe or saw during the limbing operation, as well as bumps and other irregularities that show up after peeling, might require some attention. Knots and stubs in particular are very tough, and because the cutting must be done across the grain, they are doubly difficult to work. The best approach is to trim them carefully by hand with a wide carpenter's chisel or slick, tapped with a heavy wooden mallet. You can trim with great precision using these tools, and the resulting surface is much smoother and better dressed than if you use a saw. There is also less chance of barking up the surrounding wood. You can use the same tools to clean off any other irregularities, and sometimes a drawknife or a hand plane works as well or better.

Making a perfectly straight cut through a thick log with either a handsaw or a chainsaw is difficult to do freehand. A handsaw blade is apt to wander off the line, while a chainsaw cuts so rapidly that accurate control is sometimes difficult. The best way to get smooth and square cuts, such as those that are necessary next to window and door bucks, is to set a simple miter guide in place, secured with a couple of nails (Fig. 3-12). Nominal 1-inch boards can be used for this purpose, but 2-inch stock provides a better guiding surface for the saw blade. Keep the blade lined up with but not tight against the guide as you saw, and you'll end up with a nice straight cut.

Though log homes are sometimes built with logs that remain completely in the round, more often they are flatted top and bottom, at least slightly, for easier and tighter construction. Sometimes the interior faces are flatted as well. (Some builders hew, saw, or mill the logs flat on all four sides and call the structures made from them log houses. To many folks, these do not have the appearance of log houses, and in fact they are variously called solid wood beam, precut, hand-hewn, or timber houses.) Even with round log construction, log joists are usually flatted on the top surface.

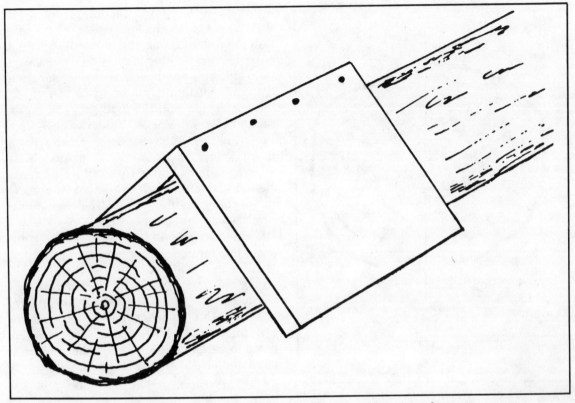

Fig. 3-12. This simple miter guide set over logs aids in making straight cuts.

The time-honored method for flatting logs, whether on one face or all four, is with a broadax followed up with an adze. This gives the highly prized hand-hewn look that is nowadays so often imitated using other methods—with a notable lack of success. If you care to take the time and trouble, and have the patience to develop the necessary skill, hewing with broadax and adze is the most satisfactory, and to many the most satisfying, way to shape logs. It is also the most difficult and time-consuming.

The process begins by propping a log up off the ground on short chunks of wood and jamming it in place with log dogs or wedges. The log should be positioned just as you want it to lie when in place in the building. Mark a plumb line down across the butt of the log, bisecting it (Fig. 3-13). Do the same at the tip end. Drive a small nail into this line about an inch down at each end. Secure a carpenter's chalkline from nail to nail along the centerline of the log, end to end. Then stand a level up plumb at the midpoint of the log, next to the chalkline (Fig. 3-14). If the log is bowed right or left, move the level so that the edge facing the line is, by eye, about at the true centerline of the log at that point. Then raise the line, keeping it just slightly away from the still-plumb level, and let it snap down.

Next, decide the width of the flat. With a steel rule laid across the top of your level, rest the side of the level against the butt end of the log, and adjust it until half of the required flat dimension is to either side of the plumb centerline. Zero on the rule should be at the edge of the log on the left and the full dimension figure on the edge of the log at the right, with the

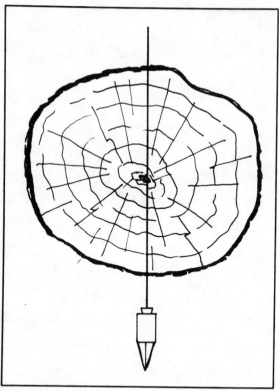

Fig. 3-13. *The first step in establishing hewing guidelines is to bisect the log butt and tip.*

level dead level. Draw a line across (Fig. 3-15), then go to the tip end and repeat the process. Roll the log until one end or the other of that cross-line or the other is at the 12 o'clock position, and snap another chalk line the length of the log, adjusting as necessary as you did for the centerline. Roll the log back, and do the same on the other side. You now have three lines (Fig. 3-16), the centerline which will get hewn away, and the two side guidelines, which you must hew to (hence the old expressions, to "hew the line" or "hew to the mark"). Incidentally, setting these lines sometimes needs some judgement, some "eyeballing," and some shifting of lines—it's not a terribly exact procedure.

The next step is to score the log (Fig. 3-17), which you can do with either a handsaw or a chainsaw. To do so, work with the saw in three positions. Cut the near side first, with the saw tip canted upward 10 or 15 degrees, and cut down to the guideline. Then tilt the saw downward and cut down just to the line on the opposite side. Finish the cut with the blade held level, straight across the log, but don't go below the side guidelines (Fig. 3-18). Do this

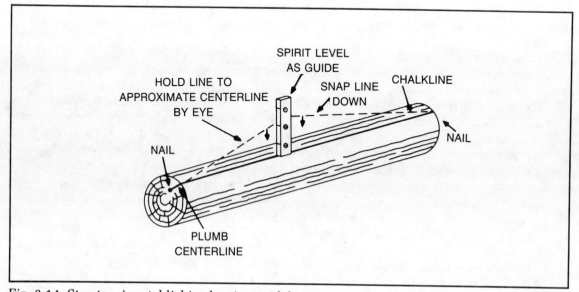

Fig. 3-14. *Step two in establishing hewing guidelines is to strike a longitudinal centerline along the log from butt to tip.*

every 6 or 8 inches along the log top, or a little more or less depending on how well your particular species of wood splits.

Next, chop out the chunks of wood from score to score. You can do this with an ordinary axe, which will leave a rough flat with the bottoms of the saw cuts still visible. Or, you can stand on the opposite side of the log and knock the chunks out with a broadax, working backward from score to score (Fig. 3-19). Because of the way the broadax is made—with the blade flat on the inside, the cutting edge beveled to the opposite side, and the handle offset—you can swing the broadax straight down and straight back, leaving a clean face. One blow for each score should do the trick. This takes a bit of getting used to, but with some practice you'll do the job with great precision. Old hands at the task can stand atop the log and work steadily along, never missing a beat and leaving a true surface behind (not recommended for beginners). As you gain experience, you might be able to move the scores further apart, depending upon the wood species.

For general construction purposes and where the flatted faces will be hidden anyway, no further work is usually necessary if you've done a good job with the broadax, save perhaps to whittle down a few high spots. For a more

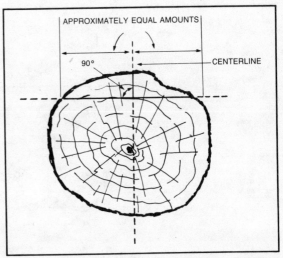

Fig. 3-15. Step three in establishing hewing guidelines is to set the flatting lines at the log butt and tip.

Fig. 3-16. The last step in establishing hewing guidelines is to strike the side guidelines along the length of the log.

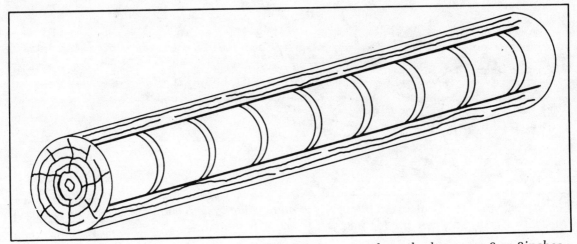

Fig. 3-17. To begin the hewing process, make scoring cuts along the log every 6 or 8inches.

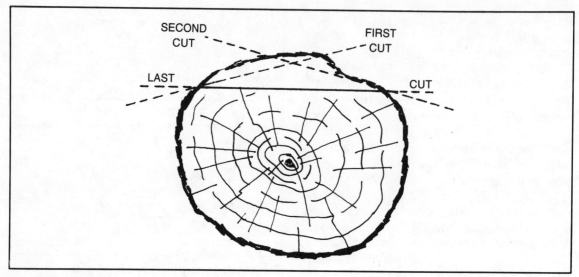

Fig. 3-18. Make the scoring cuts in three steps: upward, downward, and straight across to meet the side guidelines.

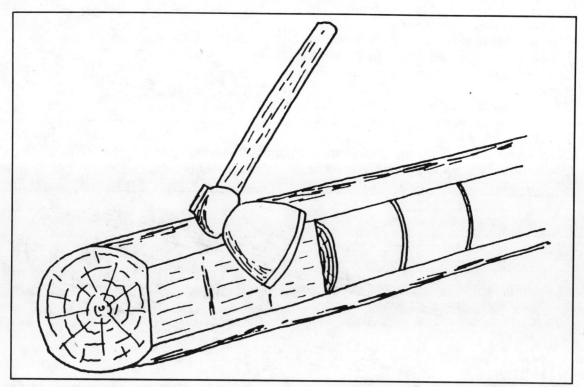

Fig. 3-19. Use a broad hatchet, a broadax, or an ordinary axe to chop out the chunks between the scoring cuts, and hew the log face flat to the side guidelines.

finished appearance, as on wall log interior faces or portions of joists or beams that will be exposed, the next step is to smooth the flat and leave the characteristic hand-hewn finish, and here you have some choices.

In the first method, place the log on waist-high sawhorses, set and secured so the flat faces your best working side, Then hew with a broadax held close to the head, rather like a big hatchet, moving forward down the log from one end to the other. Or, you can leave it low to the ground on chunks, and straddle it or stand on the opposite side. Swing the broadax full length, working backward along the log (wear sheet-metal leg protectors, like a cowboy's chaps if you do this). Or, you can leave the log face upward on the chunks, straddle the log, and hew backward along the face with an adze. This is usually the preferred method (Fig. 3-20). Swing the adze in short, choppy, controlled swings, straight down between your legs. Be sure to keep your feet and legs well out of the way. Each stroke should take out a small chip or curl, finishing the surface with a slight rippling effect. The finished patterns left by the different methods do not look quite the same, but all look good.

Fortunately there are easier methods of flatting logs. You could use a handsaw, and saw the log flat to the line instead of hewing to it, but there's lots of exercise involved with this method too. By far the simplest method is to use a device known as a chainsaw mill. This machine uses two chainsaw motors with a long

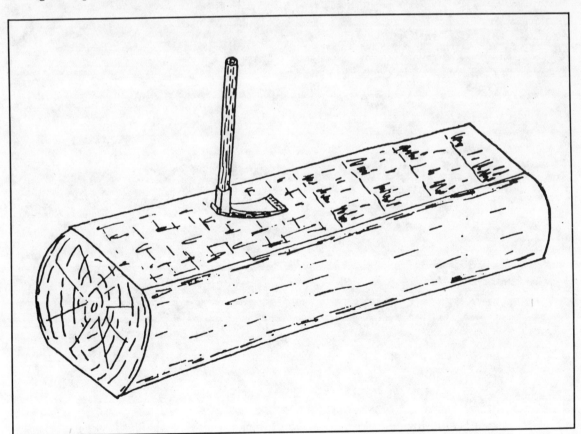

Fig. 3-20. To further smooth the hewn log face, chip away at it with a straight-edged adze.

continuous bar and chain between them, and is outfitted with a series of rollers and guides. Operated by two men, one on each end, it is simply set to the proper cutting depth and drawn along the top of the log, against a guide, to flat it off. The same machine can be used to cut successive boards or planks from raw logs in the field. Smaller, single-motor mills are also available (Fig. 3-21). If a large amount of cutting must be done and if the cost can be justified, a portable bandsaw mill (Fig. 3-22) does a fine job.

Note that if you are buying logs from a mill or supplier you can order them flatted in any way you wish, for an extra charge.

Log construction requires that the logs be interlocked with some sort of joint where they meet at corners. This requires cutting a great many notches of one sort or another, and complete details will be discussed in later chapters. Suffice it to say at this point that the notches are made with the same sort of tools used for other kinds of log shaping, including an axe, hatchet, or broadax, saws, and carpenter's slick and mallet.

Splining is one of the common methods of

Fig. 3-21. A small chainsaw mill like the Alaskan® makes flatting logs relatively easy. (Courtesy of Granberg International.)

Fig. 3-22. *A portable bandsaw mill like this one not only flats logs easily, it also will produce large quantities of boards or dimension stock in short order.* (Courtesy of Delta International Machinery Corp.)

joining stacked logs, usually but not necessarily flatted. This helps hold them in place during construction and aligned afterward, and provides a better weather seal. Setting splines requires first that matching grooves be cut to accommodate the spline itself. This can be done in several ways. Narrow and relatively shallow spline grooves can be easily cut with a router. Insert a suitable bit in the router and align the machine so that the cut will be made down the centerline. Nail a guideboard to the log that will keep the router properly positioned and traveling in a straight line. Set the router bit to the desired depth and run the groove the full length of the log (Fig. 3-23). Use a carbide bit for longevity, and make two or

more passes if the grooves are deep. In some cases double splines are used, and the procedure is the same.

Narrow grooves as well as relatively wide and deep ones can be made with a circular saw in much the same way. Nail a guideboard to the log to act as a straightedge for the saw, and set so that the center of the saw cut splits the centerline (for a single spline) of the log. Repeated passes can be made—resetting the straightedge each time—with a standard saw blade, leaving about a ⅛-inch groove each time. This is a tedious process, however. A better system is to use an adjustable dado blade of the type that is made specifically for portable circular saws. Just set the blade to the

Fig. 3-23. This demonstration shows one way of routing spline grooves in logs. The more guides the better, so that the router does not wander.

desired width of cut and the shoe of the saw to the desired depth; the groove can be cut in one pass.

If you happen to be an artist with a chainsaw, you can make a wide spline cut down the centerline of a log flat free hand. Experienced workers often do just that, especially if the spline is a relatively loose-fitting one. However, for a cleaner and more accurate job, and to compensate for the average unsteady hand, the best bet is to use a special attachment that bolts to the chainsaw bar and guides the chain.

These have to be made up specially for the job by a local machinist, but are worth the effort spent. They result in accurate control of cut depth, place the cut in the same relative position on each log face, ensure a straight groove, and save a lot of time.

V-cuts are sometimes used in fitting wall logs together instead of flats or other methods. There are two ways they are used. One consists of a V-cut along the centerline in the bottom of each log, so that the cut just rests down over the rounded top of the log below. The other method uses a V-cut in the bottom of the log with a matching V-shape—a peak—on the top of the log below. The single V-cut is made by first placing the log to be cut temporarily on top of the one on which it will eventually rest. The log is then secured in place so that it can't shift about. The next step is to scribe a line with a pair of dividers the full length of the log and on each side (Fig. 3-24). If you keep the dividers always at a 90-degree angle from the surfaces being scribed, the line on the upper log

will faithfully follow the contour of the top of the lower log. Thus, when the cut is made along these lines, the log will drop into place with a good fit. After scribing the lines the log is removed and a 45-degree (or shallower) V-cut is made with a chainsaw, freehand but carefully controlled. If the cut is well made, the fit between the logs should be very good, needing only a little trimming along the feather edges of the V with a small coping saw to mate the logs.

Mating V-cuts can also be made completely with a chainsaw, or with a large portable circular saw for the V and a chainsaw mill for the inverted V. Scribing is necessary for a good fit, and the angles of the cut should remain constant if the edges of the inverted cut are to remain unobtrusive. This process requires exact control over guideboard placement and cut dimensions and angles, as well as exact positioning of the top and bottom cuts opposite one another.

Another method of mating logs is by cup-

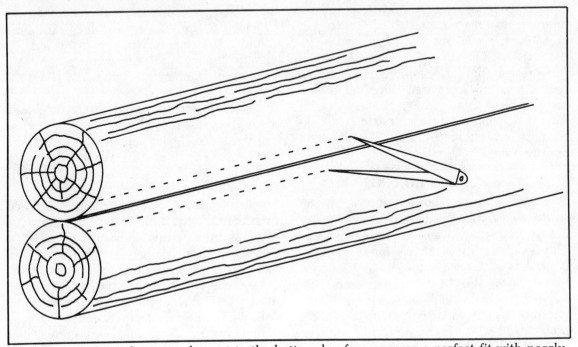

Fig. 3-24. Scribing the upper log cut to the bottom log face ensures a perfect fit with nearly identical contours.

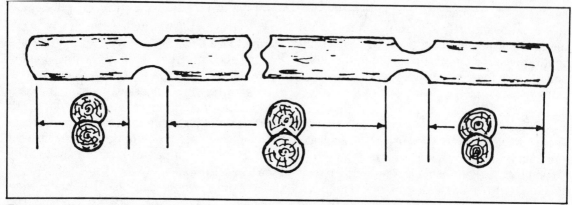

Fig. 3-25. *Logs can be V-grooved through most of their length for ease of cutting, then cupped only at the ends for appearance and a tight fit.*

ping or coping, a process of cutting a rounded groove the full length of the bottom of each log. The traditional way of doing this is with a gutter adze. This tool is similar to the straight-bladed adze except that the blade is curved, and the cuts are made with a continuous scooping action. This is a long and tedious job. When the cope method is used nowadays, the process is hastened by using a chainsaw to rough out grooves, then the remaining wood is cut out and the groove finished with gouges. Sometimes the cope is used only on the endwork of the logs, from the corner joints out to the ends, with a V-groove joint used along the middle section of each log (Fig. 3-25). This gives a tight fit with no gapping at the visible log ends, allowing a more attractive and more weathertight construction.

MANEUVERING LOGS

Logs certainly are not the easiest things in the world to handle and maneuver about. They are heavy, clumsy, awkward, and often contrary. This is especially true of green logs, and of the large sizes often used in building a log house from scratch. Most of the kit logs tend to be somewhat smaller and usually have a low moisture content, which helps with the weight problem. Logs wet from rain can be murderously slippery. Milled logs with one or more flat edges are easier to handle than round ones.

Unfinished logs or those that won't be adversely affected by the addition of a few scrapes and scratches are most easily shoved and rolled around with a peavey or a cant hook (similar to a peavey but with a blunt instead of spiked tip). Carrying logs and setting them in place at the lower levels can be done with two or more lug hooks, which require two persons each to act as bearers. Temporary-duty lug hooks can be made by running a stout length of pipe through the rings of two or more sets of grapple hooks or loading tongs. A pair or more of short nylon-strap cargo slings attached to pipe or wood beam crossbars work nicely for carrying milled or finished logs around, because the nylon straps will not damage the wood. Nylon automobile tow straps work just as well, and are easier to come by. Sets of big old ice tongs also work well for shifting logs about.

If you need to haul the logs a fair distance from the storage lot to the building, consider cobbling up a narrow dolly, perhaps using a pair of wheelbarrow or go-cart wheels, or other fat tires that won't dig into the ground. Fashion some sort of cradle on a two-wheeled axle, to which the log butt can be lashed. Lift the tip with tongs, and trundle the log into position. Alternative for short logs: a high-wheeled (bicycle-type) garden cart.

Boosting heavy logs onto upper courses or

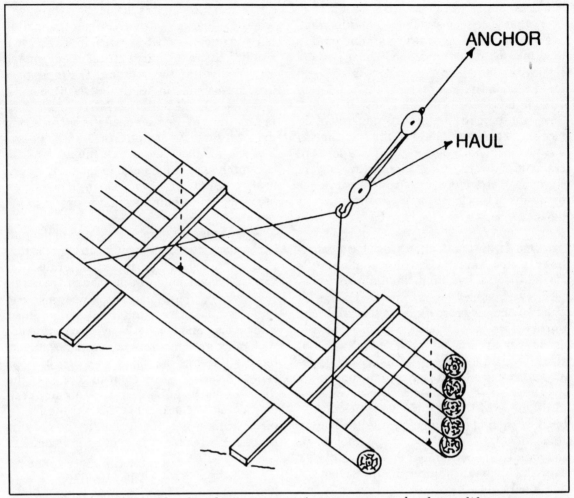

ANCHOR

HAUL

Fig. 3-26. One method of hauling logs up ramps is to use a cross-haul rope lift arrangement.

into position as rafters or girders often requires some ingenuity, as well as a lot of caution. One method is to raise the logs bit by bit up a stair-step scaffolding. The scaffold can be built up from dimension stock, but adjustable steel scaffolding or staging is easier and safer to use. This can be rented for a nominal sum on a daily or weekly basis from an equipment rental house or a building contractor. By arranging staging at various levels and flooring the sections with heavy planks, you can maneuver material into place more easily and work from a better vantage point.

The most efficient way of handling this problem is with machinery. Assuming good access around the building, a high-lift type of forklift will make short work of lifting logs into place. A backhoe or a big front-loader equipped with slings will also work. There are also several kinds of elevator-like building material hoists that can be erected against the side of the building; these can be rented, and save a great deal of time and effort.

Perhaps the most common way of hoisting high logs into place is one that could loosely be called rigging. Rigging consists of using lines, block and tackle sets, come-alongs, chain falls, inclined planes, anchors and deadmen, jammers, props, gin poles, levers, and whatever other gear seems indicated and in whatever combination necessary to lift and guide a load into the proper position. The aspects of rigging are difficult to explain because they differ in each individual case and there are literally hundreds of possibilities involved. Basically, though, the process consists of attaching one or more lines to the log, finding a suitable anchor point, providing a lever or crane for outward lifting or ramps for inward lifting, and arranging a mechanical advantage by means of block and tackle or some similar device so that a heavy load can be moved with a small force.

One of the most often used basic variations, which works well, consists of a simple arrangement of haul rope, an inclined plane, blocks and tackle, and an anchor (Fig. 3-26). The two ramp logs or beams are secured to the top of the wall with the log to be raised resting at the bottom. The haul rope is well secured at each end on the other side of the wall, probably at floor level, and passes to the outside of the ramps, under the log at each end, and back to the hook of the forward block. The other block is secured by an anchor line attached to some immovable object like another portion of the building, a convenient tree, a vehicle, or a deadman sunk in the ground. The anchor line and blocks must be directly in line with and centered between the two ramps. A relatively light pull on the free line of the blocks rolls the log up the slope and into place.

Hauling flatted logs into place this way has to be done carefully to avoid damage or rope burns as they drag along. Tapered round logs will roll unevenly, moving along faster at the butt end than at the tip, so the ropes must be adjusted and the log shifted on the ramps to compensate. It is helpful to have someone stationed at each end of the log to guide it and keep it in position. But for safety's sake always stand outside the log and away from the haul rope so that if something slips or breaks loose there is no danger of getting caught.

A variation on this theme that works well when the logs are fairly light and the incline fairly gentle, uses two separate ropes and two sturdy haulers. One end of each haul rope is anchored within the building. The ropes pass over the wall and under the log near the ends, and back into the building. Two persons pulling on the ropes with equal strain can scoop the log right into position (Fig. 3-27). This system has an advantage in that the haulers can control the log as it comes up the ramp by adjusting the pull on each rope to the rate of travel of the log tip or butt, keeping it square to the ramps.

In either case, the trickiest part of the pull comes when the log is about to go over the top. Full-length logs with extra length for the end-work can be accurately positioned on the ramps so that they will roll out onto the sidewalls. The ropes can then be removed and the log fitted into place. Short logs have to be stopped, preferably by something rather than someone (unless the logs are small and light). Stops should be provided by securing 2 × 4s to the inside of the wall. If necessary, more stops can be secured to the outside to hold the log in place while it is being worked. Much of this process is a matter of ingenuity and common sense.

Placing very high logs, especially big truss logs or a massive ridge log, or even some of the smaller vertical or angled truss members, can be very tricky. The use of hoists, block and tackle sets, steady lines, and usually a series of props, supports, and staging is required. This is difficult work that should be done slowly and carefully and with forethought for every move; it is also dangerous work for all concerned. Several hands are often needed, and a good knowledge of rigging is handy, too. If you are at all unsure about what approach to take, you might be better off to hire some experienced help or consider a different method. Or investigate the possibility of hiring a boom truck or a crane. They are expensive, of course, but so are hospital bills, and they can accom-

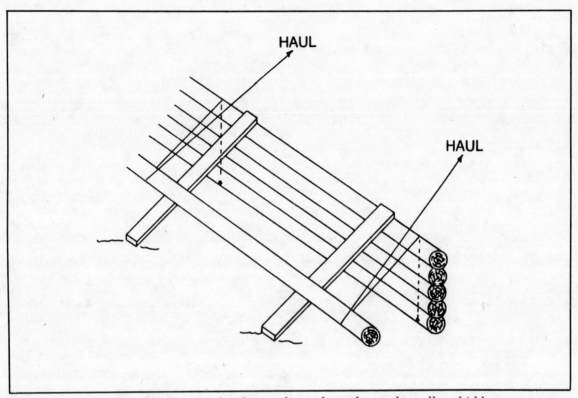

Fig. 3-27. Two separate haul ropes, closely coordinated, can be used to roll or skid logs up ramps.

plish in a matter of hours the work that might otherwise take weeks to finish up. Have all the high-lift work lined up and ready to go, along with a crew of two or three workers, and you'll have the whole job done in less time than it takes to describe it.

4

Foundations

IN THE EARLY DAYS, MANY LOG CABINS WERE CONsidered as only temporary shelters, something to get by in until a "real" house could be built. Consequently a lot of shortcuts were taken, especially with the underpinnings. The pioneer in a hurry just dug a shallow furrow in the ground, dropped the first course of logs in, and packed the earth around them. The floor of the cabin was often packed earth as well. Many of the pioneers took the process a step further by placing a few stones on a level patch of ground and resting the first course of logs upon them. This worked a little better, but the stones eventually sank down and left the first course on the ground anyway.

The next improvement was a trench dug a couple of feet deep, in which was built what amounted to a low stone wall. This was extended a foot or so above grade level and the cabin rested on a more or less solid foundation. Today, though, our building styles and standards, not to mention building codes, demand

a more stable and substantial foundation under our houses.

There are a number of different kinds of foundations that are suitable for log houses, and no one is markedly better than another. Any of them will do the job, and selection rests upon local building codes, house design, building site conditions, and personal preferences.

TYPES

You have five basic options as far as foundation types are concerned, and you can use any combination of them beneath different parts of the house if that seems desirable.

The first and simplest variety is the open foundation in which the building rests upon a series of piers, piles, or posts spaced around the perimeter of the building and at certain interior points. The structure might be only 6 inches or so above grade level (not recommended because of lack of access) or might be elevated to a height of 3 or 4 feet or even more, with free air movement beneath the building. This style is not widely used for houses, mainly because of appearance, but is sometimes used for summer cottages, hunting camps, and storage buildings. The system is widely used for deck and porch support, too, especially those that extend out over a steep drop-off. This is the only foundation style that obviates any possibility of the buildup and infiltration of radon gasses into the structure.

The second style is a modification of the first, with the house (or parts thereof) set on piers. Instead of being completely open, all spaces between grade level and the structure proper are filled in with some sort of nonstructural trim material, thus forming a skirted foundation (Fig. 4-1). Again, the structure may be low to the ground or high enough to provide a sizable crawl space underneath.

This is a satisfactory arrangement which combines low cost with a neat and attractive appearance, while affording some extra, dry storage space. The skirting material can be nearly anything. Textured plywood attached to a framework is often used, as is corrugated or patterned sheet metal roofing. Latticework was once very popular for this purpose and is still used to some extent. Other possibilities include stonework, planking, brick or imitation brick, and decorative concrete block. With complete skirting, provisions must be made for ventilating the area so as to prevent moisture buildup. This can be done by installing wood or metal louvers, sections of latticework, gratings, or

Fig. 4-1. Pier foundation skirted with resawn boards on a framework.

Fig. 4-2. *Note the piers for girder support used in conjunction with this typical continuous-wall crawl-space foundation.*

other types of vents in the skirting. However, neither ground moisture nor surface water run-off poses much of a problem for the foundation system itself (as is also true of the open foundation).

The third choice is a continuous-wall crawl space arrangement, which is today perhaps the most popular of all. In this type of construction a continuous wall is built around the perimeter of the structure, extending from a below-grade level at or slightly below frostline (usually about 2 to 4 feet deep but not less than 18 inches) to any suitable height above grade level (Fig. 4-2). The bottom of the house itself might be only a few inches above grade, or in some instances 3 feet or more. Or the distance can be varied all around the house by stepping the foundation. The continuous wall supports all the weight of a small structure, while in larger structures a portion of the weight is

borne by girders, piers, or other support arrangements beneath the floor. The foundation may be made of poured concrete, concrete blocks, stone, brick, a specially treated wood foundation system, or various combinations of materials. As with the skirted foundation, suitable ventilation has to be provided to prevent moisture buildup.

The fourth possibility is a full basement, and there are two varieties to consider. The choice of one or the other rests to a great degree on the topography of the building site and the design of the house. One type is the hole-in-the-ground basement, made by excavating to a depth of anywhere from about 5 to 8 feet over the entire area of the building footprint (the specific, outlined area that the building will cover when constructed). Then full-height walls are built around the perimeter of the structure, or that portion that will lie above a full basement. The foundation may rise to just above grade level, go up 2 or 3 feet, or be variably stepped. Some foundations contain no windows, while others can have small ones either exposed between grade level and the foundation top or set in wells sunk into the ground alongside the foundation walls. By far the greater proportion of the foundation is underground on all sides of the house.

The other variety, a daylight or walk-in basement (also sometimes called a "garden level"), contains one or more walls that are almost or entirely exposed and above grade level (Fig. 4-3), an arrangement satisfactory on steeply sloping sites. Though these basements are built in essentially the same way and support the perimeter of the house, the exposed walls are fitted out with doors and windows and finish exterior siding, and from at least one direction actually become ground-level floors.

Full basements of either type are most often built from poured concrete or concrete block. The exposed wall portions may be constructed of the same materials, or framed up with wood, or otherwise built in the same manner as the rest of the above-ground structure. Exposed masonry walls can later be veneered with brick, stone, or other building materials. Another possibility for constructing full basement walls is the Permanent Wood Foundation (PWF) system, which is rapidly gaining acceptance throughout the country. Stone and brick have also been used in the past for this purpose, but seldom are anymore.

And last, you might choose to build your house on a slab foundation (Fig. 4-4). Slab foundations are made entirely from concrete poured onto a previously prepared surface, which is approximately at grade level. As with all foundations, this style has its advantages and disadvantages, and is a particularly popular method in the more temperate parts of the

Fig. 4-3. *Any log house can be built on top of a daylight basement to gain an added level of living quarters.* (Courtesy of Town & Country Cedar Homes.)

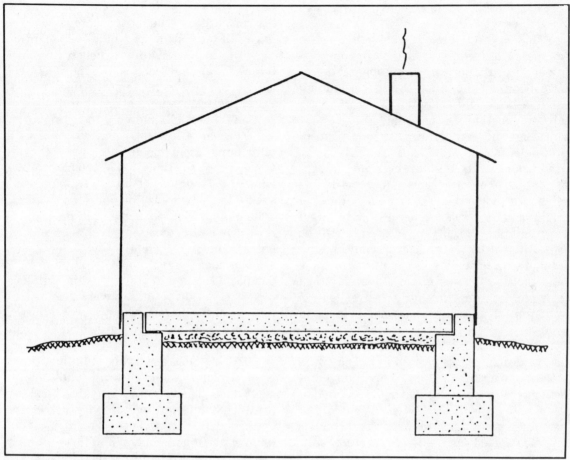

Fig. 4-4. *A typical slab foundation arrangement.*

country. It can be successfully used, however, in any climate, and often forms an integral part of solar house designs.

SIZING

The size and strength needed for foundations depends upon a number of factors. One is the total weight of the structure including dead load (the house itself plus all furnishings), live load (the occupants and their activities), and weather (wind, snow) load that will be pushing down on the foundation, plus the weight of the foundation itself. Another is the height of the foundation walls or piers; the higher a foundation is the less weight it can handle, and

the greater is its susceptibility to lateral forces. A third factor is lateral pressure, if any, that might be exerted by backfill shoved up against the outside of the foundation, and also the depth of the backfill itself.

There are a number of foundation design variables that can be controlled and matched to those factors to provide greater or lesser strength as necessary. The thickness of continuous walls can be varied, as can the width of the footings upon which they rest. Posts or piers can be made larger, set deeper, their footings increased in size, or their numbers increased to support more weight. Also, interior piers and load-bearing girders can be added to spread the load, and other design devices can be used as well.

One way to figure out what you need for foundation strength is to do a bit of engineering and calculating with the proper tables, or have it done for you. Another is to look around, ask questions, and study the literature to see what foundation designs and arrangements have been successfully used, or would be appropriate, in your area. Those that have been used before can be used again. Note, though, that the standard designs used in frame houses might not be sturdy enough for a log house, or might not be suitable for the soil conditions at your building site. If your log house will be large, it will be heavy, and if you are confronted with unstable soil conditions or some other peculiarity that might adversely affect your building program, further investigation and probably some professional help is in order.

Perhaps the most crucial factors in foundation design is *ground loading*. The entire weight of your house will rest upon the foundation. This weight plus that of the foundation itself will rest upon a few small strips and patches of ground (except for a slab, which is far more spread out). Different types of soils have different load-carrying capacities, and if you provide insufficient flotation at the footings so that the load is concentrated upon too small a ground area, subsidence of part or all of the structure is inevitable. The total area of the bottom of your footings—the base upon which the foundation walls or piers rest—must be large enough to prevent your house from slowly sinking down into the particular soil that you build on. This in turn means that you need to know two things: The weight of the building, and the load-carrying capacity of the soil where the house will be built.

To take the last first, soil load-carrying capacity is widely variable. Different kinds of soils can hold up different weights. To add to the fun, there is not only considerable variation from locale to locale, but often between nearby spots as well. How can you determine the capabilities? The most accurate way is to have soil tests made by a qualified engineering firm—not an awfully expensive proposition. If the ground seems soft or spongy, or you suspect a high water table or underground water pockets, such problems as well as other potential ones will show up in the report.

You can also bypass the test and, as is often done, use some general figures that are widely accepted (Table 4-1). A soft clay soil can handle a weight of about 2000 pounds per square foot. Firm clay or fine sand can hold 4000 pounds. Tightly compacted fine sand or relatively loose, coarse gravel will support 6000 pounds, and tightly compacted coarse sand or loose gravel about 8000 pounds. A compacted sand and gravel mixture will handle up to 12,000 pounds of weight per square foot. All these figures presuppose that the soil structure is native and undisturbed and contains no fill earth.

You can also use a rule of thumb, if you wish, which is applicable to all conditions except where the soil is obviously unstable. Keep the total weight resting upon the soil, house, and foundation together, to no more than 1000 pounds per square foot. While this will often result in some overbuilding—you'll have more foundation than you really need—it also affords excellent stability and does no harm.

The next problem is to figure out the weight of the house. This weight is divided into two categories: dead weight, which, as mentioned, is the weight of the structure itself, and live weight, which includes the occupants and their belongings and also the wind and snow load on the roof. You can figure the weight of a building by consulting the proper tables and adding up all the weights of all the parts of the building. For logs, use the average diameters of the various members, determine the total cubic footage for each category, multiply by the approximate density of that species at air-dry weight, and add up all the results. There are tables for live occupancy load

Table 4-1. Load Capacity of Various Soils in Pounds per Square Foot.

SOIL	CAPACITY
Compacted gravels, gravel-sand	10,000
Well-graded sands, gravelly sands	8,000
Poorly graded or gravelly sands	6,000
Silty gravels, gravel-sand-clay	5,000
Clayey gravels, gravel-sand-clay	4,000
Silty sands, sand-silt mix	4,000
Clayey sands, sand-clay mix	4,000
Inorganic silts, very fine sands, clayey silts, clayey sands	2,000
Inorganic clays, gravelly, silty, or sandy clays	2,000
Inorganic silts, elastic silts, fine sandy or silty soils	2,000
Inorganic clays with high plasticity	2,000
Organic clays or silts	400
Highly organic soils, peat	0

under various kinds of occupancies, and tables for wind and snow loads (which vary from one geographical area to another) that you can consult for those figures. Or, your local building department might have all of the locally-used figures on hand. Tracking down and tallying up all this information is tedious, but necessary.

Most residences are figured according to some averages that have proven themselves over years of construction experience, plus locally applicable load figures for wind and snow. One way to make your calculations is to allow 100 pounds per square foot of living area for the dead weight, plus 50 pounds per square foot for the live load of occupants and belongings. To this add the weight per square foot of the entire roof area, which is usually about 50 pounds (more for exceptionally heavy beaming or heavy coverings like slate or tile). Add also the wind/snow live load factor. Again, 50 pounds is usually adequate, but can run over 100 pounds in some places; this bears checking on a local basis.

To work out an example, a 25- × -40-foot, single-floor residence has a living area of 1000 square feet. The roof area is variable depending upon the roof style and pitch, but let's assume it to be 1200 square feet. Multiply the floor area by 150 and the roof area by 100 and add the two answers together. The first figure is 150,000 pounds, the second is 120,000, and the total is 270,000 pounds for the full weight of the building. This is the load that is transmitted to the ground by way of the foundation walls, piers, or slab.

Taking the figures a bit further, it's apparent that in order to keep the ground loading factor at 1000 pounds per square foot, you will have to have 270 square feet of footing area to bear upon the soil. A continuous-wall foundation for this house would contain 130 linear feet (both sides plus front and back). If the footing beneath the wall were 2 feet wide, the total bearing area of the footing would be 260 square feet. This would be satisfactory, especially in view of the fact that additional support would doubtless be provided, perhaps in the form of a girder and posts, down the centerline of the building to cut the floor joist span to 12½ feet. Additional support for the weight of the building would be gained there.

These figures can also be used to calculate the number of piers or posts needed for that type of foundation, along with the necessary size of the footings. For instance, by making each pier footing 4 feet square for a total of 16 square feet each, you would need 17 piers. The smaller the footings, the more piers you would need, and vice versa. The actual number of piers must also be balanced against the sizes and spans of the timbers used in the floor frame. Timber size, span length, and number and placement of piers all interrelate in terms of overall strength and stiffness of the structure. A span between piers of 8 to 10 feet is a good working maximum, with the other factors selected to suit.

Note that if you were positive that all of the soils at your building site were fully capable of carrying 2000 pounds per square foot, the bearing surfaces of the footings could be halved. The continuous-wall footing could be 12 inches wide, (but in any event should be double the wall thickness dimension) and the pier footings could be reduced to 2.8 feet square. Further variables might be introduced in the weight figures themselves. For instance, in your locale there might not be any snow load, and only a light wind load. If your plans call for building with 12-inch logs, the dead weight of 100 pounds per square foot of living area might be exceeded. Such differences would of course have to be taken into account.

Note too that for purposes of this example the weight of the foundation itself was not included. But wherever this weight is appreciable, as in poured concrete continuous-wall foundation which amounts to approximately 145 pounds per cubic foot, these figures should be included in the total weight resting on the soil. The weight of posts, on the other hand, would be negligible and could be discounted. Posts that are sunk directly into the ground, by the way, pick up ground loading area not only at the bottom but to a certain extent from the sides as well, through friction.

CONCRETE FOUNDATIONS

Poured concrete foundations are among the most widely used of the several types, largely because of their strength and solidity. They are particularly good in areas of severe weather or high ground moisture content, and serve equally well for low crawl-space or the full-basement types of foundations. From a practical standpoint, making poured concrete foundations demands that ready-mix concrete is available within a reasonable distance and can be trucked to the building site. If the service is not available or your location is such that the huge, extremely heavy mixer trucks cannot get to your site, you might want to consider another type of foundation. The alternative to ready-mix concrete is to mix up a good many cubic yards by hand or with a small power mixer, and this is a big, big job.

The first requirement for a poured concrete foundation is a concrete footing or footer. The bottom of this footing should rest a minimum of 18 inches below the original grade level or 24 inches below a new finish grade level made up with fill dirt. Footings should always rest upon or be dug into undisturbed native soil, and never poured on loose fill dirt. Where the use of some fill under parts of the footing is unavoidable, the fill must be soaked and compacted mechanically in shallow layers, built up as necessary, and tested for density of compaction until suitably solid results are obtained. In areas of severe winter weather, the bottom of the footing should rest below the approximate average frost-line depth, which in many places means a depth of 4 feet or more.

The general rule for footing sizes is to make the depth of the footing the same as the thickness of the foundation wall, and the width of the footing twice the thickness of the foundation wall. This is suitable for small- and medium-size houses and for many log houses. However, because of the extra weight that large log houses (or houses made of large logs) impose upon foundations, tripling the wall thickness to arrive at a footing width to provide extra flotation might be necessary. Very heavy log houses made of massive logs often require even larger footings, and the foundation walls are also likely to be thicker than the usual 8 inches.

The footing forms can be prepared in two ways. One is to cut a fairly wide working trench, then build up forms of planks, plywood, or special premade concrete form sections, properly braced and staked to hold them rigidly in place and level upon the floor of the excavation (Fig. 4-5). The tops of the forms must be level in all directions.

The second method can be used where the building site is relatively flat and the undisturbed native soil is dense and tight. This involves first digging a square-sided, flat-bottomed trench of the correct width and depth, and exactly following the line of the foundation (Fig. 4-6). This can be done with a narrow bucket backhoe and then trimmed and smoothed with a pick and shovel, or the whole job can be done by hand. This system, by the way, works fairly well for small projects, but is less effective and can mean more work than the usual forming methods.

When the form is finished, lay in two or three parallel No. 4 (½-inch) reinforcing bars, set so they are about 2 inches in from the side of the footing and about at mid-depth. (This is a standard arrangement, but a fully engineered footing for a particular house might be done differently). The rods can be perched on small rocks, chunks of brick, or scraps of wood; pull these props out as the concrete is being poured. Some workers like to wet the forms and the soil down with a hose just before pouring so the moisture in the fresh concrete mix is not sucked out into the surrounding materials.

Pour the form full (or to the correct depth in the trench) of concrete, mixed in a ratio of 1 part portland cement to 2¾ parts sand to 4 parts gravel. This is a commonly used mix that works well for footings, but other ratios are sometimes used. As the pouring proceeds, rough-level the top surface with a shovel or rake, taking care not to knock dirt down into the fresh mix. With the trench form you must level the surface continuously as you go along, smoothing as necessary and pushing excess mix ahead. With the plank form, strike excess concrete off by scraping along the form top with a chunk of board or 2 × 4.

As the top surface is leveled and smoothed, press lengths of 2 × 4 down into the wet mix until the top is flush with the concrete, and relevel the surface as necessary. After the concrete has begun to cure but before it has completely hardened, remove the 2 × 4s, taking care not to dislodge any of the concrete. This will leave a keyway that will help bond

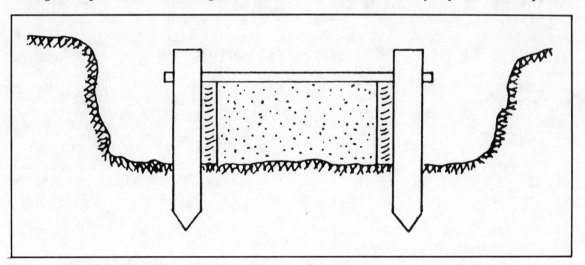

Fig. 4-5. Wood footing forms can be built up in this manner.

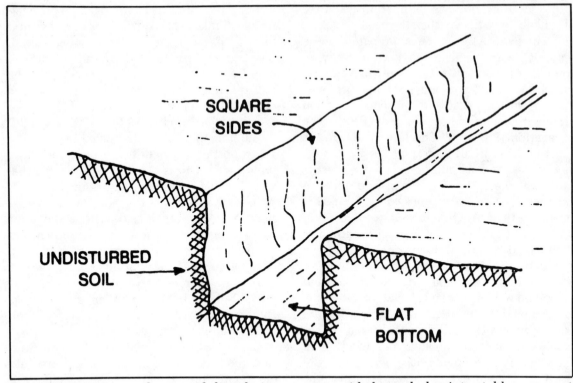

SQUARE SIDES

UNDISTURBED SOIL

FLAT BOTTOM

Fig. 4-6. *Footings can be poured directly into a square-sided trench dug into stable, compact native subsoil.*

the foundation wall to the footing (Fig. 4-7).

Allow the footing to cure for a least five days for best results, and preferably for seven days. As it cures, keep the concrete surface damp by misting occasionally with a hose, by covering with wet burlap, or by sealing the moisture in with a strip of construction plastic. This process allows the concrete to cure to maximum strength without drying. At the end of the curing period, strip away the wood forms. The trench form needs no further attention.

The next step is to construct the forms for the walls. Professional concrete workers use a premade forming system that can be reused time and again; you can do the same by renting or borrowing the necessary components and supplies. Most owner/builders, though, construct their own one-time forms, then use the materials later for other purposes. These

forms can be made from sheets of ½-inch or ¾-inch exterior-grade plywood, supported by studs and wales plus staked braces where necessary (Fig. 4-8).

Don't skimp on studs, because fresh concrete will exert a tremendous amount of pressure on the form walls. Two wales are usually sufficient, depending on the size and frequency of the studs, for a low wall. For full basement walls, several wales should be used along with extra bracing. The shoes on each side of the form bottom lie flat atop the footing so that the longitudinal centerlines of both footing and form match up. The shoes can be nailed to the still-green footing top—right into the concrete—with ordinary common or box nails, or with double-headed scaffold nails for easier removal. Provided that you don't use too many nails, this will not harm the footing.

Combination tie/spreaders, a variety of

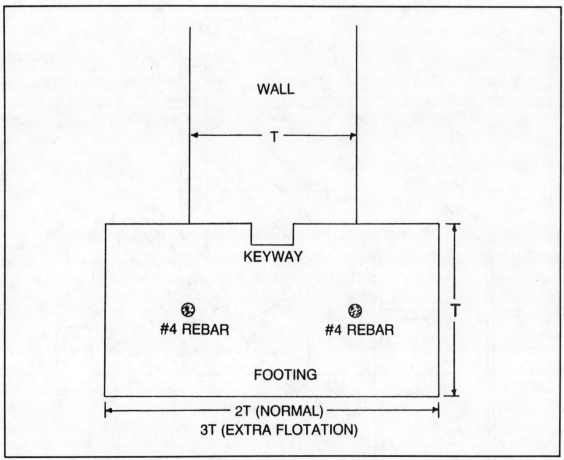

WALL

T

KEYWAY

⊛   ⊛

#4 REBAR   **#4 REBAR**

T

FOOTING

2T (NORMAL)
3T (EXTRA FLOTATION)

Fig. 4-7. Standard footing dimensions.

which are available at lumber and hardware supply outlets, should be inserted through the forms as they are built. These serve to hold the form walls in place until the concrete cures, so that the form walls can neither shift inward and out of place while still empty, nor bulge outward as the concrete is poured. After the concrete has cured, the breakaway heads of these tie/spreaders are knocked off with a hammer, and the remainder stays embedded in the concrete. Some wall designs require that reinforcing rod or mesh be embedded in the concrete; these materials are placed according to plan before the tie/spreaders are installed.

Once the forms are erected and double-checked for rigidity, accurate dimensions, and proper level, the concrete can be poured. The same concrete mix ratio can be used here as in the footings, provided that normal ground moisture levels at the building site are low. However, in many areas of the country where precipitation and consequent ground water content is moderate to high, a more watertight mix is preferable for full-basement foundations. A mix consisting of 1 part portland cement, 2¼ parts sand, 3 parts gravel, and water not to exceed 6 gallons per sack of cement (including the moisture in the sand) is a good one to use. Top the forms up full and screed the surface (scrape off the extra) with a block of wood. Embed a series of anchor bolts deep into the concrete about a foot from each corner and at

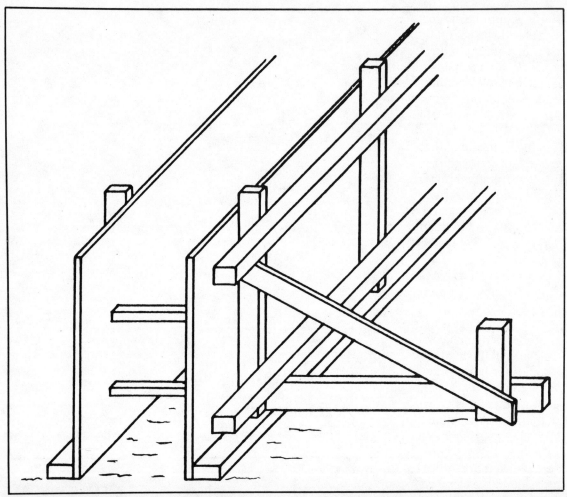

Fig. 4-8. Poured-concrete wall forms are typically built in this way.

intervals of about 4 feet elsewhere, making sure that the threaded portion sticks up far enough to go fully through the sill plate or sill.

For best results, all these concrete pouring operations should be done in temperatures between 40 degrees F and 75 degrees F, and a relative humidity of around 40 percent. The upper temperature limit can be extended to 85 degrees F with no problems if the winds are calm and the air is humid. Cold temperatures or hot, dry, and windy conditions bring about problems in concrete work, and special precautions must be taken to avoid damage or improper curing.

Cover the exposed concrete to retard evaporation, or moist cure with frequent misting, or cover with damp hay or burlap for about three days. Allow the concrete to cure for at least 5 days and preferably longer. Strip the forms away carefully and set all the material aside for later use in the building. Plywood, for instance, can be reused as subflooring or roof sheathing, while the studs and wales can be put to work as blocking, supports, hidden studs, or braces.

If openings are needed through the concrete walls, they are provided for as the forms are built. Full-height openings are made simply by stopping the forms at the appropriate points and closing off the ends. Smaller openings such as for windows or vents are made by blocking out a suitable opening in the form itself. A window opening, for example, could be made by building a rectangle of nominal 2-inch stock, with a couple of braces within the rectangle if it is very large. The frame is inserted into the form and nailed into position. Lintels or headers across the top of the window opening for strengthening can be of steel, stone, wood or other materials, set into place and secured. Then the concrete is poured all around the frame, with precautions made to ensure that there are no air voids next to it, especially underneath.

Small openings, chases, or sleeves such as might be needed for running pipes or wires through from the outside, can be made by inserting short lengths of plastic or steel pipe of appropriate diameter through the form. These can be cut flush to the wall surfaces later. Notches for bolt pockets or door sills located at the top of the wall can be formed simply by impressing pieces of wood cut to the required shape and dimensions into the wet concrete after the pouring has been completed, and removing them before the concrete sets up hard. Pockets or saddles for joists or girders can be made in the same way. Just box out an appropriately shaped area at the required locations in the forms so that the concrete cannot fill those spots.

Full basements are usually provided with poured concrete floors. This job can be done as soon as the foundation is finished, or delayed until the shell is built, provided that there is at least one suitable opening through which a concrete chute can be run. Delayed floor pouring does have one advantage: all the pouring, curing, and finishing work is done in an area completely protected from the weather, so the job is easier and the results often better. Either way, the earth floor must be cleaned up and rough-leveled.

An expansion joint is usually installed around the perimeter of the foundation to separate the wall from the floor and reduce the possibilities of cracking from expansion. The concrete is often poured directly onto the dampened subsoil of the excavation, though in some cases a layer of sand or gravel about 2 inches deep is spread first. Reinforcing mesh is best included in the floor slab, about an inch from the slab bottom. The floor slab is generally about 4 inches thick. A plastic vapor barrier and insulation might also be called for; if so, this is laid before the mesh and sometimes before the sand cushion.

After pouring, the concrete is leveled and screeded flat and excess concrete removed. Just as the concrete begins to cure, a few hours after pouring, the surface is finished with a hand float. For a very smooth surface, subsequent finishing can be done with a steel trowel. The slab should be moist-cured by misting with water or covering with construction plastic, or both, for about three days. It can then be walked on, but should be allowed to gain strength for several more days before being subjected to heavy traffic.

CONCRETE BLOCK FOUNDATIONS

Though not quite as strong and perhaps not quite as satisfactory from a few other standpoints, the concrete block foundation is easily as popular as poured concrete. There are some advantages to this type of construction: Ready-mix concrete is not really essential, the individual blocks are relatively easy to handle, and the blocks are easily laid (especially some of the new types of system blocks). The job can be done by one person alone and in piecemeal fashion as time and energy dictate. Also, the cost is likely to be less than for a poured foundation.

There are two kinds of blocks in general use: concrete, which are made with stone as the aggregate, and cinder, which contain cinders instead of stone. The concrete variety is stronger and heavier, and preferable. The standard 8- x -8- x -16-inch block is satisfactory for most jobs, but large, heavy houses might require the 12- x -12- x -16-inch size. Though there are many different shapes of block available, foundations usually require only four or five configurations at most.

The bulk of the walls consists of standard stretcher blocks, which are flanged at each end. Building up corners requires corner blocks, which are flat on one end and flanged on the other. In the standard half-overlay or running bond construction, half-blocks are needed to fill out the courses. Some masons use 4-inch-thick solid blocks as a cap or final course on the walls, and they can also be used where a half-height course is needed. Door and window openings might require the installation of beam or lintel blocks above the openings, and specially molded jamb blocks are sometimes used on the sides of these openings. Special sizes or shapes can be cut on the job with a power masonry saw, or by careful chipping with a mason's hammer or block chisel.

When figuring out the details of a concrete block foundation, you can save some labor by calculating the overall dimensions to agree with the modular sizes of the blocks. Stay with multiples of 4 or 8 inches for height and 8 or 16 inches for length wherever you can, so as to reduce or eliminate the need for cutting blocks to odd dimensions.

As with the poured concrete, a block foundation wall requires a substantial footing. This footing is designed and built in exactly the same way as a poured foundation wall, but without the keyway on the footing top. After the footing has cured sufficiently (3 days minimum), the block laying can begin. Start by spotting the first corner, and snap a chalk line all the way around the footing to denote the exact position of the blocks. The blocks should be centered on the footing; find the centerline, then measure outward (or inward) half the width of the block and snap the guideline. Check these lines for accuracy, and make sure that the overall dimensions match those of the

floor frame of the building and are properly squared. If the footings turn out to have been poured a little cockeyed, you will have to adjust the block guidelines. And if the block wall tops do not come out just right, you will have problems constructing the floor frame to the correct dimensions.

The next step is to lay out a full course of block dry (use no mortar) on the footing top, spaced ⅜ inch apart to simulate mortar joints, all around the footing to make sure that the blocks will line up properly.

Now mix up a batch of mortar. You can do this by combining bulk ingredients from scratch, using a ratio of 1 part masonry cement to 2¼ to 3 parts damp loose sand, with just enough water to make a plastic, workable mix. This is the best way to go if you will be laying a lot of block. Or, you can opt for a prepackaged mortar mix to which only water need be added; this costs more but is also more convenient if only small quantities of mortar are needed. You can mix the mortar in a wheel barrow or mortar tub by hand, or use a small power mixer. The latter provides a more uniform and workable mix, faster and with less effort. Combine and stir up the dry ingredients first, then add the water. Mix for 5 minutes at least by hand, and about 3 minutes by machine.

Start at one corner and lay a full bed of mortar along the footing top to an extent that will handle four or five blocks. Furrow the mortar out along the centerline with the trowel tip so that the bed is at least as wide as the blocks (Fig. 4-9). Set the corner block down into the mortar, held flat, accurately positioned and aligned, and push it down until there is a ⅜-inch mortar joint between it and the footing. Stand the next three or four stretcher blocks up on end and butter the flanges with mortar (Fig. 4-10). Set these blocks successively by lowering them in a combined down and forward motion to form both the bed joint and the head joint between the flanges (Fig. 4-11). This head or vertical joint should also be ⅜ inch.

Check to make sure that all the blocks are

Fig. 4-9. Laying a full mortar bed on the footing top. (Courtesy of the Portland Cement Association.)

Fig. 4-10. Buttering the block flanges prior to laying. (Courtesy of the Portland Cement Association.)

Fig. 4-11. *Setting the blocks into place in the first course.* (Courtesy of the Portland Cement Association.)

aligned with one another by running a straight-edge along their sides. Check that they are level by laying a long spirit level across the tops. Then ascertain that each block is plumb, or straight up and down. Make any necessary adjustments by gently tapping the blocks with your trowel handle (Fig. 4-12), but don't move them so much that the mortar joint breaks. If this happens, remove the block and begin again; a broken joint cannot usually be reset by wiggling or pressing on the block. When the blocks are in final position, scrape away the excess mortar that has curled out of the joints and flip it back onto the pile for reuse.

When this set of blocks is squared away, perform the same operation starting at the same corner but in the opposite direction. Then start right in again on the second course, again beginning at the corner. Lay a face shell bed of mortar atop the first-course blocks by buttering just the outside edges and not the cross-webs. Lay the second course of blocks in place in a half-overlap pattern in the same fashion as you laid the first course, leveling, plumbing, and aligning as you go, making ⅜-inch joints. The second course will be a half block short of the end of the first course. Continue building the corner in this fashion until you have a corner pyramid with only one block on the top (Fig. 4-13). Five or six courses in height is about right. Then move on to the next corner and do the same thing all over again.

At this point you can either go back and fill in between the two corners you have just completed, or you can go ahead and build up all of the remaining corners. Filling in between corners is merely a matter of laying successive stretcher blocks (Fig. 4-14) until the gap is closed. Use a full mortar bed under the first course, and a face shell bed on succeeding courses.

At some point in each course you will

come to a place where one block or half block will complete the course. This block is called a closer, and is handled a little differently than the others. Butter the face shells of the lower-course blocks upon which the closer block will rest, and the end flanges of the two blocks that form the opening to be closed. Then butter the flanges or edges (a half-block might have one or two smooth ends) of the closer block ends. Hold the closer block directly over the opening and slide it slowly and carefully straight down into place without dislodging the mortar (Fig. 4-15).

If your wall is only a few courses high, that's all there is to it. If you are building full-height foundation walls, go back to the corners and build them up into pyramids once more, to the required height. Fill out the courses to complete the wall.

Whether the wall is low or high, the final course requires some additional treatment. The last course should be sealed off so no moisture or wildlife can get down into the hollow cores of the blocks. One way to accomplish this is to make the last course of solid blocks, which are available in several modular thicknesses. These blocks are laid just the same as the others. Another method, which allows easy installation of anchor bolts to secure the sill, is to complete the wall up to the next-to-last course. Then lay a strip of screening or hardware cloth on top of the course just wide enough to cover the core openings. Lay the top course of standard block in the usual manner, sandwiching the screening into the mortar joint (Fig. 4-16). Then fill all the core spaces in the top course with mortar (Fig. 4-17). At the same time bed the anchor bolts into the mortar, about a foot from each corner and 4 feet in between.

Window and door openings are built in as the block-laying goes along. The opening sizes are calculated to match the block dimension

Fig. 4-12. Tapping the first set of blocks level. (Courtesy of the Portland Cement Association.)

Fig. 4-13. *Laying up a corner pyramid of block.* (Courtesy of the Portland Cement Association.)

modules wherever possible, to save cutting. Sturdy and well-braced wood frames, or ready-made door bucks, or sometimes steel frames, are set in place at the proper course level and the block laid up around them. Special-purpose blocks are sometimes used here. Lintel blocks are laid over the openings and then filled with mortar or concrete along with a few lengths of reinforcing rod. Placing window openings so their tops are even with the wall eliminates the need for lintels, and the sill or sill plate acts as a header over the opening.

There are two kinds of block systems, relatively new to the market, that are ideal for do-it-yourself block foundation building. Both are code-approved and available in most places. These are the stack-block or interlocking block system, and the surface-bonded masonry system.

Working with stack-blocks (Fig. 4-18) is simplicity itself. The first course is laid in the usual manner in a mortar bed on a footing, but without any mortar between the end joints. The blocks are made with interlocking tongues and grooves, and are just slid together until they mate. From there to the top of the wall, no more mortar is used. Simply stack the blocks in the half-overlay pattern, dry, with the tongues and grooves mated. Leveling and plumbing and adjusting each block is not necessary, though the walls should be checked for plumb after stacking.

Special sash blocks are used to box out door and window openings, with bond beam blocks set over the tops of the openings. The top course of the wall must also be made up of bond beam blocks, all the way around. The top corner blocks are fitted with both vertical and horizontal lengths of reinforcing rod, and then the corner cores and the bond beam blocks are filled with grout, a slurry of cement and sand. In some cases, especially very high walls, extra vertical reinforcing rods are inserted and grouted into place for extra strength. All of the details, which vary a little depending upon the manufacturer, can be obtained from the supplier.

The surface-bonded masonry system (Fig. 4-19) uses conventional concrete blocks, available anywhere. Like stack blocks, the first course is laid in a bed of mortar atop a suitable footing, with the ends butted up against one another without any mortar joint. In this case, allowances must be made for the lack of mortar joints in a block wall that is supposed to have ⅜-inch joints vertically and horizontally; each block will leave you ⅜ inch short of the standard module. As with a standard block wall, great care must be taken to keep the blocks properly aligned and perfectly plumb.

Once the first course is laid, the blocks are just stacked up dry in whatever configuration is required. Then both surfaces of the walls, inside and out, must be plastered over with a special coating, which is laid on ½ inch thick with a trowel. This coating, made up of cement, ad-

Fig. 4-14. *Laying a stretcher block, using a taut line as a guide.* (*Courtesy of the Portland Cement Association.*)

Fig. 4-15. Setting a closer block to complete a course. (Courtesy of the Portland Cement Association.)

ditives, and glass fibers, bonds the blocks to-gether and seals them against dampness and the weather. As with the other systems, the top courses should be filled with mortar or grout and anchor bolts placed as necessary. The end result is a clean, smooth, virtually weather-proof, sturdy foundation that is easy to lay up.

DAMPPROOFING AND WATERPROOFING

Even in areas where the ground moisture con-tent is relatively low and appears to stay that way all the time, both poured concrete and con-crete block full-basement foundation walls should be at least dampproofed. Where the ground moisture content is known to be moder-ate to high at least part of the year—in spring,

for instance—waterproofing is in order. Neither process is necessary on crawl-space founda-tions, although deep-set crawl spaces can ben-efit through a reduction in potential moisture infiltration into the area, thus keeping the in-terior somewhat drier. In the case of full base-ments, a complete perimeter foundation drainage system should also be installed.

Dampproofing can be done by either of two methods. One is called parging, and consists of coating the entire below-grade portion of the foundation walls with a ¼-inch layer of mor-tar plastered on with a trowel. This process may also be done in two layers for added pro-tection, with the first liberally scratched to form grooves which the second coat will grip. The final surface is steel-troweled to a smooth, dense finish just as it begins to set up. The other method, a more common one, involves painting the entire below-grade area of the walls with a thick, tar-like waterproofing compound made for the purpose. Either coating should be allowed to cure for several days before backfilling proceeds.

Waterproofing is a more complex process designed to actually hold back a static head of water rather than merely a slight seepage or dampness by capillary action. The measures taken are much more involved, and a considerable amount of study continues in quest of a reasonably simple, inexpensive, and fully effective means of waterproofing. So far, that goal has not been adequately reached.

There are a number of possibilities. One is to cover the below-ground portions of the foundation with a single membrane, sealed in place. This could be polyethylene sheeting glued on with heavy mastic, or a butyl rubber or neoprene membrane applied the same way, or spraying on any of several varieties of liquid polymer. A membrane can also be built up in layers. The oldest method is to mop on several coats of hot coal-tar pitch. Other methods include applying successive layers of hot tar and roofing felt, hot coal-tar pitch and overlapping layers of fiberglass fabric, or fiberglass fabric or mat and resin. In all cases the trick is to make a thorough job of it, leaving no seams or joints that might admit moisture. If

Fig. 4-16. *Laying the top course of block over wire lath sandwiched into the mortar joint.* (Courtesy of the Portland Cement Association.)

Fig. 4-17. *Filling the top-course cores with mortar, which bonds to the block and to the wire mesh sandwiched in the joint below.* (Courtesy of the Portland Cement Association.)

you are faced with a waterproofing job, check first to see what the latest developments in the field are, and what supplies and materials are readily available to you.

Installing a perimeter drainage system (Fig. 4-20) is not a difficult job and adds greatly to the moisture protection aspect of the foundation; generally it is used only on full-basement foundations. The job involves placing a line of clay drainage pipe or perforated or slotted plastic drainage pipe around the outside edge of the footings, set upon a couple of inches or so of ¾ inch gravel. Joints between the pipe sections can be covered with a small piece of roofing felt to prevent gravel from working down into the pipe; the sections are not coupled together. The pipe is then covered up with a few more inches of gravel and the backfill run into place. In some systems, espe-

cially where ground water is a serious problem, the drainage system includes one or more un-perforated run-off pipelines that carry free water away from the building to drywells or an

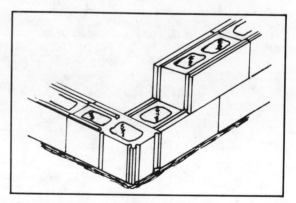

Fig. 4-18. *A typical stack-block configuration; no mortar joints are used.*

Fig. 4-19. Surface-bonded blocks are held together with a thick coating of special bonding material troweled onto both the inside and outside faces.

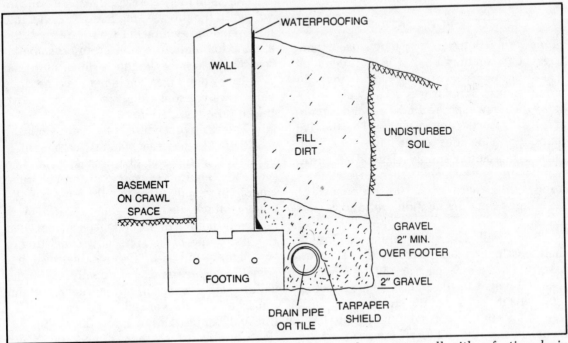

Fig. 4-20. Cross-section of a typical waterproofed poured concrete wall with a footing drain system.

open drainage ditch. But in no case should this system be piped into a septic tank or terminate in the vicinity of a leach field.

Moisture control in a crawl space is handled differently. Sometimes the walls are dampproofed, but usually not. The dirt floor should be smoothed over and covered with a layer of 30-pound roofing felt or heavy construction plastic sheeting with the seams well overlapped. A layer of sand 3 or 4 inches thick will provide protection for this vapor barrier, and—along with proper venting—is usually sufficient to take care of any moisture problems. This chore is most easily taken care of before construction of the house is begun, provided there won't be too much scrambling around in the crawl space. If there is a possibility of damage because of people working there, running pipes and wires and whatnot, the job is best done later on. Ample ventilation must be provided by making openings in the foundation walls. They should be louvered or screened (or both), and can be made to close in areas that have severe winter weather.

STONE FOUNDATIONS

Stone foundations are not much used these days, but when they are, it's often under a log house. The two seem to go together. In the right circumstances stone works very nicely, especially for a crawl-space foundation, and is probably the most compatible and attractive foundation a log house could have. And if you have a substantial supply of good stone on hand, more time available than cash, and don't mind a little hard work, the economics of building a stone foundation are mighty persuasive.

Stone walls laid up dry are more durable than those put together with mortar. They are best used in a crawl-space arrangement where the total height of the wall is about 4 feet or less. This makes a shallow crawl space, with the wall about a foot above finish grade level on the outside, 2½ to 3 feet above grade on the inside, and approximately 1 to ½ feet completely buried in the ground. The thickness of the wall should be about 2 feet at the bottom and a minimum of 16 to 18 inches at the top, with the outside face vertical (approximately plumb), and the inside face either vertical or slanted back slightly.

Full-height foundation walls can also be made from stone, but this is a big job that has to be done exactly right in order to avoid difficulty. And, of course, moisture incursion is unavoidable in such a dry-laid wall, and nearly as problematical in a mortared one. All things considered, other methods are easier and do a better job.

Even a low foundation wall must be correctly and sturdily built if it is to stand up to the weight of the house and the forces of time and the elements. But it certainly can be done. Disbelievers in this system have only to look at the 200-year-old houses—many of them quite large—still standing today foursquare and strong on dry-laid stone foundations. Proper stone wall building is as much of an art as it is a craft, and there are a great many details involved in the process, too many to delve into here. The do-it-yourselfer who wants to build a stone foundation is advised to do some research to see how the job is done, and then practice by building a small, freestanding stone garden wall or something similar before starting in on a foundation.

The basic procedure is to first lay out the foundation in the usual manner (which will be explained at the end of this chapter). Then make the required excavation or trench cuts, calculating the depth so that the bottom of the stone wall will lie about a foot or a little more below the bottom of the crawl-space floor. Bed the first course of stone (usually consisting of two parallel and partly interlocking rows, but sometimes three and occasionally only one) solidly into the subsoil at the trench bottom. Subsequent courses are laid up by carefully fitting and locking the stones together, with a little trimming or shaping if necessary, and setting tie-stones crosswise in each course about every 3 or 4 feet to help lock the rows together. The best stones should be saved for the top course, which must be laid flat and level, and should preferably be large enough to cover the full thickness of the wall. Anchor bolts are not used in a dry-laid stone foundation (which might be against code in many places), and the heavy sill logs or beams just lie on top of the foundation, held in place by the rigidity of the framing and the weight of the structure. Ventilation ports are not needed for the crawl space either, because there is ample air movement through the cracks in the stonework. Figure 4-21 shows a typical rubble-stone or fieldstone crawl-space foundation wall.

In areas where such a foundation is not permissible because of a lack of sill anchoring, there is another way to achieve the same effect. Set the house on a pier foundation, correctly engineered for the structure. Then, instead of using a conventional skirting material, fill in the spaces between the piers with short stone wall sections. With a little ingenuity, you can arrange a slight setback for the piers, so that you can face them with thin stone slabs and give the appearance of a solid stone foundation.

It should be noted that either of these stone foundation systems can be laid up with mortar, rather than dry. In some regards, this makes the job of laying a bit easier, and the result is certainly attractive enough if the mortar joints are nicely tooled and the stonework cleaned of residue afterward. There is one point to keep in mind: Don't use gobs of mortar slap-dash and make the mistake of relying upon the mortar joints to make up for the lack of strength and stability of poorly fitted stones. Fit the stones first, as you would with a dry-laid wall, for the best positioning and interlocking you can. Then make sure each stone is clean—no dirt and grit—and lay the mortar bed in relatively thin joints. Also, be sure to make provisions for ventilation ports when building mortared stone foundation walls (not necessary with most dry-laid walls).

There is another way to create the appearance of a full stone foundation wall, which can be used with either crawl-space or full-basement foundations. This method employs poured concrete foundation walls built up in the usual way. Mark a line on the forms to indicate a point slightly below the planned finish grade level. The concrete being poured into the forms should be as stiff as is practicable, and when the grade level line is reached, stop

Fig. 4-21. Cross-section of a typical crawl-space foundation wall made of field-stone.

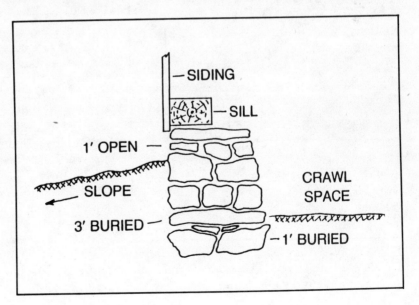

pouring. Then place preselected stones of any face size, but only about 4-inch thickness, on the fresh concrete with their faces tight against the outside form wall. As they are placed, slowly pour additional concrete so it settles around them. As the first row of stones is set the second is begun, and so on until the top of the form is reached.

This is a fairly slow process which should be done in sections, so the concrete does not start to cure before all the stones are properly embedded. Each section should be preplanned, with the stones laid out on the ground in the desired pattern and then transferred to the wall. Two or three people working in coordinated fashion to set the stones and keep the fresh concrete coming behind them helps to speed the job along.

When the forms are later stripped away, the upper portion of the concrete walls will present a rock facing (Fig. 4-22). The joints be-

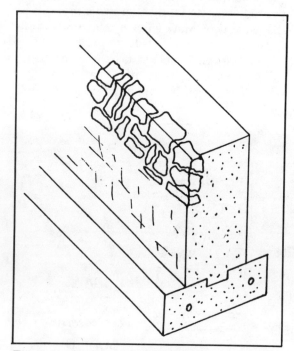

Fig. 4-22. Stone can be bedded into the exterior visible portion of a poured concrete foundation wall to simulate a stone foundation.

tween the stones probably won't have much concrete in them, and the appearance will be rough and ragged. This is easily taken care of by filling the joints with mortar applied with a small pointing trowel. Tool the joints smooth and dense as the mortar sets up, and then clean them of residue later on.

There is a variation on this theme that some masons prefer, and which might be easier in some circumstances. It also has the advantage of being usable with concrete block as well as poured concrete walls. The foundation is poured or laid up in the usual fashion up to a point just below the planned finish grade level. At this level, the outside face of the wall is stepped back 4 to 6 inches, and continued to the top at a reduced thickness; the lower section of the wall may be made thicker than usual in compensation. After the concrete or mortar joints have cured, a veneer of flat stones is mortared into place in the setback area, filling the wall out and giving the appearance of a solid mortared stone wall. Often ties or tie-wires are partly embedded in the concrete or block wall as it is built, then the free ends are bedded into the stonework mortar to help secure the veneer in place.

CONCRETE PIER FOUNDATIONS

Poured concrete piers are commonly used, alone or topped with wood posts, to support porches and decks. Properly sized they do an equally good job of supporting an entire structure. The pier foundation is an easy one to build and considerably less expensive than most other kinds. A series of piers is installed around the perimeter of the house and another set within the perimeter to support girders, which in turn bear part of the weight of the structure. Additional piers, usually of smaller size, can be used for porches, decks, carports, roof post supports, and similar elements.

One of the big advantages of pier foundations is that the piers can be of various lengths and suited to the specific topography of the building site. Though all are buried to approximately the same depth below grade, the above-grade portions can be set to whatever length, within reason, that is necessary to compensate for variations in the topography and still provide a level platform for the house. Piers also require considerably less site preparation and cause far less site disturbance than most other foundation types. Only a series of relatively small holes need be dug, instead of a huge excavation, and spoil dirt disposal presents little problem.

To build a pier foundation, first lay out the foundation lines and locate the points where the pier holes must be dug. Poured concrete piers are generally round, though they can be formed square as well. Round ones are usually about 12 inches in diameter, and other form sizes are also available. Set the pier centers so that the outer edge of the sill or floor frame will be even with or set back a bit from the outermost edges of the piers. Interior piers should be centered under appropriate support points along the girders.

Dig a series of holes down to frost line or slightly below but at least 2 feet deep, and the same size as the required pier footing (which an be either square or round). Rough-level the bottoms of these holes and pour in concrete to a depth of 4 inches or more, depending upon the foundation design. Short lengths of reinforcing rod crossed and wired together at the crossing points in a # pattern may also be set in place, about at mid-depth of the footing. Level and smooth the top of the footing with a chunk of wood or a small hand float, then bed a pair of right-angled (and bent cold, not with a torch) reinforcing bars in the concrete. Place the elbows of the bars at about mid-depth of the concrete pad, with the stubs pointing straight up (these can be wired to the rebar, if used, and set at the same time). This arrangement forms a footing or punch pad for the pier, and a pair of anchors to bond the pad and pier securely together (Fig. 4-23). Allow the pads to cure for 3 or 4 days before pouring the piers.

Note that in some cases the footings are not

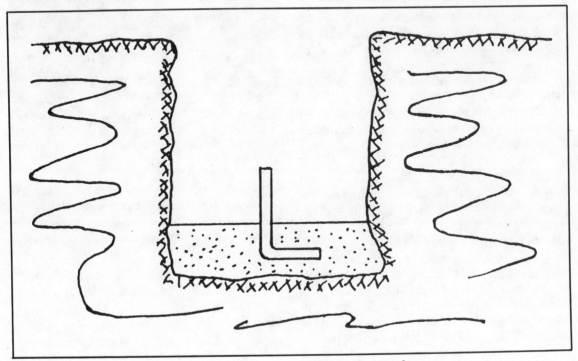

Fig. 4-23. Typical concrete pier pad with an angled reinforcing bar.

needed, if the piers themselves are of sufficient size and number that their total bottom area provides enough bearing surface to support the weight of the house. In that case, the forms can dug just slightly larger than the pier forms, the forms can be set directly in the holes, and the piers poured immediately.

To pour the piers, first set a series of level lines over the pier locations so you can tell where the pier tops should be located, and so you can determine the location of their center-lines and the total length, or height, of each form. Cut sections of the specially made card-board pier form tubes—which are available at most lumberyards—to the correct lengths and stand them in place in the holes. Or, make up your own forms from plywood, well braced. Locate the forms accurately, using your level lines. If you are using tube forms, shovel clean dirt (no rocks bigger than fist-size) in around the tubes to lock them in place, checking their positions as you do so. Tamp this fill down firmly, but be careful not to knock the form askew, or you might have to start all over again. Fill around the tube up to grade level. Wood forms must be securely braced in place in the holes with stakes, braces, and rocks, all of which must be removable.

Pour the forms full of concrete, periodically shoving a stick or old broom handle up and down in the mix, like churning butter, in order to consolidate the mix and work the air bubbles out. After you have poured each form to about the 2-foot level, stick a pair of precut pieces of No. 4 reinforcing bars down into the fresh concrete untill they bottom. Top up the forms (Fig. 4-24), then level the tops and insert anchor bolts or pins deep into the mix and plumb. Cover the top of each form with a plastic bag secured with string or mechanic's wire.

Allow the piers to cure for at least a week before you load any weight onto them. If possible, wait 2 weeks, because by that time the concrete will have nearly reached maximum strength. The cardboard form can be peeled away after 5 or 6 days, but is better left for a

Fig. 4-24. A heavy cardboard pier form topped up with freshly poured concrete.

couple of weeks. The below-grade portion can be left on; it will do no harm and will eventually rot away. Wood forms and braces can be dismantled and stripped away, and the backfilling finished after about a week.

CONCRETE BLOCK PIER FOUNDATIONS

Piers can also be made of concrete block, wherever ready-mix concrete is not readily available or the greater ease of construction suggests that this might be a better way to go. Concrete blocks are easy and convenient to handle and the piers are simple to build. They have ample strength to support a log house and there are several pier variations, each with increased strength.

Concrete block piers are built with standard pier blocks that are squared at each end, usually in the 8- × -8- × -16-inch size. Where a great amount of strength is needed, 12-inch blocks can be used, but this is usually not necessary; in any event, the number of piers employed can be increased to provide extra support. Small piers are built by simply stacking a series of blocks, one atop another.

For more strength the hollow cores of the blocks can be filled with concrete or mortar, and a No. 4 reinforcing rod bedded in one or more of the core spaces. A more substantial pier can be made by stacking pairs of pier blocks (stretcher blocks can be used, too, if appearance is not important) with each pair at right angles to the pair below (Fig. 4-25). For yet more strength, fill two diagonally opposite cores with concrete or mortar and embed a length of No. 4 rebar in each. For maximum strength, fill all the cores with rebar and mortar or grout.

Building block piers begins with a series of appropriately positioned holes, just as for the poured concrete piers. Line them up so that the outside edges of the perimeter piers line up with the outside edge of the floor frame or sill. Pour concrete footings, but eliminate the reinforcing bar stubs. After the footings have cured, stack the pier blocks with a 3/8-inch mortar joint between each. Cover the next-to-last block with a layer of screening, place the top block, and fill all the cores with mortar. At the same time, embed a sill anchor bolt. Or, if the cores are to be filled full height, do so after placing the last blocks. Scrape away any excess mortar that curls out of the joints as you go along, and tool the joints hard and dense as they begin to set up.

Note that as you dig the pier holes and pour and level the concrete footings, the position of the footing surface relative to the posi-

Fig. 4-25. A typical concrete block pier.

tion of the top surface of the completed piers must be exact. All the pier tops must come up to the proper elevation and all be level and in line with one another. And, of course, all the piers must be plumb. You can make slight elevation adjustments as you build the piers by taking constant measurements and slightly thickening or thinning the joints. However, too much of either can weaken the joints. Also, any piers that come out too low can be shimmed, or sills can be notched slightly if some piers are a bit too high. However, accuracy at the outset is important because you don't have much leeway; shimming and notching should be kept to a minimum.

Allow the mortar joints to cure for at least 3 days, and preferably 5 or 6, before you impose any great weight upon the piers or begin backfilling. A dense and solid backfill can be obtained by shoveling in a foot or so of earth, tamping it firmly with a tamper or posthole bar, and then soaking the dirt with water. When the fill has dried out some, shovel in another foot or so, tamp, and soak once again. Continue until the backfilling is slightly above the finished grade level.

POST FOUNDATIONS

Though not as widely used as it could be, the post foundation has a lot to recommend it. It is by far the easiest for the do-it-yourselfer to construct, and has the great advantage of low cost and extreme flexibility. No equipment is needed, except for tools to dig the holes and a saw to cut and trim the posts. No concrete or mortar is necessary. An absolute minimum of site preparation and excavation is needed, and site disturbance is practically nil. As with piers, the above-grade lengths of the posts can be set to suit any sort of topography. Construction time is short, and once the posts are in the ground you're ready to commence building the structure. Posts, like piers, will also support a tremendous amount of weight, and if properly set in good firm soil, they are unlikely to settle; in any case they can be footed with large stone punch pads. Their biggest drawback is a susceptibility to rot or insect attack, but this can be almost completely eliminated by the use of posts properly pressure-treated with preservative. A good post foundation can be expected to last for many decades.

There are a number of possibilities for post materials. Large beams work well. The minimum size to use is 8- × -8-inch. If you can locate them, 12- × -12-inch is the best for most purposes. New railroad ties work well, as do new telephone poles and pilings; the biggest chore is to find them. Whatever you select, make sure that the material is commercially pressure-treated with preservatives in a density suitable for direct burial in the ground. Trying to treat your own logs for this purpose is not recommended, for two reasons. First, the best preservatives, like creosote and pentachlorophenol and the arsenic-type solutions, are no longer available for public use; only licensed companies can buy and use them. And second, only pressure-treating is effective for this purpose, a process well beyond the capability of any do-it-yourselfer. Also, don't be fooled into buying used poles or railroad ties. Most are old, were not as effectively treated as they are nowadays, and have been taken out of service because they are nearing the end of their safe usefulness.

The initial proceedings for building a post foundation are the same as for either of the two pier foundations just discussed. The holes, however, should be dug to a minimum depth of 2½ to 3 feet into the ground; 4 feet is even better. The hole diameter should be just a little bit bigger than the post cross-section. The holes should be dug fairly straight. This can be done with a posthole bar and posthole shovel, or with a one- or two-man power auger, or by an auger-bit posthole digger mounted on a tractor. The latter method is by far the easiest, but is also the toughest on surrounding vegetation. The hand-held power augers will lead you a lively dance in rocky soil and don't really work very well in those conditions—but then, neither does anything else.

Set the posts in place (tip down for tapered poles), shovel a few inches of dirt around them and tamp the earth down firmly with a posthole bar or tamper. Check the plumb and alignment, add another foot or so of dirt, tamp that down, and soak it. Continue filling, tamping, and soaking, all the while keeping a sharp eye on plumb and alignment, until you have filled to slightly above grade level. The more you tamp and compact the soil, the better.

You have two options regarding the setting of the posts so that the tops come out level and aligned. One is to cut the posts to the required length, and then adjust the bottom level of the posthole to the proper depth by scooping out a little soil; adding some and tamping can be done if you dig down too far, but is something to be avoided. The second method is to cut all the posts a little oversize so that they stick up beyond the level lines. Bed the posts firmly, then trim them off to accurately match the level lines (Fig. 4-26). It's a toss-up as to which involves more work, but the latter method is likely to result in more accurate leveling, provided your saw cuts are square and true.

A modification sometimes used is to add punch pads which act as footings beneath the posts, creating a larger bearing surface. In this instance, the posthole must be considerably larger than the post. A large hard rock (granite, for instance), flat on the top and bottom faces, is dropped into the hole first. Poured concrete footings could also be used to accomplish the same purpose, of course, and would be made in the same way as for the poured concrete piers. But unless the punch pad is considerably larger in surface area than the post end, there is no point in bothering. Often it is

better, or just as easy, to use more posts without punch pads than fewer posts with them, to carry identical loads. And under most circumstances the post alone is sufficient, and because of the substantial holding power of the post sides against the soil it is unlikely to move much.

SLAB-ON-GRADE FOUNDATIONS

The slab-on-grade foundation is another type not widely used in log construction, but it easily could be because it is quite effective and popular with other types of houses. Its disadvantages for the do-it-yourselfer are that it requires a source of ready-mix concrete; a considerable amount of site preparation that often includes laying a sand or gravel cushion on which to pour the concrete; and a crew of workers to form, emplace, and finish the slab.

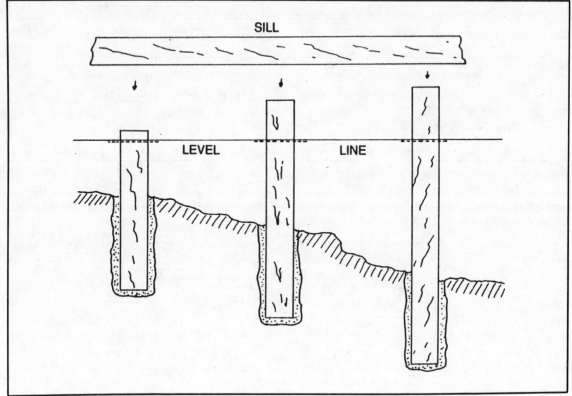

Fig. 4-26. A post or pole foundation can be set in uneven topography and trimmed to level.

This is a big job that must be compressed into a relatively short period of time, and done just right. In addition, certain elements of the electrical, plumbing, waste disposal, and sometimes heating systems must be carefully planned out and installed in exactly the right places before the concrete is poured. Once the slab is in place, any mistakes cannot be rectified without a great amount of difficulty.

Slab-on-grade foundations can be made in one monolithic pour, or in three steps. The first system is accomplished by pouring the footings, short stem walls, and floor slab all in one operation (Fig. 4-27). The second system consists of making footings first, then the stem walls, and finally pouring the slab (Fig. 4-28).

Preparation involves digging the footing trenches and smoothing out the slab area, and adding a layer of compacted sand or gravel if necessary. The footing trenches and the gravel cushion are covered with a layer of overlapped heavy plastic film to form a vapor barrier. Rigid thermal insulation is often placed beneath the vapor barrier. Side forms are erected around the perimeter of the foundation to contain the wet concrete. Reinforcing mesh is laid out in the floor area, and reinforcing rods set throughout the footings. Meanwhile, all pipes, electrical conduits, heating ducts and other necessary items are set in place. When all this is completed, the pour is made, leveled and screeded, and then finished and cured. Anchor bolts are set in the fresh concrete as necessary. After curing, the side forms are removed. Rigid thermal

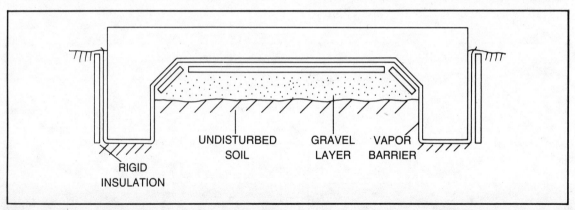

Fig. 4-27. A monolithic or one-pour slab-on-grade foundation.

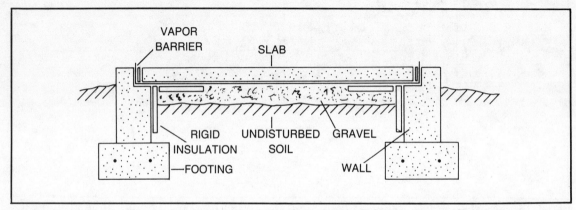

Fig. 4-28. A slab-on-grade foundation made in three parts: footing, stem walls, and floor slab.

insulation may be placed along the footing perimeter, and then the remaining excavation is backfilled.

Among the advantages of this type of foundation is that it can be built in a relatively short period of time without an excessive amount of site disruption (usually). It also provides great flotation and stability for the structure by reducing ground loading to a low point—and thus is useful on unstable or soft soils, and it provides an extremely solid first floor. However, it must be fitted with a vapor barrier, and with insulation in cold country, and be properly engineered and built to avoid the common problems of cracking, buckling, or distortion.

GRADE-BEAM FOUNDATIONS

The grade-beam foundation (Fig. 4-29) is yet another type that is seldom used in residential construction, but there is no reason that it can't be. This is a combination of piers and slab-on-ground, and is effective and more economical and easier to build than the previously discussed slab-on-ground systems. The piers actually support the load of the building, while the grade-beam acts as a sill and containment for the slab. This foundation is also a good choice where the site soils are weak or unstable.

This foundation is built on a flat pad of preferably undisturbed native subsoil. After pe-

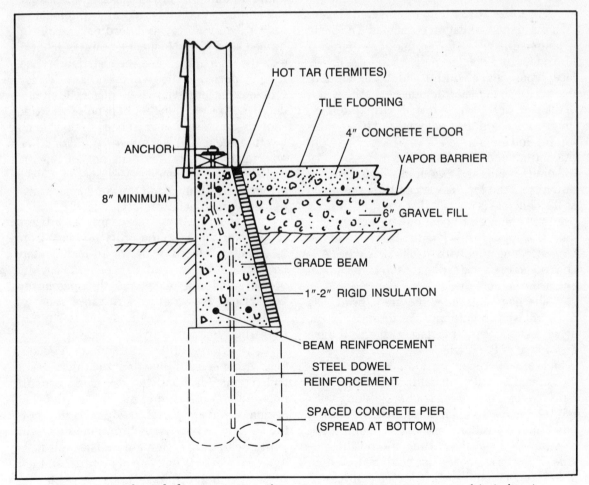

Fig. 4-29. A typical grade-beam construction. (Courtesy of the U.S. Department of Agriculture.)

rimeter guidelines are laid out in the usual fashion, holes are drilled just inside the foundation perimeter line for a series of 8- to 12-inch diameter (depending upon load and other engineering factors) poured concrete piers. These piers may be poured directly in the ground, or in special form tubes, a few inches below the working grade level. They are best tapered slightly so as to be about 2 inches greater in diameter at the bottom than the top, and are usually spaced about every 6 to 8 feet, depending upon specifications. Each pier contains a length of reinforcing rod, usually No. 4 or 5, protruding above the pier top to extend within about 2 inches of the top of the grade beam.

The forms are built up for the grade beam, all around the foundation perimeter. The beam is poured directly on the ground, flat on the exterior face and slanted outward on the inside face, tapering to a width equal to the width of the sole plate in platform framing, or the width of the bottom log course in a log structure. Two longitudinal continuous lengths of No. 4 reinforcing rod are placed about 2 inches up from the bottom and 2 inches in from the sides of the grade-beam, and two more about 3 inches down from the top. These can be set in place as the concrete is poured. The rods protruding from the piers can be bent outward slightly to meet the upper inside lengthwise rod, and the two wired together with mechanic's wire. Anchor bolts are embedded in the top of the grade-beam in the usual way.

The next step, after the grade-beam has been allowed to cure and the forms stripped away, is to lay rigid insulation against the interior face of the grade-beam, then lay a 4- to 6-inch gravel or sand cushion over the entire slab area. Floor slab insulation may be placed here too, and a vapor barrier laid, along with reinforcing mesh. Then the slab can be poured (after all the utilities are in place), a minimum of 4 inches thick. Backfilling around the outside of the grade-beam can be done any time after the concrete has cured. Leave at least 8 inches of the grade-beam exposed (12 inches is better).

PERMANENT WOOD FOUNDATIONS

The Permanent Wood Foundation (PWF) foundation system, which used to be called the All Weather Wood Foundation (AWWF), has been around for many years, but only over the past decade or so has it started to gain widespread use. It is efficient, practical, effective, and relatively inexpensive, the materials are available almost anywhere, and the system is approved by all the model building codes. It is an excellent system for the do-it-yourselfer, in that the entire foundation is made from dimension-stock lumber and plywood and is put together in just the same way as an ordinary platform-framed stud wall. No great amount of labor or expertise is required, and the materials are easily transported to sites where accessibility is a problem for large vehicles. In fact, this foundation can be put together in panels in a workshop or garage and then trucked to the site for erection, a decided advantage in cold or otherwise inclement weather. And, not a bit of concrete or mortar is needed. The key to the PWF is that all the lumber and plywood is pressure-treated with special preservatives.

In a typical full-basement installation (Figs. 4-30 and 4-31) the walls are made from 2- × -6 studs placed on 12- or 16-inch centers between a sole plate and a top plate. The width of the studs and plates and the spacing on centers can be varied to suit the amount of strength needed in the foundation to support the structure adequately.

The exterior of the wall frame is covered first with a layer of plywood, the thickness of which depends upon the estimated backfill pressure and the stud spacing. The plywood is then completely covered with a dampproofing layer of polyethylene film, glued on tight with a waterproof compound. The wall rests upon a wider footing plate of nominal 12-inch stock, which in turn rests upon a wide bed of gravel, compacted and leveled and extending below frost line.

Fastening is done with stainless steel or galvanized nails or staples, depending upon just what is being fastened and where. All the below-grade wood is pressure-treated with preservatives; the top plate is untreated. A drainage system can be added around the base of the foundation if desired, and the backfilling is handled in the usual manner, though with extra care so as not to damage the walls.

This foundation system can also be used for crawl-space foundations, or for perimeter foundations with a slab-on-grade poured within, as for a garage. In these situations the job is even easier, because the plastic film barrier need not be used and the gravel bed need not go below frost line. Crawl-space ventilation and moisture protection is handled in the normal way. A PWF foundation cannot be satisfactorily used in Type IV soils (primarily organic silts and peat), but performs well in other soils, and its many advantages make it well worth investigating.

Further details—and there are a lot of them—can be obtained from the American Plywood Association at P.O. Box 11700, Tacoma, WA 98411.

LAYOUT

Perhaps the most critical part of the entire house-building process is the foundation layout. Accuracy is essential, otherwise all manner of problems will be encountered as the building is raised. Foundation plans are usually drawn up after the design of the structure has been completed, so that the details of each can be properly matched up. Once the foundation plan is complete with all necessary dimensions and specifications, it must be translated into a foundation structure. But before that can happen, the foundation must be located on the site and laid out, and the ground prepared for it. There are several ways to do this, with variations of each. Exact procedures depend upon the house design, the foundation style, topography at the site, and the general construction procedures adopted for the job.

One of the most common layout methods is the batter board system. Rectilinear foundations are easily laid out as shown in Fig. 4-32. The batter boards are set back from the actual foundation lines, which must be accurately positioned with the angles exact. Equalizing the diagonals proves that the rectangle is correctly squared. Excavation takes place within the confines of the batter boards, and reference lines are dropped from properly positioned taut lines stretched across the batter boards to locate the corners of the foundation bottom (Fig. 4-33). Further guidelines can then be set up at the bottom of the excavation, and the foundation is constructed along those guidelines. If no excavating is necessary, the taut lines are used to set reference points at appropriate locations to properly align posts or piers.

Another commonly used method is to establish a series of reference points on the building site and then begin excavating. Grades and levels are constantly checked with a transit as the excavation continues, until the final depth and configuration is reached. Further work with transit and measuring tapes, constantly checked against the reference points, serves to establish the foundation outline at the bottom of the excavation. Stakes and guidelines are set and the foundation is constructed to them.

In cases where there will be no excavating, except for a series of holes to accommodate posts or piers, another method can be used. This involves staking out a rough outline of the foundation and checking to make sure that the structure will be properly aligned on the site and facing in just the right direction. This is much the same process as outlining the house with string and stakes during the planning and site orientation stage discussed in Chapter 2. The rough outline is then "cleaned up" by starting at one point and working all the way around the perimeter of the foundation, setting out accurate stakes and guidelines and spotting the post locations. A great deal of care must be

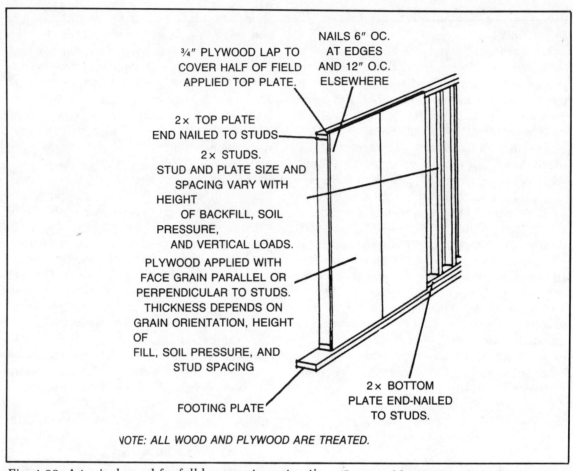

NAILS 6" OC. AT EDGES AND 12" O.C. ELSEWHERE

¾" PLYWOOD LAP TO COVER HALF OF FIELD APPLIED TOP PLATE.

2 x TOP PLATE END NAILED TO STUDS

2 x STUDS. STUD AND PLATE SIZE AND SPACING VARY WITH HEIGHT OF BACKFILL, SOIL PRESSURE, AND VERTICAL LOADS.

PLYWOOD APPLIED WITH FACE GRAIN PARALLEL OR PERPENDICULAR TO STUDS. THICKNESS DEPENDS ON GRAIN ORIENTATION, HEIGHT OF FILL, SOIL PRESSURE, AND STUD SPACING

FOOTING PLATE

2 x BOTTOM PLATE END-NAILED TO STUDS.

NOTE: ALL WOOD AND PLYWOOD ARE TREATED.

Fig. 4-30. A typical panel for full-basement construction. (Courtesy of the American Plywood Association.)

taken to make all angles completely accurate, all lines perfectly straight, and all elevations right on the dot so that the foundation top will be absolutely level, true, and accurately dimensioned in all directions when finished. This means constant checking and cross-checking with line level, spirit level, tape measure, and preferably a sight level or transit as well. Further checking is necessary as the posts or piers are placed and brought into final position.

With some modifications, this same method can be used for other types of foundations where excavating is required. Lay out the rough outline of the foundation first, and excavate to a distance of 2 or 3 feet beyond all the lines. The demarcation lines can be just a stripe of lime dusted right on the ground, like marking a football field. This forms a large, flat-bottomed pit in which the true foundation lines can then be established. Lay out grade stakes, location stakes, and guidelines through the process of continuous measuring and leveling, and build the footing forms to these established lines. Once the footing forms are properly set and accurately dimensioned, squared, and leveled, the remainder of the foundation construction follows along nicely.

One of the biggest problems that a do-it-yourselfer runs into in foundation layout, especially when not conversant with the mysteries of the surveyor's transit, is establishing accurate levels between two or more points a

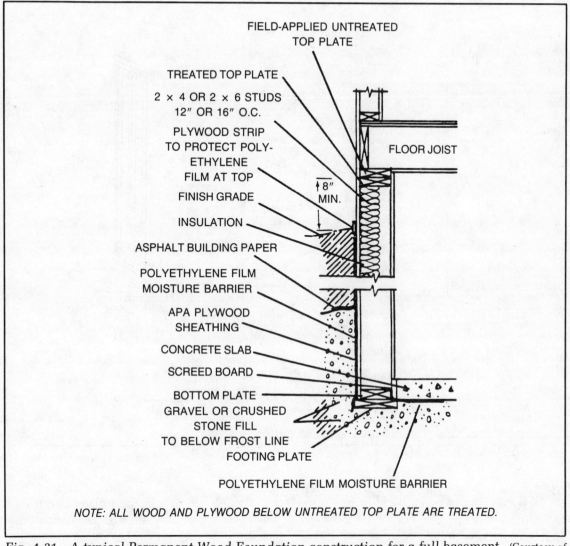

FIELD-APPLIED UNTREATED TOP PLATE

TREATED TOP PLATE

2 × 4 OR 2 × 6 STUDS 12″ OR 16″ O.C.

PLYWOOD STRIP TO PROTECT POLY-ETHYLENE FILM AT TOP

FINISH GRADE

INSULATION

ASPHALT BUILDING PAPER

POLYETHYLENE FILM MOISTURE BARRIER

APA PLYWOOD SHEATHING

CONCRETE SLAB

SCREED BOARD

BOTTOM PLATE

GRAVEL OR CRUSHED STONE FILL TO BELOW FROST LINE

FOOTING PLATE

FLOOR JOIST

8″ MIN.

POLYETHYLENE FILM MOISTURE BARRIER

NOTE: ALL WOOD AND PLYWOOD BELOW UNTREATED TOP PLATE ARE TREATED.

Fig. 4-31. *A typical Permanent Wood Foundation construction for a full basement.* (Courtesy of the American Plywood Association.)

considerable distance apart. This problem can be easily solved with a hose level. All you need is a suitable length of garden hose—it can be a couple of hundred feet or more if necessary—and a pair of hose level ends, which you can obtain through a tool supply house. These short transparent ends couple to the hose, and are equipped with caps and shut-off valves that make the leveling chore easy. An alternative that works nearly as well is a length of trans-

lucent garden hose or transparent plastic tubing from an automotive or hardware supply store.

Fill the hose or tubing almost full of water so that a few inches remain empty at each end, then plug or cap the open ends. All you have to do is set one end of the tubing at the reference level point and position the other end at the point to be leveled, then uncap the ends. Adjust the reference end of the hose until the

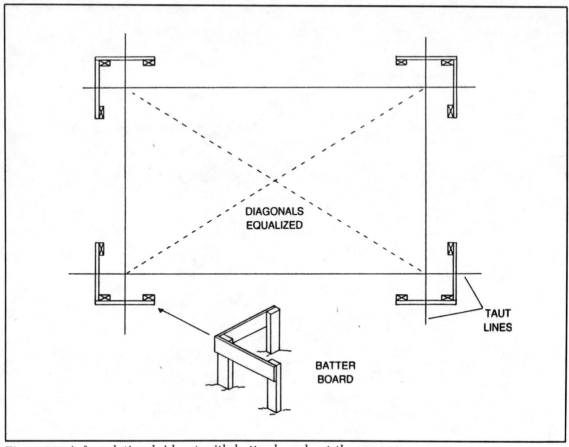

Fig. 4-32. A foundation laid out with batter boards at the corners.

water level matches the reference point. Because water always seeks its own level, the waterline in the opposite end of the hose will be exactly even with the reference end, and all you have to do is mark the point (Fig. 4-34).

In lieu of a builder's transit, a rather expensive and complicated instrument, the do-it-yourselfer will find one or another of the various smaller sight-level devices almost as useful as a hose level. They are sufficiently accurate for many purposes when sighted carefully, and are inexpensive and easy to use. There are numerous models, such as the Locke-type hand level or the pocket sight and surface level, and they are very helpful in establishing levels, determining elevations and grades, and aligning.

Foundation layout can indeed be a tricky business, but one which can be satisfactorily accomplished by the do-it-yourselfer, by exercising patience and perserverance and continually checking and cross-checking all elevations, grades, and levels. Mostly it is just a matter of keeping after the job, frustrating though it is at times, until you are absolutely sure that everything is accurate. However, because there are so many details and variables involved, a little further research in some of the many volumes available on the subject is suggested. If you still feel leery about tackling this crucial part of the house construction process, contract the job to a professional builder.

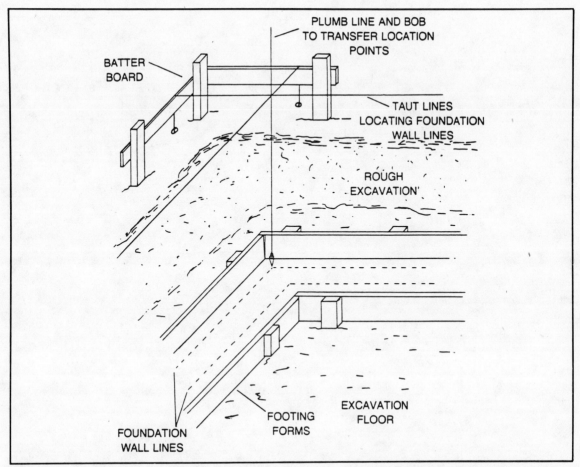

Fig. 4-33. Foundation corners are found by dropping plumb lines from taut guidelines properly positioned in the batter boards.

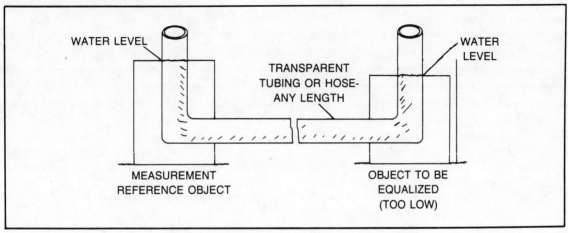

Fig. 4-34. A hose level is ideal for leveling points that are far apart.

5

The First Floor

ONCE THE FOUNDATION IS COMPLETE, THE NEXT step is to build a floor frame for the first floor level. Occasionally in small log structures with exceptionally shallow crawl spaces beneath, the walls are laid up and the first floor installed later. However, in nearly all cases it is advisable to build the entire floor frame and cover it first, so that you have a convenient and stable platform upon which to work.

There are several ways to go about constructing a floor frame and a good many variations on each, depending upon the specific house design. But no one method is necessarily better than another, so you have a free choice. There are also several ways to go about laying flooring. Whatever combination you choose, the object is to provide a level, smooth, strong floor, vibration-free and with a high degree of stiffness. There are few things worse in a house than a rubbery, sagging floor, and this is usually difficult to correct later.

The following arrangements are basic, and all are widely used in log house building. Construction variations and detail changes can and should be introduced wherever necessary or desirable.

LOG FLOOR FRAME

The combination of log sills, joists, and girders is a time-honored one which originally came about because of a scarcity of sawed planks and a plenitude of logs. This is a sturdy system that allows fairly long joist spans and spacing, depending upon the log joist size.

The starting point is the single layer of logs that lie directly on top of the foundation, called sill logs. For this purpose, select your longest, straightest, and best logs with the least amount of taper. On continuous-wall foundations, short sill logs can be spliced together at any point. On pier foundations, short logs must be spliced together directly over a pier. Wherever you can, though, stay away from splicing, because this involves extra work and also creates a weak spot in the structure.

The bottom of the sill logs should be flatted along their entire length when set on continuous-wall foundations, for ease of working and a generous bearing surface. If the sill logs are set upon piers, they need only be flatted on their bearing surfaces. If you wish, in both cases the flatting can be done so as to compensate for log taper, so the sill log tops will be level all the way around. Note, though, that if the rest of the wall logs have a fairly pronounced taper and the sill logs do not, the appearance will not match up. No construction difficulties will be caused, however.

Lay the sill logs upon the long sides of the structure first. If tapered, opposite logs should always be placed with their butts/tips opposite: on the near-side wall, butt left; and the far-side wall, butt right, or vice versa. Lay out and drill the anchor bolt holes, slightly oversize to allow for some adjustment. The tops of the holes can be countersunk so that the nut rests below the log surface, or recesses can be made in the next round of logs to accommodate the bolt ends and nuts. In the case of continuous-wall foundations, place a layer of sill seal on top of the foundation. A strip of fiberglass insulation ½ to 1 inch thick works nicely for this, and fills and seals off slight irregularities. Set the log sills in place and tighten the anchor bolt nuts down firmly (Fig. 5-1).

There are several ways to make sill corners. Most log walls use jointed corners with the log ends—the endwork—protruding in both directions. The sill can be made in the same fashion as the remainder of the log walls, in which case the sill logs will simply extend beyond the foundation corners for the desired length (Fig. 5-2). Logs that are flatted top and bottom and are of relatively uniform thickness usually are set with a joined corner. In this case, the long log sills protrude beyond the foundation corner, but mortises are cut first so that tenons of the short sill logs will fit in (Fig. 5-3). The short sill logs do not extend beyond the foundation corner, but subsequent wall courses do, alternately. Corner-post construction requires that the sill logs stop short of the foundation corners with the ends cut exactly to accommodate the corner posts (Fig. 5-4). These are sometimes installed first, but often after the sill logs. Full details of the various corner constructions and endwork are covered in Chapter 6, and will have a direct bearing on exactly how you set your sill.

The short sill logs are set next. In corner-notched construction these sill logs will also protrude beyond the corners of the foundations, overlapping the long sill logs. Align them and cut the necessary corner notches and set the logs in place. Bolt them down and spike the notched ends together. Tapered short sill logs should be placed with opposite butt/tip ends, with their tips notched into the butts of the long sill logs. Thus, tapered logs always fol-

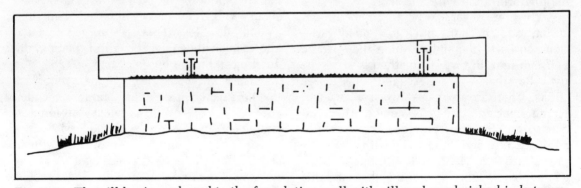

Fig. 5-1. *The sill log is anchored to the foundation wall with sill seal sandwiched in between. The taper of the log is exaggerated for illustrative purposes.*

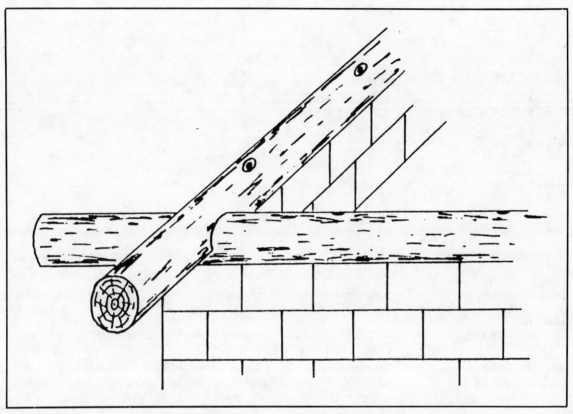

Fig. 5-2. In this log sill corner, both logs are extended past the foundation.

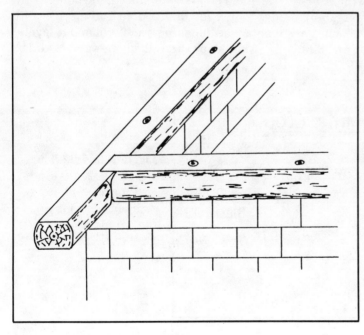

Fig. 5-3. This type of log sill corner is made with one log extended beyond the foundation and the mating log tenoned into a mortise.

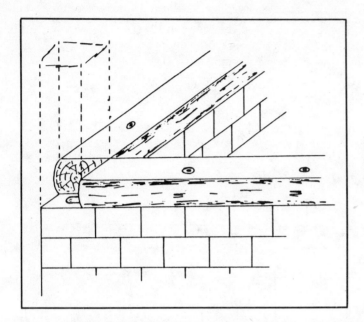

Fig. 5-4. Full corner posts are used in this kind of log sill corner.

low each other around the foundation tip to tail, like elephants in a parade. If the sill logs run clockwise, the second round will run counter-clockwise, or vice versa, and alternate on every round.

Setting round or bottom-flatted logs in half-notched style results in a gap between foundation and log at the two ends of the structure that is roughly a half-log width (Fig. 5-5). In a continuous-wall foundation this can be corrected by preplanning and adding an extra half-block (or half-log) of height to these foundation walls during construction. This can also be accomplished by placing a split half-log in these locations, or by filling the gap with mortar or concrete afterward. With pier foundations, the short-wall piers can be made higher at the outset, or shim blocking can be fitted between the pier top and the sill log bottom. Sill logs flatted top and bottom and mortise-and-tenoned at the corners will come out level.

Most plans also call for one or more girders

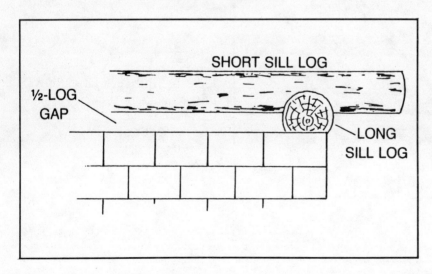

SHORT SILL LOG

½-LOG
GAP

LONG
SILL LOG

Fig. 5-5. Saddle-notched sill logs leave a gap that must be filled, or compensated for when the foundation walls are built.

to help support the floor joists. Girders can be set in pre-planned notches in the foundation walls, calculated so that the girder tops are level with the floor joist bottoms (Fig. 5-6). This type of girder is set before the sill logs are placed. Girders may also lie wholly within the foundation, attached to piers or other supports. In that case, they can be installed after the sill logs are placed. They may, in fact, be attached to the sill logs themselves at some points (Fig. 5-7). In any event, girders must be secured in place before the floor joists can be laid down.

Log joists are usually made from smaller log sections about 6 to 8 inches in diameter. Spans should not exceed 10 feet for this size, and even this short length is apt to make for a springy floor, depending upon the relative stiffness of the wood species. Each joist should be flatted the full length and a minimum of 2 inches wide to receive the flooring. The taper in the joist logs can be compensated for as the flatting is done, or the joist ends can be set so

that the flat is level. One end of each floor joist is cut to a squared tenon, which will fit into a matching mortise in the sill log so that the flatted surfaces of each are flush (Fig. 5-8).

If the opposite end of each floor joist log is held by a girder placed at the same level as the sill log, that end is also tenoned and the girder mortised in the same fashion. If the joist log lies on top of a girder set at a lower level than the sill, it must be accurately flatted on the bottom to lie level and even upon the girder when spiked into place (Fig. 5-9). Some amount of shimming might be necessary to bring all of the joists into accurate alignment. Flatting should be done with caution, however, so as not to take away so much wood that would weaken the joist at its bearing point.

The mortises are usually spaced on 16-inch or 2-foot centers along the sill logs, and also in girders as necessary. The bottom of the mortise cuts may or may not be on a level line; they may be cut to fit each tenon individually.

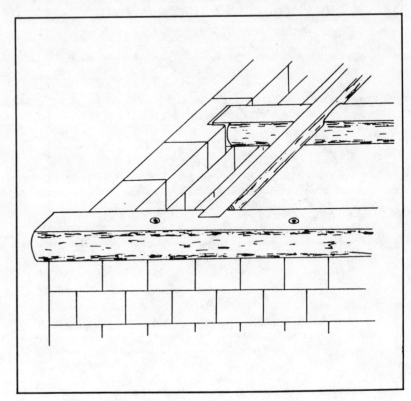

Fig. 5-6. A girder notched into a foundation wall should be calculated to be level with the floor joist bottoms.

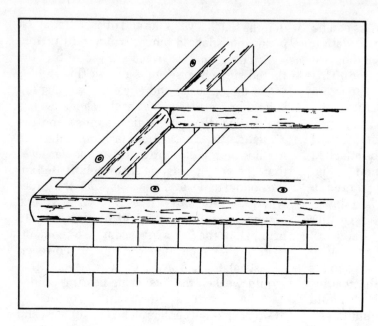

Fig. 5-7. In this arrangement the girder is notched into the sill log with its top level with the sill tops.

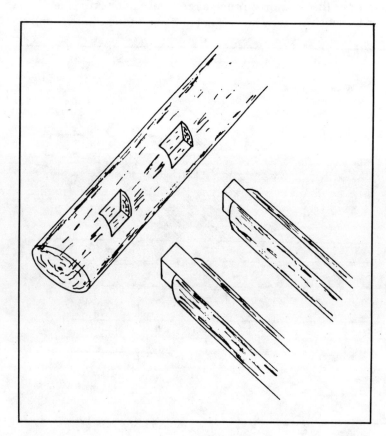

Fig. 5-8. Joist logs can be attached to the sill logs with a mortise-and-tenon arrangement.

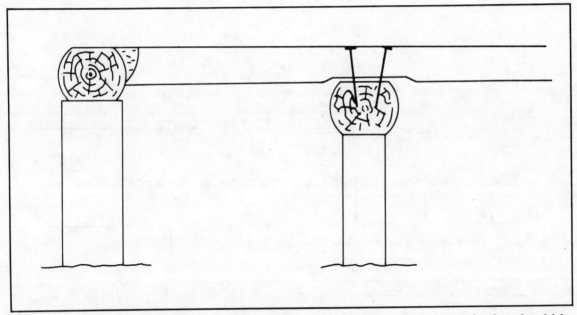

Fig. 5-9. *Flatted logs mortised into the sill logs and resting on top of a girder log should be shaved or shimmed as necessary for a level fit.*

Note too that the mortises may or may not be the same distance from either the top or the bottom of the sills, depending upon the taper of the logs and the varying sizes of the joist logs at the tenons. The object, however, is to line out a level and even floor by setting all of the joist tops in the same plane.

One drawback—aside from the amount of work involved—in tenoning the joist ends and mortising the sill logs is the loss of strength from cutting away portions of the logs. Each log then has only the strength attributable to the size of the tenon, not the uncut portion of the log itself. An alternative method that retains the strength of the log and at the same time allows the use of somewhat smaller logs for the same conditions, is to saddle-notch the joist logs close to their ends so that they will lie on the sill logs (Fig. 5-10). Thus on the long sides of the building the joist logs protrude through the wall and are visible from the outside.

This is a strong and sturdy system, but also creates a few problems of its own. Some of the second-round logs must be saddle-notched to accommodate the top portions of the joist logs, and exact fitting is not an easy job. Also, the added joints and the protruding joist ends afford a number of additional spots for moisture to attack the structure. The joist logs can also be extended several feet, be supported at their ends by piers or posts, and form the floor frame for a porch that would protect them anyway.

In any case, after the joists are trimmed, fashioned, and fitted (or as you go along), set them in place and check for accurate level by using both level lines stretched across the structure and a long spirit or hose level. Shim up or pare down slightly as necessary, and when each joist is just right, secure it with one or two spikes driven into the sill or girder. Bear in mind that when you do so, you will probably settle or compress the joint somewhat, depending upon the species of wood. You might find that each joist face will have to sit just a tiny bit high in order to be flush and properly level when spiked down. Also, if there is any danger of splitting (some kinds of wood split

123

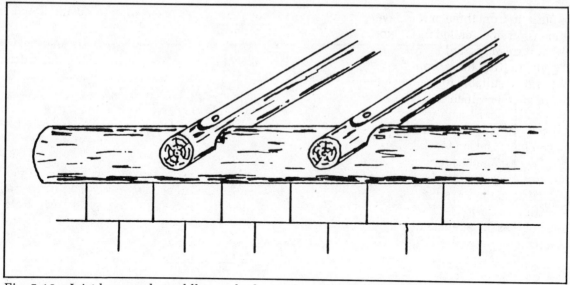

Fig. 5-10. Joist logs can be saddle-notched over the sill logs and left to protrude on the exterior of the building.

much more readily than others), drill pilot holes for the spikes first. Figure 5-11 shows a typical log floor frame layout.

LOG AND
DIMENSION-STOCK FLOOR FRAME

Dimension stock is the term given to standardized lumber that is 2 to 4 inches thick and 2 or more inches wide. Stock less than 2 inches thick is called board or plank, while that over 4 inches is called timber. Rough-cut, full-sawn dimension stock is left rough from the saw and can be cut to any dimensions, but usually follows an even thickness of 2, 3, or 4 inches and widths in even increments of 2 inches. This stock can be bought through lumberyards on special order, or purchased directly from sawmills. Nearly all dimension stock purchased from lumberyards has been planed on all four sides (occasionally on three) and is called S4S (or S3S). It also is somewhat smaller than its nominal or named dimensions—trade size—would indicate. Thus, a 2 × 4 actually measures not 2 inches by 4 inches, but approximately $1\frac{5}{8} \times 3\frac{1}{2}$ inches.

The combination of log sills and di-mension-stock joists is a commonly used one because the floor frame goes together much more easily and rapidly than does an all-log floor frame. The S4S variety of dimension stock is the common choice because it is readily available and can be quickly assembled into a level, uniform, and strong structure. However, rough-sawn stock from local mills is frequently less expensive and nearly as easy to handle, and is just a bit stronger per nominal size because the actual size is greater. You can also cut your own dimension stock from logs you have felled yourself by slicing them up with a chainsaw mill. Or, you might be able to arrange for a local sawmill to cut your logs for a small fee.

Building this type of floor frame begins in the same manner as an all-log floor frame. Set and secure all the sill logs in the same way as discussed earlier. Set any necessary girders as well, positioned to allow whatever joist spans you have decided upon. The spans are variable depending upon the spacing of the joists, the species of wood used, and the dimensions of the joists. Some typical spans are shown in Table 5-1. The girders can either be stout logs or built up from three or four layers of suitable dimension stock nailed tightly together. Either are in turn supported by piers or posts below.

Begin the floor frame construction by choosing a suitable reference point at one corner or another which will be the level guide for the entire floor assembly. Start at this point and spike headers of dimension stock the same size as you have chosen for the joists to the log sill (Fig. 5-12). The headers run at right angles to the joist direction. Then in the same way spike end joists to the log sills; these lie in the same direction as the joists. Keep a sharp eye on the level of these headers and end joists to ensure that their tops are all at exactly the same height.

They must also be kept straight up and down, or plumb.

Mark off centerlines for all the joist positions along the headers and also on the girder tops. The most commonly used spacing is 16 inches on centers, and this is the most workable arrangement. A 24-inch spacing is adequate in some instances if the flooring is to be a heavy decking material or one of the special plywood systems. The 12-inch centering affords greater strength and stiffness, but at the expense of additional labor and inability to use standard-width thermal insulation batts. Butt the ends of the joists tight against the headers and secure them with metal joist hangers nailed

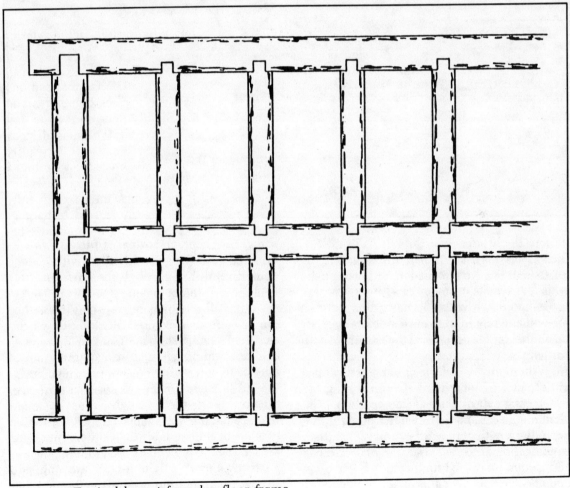

Fig. 5-11. Typical layout for a log floor frame.

Table 5-1. Maximum Length of Dimension-Stock Floor Joists.

Nominal Size (Inches)	Spacing (Inches)	40-lb. Live Load (Plaster or Wallboard Ceiling)	(Open or Tile Ceiling)	50-lb. Live Load (Plaster or Wallboard Ceiling)	(Open or Tile Ceiling)
2 × 6	12	10'8"	13'2"	10'0"	12'0"
	16	9'8"	11'6"	9'1"	10'5"
	24	8'6"	9'6"	8'0"	8'7"
2 × 8	12	14'1"	17'5"	13'3"	15'10"
	16	12'11"	15'3"	12'1"	13'10"
	24	11'4"	12'6"	10'7"	11'4"
2 × 10	12	17'9"	21'10"	16'8"	19'11"
	16	16'3"	19'2"	15'3"	17'5"
	24	14'3"	15'10"	13'5"	14'4"
2 × 12	12	21'4"	26'3"	20'1"	24'0"
	16	19'7"	23'0"	18'5"	21'0"
	24	17'3"	19'1"	16'2"	17'4"

to both the headers and the joists (Fig. 5-13). Sometimes it is easier to nail the hangers to the joists first, then to the headers. If the opposite ends of the joists lie on top of a girder, they are toe-nailed down with 10d nails, one through the end and one in from each side. If the joists meet the girder, they can be secured with hangers.

When you are setting floor joists atop a girder, nail in lengths of solid blocking between each pair of joists as you go along. The blocking pieces should travel in a straight line down the length of the girder, and secure them by toe-nailing into the closed end of each block and through-nailing into the ends at the open end of each block. An alternative method is to stagger each block so that if offsets from its neighbor, allowing room (except with 12-inch centering) to nail through the joists and into each end of the blocks (Fig. 5-14).

After all the joists are set, nail in another run of solid or staggered blocking down the center of each joist span. You can also use X- or cross-bridging, which can be made up of lengths of nominal 1- × -4 stock or metal bridging struts made for the purpose. In this case, the upper ends of the bridging must be nailed in place but the lower ends left loose. After the subfloor has been laid, then the bottom ends are secured. In either case, the bridging ties the joists together solidly to reduce warping, add strength, and help to minimize vibration and

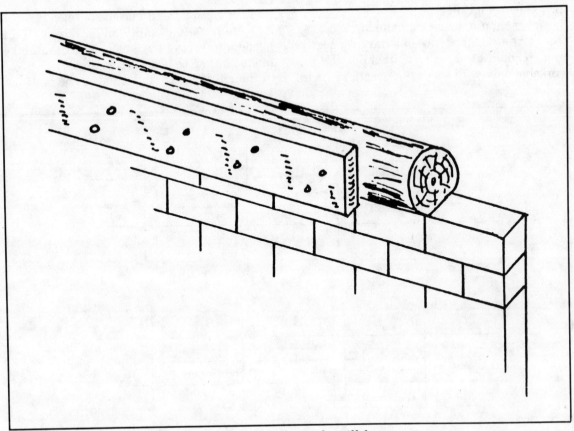

Fig. 5-12. A joist header can be nailed directly to the sill log.

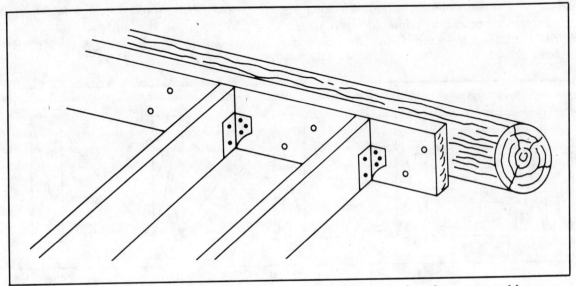

Fig. 5-13. A sturdy method of attaching joists to a header is to anchor them in metal hangers.

springiness (Fig. 5-15).

Joists should not be toe-nailed to headers, because this method doesn't provide nearly enough holding strength. Another possibility, workable only with small floor sections, is to nail the headers and end joists together in a built-up rectangle, and then nail through the headers to secure the joists. Then the entire frame unit can be boosted into place and spiked to the sill logs. Though this can be (and has

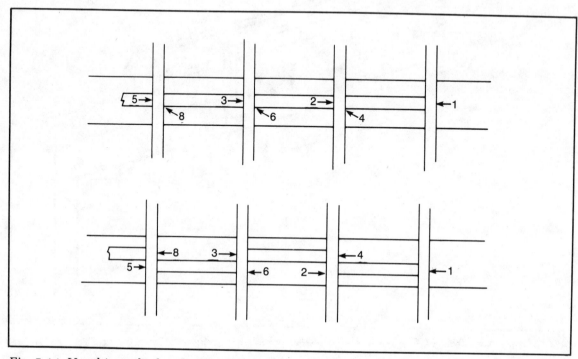

Fig. 5-14. Use this method and nailing sequence for installing straight-line solid blocking (above) and staggered blocking (below) between joists. This drawing shows the joists resting upon a girder, but the same method can be employed in open spans to reduce springiness and joist twisting.

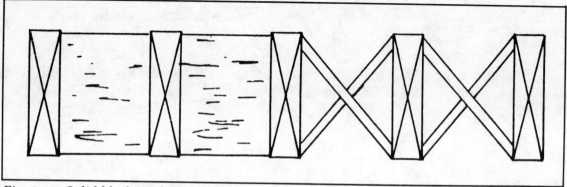

Fig. 5-15. Solid blocking (left) of X-bridging (right), shown in cross-section between the floor joists, increases the strength and stiffness of a floor.

been) done, it is a decidedly awkward method and proper fitting and aligning of the frame and sill can be problematic and frustrating.

Another method uses ledger plates. Ledgers are usually 2 × 4s or 2 × 6s spiked to the log sills at right angles to the lie of the joists. The first wall course of logs (or more) is set upon the sill logs, and these logs are flatted back on the inside face. The joists are set on top of the ledger and butted to the log flat, and toe-nailed to both ledger and log (Fig. 5-16). The opposite ends of the joists may be handled the same way on a narrow span, or laid across or butted to a girder at some intermediate point.

Sometimes another method is used, consisting of a header with a narrow ledger nailed along the bottom edge. The joists are notched to rest upon the ledger and are toe-nailed into the header (Fig. 5-17). Though this looks like a good arrangement, it isn't, and should be avoided. If 2- × -10 headers and joists are used with a 2- × -4 ledger, a 3½-inch notch must be taken out of the bottom of each joist. The net effect is to reduce each joist to the rough equivalent of a 2 × 6 because a joist is only as

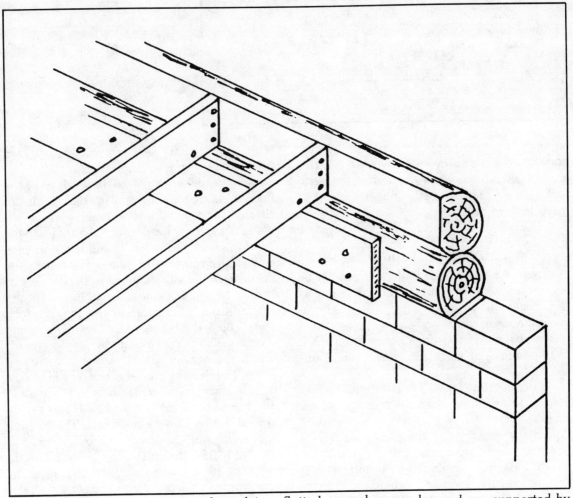

Fig. 5-16. These floor joists are abutted to a flatted second-course log and are supported by a ledger strip nailed to the sill log.

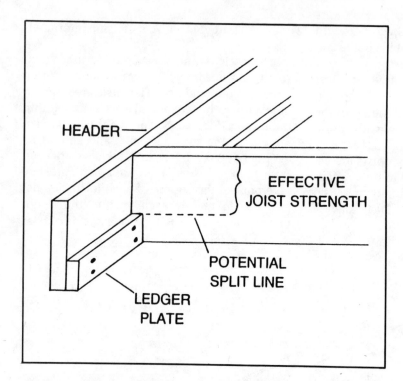

HEADER

EFFECTIVE
JOIST STRENGTH

POTENTIAL
SPLIT LINE

LEDGER
PLATE

Fig. 5-17. The practice of notching a floor joist, as shown here, to fit over a ledger plate is not recommended.

strong as its narrowest width will allow. Going to wider joists and headers to overcome this deficiency is just a waste of good material, especially where other, better systems could be used instead.

DIMENSION-STOCK FLOOR FRAME

A dimension-stock floor frame can readily be made for a log house. It is exactly the same as the system used in conventional platform-framed houses, sturdy and easy to build. There are two basic varieties, one for continuous-wall foundations, and another for pier or post foundations.

On a continuous-wall foundation, the first step is to lay down a continuous sill plate, usually either a 2 × 6 or a 2 × 8. Building codes now require that the plate material be pressure-treated with preservative to minimize rot from damp concrete foundation tops; redwood or perhaps cypress might also be allowable. Either way, the idea is a good one.

The plate lies flat on the foundation top

with a layer of sill seal sandwiched between them, and is firmly secured with anchor bolts. Stand a header of the same dimensions as the floor joists up on edge and toe-nail it into position flush with the outside edge of the sill plate. Place these headers at right angles to the lie of the floor joists. Stand end joists on edge and secure them in the same fashion as the headers, to the sill plate and to the headers as well. Line up the joists and nail them into position through the headers and into the joist ends (Fig. 5-18). Before setting each joist, stand it on edge and sight along it to see whether it is straight, or bows slightly up or down. Then place it so that the crown of the bow is uppermost. Secure the joists to girders by toe-nailing, and install blocking between each pair as discussed earlier, down the centerline of each span and along the girders if they are present.

Note that the joists can be full length, reaching from wall to wall but supported by one or more girders beneath and at right angles to them, or they can be short ones that reach only from wall to girder, or girder to girder.

Short joists are easier to handle, but require more nailing. Full-length joists require a little less labor and time, and the effective strength and stiffness is somewhat greater than two or more short ones.

For pier foundations the situation is a bit different. A 2- × -6 sill plate (this may be untreated wood) is first secured flat to the pier tops with anchor bolts. Splicing must be done atop a pier, and requires that two anchor bolts be set. Then the headers are set atop the sill plate, on edge and flush with the outside edge. These headers, though, must be doubled at least and are often tripled in thickness, depending upon the span between piers. The end joists are likewise doubled or tripled, and all are attached to the sill plate in the same way as for a continuous-wall foundation (Fig. 5-19).

The headers and end joists can be nailed together first and then set into position on the sill plate. In this case, the joists are attached to the headers with metal joist hangers if the sill plate is the same width as the thickness of the headers, or rested upon the sill plate and toe-nailed to the headers if not. If you would prefer to end-nail the joists, set a single-thickness header back from the outside edge of the sill plate by a distance equal to the thickness of the headers that must be added—that is, usually one or two more headers. Secure that header to the sill plate, then set the joists and nail through the header and into the joist ends to secure them. Nail on the one or two remaining headers, as well as the end joists, so that the outside face of the completed header is flush with the outside edge of the sill plate.

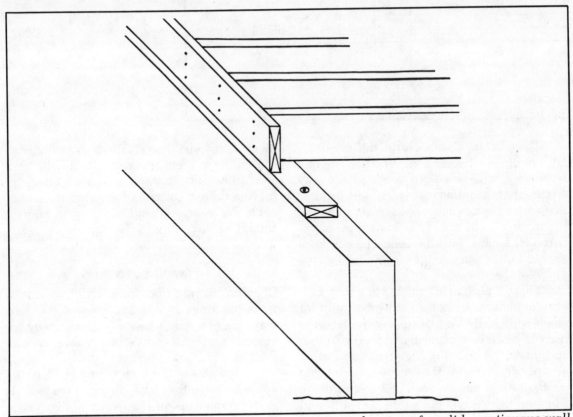

Fig. 5-18. In this system, sill plate and header are mounted on top of a solid, continuous-wall foundation.

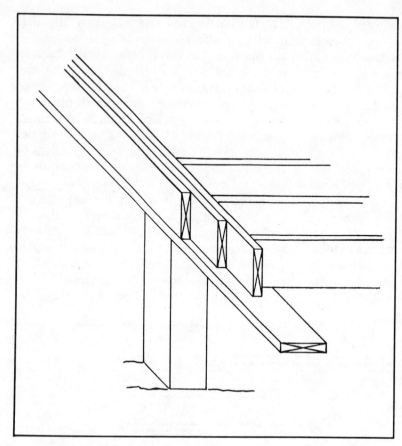

Fig. 5-19. Where a pier foundation system is used, a full sill beam must be installed, or a sill girder can be made up from dimension stock.

There is an alternative to the multiple-layer or built-up header and end joists, and that is to set a solid-wood sill beam all the way around the foundation perimeter. This requires that suitably long anchor bolts be set when the foundation is built, and the joists must be secured with metal joist hangers. The sill beam should be the same height, or higher, as the depth of the joists.

There is also an alternative to using ordinary dimension stock for floor joists, and for headers as well. You can use manufactured truss joists of the type designed for residential applications (Fig. 5-20). These are solid wood and plywood fabrications made in an I-beam configuration, usually about 12 inches deep. They are lightweight but strong and stiff, and are easy to install. Special girders, hangers, and other components are available for use with

them. Truss joist sizes should be fitted for each individual job, but you can obtain help from a supplier or factory representative in selecting the correct joists and associated components for your application. This, of course, should be done during the planning stage.

FLOOR OPENINGS

Chances are your floor frame will have one or more openings in it to accommodate a stairway, crawl-space access hatch, chimney, or something of that nature. Such holes require a bit of additional framing.

If the size of the hole is smaller than the space between the joists, all you have to do is nail a framework of the required size, made from dimension stock, into place between the joists. Generally 2 × 4s are adequate for small holes; the principal object is to provide a nailing strip for the flooring edges.

Larger holes that span two or more joist spaces require a considerable amount of extra strength in the framing to compensate for the loss of joist material and continuity. In all-log floor frames, joists that will intersect an opening in the floor are left out temporarily. A pair of header joists is installed with mortise-and-tenon joints between the two joists bordering the opening on each side and at right angles to them, to act as two sides of the opening and forming a rectangle. Then tail joists are installed, also mortise-and-tenoned. They run parallel to the main joists and are at normal spacing, from sill (or girder) to header joists on both sides of the opening. If the opening must be narrowed further, a pair of trimmer joists is installed, again with mortise-and-tenon joints, between the two header joists. This construc-

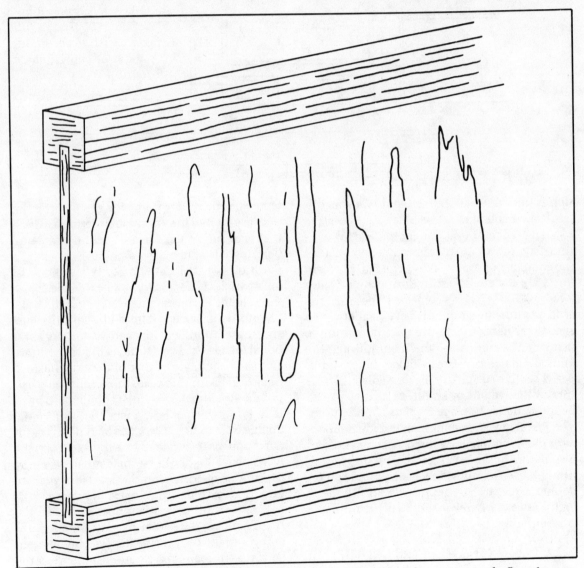

Fig. 5-20. Installing truss joists like this one is the modern way of building up a sturdy floor frame.

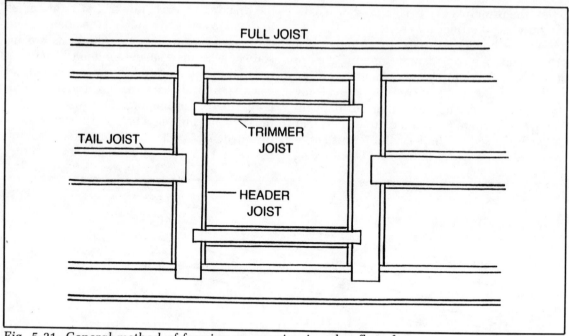

FULL JOIST

TRIMMER JOIST

TAIL JOIST

HEADER JOIST

Fig. 5-21. General method of framing an opening in a log floor frame.

tion is outlined in Fig. 5-21, and is not as difficult as it sounds.

The situation is much the same with dimension-stock floor frames, except that all the components are doubled. The outside main joists are installed first, followed by primary headers. The tail joists come next, between the sills or girders and the primary headers. The secondary header joists are then nailed to the primary headers and to the main joists at the ends. Trimmer joists are installed, if necessary, between the secondary header joists. These carry little weight or strain, as a rule, so can be toe-nailed into place from top and bottom. The last step is to install doubling joists alongside the main joists, secured at each end and also nailed to the main joists. The diagram in Fig. 5-22 shows how the various pieces go together. For extra strength, you can use metal joist hangers wherever they will fit in.

EXTRA-STRENGTH CONSTRUCTIONS

There are occasions when a lot of extra strength

is needed in a floor frame for some particular purpose—often to support an interior partition that is to run in the same direction as the underlying joists. In a log-frame floor system, the partition is best located directly above a joist log, which, if necessary, can be made larger than the other joists.

If this is not feasible, don't shift the joist spacing around, but instead install an additional joist to lie directly beneath the partition. The same situation is true of dimension-stock floor frames. In this case, though, if the partition is directly above a joist, double the joist. If it is between joists, install an additional double joist to help carry the load. If the partition happens to be a load-bearing one itself, the joists beneath should be further beefed up by tripling or quadrupling the joist to become a girder, or by placing an extra or a larger joist log, or by adding post support beneath.

There are also other reasons for strengthening certain sections of the flooring. A concert grand piano is a case in point, or a 200-gallon hot tub, or a 1000-pound, slate-bed

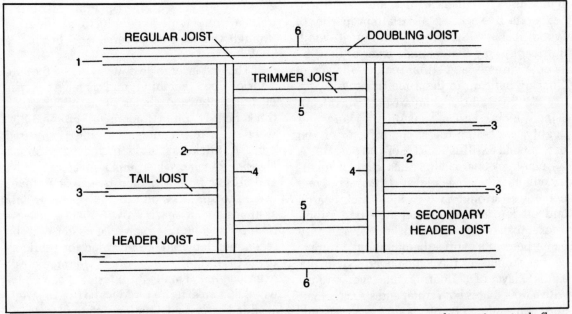

Fig. 5-22. *Follow this sequence of steps when framing an opening in a dimension-stock floor frame.*

billiard table. Wherever a semipermanent massive deadweight of this sort is anticipated, it's a good idea to double dimension-stock joists, increase log joist sizes, or decrease the joist spacing in that area. Additional post and girder support might also be convenient or desirable. However you do the beefing up, do so to that entire section of floor frame where the load will rest, rather than trying to insert assorted headers and trimmers here and there.

DECKED FLOORING

There are any number of ways to go about laying a floor, but perhaps one of the best uses heavy decking. Standard decking is usually of a 2-inch nominal thickness and 6-inch nominal width, with either one or two matching tongues and grooves that lock the stock together. It is available in several woods, and can be used as a finish floor simply by sanding and applying a floor finish, or it can be covered with another layer of finish floor covering. Decking has tremendous strength and allows

for a particularly firm, tight, stiff floor. When used as a finish floor it is both labor-saving and inexpensive by comparison with many other conventional floor systems. Decking can also be laid to provide a finish ceiling below—as over beams between a first and second floor—with another layer of finish flooring applied on the upper or floor side.

To install decking material, first provide a vapor barrier of plastic film if necessary. Then fit the decking piece by piece at right angles to the floor joists. Toe-nail through the leading edges of the decking planks and into the joists for finish flooring, or top-nail where the decking will later be covered. Lock the tongues and grooves tightly together as you go. Make any necessary butt joints directly over joists. Fill out the entire floor area in this way, fitting the decking close to the walls at the edges and trimming around the floor openings.

There is also another type of single-layer flooring that you can use. Though not as thick as decking, planking—which is known as "five-quarter"—makes excellent flooring. This planking is 1¼ inches thick and is surprisingly effective because of certain properties of wood fibers. Without going into great detail, suffice it to say that a single layer of flooring is both stronger and stiffer than two layers of flooring built up to the same thickness.

To give you a comparison, consider a 1-inch-thick board of a particular kind and quality and assign it a strength factor of 100 percent and a stiffness factor of 100 percent. A ¾-inch-thick board of the same kind and quality will be only 42 percent as stiff, and only 56 percent as strong. Two ¾-inch-thick boards laid on top of one another will be ½ inch thicker than the 1-inch board, but will still only be 84 percent as stiff—though about 112 percent as strong—as the 1-inch board. By using a single layer of ⁵⁄₄ flooring, then, you end up with a floor that is both stiffer and stronger than most conventional two-layer floors, having put out a good deal less labor and usually less cost. This type of flooring is installed in much the same manner as decking, either top-nailing or toe-nailing as the occasion demands. There is a drawback if the floor is to be finished: it must be well protected against damage and staining during construction.

LAYERED FLOORING

The layered method is the more conventional way of installing flooring, and consists of at least two and sometimes as many as four or five layers of material to achieve a finished floor. Though usually involving more labor and greater expense than the single-layer floor, there are advantages of flexibility and convenience, and often this is the only way to end up with the desired floor finish or finish covering. The subfloor layers provide excellent working surfaces where dirt and minor damage are of little consequence, and there is a wide range of finish flooring that can be applied over the subfloor with whatever variations are desired from room to room or area to area. Furthermore, the finish layers can be ripped up and replaced with new and differ-

ent materials at any time, something that cannot be done with single-thickness flooring (though that can be covered and become a subfloor).

The first layer to go down is called the subfloor or floor sheathing, and usually consists of either plywood sheets or nominal 1-inch thick boards, often tongue-and-groove. Plywood saved from concrete forming can be used here. A thickness of ⅝ inch is a common choice, ¾ inch can be used for greater strength and stiffness, and ½ inch is also sometimes used, though it is a bit thin and springy. This assumes a joist spacing of 16 inches; use ¾-inch plywood for 24-inch joist centering. The recommended grade of plywood for subflooring is CD INT-APA with either intermediate or exterior glue. This is an interior type of plywood, but an exterior type can be used as well, at added expense. Sometimes, though, exterior grades are more readily available, and they will better withstand the weather while the house is still under construction and open.

Plywood subflooring should be laid by starting at one corner of the floor area and laying a full sheet so that the face grain runs at right angles to the joists. Lay out a full row of sheets in this manner, trimming to fit as necessary; all end joints should lie directly over joists. Use 6d common or box nails for ½-inch plywood, and 8d for ⅝- and ¾-inch plywood. For extra holding power, substitute ring nails of the same size. Space the nails 6 inches apart at the ends, and 10 to 12 inches apart at the intermediate supports. Cut pieces should span a minimum of two joist spaces, so they bear on three joists. For sections of a half sheet or less spanning 48 inches or less, use the 6-inch nail spacing at every bearing point. The rows of panels should be staggered so that end joints do not coincide at adjacent rows. Leave a gap of ¹⁄₁₆ inch at all panel end joints and ⅛ inch between all edges. In climates that are persistently humid, double these gaps.

Subflooring boards are usually 6 inches wide, but 8-inch stock can also be used, in whatever lengths are convenient. Square-edged boards are all right, but tongue-and-groove boards are better. Lay the boards at right angles to the joists, staggering the end joints, and nail them down with 8d common, box, or ring-shank nails. For greater structural strength and rigidity, you can lay the boards diagonally to the joists. All end joints, of course, should lie directly over a joist edge.

If there is no plastic vapor barrier lying directly over the joist tops, you can modify the installation a bit to provide a better floor. Lay a bead of construction adhesive along the top of each joist as the plywood sheets or the flooring boards are laid down. This adhesive is available at all lumberyards; all other details of laying the floor remain the same as just discussed. The adhesive fuses the subflooring to the joists and greatly increases floor stiffness, while at the same time virtually eliminating squeaky floors that are otherwise bound to show up in time from shrinkage and aging.

Whether you use plywood or boards, the edges close in to the walls, or in the case of a platform-framed floor, flush with the header faces. Tiny gaps and irregular edges make no difference because they will later be caulked and covered with trim or hidden by the wall construction. A true, clean fit around floor openings is a good idea. As you go along, also check that there are no large humps or deep droops in the joist tops, especially if you are laying the flooring on hand-hewn log faces. If you find some obvious bumps or rises, trim them off with a plane. Shim low spots before the flooring is installed. Some carpenters check all the joist tops with level lines, then plane off any crowns with a power plane so that they are all dead even. Whatever your method, extra attention to these details now will give you a smooth and even floor later.

The subflooring is all that requires attention at this stage. Once it is laid down, work can proceed on the house shell. Subsequent flooring may consist only of a finish layer or may also include underlayment. These are installed after the shell has been completed, and will be discussed later.

6

The Walls

LAYING UP THE WALLS OF A LOG HOUSE IS ESSEN-
tially a repetitive process. It involves notching,
stacking, aligning, sealing, and securing the
pieces, while constantly checking plumb and
level and either leaving whatever openings are
necessary, or notching starter cuts for them.
There are two possibilities: stacking the logs
horizontally one atop another, or standing
them up vertically, side by side. Either concept
is simple enough, but the actual work is not,
and must be done with care, patience, and
good craftsmanship if the results are to be good.
In addition, there are a number of details and
construction variants that need explaining.
You will have to make some decisions at the
outset as to just how you want to construct the
walls, and those methods will carry through for
the entire construction process.

LOG LAY-UP

Logs that have been milled or flatted top and
bottom to a uniform thickness and no taper
need only be dropped into position, aligned
properly, and secured. With some kinds of corner joints, such as a mortise and tenon, each
layer of logs is at the same level all the way
around the structure—a course, like bricks or
blocks in a masonry wall. With other kinds, opposing sets of wall logs are roughly a half-
thickness above or below each other; this might
be compensated for in the foundation or at the
top plate.

When fully round logs—those that have
been hewn or sawn flat top and bottom but retain the taper—are used, the situation is different. Then the logs are placed tip on butt around
the perimeter of the structure first in one direction, then in the other, in rounds. Assuming
tapered sill logs to be the first round, set clockwise, the second round will be set counter-
clockwise, tip on butt. At this point, the
corners will be roughly the same height from
the foundation, provided that you have

selected logs of comparable diameter and taper. When the third round is set, diagonally opposite corners should be about the same height, but for four corners there will be two different heights—the round will be uneven. The fourth round will even out, and so on. Odd-numbered rounds are uneven, even ones are approximately level. For this reason, it is best to plan for an even number of rounds; this avoids extra work at the top of the wall. When the plate log is placed, the entire top of the wall structure should be in the same plane, otherwise there will be trouble later on in building up a true, squared-up roof.

There are also two ways of setting up the walls. You can use logs of similar diameter all the way up, or you can start with large logs at the bottom and diminish the log diameters successively with each added round. The top log, however, should not be dramatically skinnier than the bottom one. The method you choose is a matter of personal preference. Either way, the trick is to match and fit the logs very carefully, checking plumb and alignment and corner heights all the while, and judging the taper and overall shape of each log as it is added, to best fit each situation. There are no hard and fast rules here, it is largely a matter of common sense, judgement, and a good eye for form and fit.

CORNER CONSTRUCTION

The corners of log houses are constructed in two general ways: extended and flush. In an extended corner the logs pass by the foundation corner point and protrude beyond the sidewalls anywhere from 6 inches to several feet, depending upon the decision of the builder. These log protrusions are called wings or endwork, and can be formed in a number of ways, both plain and fancy. In a flush corner design, the logs meet and match right at the corners.

Both of these methods can be used for inside corners, where the log ends are to the inside of the building, or for outside corners where the log ends are exposed on the exterior.

Actually the term is a bit of a misnomer, because flush exterior corners should not really be cut off truly flush with the wall surface (though they sometimes are). At least 6 inches of free log should be left, so that the inevitable end-checking of the log and subsequent entrance of moisture will occur outside the structure and not within the corner joints where it can cause damage. Combination corners can also be made, with extended corners on the exterior and flush in the interior—they can be truly flush here—to conserve space and allow a less rustic appearance.

In most types of corners (there are some exceptions) the logs are locked together with joints. There are many that can be used, each with advantages and disadvantages. By and large, the more complex the joint the stronger the construction. However, modern log houses seldom depend entirely on the corner joinery alone for strength; mechanical fasteners are used as well.

Some joints are easier to make than others, and some are more susceptible to water penetration than others. Most can be used with either flatted or round logs, and some with squared logs or beams as well. Whichever one you choose (or two, if you plan to combine both extended and flush corners in the same structure), follow through the entire construction process with them, including the sill logs.

The most critical part of constructing corner joints, and all others in the building, for that matter, lies in the fitting. The cuts must be accurate and well fashioned so that the mating surfaces fit together correctly and snugly like the parts of a Chinese puzzle. This is largely a matter of careful and accurate scribing, making clean and exact cuts, patient and precise trimming, and time. Lots of time. Sloppy joints are not only bad workmanship, they weaken the structure and allow excessive moisture penetration and air infiltration.

One further note: If you are not sure just how one or another of these joints will actually look when completed, or if you have never done any log joinery, it's a good idea to take a few hours and do some practice notching on a few log chunks, or even poles. This will give you an idea of what you like best, how to proceed, and a little experience as well before you start whittling away on the nice sill log.

Butt Corner

The butt corner joint (Fig. 6-1) is a fairly simple one to make and relatively weatherproof, but lacks strength because neither the logs nor the courses lock together. One log extends to or beyond the corner point, while the other in the same course butts tight against the side of the first. Scribe the butting log to the side of the extended log and cut or cope to exactly the same contour for a tight fit. Drive a pair of spikes through the extended log side and into the butting log end. On the next course up, reverse the pattern so that the extended logs alternate with butting logs in each respective wall.

Saddle Notch Corner

The saddle notch corner (Fig. 6-2) is one of the most popular joints because it is effective, sheds moisture well, makes a relatively strong joint (both logs and rounds lock together), and is easy to fashion. This joint can be used only with extended corners.

The joint is made on the log bottom only, and extends about halfway through the log. It is made by first resting the log on top of the one to which it will be joined, and carefully scribing an outline of the rounded notch to the same contour as the upper surface of the log below (Fig. 6-3).

Roll the log over and make a series of sawcuts straight down in varying depths to almost meet the notchline. Cut the remaining chunks away with a chisel and mallet, and at the same time take the bottom of the cut down to the scribed line (Fig. 6-4). The interior face of the cut should be dished slightly downward and inward so that it forms a very shallow bowl.

Fig. 6-1. A butt joint corner with alternate extended logs.

Fig. 6-2. A saddle notch corner.

Then the final shaping is done so that the fit is exact. Final settling can be done by running a small coping saw around the thin edge of the notch as the log rests in place; when the cut is finished, the log will set down tight. The joint is usually secured with one spike driven down through the center of the upper log.

Double-Round Notch Corner

The double-round notch corner (Fig. 6-5) is a more difficult construction, but it is also somewhat stronger than the saddle notch because of the double locking. It has one drawback in that moisture can seep down into the upper notch.

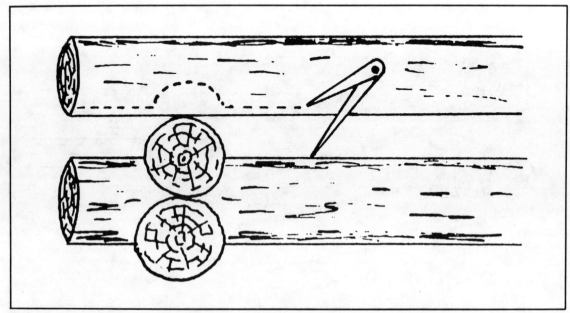

Fig. 6-3. Use dividers to scribe a log for a saddle notch cutting guideline.

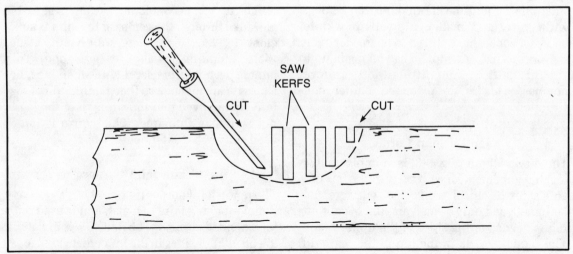

Fig. 6-4. Cutting a saddle notch.

Make the notches in both top and bottom of each log, extending about a quarter to a third of the way through in each direction, so that the joined logs lock together completely. The bottom notch is rounded inward just as the saddle notch is. The upper notch must be rounded upward in the same conformation as the lower notch of the log above. This requires a con-

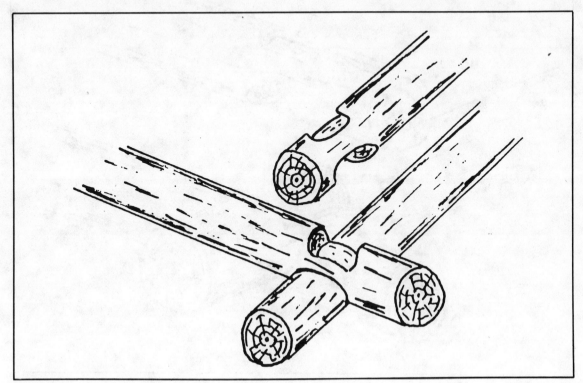

Fig. 6-5. A double-round notch corner.

siderable amount of shaping, but can be done with chisel and mallet, a small drawknife, and/or a spokeshave. If the logs are relatively uniform in size, a template can be made up to aid in cutting snug-fitting and uniform notches. This is an extended corner construction.

A-and-V Joint Corner

The A-and-V joint (Fig. 6-6) is a simple double-locking joint to make with a few quick saw cuts and a bit of chisel work. The cuts are flat-bottomed, and only a small amount of contouring is needed at the sides of the upper notch. The A-cut is made in the top of the log, with the V-cut directly below. Size of the cuts is determined by the size of the logs, and calculated so that when the joint faces come together there

will be no gap between the mating logs. A single spike through the center of the joint is sufficient to lock each log solidly in place. Water-shedding capabilities are good. This joint is particularly useful with small logs, because it can be made so that a minimum of material is removed and the strength of the log is not seriously impaired. This construction is used only with extended corners.

Tenon Joint Corner

The tenon joint corner (Fig. 6-7) is also an easy double-locking joint to make, and is used only for extended corners. The first step is to flat the log on all four sides in the immediate joint area; this can be done with an axe, adze, or hatchet. With like-size beam sections to work with, you can then fashion the tenons by making several

Fig. 6-6. An A-and-V joint corner.

144

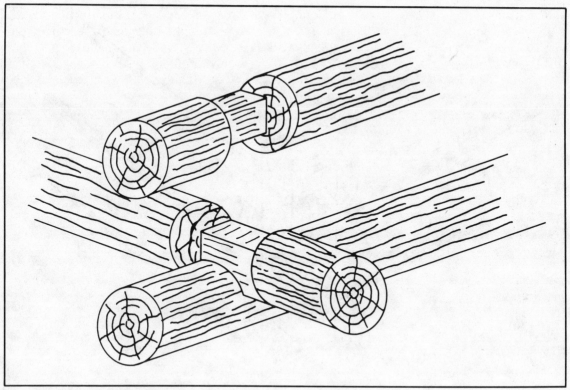

Fig. 6-7. A tenon joint corner.

parallel saw cuts, and chip away the excess wood with a chisel to make a flat-bottomed, square-sided cut. This is a strong and tight joint that locks well and is reasonably weathertight. A single spike will tie the joint on small logs, and two slightly angled ones will serve for large ones.

Dovetail Joint Corner

The dovetail joint corner (Fig. 6-8) is used in flush corner constructions and is one of the more difficult to make. The log ends are subject to checking and opening over time right at the joints, which is a drawback, but it is a strong locking joint of classic appearance.

The log ends must be squared first, which can be done by cutting a few inches of the log end into a beam; the cut faces must be at right angles to the beam surfaces. Then each end is fashioned by cutting and chiseling into dove-

tail keys and slots. There are two variations: the common dovetail where the cuts are squared on one joint face and angled on the other, and the compound dovetail where the joint lines are angled on both faces. Either way, careful cutting and fitting is necessary to get the joints to fit together snugly while at the same time keeping a tight mating fit along the lengths of the logs. The common dovetail is held together with one spike down through the center of the joint. The compound dovetail totally interlocks, though, and if the joint is well made, spiking is superfluous. Both joints are best suited to fairly large log diameters that allow plenty of material to work with.

V-Joint Corner

The V-joint corner (Fig. 6-9) is another system whereby one log extends and the other joins it, in alternating courses. The butting log is

Fig. 6-8. A dovetail joint corner.

shaped in a sharp V, with a matching V-notch cut into the passing log. This is a fairly strong joint when properly joined with two spikes through the passing log and into the end of the butting log, and a third spike toe-nailed down from the top into the angle of the V. Note, however, that as with the butt joint corner, the successive courses of logs do not interlock with one another.

Half-Cut Joint Corner

The half-cut or half-lap joint corner (Fig. 6-10) is one of the easiest joints of all to make, and probably the least satisfactory. It is not a strong joint because neither the joining logs not the courses interlock at all. Both the joining logs and the courses must be spiked together or otherwise secured to hold them in place. This joint also does a poor job of shedding moisture,

and can even trap it to the extent of funneling it inside the structure. Even so, it is sometimes used because of its simplicity. The joint is made by merely sawing halfway through the top of one log and the bottom of the next and splitting the half-sections away.

Saddle-End Joint Corner

The saddle-end joint corner (Fig. 6-11) is nearly as easy to make as a half-cut joint corner but is more effective. The joint is made by shaping an inward-curving cut on the bottom of the log and then splitting away the entire end half. For best results the curved portion of the cut should be contoured to the log which it will join, by scribing, coping, and fitting it snugly. This joint can be used for either flush or extended corners, and sheds moisture well. Each joint should be secured with a pair of spikes

Fig. 6-9. A *V*-joint corner.

Fig. 6-10. A half-cut joint corner.

Fig. 6-11. A saddle-end joint corner.

driven down from the top at opposing angles.

Full Post Corner

Installation of a full corner post (Fig. 6-12) makes a neat and clean corner construction suitable for either inside or outside corners. The corner post should be carefully selected to be straight and true and of as uniform diameter as possible.

Cut two wide grooves or dados the full length of the log and at 90 degrees to one another. Stand the log up on the foundation corner, secure it in position with a pair of long pins bedded in the foundation for that purpose, and solidly braced plumb. Square the log ends off, and cut vertical tenons matching the post dado width on them.

The cut log face can be left at right angles to the tenon faces, but a much better and more attractive joint can be made by setting the log in place, scribing the post contour, and coping the joint to fit snugly. Mate each successive log along its length to the log below, as necessary. Set the log with the tenon fully home in the dado and make the final fitting. Spike the logs to one another; they can be secured to the post by driving one spike through

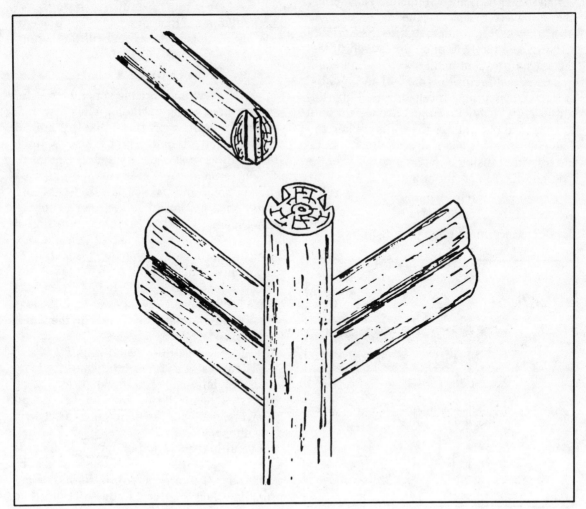

Fig. 6-12. Full corner post construction.

and into the tenon, but only if the tenon is wide and unlikely to split. The post is held in place at top and bottom. Properly constructed, this makes a reasonably strong corner, and if well caulked and sealed it is also quite weatherproof.

Quarter-Post Corner

Though easily made and attractive, the quarter-post corner (Fig. 6-13) is less satisfactory from several standpoints. The construction is not very strong and is held together only by a lot of spikes. Shrinkage can cause joint separation, which in turn can cause problems. The method of spiking also means that the logs cannot settle as they shrink in diameter, so the horizontal joints are likely to open up as well unless the logs are exceptionally well-seasoned. In this construction the logs are laid and squared at the ends, mating with the inserted quarter-round post. Heavy bracing is needed for both the post and the walls as the walls are laid up. The cuts are simple and this method is suitable for either inside or outside corners, but is best confined to small structures.

Plank Corner

Plank corner construction (Fig. 6-14) is a vari-

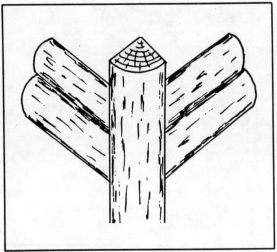

Fig. 6-13. Quarter-post corner construction.

ation upon the above. The corner is both stronger and more weathertight and the possibilities for shrinkage opening up the vertical joints is alleviated to some degree. However, because the logs are securely spiked to the corner planks, there is no way they can settle properly. Unless the wood is exceptionally dry to begin with, the horizontal joints between the logs are likely to open up from shrinking. Construction is accomplished by inserting a right-angled pair of nominal 2-inch dimension stock of appropriate width into the valley between the log ends. Mortise these planks full-thickness into the log ends, leaving an exterior overlap of log facing, and spike to the log ends. Then spike a quarter-round log into place to hide the dimension stock and fill the corner.

ENDWORK

Endwork or ''wings'' are the general terms for the treatment given to the log ends of walls, whether interior or exterior. If the logs are cut off flush or are all butted at the corners, there are no wings, just ordinary squared corners. But where the corners are made with logs extended in butt-and-pass or pass-and-pass configurations, this is endwork. Often as not the arrangement is very simple and almost automatic—as the logs are laid up, the ends are left to project somewhat beyond the wall lines and are merely cut off even from top to bottom. At least 6 inches of log should be left, and the choice is often about 12 inches or so. If the logs are laid butt-and-pass, this results in the familiar staggered pattern; if pass-and-pass, the result is a short wall extension (Fig. 6-15).

There is also an opportunity here for more artistic renderings. For example, by extending one or two logs at the top and bottom of a wall for several feet, you can then frame in between them and create a privacy screen; an extension of several logs top and bottom could include a grille (Fig. 6-16). The wall logs can also be extended at the corners for predetermined approximate lengths during construction, then cut to any of various patterns after completion.

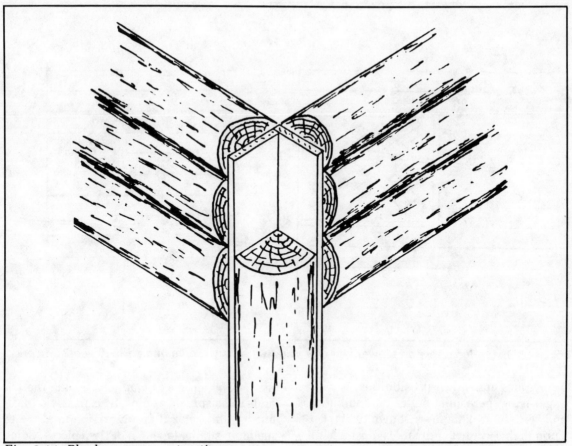

Fig. 6-14. Plank corner construction.

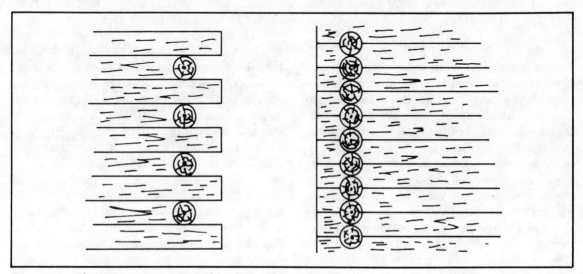

Fig. 6-15. The most common endwork configurations.

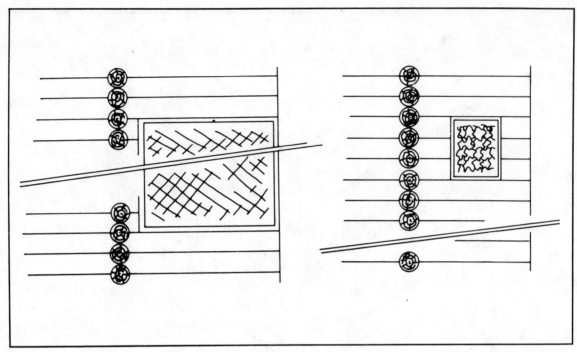

Fig. 6-16. Extended upper and lower logs can frame a privacy screen or a grille type of endwork.

There are numerous possibilities, such as angel-wing, parabolic, butterfly, and buttress endwork; some of these are shown in Fig. 6-17. Though this kind of endwork is most effective when the logs are laid up in rounds and each log end passes the corner, it can also be done with alternate passing logs.

SPLICING LOGS

Except in the smallest of log structures, a certain amount of log splicing is practically impossible to avoid. It is a good idea, though, to keep the number of splices as low as possible, because each one tends to weaken the overall structure by a small amount. Splices should always be well staggered so that they never lie above one another anywhere in the same wall. Try to avoid splicing more than once in a single continuous run of log, because two or three splices can seriously diminish the strength of that course, and detract from the appearance. Also, splices should be made well away from window or door openings, well out into a span

of wall. When making splices, match the log ends to be spliced as closely as possible in diameter and general configuration, and try to maintain similar tapers in the two pieces. Some trimming with plane or spokeshave can be done around the splice after it has been put together to make the two logs meld well.

There are several methods of making a splice joint. The simplest is called the half-lap (Fig. 6-18). Make the lap at least a foot long, and more if you can. Spike or bolt the splice solidly together. You could also use the squared splice (Fig. 6-19), which is more difficult to make but is also a good deal stronger. This joint requires accurate measurements and clean, precise cuts in order to fit together properly. Make the laps as long as you can and spike or bolt the two ends securely together. Yet another possibility is the tongue splice (Fig. 6-20), which is a form of mortise and tenon. The log ends are squared, and a long tongue or tenon is cut on one log end with a matching slot or mortise cut in the other. The two are then

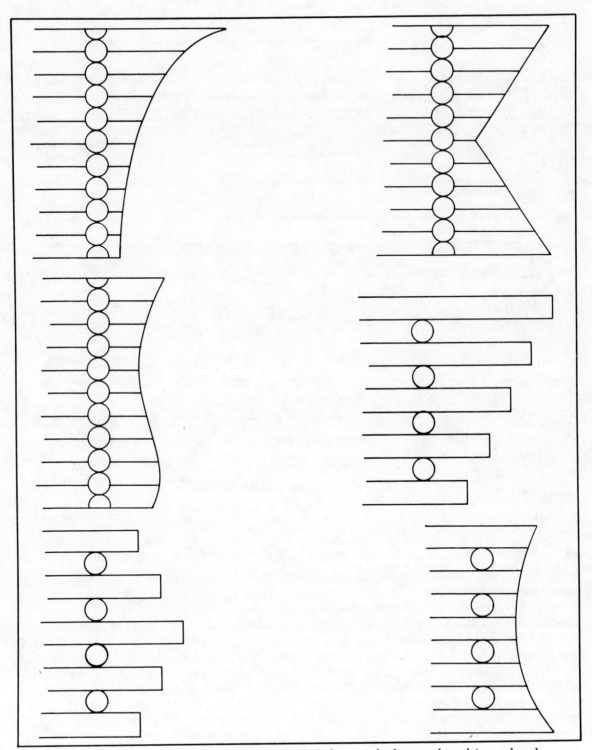

Fig. 6-17. These are a few of the various patterns that might be employed in endwork.

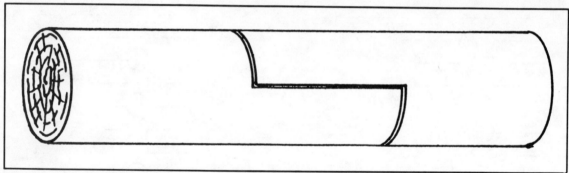

Fig. 6-18. A half-lap log splice.

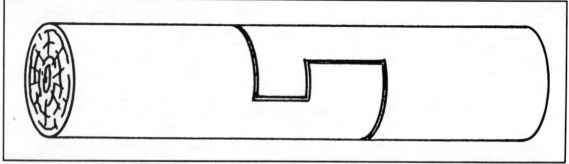

Fig. 6-19. A squared log splice.

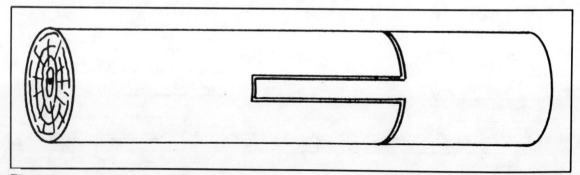

Fig. 6-20. A tongue log splice.

slipped together and spiked or bolted.

The last method is the spline splice, one commonly used by log house kit manufacturers. This entails first squaring the log ends so that they match. Cut matching mortises or dados into the log ends, positioned so that they will be vertical when the log is set in place. The width and depth of this groove is not a crucial

matter, so long as it is substantial. Drive a tight-fitting wood (or sometimes rigid insulation) spline into the dados, locking the logs together and sealing the joint (Fig. 6-21). Spikes or nails are not used here, because the logs are otherwise secured solidly in place. The spline itself strengthens the joint, keeps the logs aligned, and provides a weather seal.

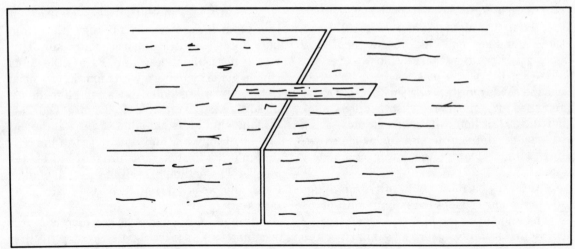

Fig. 6-21. A spline log splice.

JOINING LOGS

Joining the logs together where they bear upon one another along their length must be done just as carefully as building up the corners. If properly fitted, these joints make for a stronger and tighter house; conversely, if they are sloppily done, problems are sure to arise later on. The joints provide additional stability and strength to the log structure, while helping to keep the logs properly aligned as they shrink, settle, and try to warp or twist. Tight, firm joints, especially those with plenty of bearing surface between the log faces, afford much greater stability and a tighter weather seal than do poorly made joints. The better the joints are made and fitted, the more easily they can be sealed off to provide a snug and thermally efficient building, and the better the sealing will stand up over the years. And because better joining means better and more effective sealing, there is less opportunity for moisture to work its way under the seals and into the joints as the seals begin to sluff away or deteriorate. Paying close attention to the proper joining and sealing of all the logs at the outset, even though this increases construction time, pays big dividends and reduces difficulties over the long haul.

The simplest log construction uses no lengthwise joints whatsoever, and obviously is the least effective construction as far as strength, stability, and weathertightness is concerned. It is also the most difficult to seal. The logs are just stacked one atop another with the corner joints doing all of the work, and with the meeting lines of the logs (which don't accurately meet) full of gaps from irregularities in the log surfaces, poor log matching for taper and configuration, and/or poorly calculated corner joints. As the logs shrink, the gaps become wider. This was the traditional method of building back in the good old days, and it is still used to some extent today by those who don't care or don't know any better.

The cracks between the logs—or in good construction, the seams—are filled with chinking, which traditionally has consisted of just about any material and method that happened to be handy. The usual system in the early days was to jam in moss and then plaster it over with mud or a mixture of clay and twigs or hay. This system obviously was not very permanent, and in fact patching and replacing it used to be an annual spring chore. Another method, sometimes used today and effective if done right, is to load seams or spaces between logs with a filler of some sort—moss, oakum, clay, mortar, fiberglass, or mineral wool have all been used—and then nail fully-round lengths of saplings or strips of narrow board over the joints (Fig. 6-22). This makes a reasonably tight seal and sheds moisture fairly well. If the strips are nailed into only one or the other of each log pair instead of both, the logs can move from expansion, contraction, and shrinkage or settling without tearing the joints completely apart.

Another possibility with fully round logs is to first allow the logs to undergo most of the settling and shrinking that will take place by letting the structure age for a year or so before chinking. Then wood wedges made from shingles or clapboards are driven firmly into the spaces as necessary. The next step is to plug the interior portion of the joint space (working from the outside) with a layer of mortar or stucco. Then a narrow strip of wire lath, screening, or hardware cloth is tacked or stapled along the entire length of each joint. Finally, each joint is plastered with another layer of mortar or stucco (Fig. 6-23).

An ordinary mortar mix can be used for this procedure, made by mixing either from bulk ingredients or using bags of dry-mix. This results in a cement-gray joint. Pure white joints can be made by using a white mortar or stucco mix, and various color tones can be made up by adding the proper dyes to the mix. The mortar joint should be indented slightly at the top and slant outward and downward to the bottom in order to shed moisture rapidly. This is an effective method of sealing that will endure for many years if regularly maintained as necessary.

Round logs can also be put together with a center spline (Fig. 6-24). Do this by first slightly flatting the logs top and bottom and rough-matching and aligning them in place. Then cut a full-length groove the length of the top and bottom of each log. Mating grooves, of course, must match up. The width of the groove should be at least ¼ inch, but can be made to match any size of readily available spline material. A depth of about 1 inch is plenty, but more is fine. If the logs are green, the spline should fit a bit loosely in the grooves

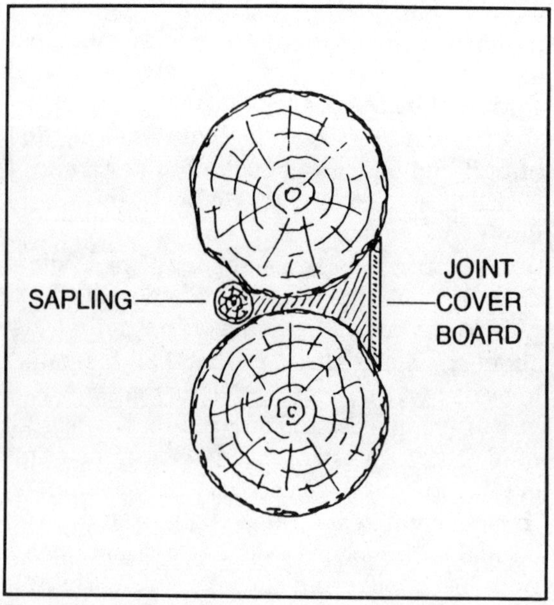

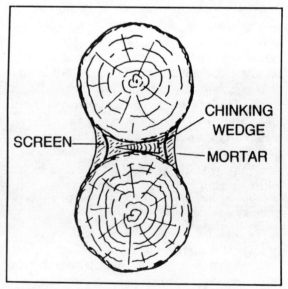

Fig. 6-22. Round logs sealed with caulking and a cover strip or sapling.

Fig. 6-23. Round logs chinked with wood wedges and sealed with mortar or chinking compound retained by screening.

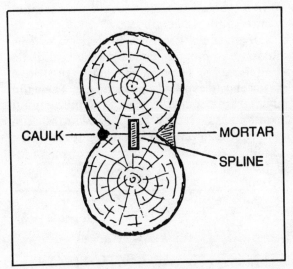

Fig. 6-24. *Flatted logs splined and sealed with caulk, mortar, or chinking compound.*

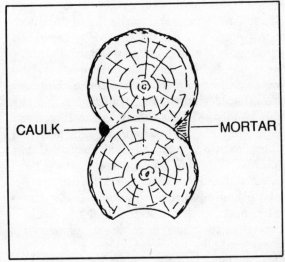

Fig. 6-25. *Cupped logs sealed with caulk, mortar, or chinking compound.*

to allow for some shrinkage. The spline in fully cured logs should be fairly snug, but not a jam fit. This center spline aids in holding the logs in position during construction, helps to keep them aligned permanently, and serves as an additional weather seal. A thick bead of caulking or a layer of mortar or mastic can be added along the seam on either or both sides for the final sealing.

Another procedure that is used with round logs, making an effective joint and seal, is shown in Fig. 6-25. The log bottoms are cupped with a gutter adze and trimmed along scribed lines so that each log fits snugly upon the log below. Often called the Swedish cope because of its origin, this construction is very sturdy and provides an airtight seal that sheds moisture extremely well. The job is finished by running a heavy bead of caulking along the seams both inside and out. A variation is to make the cup slightly deep, leaving a hollow center channel which is then filled with fiberglass insulation for added protection.

The V-groove joint, a Norwegian style, is similar but somewhat easier to make in that a power saw or a mill can be used to do the initial cutting. The log consists of cutting a deep

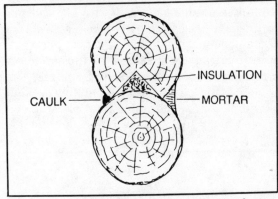

Fig. 6-26. *V-notch joint filled with insulation and the joints sealed with caulk, mortar, or chinking compound.*

V-notch in the bottom of each log, following lines scribed from the log below to make a contoured fit. The hollow portion of the notch can be left empty, or stuffed full of fiberglass or mineral wool insulation. To hold the insulation in place as the log is rolled into position, first staple a strip of cheesecloth along the groove edges to serve as a retainer. Seal the seams on both sides with a narrow bead of caulking worked well into the slight gap along the V-edges (Fig. 6-26).

157

Another possibility is to cut the top of each log to an A-shape, and incise the bottom with a V-groove. The angles should be broad; by making the A-angle a degree or two shallower than the V, the joint will pull together well when the logs are spiked in place. The cuts need not be made along scribed lines, but the logs should be of reasonably uniform taper and diameter. This makes a tight and solid joint that sheds moisture very well and keeps the logs aligned. The seams are deep enough that a bead of caulk or a layer of mortar can be easily applied (Fig. 6-27). One drawback is that some edge portions of the A-cut might be visible. However, the sharp edge can be planed to a curve and faired in.

Flatted logs are much easier to build with and to join and seal than round logs. The wider the flats are the greater the stability of the walls and the easier the logs are to join and seal. One common arrangement is to provide a center spline between each log by grooving down the top and bottom center lines. As each log is set, a bead of caulk is run along the top surface of the log below, on each side of the spline. The weight of the logs presses the caulking out into a wide seal. An additional bead of caulk can be run along the seam on one or both sides.

This combination makes a very weathertight joint (Fig. 6-28).

If the flats are wide, the system can be modified to provide an even better seal. Set a double spline between the logs, with three beads of caulk spaced across the flat. Then add another line of caulk on both the interior and exterior seams (Fig. 6-29). This requires extra time and materials, to be sure, but makes an excellent seal that should remain effective indefinitely.

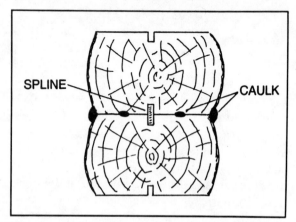

Fig. 6-28. Flatted logs splined and sealed with weatherstrip or caulk between, with caulk at the joints.

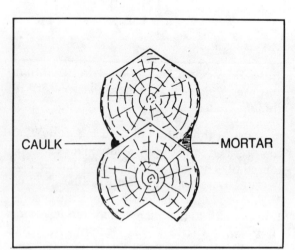

Fig. 6-27. Logs joined with mating V's and sealed with caulk, mortar, or chinking compound.

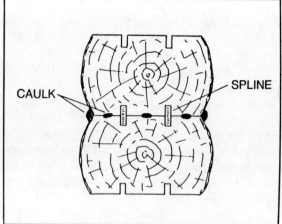

Fig. 6-29. Flatted logs double-splined with three interior strips of caulk or weatherstrip, caulked at the joints.

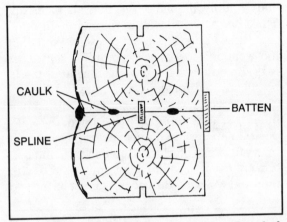

Fig. 6-30. Three-flatted logs splined and sealed with caulk and weatherstrip, and battened at the inside joints.

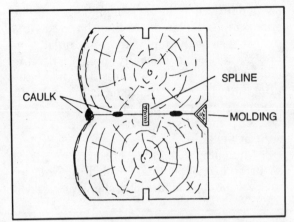

Fig. 6-31. Three-flatted logs splined and sealed with weatherstrip and/or caulk, with an inset decorative molding or an open V at the inside joints.

Where the logs are flatted on three sides, a double or triple caulk bead—with or without one or more splines—plus a caulk bead along the outside seam and a batten nailed as a cover over the inside seam, makes an effective arrangement (Fig. 6-30). If the appearance of interior battens is objectionable, an alternative is to make a deep bevel on the inside log faces. This forms a small V, along the bottom of which a bead of caulk is run. The V is then filled with a strip of matching molding, placed flush for a smooth effect or inset slightly for a shadowline effect (Fig. 6-31).

Regardless of the shape of the logs or the form of the joints between them, many log house owners prefer the visual effect of relatively wide bands of chinking between the wall logs, whether needed for effective sealing or not. There are new chinking materials now available that can be used even for joint lines too narrow to hold mortar, as well as for wide joints and for rechinking over old materials. These are quick-drying, lightweight, mortarlike compounds that are easy to apply, adhere tightly to the log surfaces, and remain flexible; they will not crack or pull away. They are also very long-lived and virtually impervious to the weather.

SECURING LOGS

The most common method of securing logs is to spike them down tight. This is usually done about every 3 or 4 feet along full-length logs, and wherever necessary to secure short pieces. One spike at each nailing point is sufficient, driven straight down through the middle of the log or slightly offset to clear splines. The spikes should be long enough to extend at least halfway into the log below. Ordinary round spikes are fine, but spiraled spikes drive more easily. They also hold tighter because of the way they screw themselves into the wood.

Drilling pilot holes for nails is not usually necessary, especially in most softwoods. With spikes, the situation varies. Generally pilot holes are necessary, especially when the wood is dry, hard, or a species prone to splitting. Pilot holes should always be drilled when the spike is being driven close to the end of a log, or near or in a joint. They might not be needed in very green or soft wood. The pilot holes should be somewhat smaller in diameter than the spike. They extend through the log being fastened down but just a bit, if at all, into the holding log. Shorter spikes can be used by drilling a pilot hole first, then boring the hole out larger to the diameter of the spike head, about one third of the way through the log. The spike can be driven down into the log with a drift to seat at the top of the pilot hole. A 6- or 8-pound sledge is usually ample for driving spikes. When working green wood, make the pilot hole size about the same as the spike diameter. When the wood cures and shrinks it will grip the spike tightly but is unlikely to split at the hole.

Dowelling is another effective means of securing logs. This involves drilling holes at intervals through all the logs, slightly oversized and carefully aligned so that they all match up. Thick hardwood dowels or rounds are inserted into these holes (Fig. 6-32). The fit is snug but loose enough so that as the building settles the logs slip down on the dowels. Steel rods could be substituted for the wood rounds.

A variation on this theme is to drill smaller holes that align from top to bottom of the wall, positioned close to corners and at 3- or 4-foot intervals. Long steel rods threaded top and bottom are inserted in the holes and secured with nuts and washers. Bolt pockets must be formed

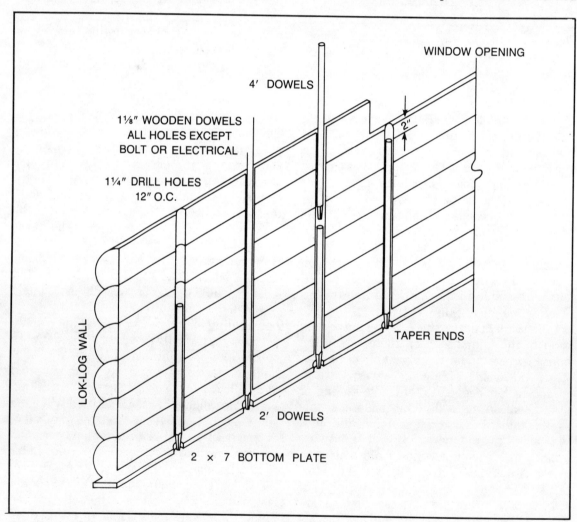

Fig. 6-32. This cutaway shows a method of strengthening and securing log walls with dowels. (Courtesy of Building Logs, Inc.)

160

in the top of the foundation if it is a continuous-wall type, positioned to allow free access from the inside, under the floor. After installation, the bottom nuts are tightened every two or three months for a few years until the structure is fully settled out.

Yet, another method uses steel cable and turnbuckles. The cables are actually tie-downs, anchored at one end to the roof frame at each exterior corner. The bottom end is attached to a turnbuckle which is in turn attached to a sturdy anchor bolt built into the floor frame, or preferably the foundation or a deeply buried deadman. The turnbuckles are taken up periodically and kept taut as the building settles, compressing the wall logs firmly together. This is a good method in high-wind country.

THE PLATE LOG

When you reach the top of the walls, the last log to be placed is the plate log. This is the log upon which the roof rafter ends will rest. The extent and position of the plate log varies. In a rectangular house with a typical gable roof, for example, there will be a plate log across the top of the front wall, and another across the back, both at the same level; the end walls just keep climbing to the peaks of the gables. If the house is rectangular with a hip or mansard roof, sill logs will go all the way around the top at the same level. On a house with a shed roof, or a saltbox style, the plate logs will be at front and back but at different levels.

Whatever the case, the plate logs should be specially selected for straightness, uniformity of taper, and soundness. They must be fitted with great care so that the corner tops are at an equal height from the floor line, the top surfaces are level and all in the same plane, and the angles of all exterior wall corners are on target (usually 90 degrees). This is the last chance to make sure that there will be no difficulties in building the roof, and the roof alignment will be correct and not racked, cockeyed, sway-backed, or otherwise out of true.

In some round-log constructions the plate

log is left fully round. When the rafters are set, whether round logs or dimension stock, the plate log is notched to accept each individual rafter. In some smaller buildings no rafters are used; instead the roof sheathing is secured to purlins that parallel the roof ridge. In that case, the eave ends of the roof sheathing boards are simply nailed directly to the plate log. In most cases, however, the plate log is flatted at least on the top, often on the top and exterior face, and in flatted-log construction on three faces. Then the rafters are either cut off at an angle and seat directly on the plate log with no overhang, or more commonly are notched with a bird's mouth to rest on the plate and also overhang to form the eaves. More information on this part of the construction will appear in Chapter 8.

At this stage, the key point is that when you have finished laying the plate logs, if you were then somehow able to drop a huge lid over the whole structure the under surface should lie down snugly all around and the top surface should be as flat and level as a pool table.

STOCKADE CONSTRUCTION

Though the majority of log buildings are constructed by stacking the logs horizontally one on top another, they can also be placed vertically in stockade construction. This is a less common method. It has a somewhat unfamiliar appearance, reminiscent of pioneer fort days, but nonetheless is attractive and has some advantages for the do-it-yourselfer.

Corner construction is simple in this type of building. Either full or split logs can be used, and because the lengths are short they can be handled and installed by one person (at least in the smaller diameters). The logs can be of small diameter as well as short length, and so might be more readily available and/or less expensive. Settling is not a problem, because logs shrink mostly in volume and hardly at all in length. Extensive shaping, joining, and splining is not necessary, though all three are or can be done to some extent. About the only cutting that really has to be done, depending upon the construction details, is to square the log ends and perhaps do some trimming and fitting around window and door openings. This method can also be used to build walls that are extremely thermally efficient and will meet or exceed the strictest building code requirements.

The foundations needed for stockade log construction are essentially no different than for the horizontal type. With pier or post foundations, however, the spans must be kept quite short and/or the sill beams or logs quite sturdy. Floor frames made from dimension stock should include built-up headers made from three or four layers of planks. This is because the weight distribution and downward press of a stockade wall is different than for horizontal construction; while horizontal logs are partially self-supporting, the vertical ones are not. There is one further detail to add: metal flashing strips between the wall and the sill to prevent moisture from seeping into the structure.

The simplest type of vertical log construction is to stand a single row of fully round logs up on the sill and run a plate plank, beam, or log across the top (Fig. 6-33). The logs can be toe-nailed or pinned at the bottom, and are spiked through the plate at the top.

This method carries one of the problems of fully round horizontal log construction: Shrinkage is bound to occur and open up the seams between the logs. Effective sealing is difficult, and the overall construction is not particularly weathertight. Sealing at the sill is difficult, too, and the flashing installation is troublesome and unsightly. At best, the logs should overhang the sill by a considerable amount to reduce the possibility of moisture entering. Liberal amounts of caulking and chinking must be applied, and then maintained religiously. Flatting the logs along their sides helps, and splining and double sealing with caulk beads makes for a much more weatherproof wall.

Another possibility, considerably more weatherproof, thermally efficient, and airtight, can be made by erecting a double wall (Fig. 6-34). This has the disadvantage of using more material (though the logs can be slimmer) and involves added labor, but is also a tremendously strong method.

Single-thickness sills should be provided at the bottom and double-thickness plates at the top. The logs are flatted on three sides for a tight

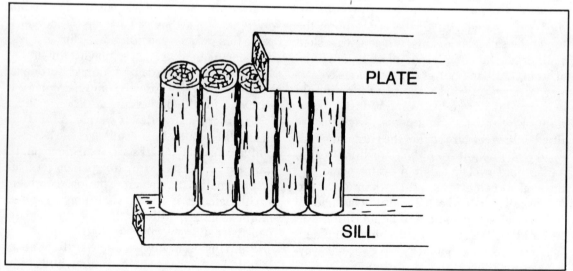

Fig. 6-33. A single-thick, full-round log stockade construction.

fit. They can also be splined between logs if desired, and single or double beads of caulking laid as construction progresses, at least on the outside course.

Construction begins by setting the outside logs in place in a continuous row, allowing them to overhang the sill corner by a considerable margin. Continuous metal flashing should cover the outside face of the sill and be bent back over the sill top beneath the wall logs, and then bent up between the two rows. Half-cut the bottoms of the outside logs to notch over the sill (Fig. 6-35). Nail the log bottoms directly to the sill and spike the tops down through the plates. Attach a core of exterior-grade plywood to the interior faces of the logs. Leave a ⅛-inch gap between all plywood joints (including top

and bottom) and fill these cracks with flexible silicone caulking.

Erect another row of logs on the interior side of the plywood, toe-nailed into the sill at the bottom and spiked through the plate at the top. Or, if the interior decor is not to be log-oriented, simply furr out the plywood surface, add insulation, and cover with paneling or wallboard to give the appearance of a conventional interior wall.

Split half-logs are easier to handle, require less material and so are less costly, and make an equally effective stockade construction. Slabs will work also and are even less expensive. However, they are much thinner and take a lot of trimming and shaping, and their structural strength is about nil.

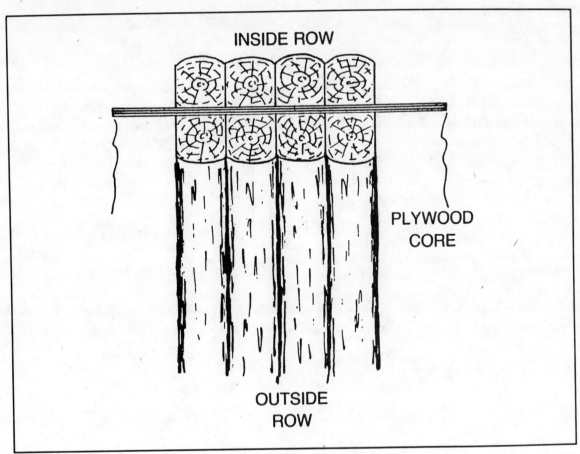

INSIDE ROW

PLYWOOD CORE

OUTSIDE ROW

Fig. 6-34. Double-thick, three-flatted log stockade construction.

The simplest construction starts with a row of half-logs, spiked to the sill at the bottom and spiked through the plate at the top. Staple a layer of tarpaper or construction plastic across the inside of this exterior wall. Toe-nail and spike another row of half-logs into place on the inside with the joints staggered (Fig. 6-36). The two layers can be nailed together for added strength. Nailing is done from the outside so that the nailheads don't appear as part of the interior decor.

A variation on this theme makes use of a plywood core sandwiched between the two rows of logs. In this case, the interior row of logs can be set first by toe-nailing at the bottom and spiking through the plate at the top. Then nail the plywood to the faces of the in-terior logs, so that no nailheads are visible from the inside. Staple a roofing felt or construction plastic vapor barrier to the plywood core, the face of which should be flush with the exterior face of the sill. Nail the outside layer of half-logs to the plywood and to the sill face, with the bottom edges extending just below the sill bottom (Fig. 6-37).

This type of construction can be expanded slightly into a core wall with as high an insulating value as you wish. The core is nothing more than an ordinary stud wall built from dimension stock, just as in any ordinary platform-framed house.

To gain a high R-value, 2- x -6s or 2- x -8s can be used when the core is filled with a full-thickness layer of fiberglass or mineral wool in-

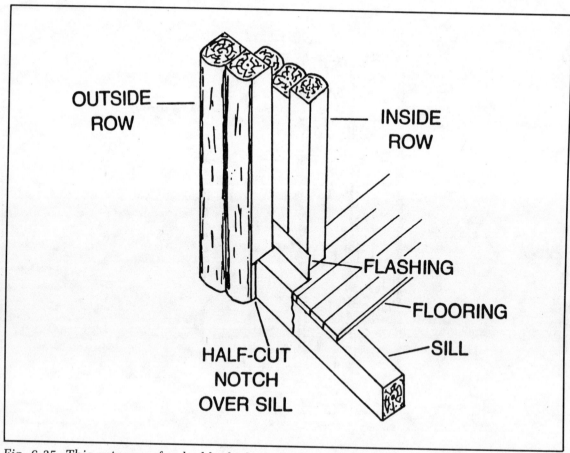

Fig. 6-35. *This cutaway of a double-thick stockade wall shows the assembly arrangement.*

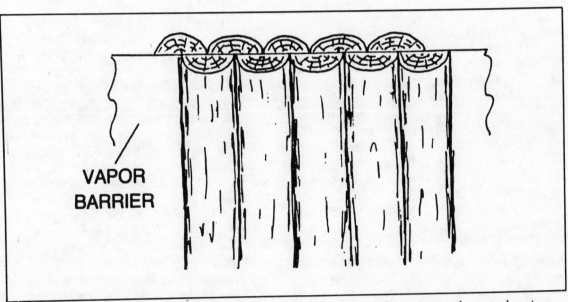

Fig. 6-36. A staggered half-log, double-thick stockade wall with an integral vapor barrier.

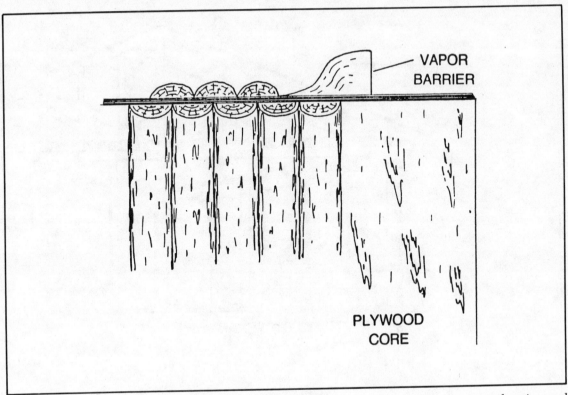

VAPOR
BARRIER

PLYWOOD
CORE

Fig. 6-37. A staggered half-log, double-thick stockade wall incorporating a vapor barrier and a plywood core. Slab facing could also be used in this construction.

sulation. The outside of the core frame is covered with plywood which extends from the top of the plate to the bottom of the sill. Nail half-logs directly to the plywood in the form of a siding material (Fig. 6-38). In this instance, slabs can be used equally well. The slab edges can be trimmed and squared for a better fit, and laid either horizontally or vertically. After the core is filled with insulation, staple a vapor barrier of plastic sheeting to the studs, and apply an interior wall covering. This might consist of standard plasterboard or paneling as in a conventional house, or an inside layer of half-logs or slabs.

Some of these constructions, as you can see, are not really log houses. But they are interesting and perfectly livable styles that at least have the log appearance.

PIECE-EN-PIECE CONSTRUCTION

Piece-en-piece construction is a method seldom seen in this country, but it is an old and well-known method in other parts of the world. It is relatively easy to do and makes a sturdy and handsome structure (Fig. 6-39). For this method, logs that are flatted on two or three faces, or beams or timbers can be used. Log thickness should be at least 5 inches in order to make effective joints; 7 or 8 inches or more is preferable. One advantage of this type of construction is that the entire structure can be made up from short chunks of logs, but without any splicing. The sections can be as short as 2 feet, or extended to 6 feet or more if desirable.

The corners of the structure can be made with one of the notched log arrangements as

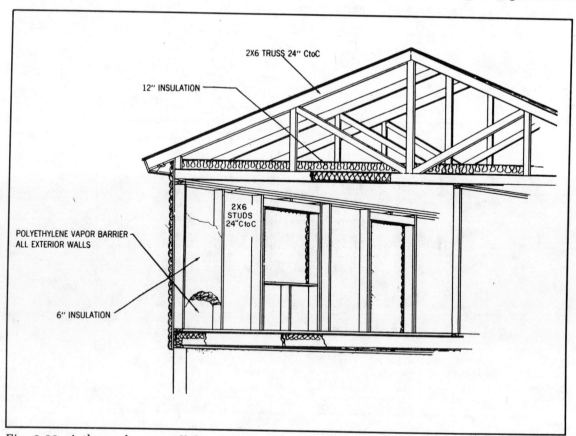

Fig. 6-38. A thermal core wall faced with matched slabs. (Courtesy of Pioneer Log Homes.)

discussed earlier, but usually feature full corner posts. The posts contain two deep, wide grooves at a 90-degree angle to one another and are shaped to a stout tenon at top and bottom. The tenons fit into mortises in the sill and top plate. The plates, sills, and posts can be logs or beams. A series of similar posts is set at the desired intervals along the sill, each with full-length dados or grooves opposite one another and parallel with the sill.

The wall logs are squared and tenoned to match the grooves and slid down into place one on top of another, and fitted to nest tightly as they are placed (Fig. 6-40). The wall logs should be flatted top and bottom for best results, and may also be splined and/or sealed with beads of caulking. The logs can be spiked together, but should not be attached in any way to the posts. This leaves them free to settle within their framework as they will. The last

Fig. 6-39. This log house was constructed with a modified piece-en-piece system called post-and-sill, incorporating a thermal core in the exterior walls. (Courtesy of Town & Country Cedar Homes.)

step is to install the top plate log or beam to tie the entire framework together. Various sealing, flashing, and caulking methods are used as necessary to make the structure weathertight and moisture-resistant.

DOOR AND WINDOW ARRANGEMENTS

There are several approaches to cutting doors and windows in a log house. As far as which one to pick—they all have their advantages and disadvantages. A lot depends upon your over-all construction methods and whether you intend to make your own doors and windows or buy ready-made units. Whatever your choice, there is one very important point to keep in mind about all door and window installations in log houses. As shrinkage and aging occurs, settling takes place, Furthermore, there is also a certain amount of expansion and contraction in the large mass of solid wood that surrounds the doors and windows, and it is not uniform from component to component. This means

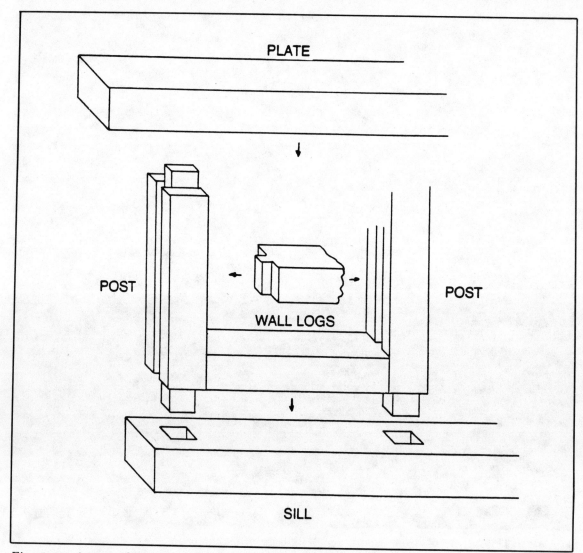

Fig. 6-40. A typical piece-en-piece or post-and-sill log assembly method.

that allowances should be made, and that installation procedures are considerably different than in a conventional frame house.

There are some builders who claim that the only way to build is to spike, bolt, and nail everything into place rigidly so nothing can shift. Perhaps that system has worked for them, but in this case two factors must be taken into consideration: The first is that the log house kit manufacturers, after years of study, designing, testing, and experience, use construction procedures that allow for shrinkage and settling. They know it will happen, and have taken steps to allow it without causing damage or problems. The second is that for centuries European log builders have always made such allowances. They have always been such superb craftsmen, and knew their woods and their construction methods so well, that they could tell to within a fraction of an inch just how much settling and shrinkage would take place at any point in a building. They not only provided slip joints wherever necessary, they also made all the corner and other joints loose by a calculated amount so that in due course the joints would properly tighten up to just the right degree. In the face of this sort of evidence, it would seem unreasonable not to follow the same course and make the necessary shrinkage and settling allowances.

Exceptionally well-dried logs in a fairly humid climate might shrink and settle as little as 1/8 inch per foot of wall height over the first couple of years, partly from compression. But that is not much for log construction, and most will settle more. Large logs that are less than half cured can easily shrink and settle as much as 3/4 inch per foot of wall height. What this means is that if you start off with a ceiling height of 8 feet, within two years or less the ceiling will lower to 7½ feet. If you arrange neat openings in the log walls and fit doors and windows snugly into them, not much time will pass before you have smashed windows and buckled doors. The force of the settling logs is tremendous and no amount of light framing or bracing can withstand that kind of pressure. Therefore, above each door and window there must be a substantial space at the outset to allow the logs to settle down around the window and door frames.

There are at least five different ways to go about cutting in doors and windows. One is to build the wall up solid, leaving no openings at all to begin with. When the walls reach full height, or at any time afterward, cut the openings in with a chainsaw. Notches big enough to start the saw in are often left as markers at the window or door opening tops; these are preplanned and cut when that particular log is reached as the walls are laid up.

Cutting is done from the inside, where the sawyer has a flat, solid floor as a working platform. The openings should be outlined by boards nailed into exact position; these also serve as guides for the saw blade to ensure straight cuts. This system works particularly well in smaller structures where the logs are mostly or entirely full-length.

The big advantage to this method is that the wall logs can be stacked up rapidly without stopping to fool around with small pieces between windows and doors and corners, that have to be propped and braced until everything gets tied together. The disadvantages are that you are forever crawling over the walls to get inside the structure. Also, you have to remember to drive spikes and secure the logs in every course or round close to where the opening will be—but not within the opening or right on the saw-cut line.

Size the openings to accommodate whatever factory-built window or door units you plan to use, plus the thickness of the bucks, and the slip-joint elements if they require extra room. Or, they can be cut to any reasonable size if you plan to build up your own doors and windows.

There are three schools of thought about placement of the openings. One says that they should fit between the upper and lower logs without cutting into either, which can be a problem if you are using stock units. Another says that for windows you should always leave the header log above the window header uncut, but cut about a quarter to a third into the lower one and carve it away on an outward slant to provide a tight, flat fit for the window sill and to allow good water-shedding. The third says cut upward about a third of the way into the log above the window or door, and into the bottom log a little if you must.

All of these work. Whichever you choose, there should be at least one full-thickness log above every opening. Door sills are usually notched into the structure sills on an outward and downward angle. This, however, can depend upon the specific design and construction of the door and its frame. The standard angle of pitch for a door sill is 12 degrees, and 6 degrees for a window sill, but you will incur no penalties for using other angles.

Another method of making provisions for doors and windows is simply to cut the logs to the proper lengths to form the openings as the log courses or rounds are laid up. Window and door locations are mapped out ahead of time, and when the correct points are reached the logs are cut to suit. Window openings are started when the correct height above the floor is reached. The bottom of the window openings usually coincide with the top of a particular course, especially if the logs are flatted, but they can also be notched into the logs if desired.

Sometimes only the window and door frames, called bucks, are set in place as the construction proceeds. Door bucks are stood up before the walls are even started. They are secured at the base and leveled, plumbed, squared, and solidly braced with angled boards tacked at the top of the frame at one end and into the floor at the other. The logs are fitted and built up around the frames. Window bucks are placed when the proper course height is reached, and are set and secured in the same way as the door bucks. The log courses are built up around them. Because the bucks are empty,

there is no danger of damage to the windows and doors themselves during construction. Cross-bracing is often installed inside the bucks to make sure that they stay in square and do not bow in as the wall logs are run up against them.

A system that is often used, particularly with kit log houses, is to set the complete units in place as construction goes along. The doors are set before the walls are started, while the windows are placed when the appropriate course level is reached. This method requires an extra degree of care and caution. The units must be precisely set, and ruggedly braced so they cannot move. Cross-bracing of the assembly frames is an excellent idea wherever possible, so that the sides don't get pushed in and render the units inoperable or damage the frames. The units must also be kept fully in square so they don't jam up. Taking premanufactured door or window assemblies apart after the units have been installed in order to plane or trim them down so they will work properly is a miserable job.

Take care during construction that the units are not damaged in any way. Doors are not quite so much of a problem, but windows are very tender. Sometimes it is possible to remove sash sections and glass without much difficulty, and store them in a safe place. Otherwise, covering the units on the inside with scrap pieces of plywood works well. The butt end of a log rammed through a big casement window won't do it or your blood pressure much good.

No matter the approach you choose, every door and window opening and installation must have a substantial allowance built in above the head jamb for the inevitable log settling. The side jambs must always be installed in such a way that they are solidly set, but still allow the logs to slip down as they settle. There are a number of possibilities in providing doors and windows with slip joints and several methods for installing them. Chapter 9 contains details on this subject.

7

The Second Floor

Once you reach the prescribed height called for in the plans, wall-building comes to a temporary halt. This height might be as low as 7 feet in an open plan where there will be no ceiling or upper story, or might go up to 8 or 8½ feet where ceilings or upper floors are involved. In high-posted rooms the height might even reach 10 or 12 feet, and there is also the possibility of two or more full levels in the same structure.

In any case, at this stage of the construction structural crossmembers are installed. Exactly how this is done depends upon the presence or absence of ceilings and upper floors, the layout of interior first-floor partition walls, the roof design, and whether or not visible logs are to serve as part of the decor. The basics of construction are much the same as for the first-floor frame, and can be done with logs only; beams, logs and dimension stock together; all dimension stock; or combinations of these.

OPEN CONSTRUCTION

Open construction simply means the absence of ceiling/floor at the normal second-floor level, with the living space carried through all the way to the roof frame. This is sometimes referred to as a cathedral ceiling design, especially where the open space is carried on past a full second-floor level and into the underroof area, for a total floor-to-roof peak height of 16 to 20 feet or more.

When open construction is used, it is usually necessary to place a number of tie beams across the narrowest dimension of the building—wall top to wall top, or at approximately the second-floor level (Fig. 7-1). In a log house these members are most likely to be fully-round logs, although beams are also sometimes used. They serve to stabilize the walls and prevent them from spreading outward under roof loading. The usual method of installation is to form tenons on the tie log ends

171

and fit them into matching mortises in the wall logs at the desired height. Then they are spiked securely in place. Another method that affords greater strength is to cut the tie log ends in dovetail tenons and fit them into matching dovetail mortises, locking the members solidly together. Spikes can be driven for added insurance.

Where open truss assemblies are to be used as roof supports, the tie beams can become the bottom chords of the trusses. Depending upon the truss design, the tie beams might extend

Fig. 7-1. Tie beams help to hold walls rigid and support the roof in open or cathedral ceiling designs. *(Courtesy of Town & Country Cedar Homes.)*

past the walls to the outside where they join the rafters, or they might be mortised or spiked into the wall tops with no overhang. They might also be installed as part of a preassembled truss, or installed first with the remainder of the truss being built up piecemeal. Further details are given in Chapter 8.

Tie logs or beams placed across a relatively narrow structure and not part of a truss assembly need not be especially heavy, because they carry no weight but their own. In a narrow structure, say 16 to 20 feet wide, tie beams could easily be as small as 6-inch, especially if several are installed. The wider the span, the heftier the log must be, if only to support its own weight without sagging. Also, greater lengths automatically mean larger logs in order to gain that length. A 9- to 10-inch diameter should be sufficient out to about 24 feet, about 12 inches for a 30-foot span, and 14-inch or greater diameter for 36 to 40 feet.

Some logs, and some species, are more limber than others. If some objectionable sagging appears to be likely, the problem can be taken care of to at least some degree by installing one or a pair of support poles in truss fashion when the roof is built (the additional roof loading this causes should be taken into account in the roof framing). Prop the sagging tie log up from below until it is level or even crowned upward slightly, but not enough to drive it out of its moorings. Secure a single support pole from the tie log to the ridge pole bottom, or angle a pair of support poles from the tie log to convenient rafter beams or purlins, or use some similar arrangement (Fig. 7-2). Of course, if there is a conveniently placed transverse partition wall, or an opportunity to set

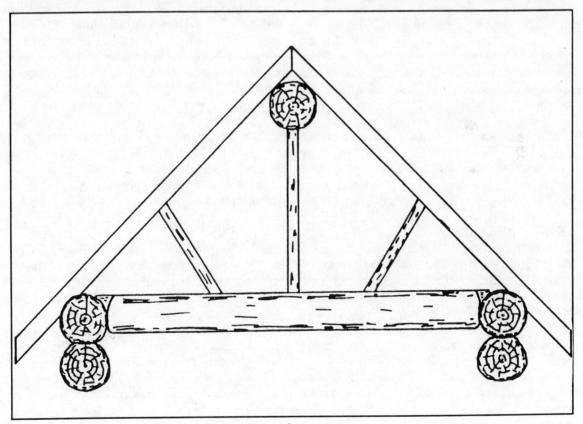

Fig. 7-2. A tie beam with ridge log and/or rafter support.

some posts, that can provide support from below.

FLOOR FRAMING

Floor framing is a good deal more involved than just setting a few tie logs. Framing for a second floor that will be part of the living quarters has to be every bit as sturdy as the first-floor framing, because it must carry a certain amount of both the live and the dead loads of the structure. Even though a portion of the second floor area might be unusable from a practical standpoint because of a low roof design, the entire floor framework has to be sturdy and substantial. Logs can be used for the entire job, flatted on top to receive the flooring. Logs or beams are used wherever the surfaces will be exposed and visible from below. Dimension stock is usually only employed when the entire framing structure is invisible because of a first-floor ceiling; more about this later.

The business of arranging a second-floor frame can be a tricky one, but the main thing to remember is to give the assembly as much support as possible. Not only must the floor bear weight, it should also be free from springiness and sag. Joists alone won't do the job, except in a very small building, so this means that girders must be set as well. Girders should be at least 10 inches in diameter, more as the girder span increases. They are usually arranged to lie directly above and parallel with the first-floor partition walls, or so that they cross partition walls and receive some support from them. Failing this, post or column supports might have to be introduced at one or several points beneath them. Such supports should in turn be supported by a first-floor girder and preferably a foundation pier as well if the load is heavy. With the proper supporting arrangements, girders may intersect one another. Load-bearing partitions that bear directly on the second-floor frame, unless made of logs the same size as the wall logs and interlocked with them (not a common construction in this country), cannot as readily be used for support

as they are in conventional framed houses because of the shrinkage problem.

Girders should also be arranged so as to shorten the span of the joists as much as possible. The joists themselves should be of a minimum 6-inch diameter, and in this type of construction are often placed on 24- or 30-inch centers. Joist diameter, joist spacing on centers, and joist span are all intertwined, so small joist diameters can be used with narrow spacing, large joists with wider spacing, and so forth.

Logs and beams, whether girders or joists, are assembled with mortise and tenon joints. Straight ones are adequate, but dovetail joints will afford greater strength and rigidity. The logs should be securely spiked down. A considerable amount of notching is involved, and this is most easily done on the ground or the first floor, before the logs are raised. Accurate measurement is called for so that the notches cut into the wall logs at one side of the joist span will line up properly and squarely with those cut in opposite wall or girder logs and so that the joists, when set, will lie straight and parallel. Good craftsmanship is desirable, too, because many of these notches will be at least partly visible.

Once the wall log notches are cut, the logs are installed atop the wall in the usual way. Then the girder ends are fashioned into tenons, mortises are cut for the joists, and the girders are spiked in place. Finally, the joists can be dropped into place from wall to girder or girder to girder. Girders and joists should be carefully aligned and leveled so that the floor surface will be level and smooth. This can be done with a little extra shimming and trimming as necessary. The process is the same as for the first-floor frame installation, except that any shimming should be kept invisible.

Where girders are held up entirely by the wall structure and there are no supporting partitions or posts beneath them, as is often the case with small structures, no further treatment is necessary. As the walls of the building shrink and settle, the girders and consequently the joists will settle along with them. But where the girders rest upon walls, the situation is different. If the partition walls are made along with the shell and are of the same log materials, the settling rate will be about the same and so will the amount of drop. However, if the partition walls are of conventional stud construction, they will neither shrink nor settle and something is going to break or pull apart. This means that girders should not rest directly upon the partition walls at construction time, but should be spaced above them a distance equal to or a little more than the anticipated total settling.

In order to provide support for the girders in the meantime, a series of shims can be installed at intervals between the top of the partition wall and the bottom of the girder (Fig. 7-3). They must be watched carefully and regularly, and adjusted periodically. If there is still a gap after the building has fully settled, shim wedges can be driven permanently into place. The same arrangement must be followed if the girders are supported by posts or columns. Otherwise, the posts can be driven through the floor, or the structure will come apart at some other point.

If the partition walls are constructed of logs placed stockade-fashion, there will be little endwise shrinking and settling of these logs, so a settling gap must be allowed between partition and girder. If the logs are horizontal but smaller in diameter and/or of a different species than the wall logs, there will be some shrinkage and settling, but probably less than in the exterior walls. In this case, the settling space must still be incorporated between partition top and girder, but it can be a somewhat smaller gap.

The second-floor frame can also be made entirely of dimension stock. Here again girders are used to provide adequate support and permit relatively short joist spans. This is even more important with dimension stock because of a lesser amount of strength and rigidity of individual pieces. Girders should be notched into the outside log walls, and must also be supported by posts or partitions to provide adequate rigidity. The joists are then set, usually on 16-inch centers, from wall to girder or girder to girder. The joists can be attached to the girder faces with metal joist hangers. Where the joists meet the wall logs, a dimension-stock header must be spiked to the logs. The joists are anchored to the header face with metal hangers.

Again, the entire floor frame is supported at the outside edges by wall logs that are bound to settle. Therefore, a gap must be left between the supporting points and the girders to allow for this settling. Blocks or wedging can be inserted to provide temporary support while the settling continues, and rearranged every few weeks as necessary. When the settling stops, the final shims can be installed permanently.

Another possibility that works quite well is to install a series of steel posts with adjustable screw-tops. These can be hidden inside the partitions or within hollow-box wood columns with the screw-tops protruding into the settling space above the partition tops (Fig. 7-4). Then all that is necessary is to wind the threaded heads of the posts down a turn or two every once in a while. The posts are adjustable through a wide range and can remain as permanent and extremely strong supports. Steel posts should be supported by first-floor girders and preferably foundation piers as well. This transmits all strain and pressure directly onto the foundation and ultimately onto the ground. The surrounding structure absorbs little, if any, of the strain.

There are few second-floor frames that do not require some sort of an opening in them, except perhaps for some sleeping-loft designs. At the least there must be a hatch through which access can be gained to the attic area. There might be a chimney or a stovepipe or two that will pass through the framing, or there might be extensive ductwork. A 1½- or 2-story house requires at least one stairway, sometimes two. Wherever the openings are smaller than

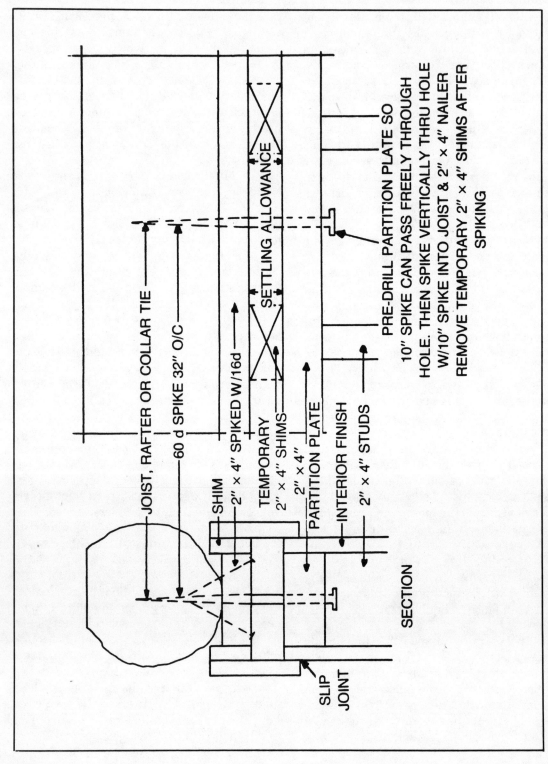

SLIP JOINT

SECTION

JOIST, RAFTER OR COLLAR TIE

60 d SPIKE 32" O/C

SHIM

2" × 4" SPIKED W/16d

TEMPORARY 2" × 4" SHIMS

2" × 4"

PARTITION PLATE

INTERIOR FINISH

2" × 4" STUDS

SETTLING ALLOWANCE

PRE-DRILL PARTITION PLATE SO 10" SPIKE CAN PASS FREELY THROUGH HOLE. THEN SPIKE VERTICALLY THRU HOLE W/10" SPIKE INTO JOIST & 2" × 4" NAILER REMOVE TEMPORARY 2" × 4" SHIMS AFTER SPIKING

Fig. 7-3. One method of constructing a partition wall slip joint with shims. (Courtesy of Vermont Log Buildings, Inc., part of Real Log Homes® .)

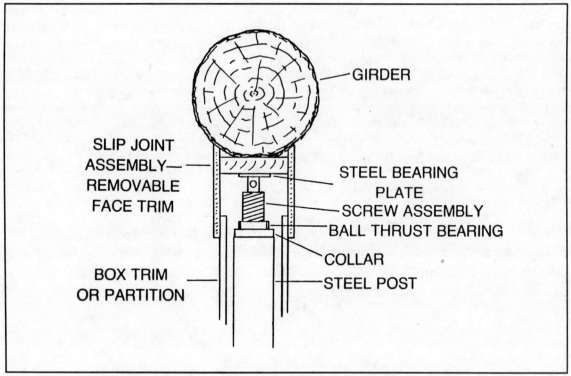

GIRDER

SLIP JOINT
ASSEMBLY—
REMOVABLE
FACE TRIM

STEEL BEARING
PLATE
SCREW ASSEMBLY
BALL THRUST BEARING

COLLAR
STEEL POST

BOX TRIM
OR PARTITION

Fig. 7-4. An adjustable partition wall slip joint using a steel column with a screw-jack top.

the distance between the joist faces, usually all that is necessary is to install trimmers to box out the desired size of opening. Where the openings are larger than the distance between joists, proceed in the same way as described for openings in the first-floor frame.

CEILING FRAMING

Wherever the first level of the building is solidly closed off from the second, be that roof space, attic, or full second floor, a certain amount of framing is sometimes needed to support a ceiling. The simplest method of doing so is to let the second-floor frame serve most or all of the purpose. Where the second-floor frame logs or beams are exposed to view from the first floor, all that is necessary is to install a deck-type floor at the second level, the bottom of which serves as the ceiling for the first level with no further construction needed. In such a situation, if the floor bottom (ceiling)

and the floor-frame logs or beams are to be left natural or all painted or stained to the same color, the finish work can be done during the interior decorating process. If the ceiling is to be treated with one finish or color and the floor frame another, either or both can be treated before installation and then touched up afterward as necessary.

Where a dimension-stock frame is used, a finish ceiling is almost invariably installed to hide the framing and present a more attractive appearance. If desirable, the same can also be done if the floor frame is made up of logs or beams. The materials most commonly used are ceiling tiles or sheets of plasterboard, though wood or other materials can be used.

Once the floor frame is complete, and usually after the second-level flooring has been put down, a series of straps or furring strips of wood are attached at right angles to the joists (Fig. 7-5). The strapping is carefully shimmed or notched in to provide a flat and level mounting for the tiles or plasterboard. The strips are nailed entirely around the perimeters of the rooms or ceiling areas, with more strips spaced on 12-inch centers across the opening. Where the joists are on 16-inch centers, the strips can be inexpensive 1- x -2 S3S spruce or pine. As the spacing between joists widens out, thicker and/or wider stock should be used. When the ceiling area is fully strapped, the plasterboard or tile is secured directly to the strapping. Tile is installed with staples, plasterboard with special drywall nails or screws.

An alternative system that can be used with tiles is to mount special metal runner strips in much the same way as the wood furring, and insert the tiles into them. Yet another possibility for many kinds of ceiling tile is a metal gridwork that is suspended on wire hangers from the joists. This system requires about a foot of open space between the joist bottoms and the finish ceiling level.

If the floor frame is constructed of beams or logs and it is desirable to cover the bottom of the floor above but at the same time expose the major portion of the beams or logs, other methods are effective. Where the beams are straight-sided, pieces of plasterboard can be cut and fitted tightly to the beam sides and nailed directly to the flooring above (Fig. 7-6). Cracks between the beams and plasterboard can then be filled with plaster or spackle, the indented

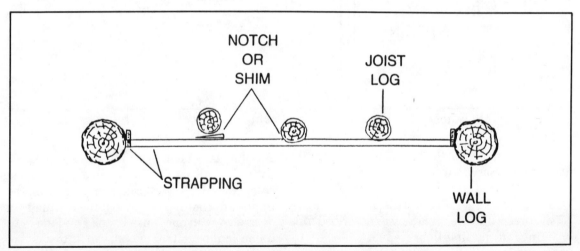

Fig. 7-5. A cross section of a finish ceiling framework using strapping.

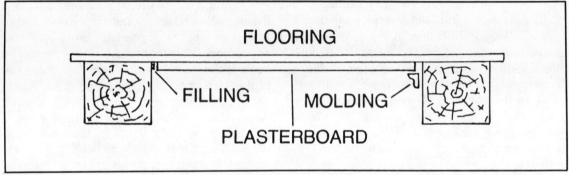

Fig. 7-6. A cross section of a finish ceiling attached to the underside of the second-level flooring, between exposed floor frame beams.

nail or screw heads plastered over, and a finish applied—a time-consuming job. Or, you can put up prefinished lengths of molding, cut to fit, and then plug and touch up the nail holes afterward, which is much easier.

Working with rounded logs is more difficult because their sides are far more irregular and the pieces of ceiling material must be bowed or bellied down in order to slip them up between the log sides where they meet the underside of the upper floor. If the spaces between the logs are narrow, plasterboard can't be used because it won't bend sufficiently. Fiberboard or insulating board of one sort or another, especially if very thin, can be used successfully and installed in much the same way, but by using mastic or construction adhesive instead of nails or screws. Cracks along the edges cannot be successfully filled with most fiberboards, so a small molding must be installed to hide the gaps.

If only a portion of the log or beam frame is to show, the job is a bit easier. Each nailing space between joints should be boxed around with nailing strips of 1- × -2 stock. On flat-sided beams they can be tacked in place at any appropriate distance above the bottom face, depending upon how much of the beam is to be visible. On logs the nailing strips should be secured just above the average greatest width of thé logs so that the ceiling panels will fit into place at the narrowest point between two logs

and show a minimum crack. Panels of plasterboard or insulating board are edge-nailed to the nailing strips, and the nail heads and joints are then covered with a small wood molding (Fig. 7-7).

Where the plans call for a first-floor ceiling but no floor above, or only a small section or two of flooring to provide service crawlways or extra storage space, the ceiling framing can be done a bit differently. All that is really needed is enough of a framework to hold up the ceiling itself and also tie the walls of the building together. Logs can be used for this purpose and so can beams, though the expense would be greater. Because the framework would be hidden anyway, dimension stock is probably the best choice.

For a lightweight tile ceiling all that is necessary is a series of 2- × -6 joists secured on 16-inch centers. A plasterboard ceiling is much heavier, and so requires 2- × -6s on short spans, or 2- × -8s or 2- × -12s on longer spans. With either stock the joist bottoms should be strapped with 1- × -2s—shimmed and/or notched to provide a level frame—on 12-inch centers. The joists are attached to the sidewalls by spiking headers to the logs and using metal joist hangers, or they can be notched into the wall logs. Depending upon the spans involved, girders and supports must also be installed to keep the spans short and give the overall framework sufficient strength (Fig. 7-8).

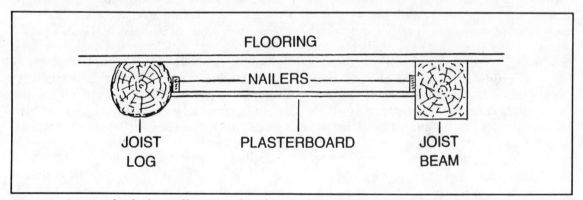

FLOORING

NAILERS

JOIST LOG

PLASTERBOARD

JOIST BEAM

Fig. 7-7. One method of installing a ceiling between partially exposed floor frame logs or beams, in cross section.

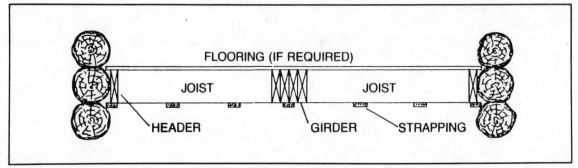

Fig. 7-8. Ceiling strapping applied to a typical dimension-stock floor frame.

If a suspended ceiling hung in a metal grid is called for in the plans, even less framing is required if there is to be no floor above. Just install enough tie logs or beams to keep the walls square and plumb and the structure intact. The ceiling grid can be suspended by wires from the tie logs and whatever else happens to be handy, even roof rafters. A suspended grid tile ceiling is so lightweight that it won't impose any appreciable strain on a well-constructed building, especially where heavy log framing is involved.

At this stage of the construction, only the structural members (girders, joists, tie beams, temporary or permanent supports need be installed. Strapping is left until work begins on the interior, and ceiling tile or plasterboard are among the last items to be installed. The same is true of suspended metal grid ceilings. Girder support posts or columns can be installed now or later. Interior partition walls are sometimes built before the second-story frame is begun, and sometimes not until the shell has been completed. In conventional platform framing, interior partition frames are almost always erected first so that portions of the second-floor frame can be anchored and supported by them. However, in log construction it is often just as easy to build these partitions later. Temporary supports can be stood in place under girders if necessary until the shell is complete.

LAYING FLOORING

The second-level flooring is best laid down as

soon as the floor frame is finished. This helps to tighten the structure up and keep it well aligned, and also affords a convenient platform from which to work while completing the upper story and roof. And, the working conditions are a lot safer than trying to trod around on planks or loose chunks of plywood. The general procedures for laying flooring are the same as for the first-level floor.

If the underside of the floor will not be visible from the first level, a subflooring or sheathing of plywood, or a layer of boards, can be laid. If the second level is designed only as a dead-storage attic, the single layer of sheathing is probably sufficient. If designed as living quarters, the subflooring is covered with an underlayment or a finish covering, or both. At this point in the construction, only the subfloor is laid.

When the underside of the flooring will be visible from the first level and actually constitutes the ceiling, an added measure must be taken in laying the flooring. Decking or deck planking is frequently used for this purpose, though other types of boards or special plywoods could be used as well. In most cases the flooring material is laid with the best or finish side down, so care must be taken not to scratch or gouge the visible surface as the material is installed. Pieces should be carefully fitted together to show a minimum of joints, and nailing carefully done so that none miss the mark and show from below.

If the upper surface of the flooring material will also be a finish floor surface, as is sometimes done with thick decking, all the pieces must be blind-nailed to maintain a presentable appearance. It is a good idea to cover the floor surface with building paper, plastic sheeting, or sheets of plywood for protection from mechanical damage as construction continues. If another layer of flooring such as underlayment or a finish covering will be added later on, slight mechanical damage won't matter. Water might, though, no matter the arrangement. There is always the possibility that an untimely rainstorm could leave watermarks or stains on the visible surfaces, upper or lower. If the finish is to be natural, these stains will be difficult to remove, especially on the underside of the floor. Covering the whole flooring area with plastic sheeting and keeping the floor clean of debris and sawdust is a good idea.

In many house designs only a portion of the second-floor level is given over to living quarters, with the remainder being storage or just crawl areas under eaves. The flooring should be installed in such areas as well—not just in the living area—in order to strengthen the structure and also to provide a platform for storing goods or for crawling around on service missions. Underlayment and/or finish flooring is put down later, in the living quarters only.

SECOND-STORY WALLS

As soon as the tie beams and/or second-story floor frame is complete, construction of the shell can proceed. In some instances the sidewalls need no further attention, and the roof rafters rest upon them approximately at the second-floor level. In other designs one more course or round of logs may be laid on the sidewalls to form the top plate, upon which the rafters will rest. In most designs, there are end walls that must be carried up higher to form a partial or full second story, and to conform to the roof design. Five of the most common roof styles are shown in Fig. 7-9. All of these end-wall configurations (or combinations and

variations) are put together in pretty much the same way. There are two general construction methods you can follow: full-log, or dimension-stock framing.

In full-log construction the courses are simply built up in the same way as the first-floor walls were, except that at one point or another there are no longer any corner joints to fashion. With the gable style roof the log outer ends must be cut to an angle that matches the roof pitch, and the logs must be accurately trimmed to form a smooth and continuous face that will match the rafter levels and present no gaps. The situation is much the same with the gambrel roof end walls except that at a certain point on each side the roof pitch, and thus the log-end cut angle, changes from relatively gentle to relatively steep.

Setting the logs for a shed roof is done in much the same way. The principal difference is that a course of logs must be laid along the front wall first. Then an end-wall course is joined to the front-wall course, with the back ends cut to match the angle of the shed roof (Fig. 7-10). Another front-wall course follows, and so forth, until the full height of the front wall is reached and all of the end-wall courses are laid.

The saltbox in effect is nothing more than a gable style with mismatched roof sections and an off-center ridge line; the pitches of the sections may be the same, or different. Depending upon the roof line, wall construction may be the same as for the gable end walls, with the log ends cut to a steep angle at one end and a gentle one at the other. Or, the saltbox style could be used where the front wall and thus the starting point of one roof section is elevated above the floor level while the rear roof section meets with the floor level. In that instance, the lower portion of the end wall is assembled as though it were a shed roof style, while the upper portion resembles a gable end wall.

Whatever the configuration of the roof lines, the wall logs are all assembled, joined as necessary, secured, and sealed just as the first-floor wall logs are. Window and door

181

openings are also handled in the same way.

Dimension-stock construction of end walls that rise above a top plate is most often done at this stage, though some builders prefer to wait until the roof frame is finished. Then they build up the end walls to suit the roof shape by simply boxing in the open area with a framework that is later sheathed. Either way works out fine, though most people consider the former method to be the easier.

Construction of dimension-stock walls is undertaken in the same fashion as for any con-

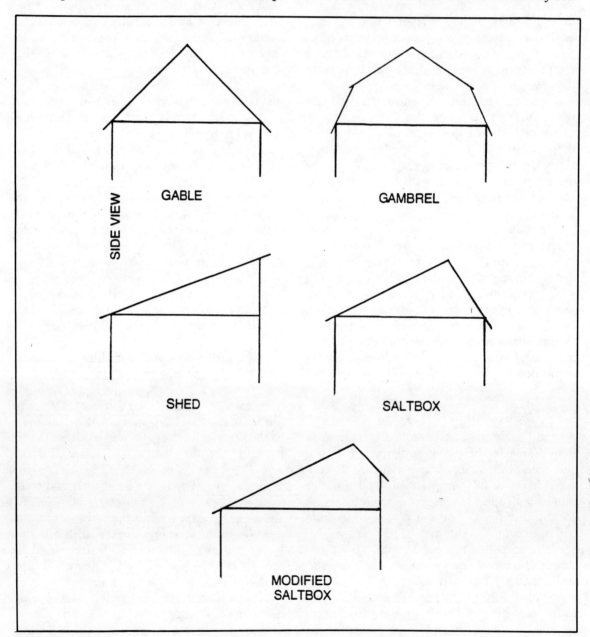

Fig. 7-9. Some of the roof lines frequently used in log houses.

ventional platformed assembly, with some variations introduced where logs are part of the scheme. The sole plate, studs, and top plates of 2- × -4s or 2- × -6s are laid out on the second-level floor and nailed together. The top angle of the studs and the lie of the top plates match the pitch and placement of the roof. Door and window openings are framed in the conventional manner. When the assembly is completed, it is stood up in position and nailed in place (Fig. 7-11).

If a large ridge log is part of the plan, a saddle notch is framed into the peak of the end-wall assembly to receive and support it. A solid or built-up post is included in the assembly directly below the saddle to support the ridge log sturdily (Fig. 7-12). If log purlins are to be used, frame in more saddles at the appropriate locations to hold them. Note, however, that in some designs the ridge log or purlin logs might lie fully above the top plate of the end-wall assembly and rest on them, rather than being enclosed in saddles.

The exterior of the end-wall frame can be covered with a variety of siding materials. A sheathing of plywood might first be attached to the frame, but sometimes is not. The finish siding might consist of log slabs or split half-logs laid up horizontally and spiked to the framing members. Log facing can be applied vertically by first nailing blocking sections between the studs to which the vertical log sections can be spiked. Conventional siding materials can also be used, such as horizontal clapboards, vertical weathered barn boards, cedar shingles, or exterior-grade siding plywood in any of several types. The bottom edge of the siding should lap down over the top log course an inch or so and be sealed off. Any kind of interior finish can be applied.

STUB AND FULL WALLS

One-and-a-half-story is the term given to those houses that have low roof lines but still contain a certain amount of living area located beneath the highest portion of the roof. The standard Cape Cod design is an example. In some cases the roof joins the wall at the second-floor level. In other cases, however, stub or stem walls are installed to elevate the entire roof structure somewhat above the second-floor level. Stub walls may be anywhere from 1 or 2 to 5 or 6 feet high. Beyond this approximate point they are considered full walls.

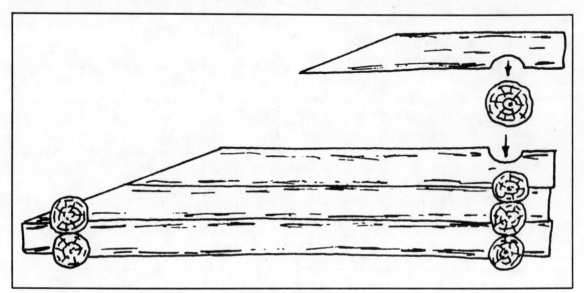

Fig. 7-10. Setting end-wall logs in a shed roof design.

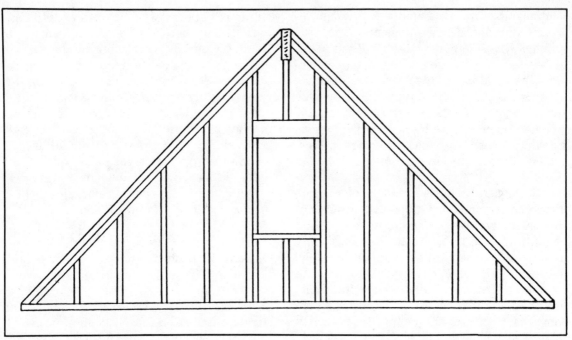

Fig. 7-11. A dimension-stock framework for the end wall in a gable roof design. The assembly can be built on the floor and erected in one piece.

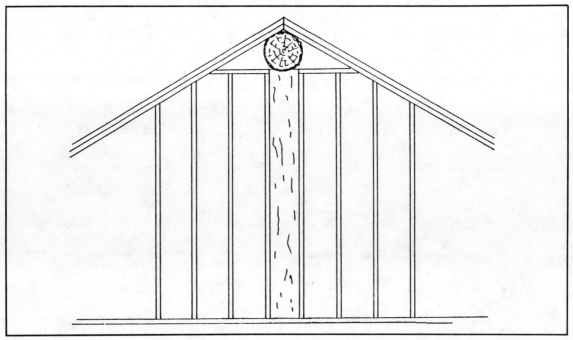

Fig. 7-12. A dimension-stock end-wall framework for a gable roof design with the ridge log and center support framed in.

Stub walls are constructed in exactly the same way as the first-floor walls and are really just a continuation of them. Once the second-level floor is built, the walls are just carried up further to the desired final height. The top course of side stub walls then becomes the plate course that supports the roof framing. The stub walls can be of varying height or the same all around the perimeter of the structure. In the case of a saltbox style with a raised front roof, there might be only a stub wall at the front, for example, or there could be a tall one at the front and short one at the rear. All manner of combinations are possible.

Full walls are those built to full height, usually 6 feet or more, as used in a house that contains two full stories with the roof beginning at the third level. These walls are also constructed in the same fashion as first-story walls, with door and window openings provided for in the same way. Upon reaching a prescribed wall height, a third-level floor frame or suitable tie beams are installed along the same lines as described previously for second-level arrangements.

KNEE WALLS

Knee walls are a form of interior partition walls, installed to separate usable living space from under-eave crawl or storage areas in story-and-a-half structures with low roof lines (Fig. 7-13). These walls are set at right angles to the roof rafters and may be 3 to 5 feet or so high.

In conventional construction knee walls are almost always installed after the shell has been completed and as a part of the interior work. However, in some types of log construction it is easier to lay up knee walls after the second-level flooring is complete and before the roof framing beings. If the knee walls are to be made of dimension stock, they might be best installed after the roof rafters—whether log or dimension stock—are in place, but before the roof sheathing is applied. If the knee walls are log and locked into the end walls, they must

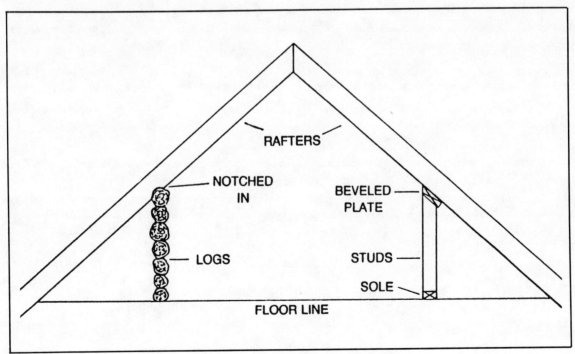

Fig. 7-13. A cross section of log and dimension-stock knee walls.

of course be laid up together. If the knee walls are log but not integrated with the end walls, they can be laid up before the rafters are set, then the top course of the knee wall can be appropriately flatted or notched to receive the rafters. Thus the rafters will help stabilize the knee walls, while the knee walls serve as bearing points for the rafters. The knee walls might also be arranged to lie directly beneath purlin logs in that type of roof construction. When built in that fashion, knee walls can become an important structural part of the building rather than tacked-in, hide-it panels.

Here again, log construction of knee walls is similar to exterior wall construction. Differences lie in that the logs need not be of as great diameter, nor need they be splined or fully sealed. They should be ruggedly secure for stability, with the ends carefully matched and mated to whatever cross-walls they butt up against. If the storage or crawl spaces they close off are unheated, the back side of the knee walls should be covered with a vapor barrier and suitable insulation, if the climate warrants it, and the seams and butt joints caulked to prevent drafts and keep out insects.

8

The Roof

THERE ARE A GREAT MANY STYLES OF ROOFS, AND
many roof systems. Some differ remarkably in
both appearance and construction, while others
vary only in relatively minor details. In fact,
it would take an entire book just to discuss
roofs. In theory, just about any kind of roof can
be applied to a log building. In practice, however, the ones actually used are few in number
and their construction is comparatively simple
and straightforward. The more important ones
will be considered here.

ROOF PITCH

The slope or slant of a roof above a horizontal
line is called the pitch of the roof. Pitch is the
number of inches the roof rises divided by the
number of feet of run that the roof covers. The
rise is the vertical distance between the wall
top and the roof peak. The run is the distance
between the lowest supporting point and the
highest supporting point. For example, consider a 20-foot-wide building with a shed roof.

The run of the roof is the distance from the outside of the front wall to the outside of the back
wall (eave overhangs don't count), and the roof
run is therefore 20 feet. If the leading edge of
the roof is elevated 20 inches above the rear
edge, this is called a 20-inch rise. Because the
20-inch rise takes place over a run of 20 feet,
it is a 1-inch-per-foot or 1-inch-in-1-foot rise,
which is called a one-in-one pitch or simply a
one-pitch (Fig. 8-1).

For comparison, consider a 20-foot-wide
building with a gable or peaked roof, and the
ridge running along the centerline of the building. Here the roof run is not 20 feet, but only
10 feet, the distance between the lowest and the
highest supporting points. If the roof peak is
elevated 20 inches above the lower edges, or
the wall tops (again, eaves don't count), this
is still a 20-inch rise but over a run of only 10
feet. Thus, the amount of rise is 2 inches for
every foot of run, and this roof would be designated a two-in-one pitch or a two-pitch (Fig.
8-2).

If the roof peak were 40 inches above the wall level, the rise would be 40 inches over a run of 10 feet for a four-in-one pitch, or simply four-pitch. If the roof were perfectly flat, a style seldom if ever used on log buildings, it would be a zero-pitch roof.

The business of roof pitch is important from several standpoints. One is style and ap-

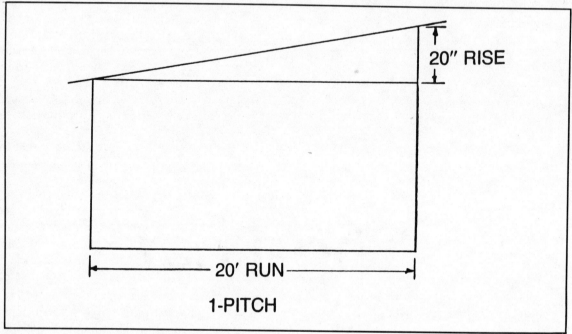

20" RISE

20' RUN

1-PITCH

Fig. 8-1. A roof with a one-in-one pitch.

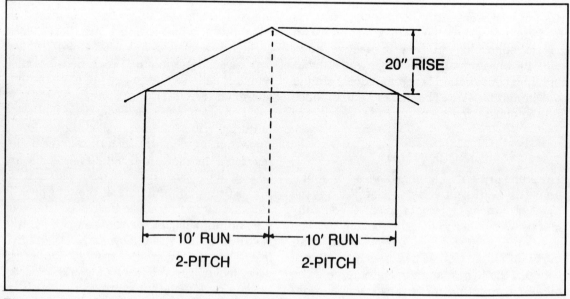

20" RISE

10' RUN **10' RUN**

2-PITCH **2-PITCH**

Fig. 8-2. A roof with a two-in-one pitch on each side.

pearance, because the arrangement and slope of the roof sections is one of the major architectural design features of a building. More importantly, however, there are some purely practical matters involved. The degree of pitch determines the rapidity and ease with which a roof can shed rainwater or snow, which in turn affects weatherability and tightness. Pitches from one-in-one to about three-in-one shed water fairly well but hold snow. From four-in-one up, water runs off rapidly, and from about eight-in-one or ten-in-one on up, snow will usually zip right off as well, depending upon the composition of the roof surface, the makeup of the snow, and the weather.

The pitch of a roof also determines to some degree the manner in which it can be built. A flat roof, for instance, must be timbered and braced to withstand the heavy loads and stresses imposed upon it, including its own massive weight. The steeper the roof, the less of a problem this becomes. Steeply sloping roofs can be built with economical beams and/or truss bracing to add strength. They shed loads more rapidly and easily, and strains and stresses are partially transmitted to the remainder of the structure rather than being sustained by the roof frame and supporting members.

On the other hand, the steeper the roof the greater the cost of construction, though there are various balance points depending upon exactly what materials are used and how, and upon what the loading factors are. A flat roof, for instance, usually has just about the same area as the floor area beneath it. A flat roof over a 1000-square-foot floor area, for example, would be just about 1000 square feet itself, or perhaps a little more if there were slight overhangs around the building perimeter. But as the roof pitch increases, so does the roof area—therefore the amount of material needed to build the roof frame and cover it. A twelve-in-one simple gable roof is almost 1½ times as large as a flat roof on the same building, disregarding overhangs.

There is another factor involved, too, and that is the cost of labor. Or, if you are building the roof yourself, the time and effort required. From zero pitch to about four-in-one, a roof is easy to work on. You can walk around, and tools and materials don't skitter off to the ground when you set them down. Above four-in-one the work becomes increasingly harder, until finally the workers must move slowly and cautiously and proceed with the aid of elaborate scaffolding, roof jacks, bosun's chairs, slings, safety lines, and material-feed systems.

Another point to keep in mind is that the steeper the roof and the larger the area, the more exposure there is to the weather. This means several things to the homeowner. First, the roof is a huge radiator that throws off heat from the inside during the cold weather, and absorbs heat into the structure in the warm weather. The larger the roof, the greater the insulating problems, and the greater the heating and cooling loads. Second, the roof is the part of the house that suffers the most wear and tear from weather. After a time the roof surface will actually wear out, sooner or later depending upon the material used. The larger the roof, the greater the expense will be to replace the weather surface, and the greater the amount of possible maintenance needed in the meantime. Third, the larger and more complex the roof, the greater will be the wind loads and the susceptibility of the roof to wind damage. The smaller the roof, the less resistance it offers. And last, the larger the total roof area, whether steep or shallow, the greater the likelihood of mechanical damage and leaks.

The pitch of the roof also determines to some extent the type of finish material—the weather surface—that can be put on it. For instance, slate or tile is used only on steeply pitched roofs. Some kinds of metal roofing can be used on pitches as low as two-in-one; others are suitable for four-in-one and up, but not below. Shingles of any kind should not be used below a four-in-one pitch. Double-coverage roll roofing can be used down to two-in-one pitch. Flat and low-pitched roofs must be covered with crosslapped layers of roofing felt bonded together with hot tar and topped with roofing stone.

DIMENSION-STOCK ROOF FRAME

This type of roof used on log houses is no different than is found on conventional platform-framed houses. The entire framework is made box-frame fashion from dimension stock, usually 2 × 8s, 2 × 10s, or 2 × 12s, depending upon the span, pitch, and loading factors of the roof. Rafter spacing is usually 16 or 24 inches on centers.

About the simplest roof construction is involved where only one unbroken roof section is needed, with no attached additional roof sections going off in different directions. All that is required is a continuous series of rafters extending from the ridge or peak at the top to the supporting plate resting atop the walls (Fig. 8-3). These full-length rafters are called common rafters, and there are two methods of installing them.

For the first method, place a ridge board in position, establishing the longitudinal centerline of the roof peak. This consists of a 1- × -8 or wider board stood on edge and running from the highest point of one end wall to the other. Several boards are usually needed to make up the full length, and they are propped and secured in place by whatever means are handiest. Stand up the first rafter, with both ends cut to the appropriate angles, and with one end resting on the plate and the other placed flat against the ridge board. The rafter is aligned by means of marks previously made, and nailed in place at top and bottom. The opposite rafter is raised in the same manner, nailed at the bot-

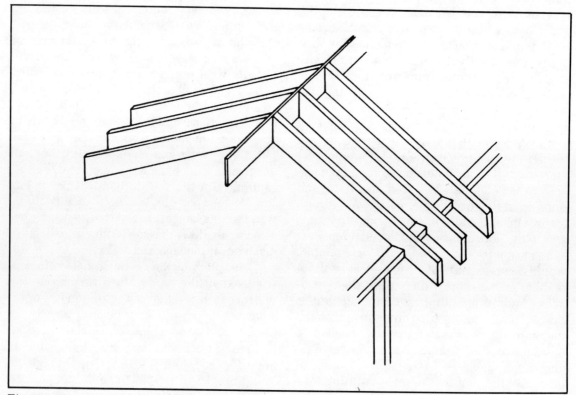

Fig. 8-3. In a simple pitched-roof construction only common rafters are used.

tom and toe-nailed to the ridge board and into the opposing rafter tip (Fig. 8-4).

The second method dispenses with a ridge board and the rafters are placed in sets or pairs. Cut the proper mating top angles first, as well as the bottom angles where the rafters rest upon the plate. Join the rafter tips together and securely nail them while they are lying on the second-level floor, or up on sawhorses. Temporarily nail a couple of boards across the rafters to form a large A. Drag the pair of rafters into position so that the bottom ends rest in approximately the right spots on the plates, and tip the A up to a vertical position. It is aligned and the bottom ends are nailed to the plates, with the top held in place by means of temporary props. When the second set is swung up into position, it is held in alignment with its neighbor by nailing two or three boards across the outside faces of the rafters (Fig. 8-5). As subsequent sets are erected, they too are held by temporary boards. As the roof sheath-

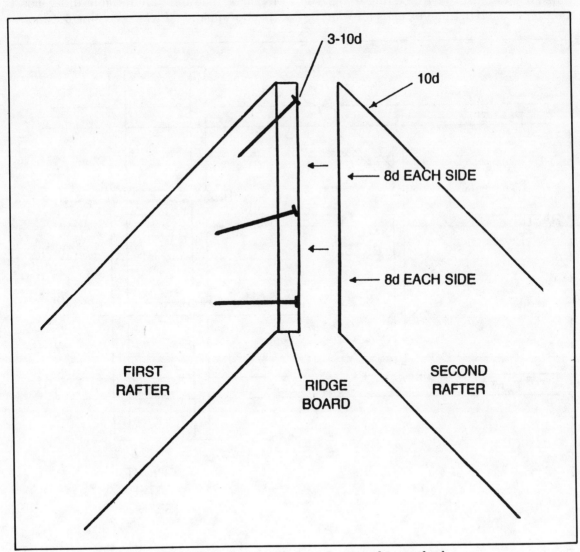

Fig. 8-4. The rafters are attached to the ridge board using this method.

ing is put on, the temporary boards and props are removed.

There are several methods of attaching the rafter bottoms to the plates. The most common is to cut a bird's-mouth notch at an appropriate point on the underside of each rafter. The angles of the notches are calculated to rest exactly upon the plate for a given roof pitch. The plate must be flat on the top and outside surfaces, which in log construction means the plate log must be two-flatted (Fig. 8-6), or suitable notches must be cut in a round log. The portion of the rafter that extends outward be-

the wall is called the tail, and this length can be varied to suit the desired amount of roof overhang. This could be as little as 6 inches, allowing just enough room to trim out, or could be as much as 3 or 4 feet.

Another method of attaching rafters is to make half-cuts or shaves at the rafter tails, with a flat angle-cut which rests on the plate (Fig. 8-7). Toe-nail the rafter to the plate just as though a bird's mouth were used, and there is no diminution of strength or structural effectiveness. The only appreciable difference is that the apparent thickness of the roof and the

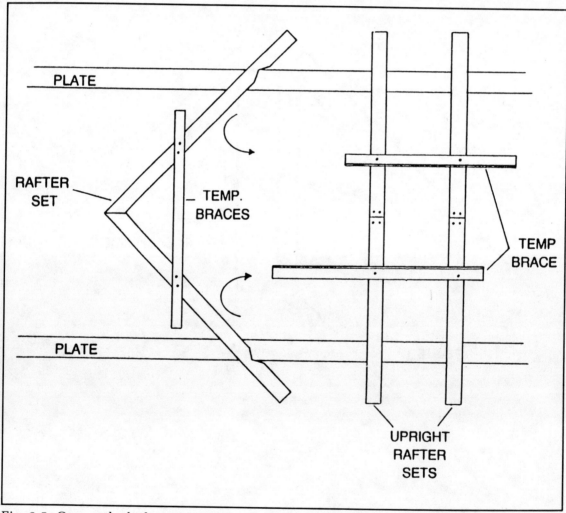

Fig. 8-5. One method of erecting rafter sets made without a connecting ridge board.

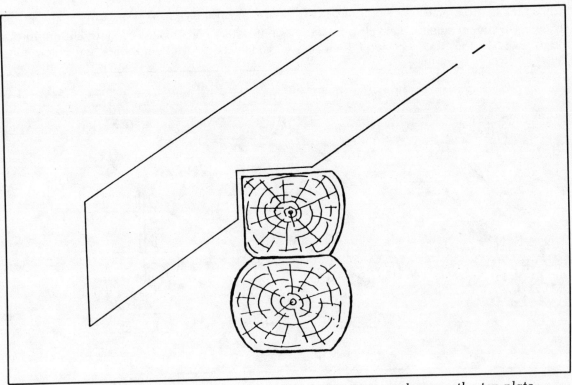

Fig. 8-6. A bird's mouth cut into the rafter allows it to sit squarely upon the top plate.

trim board of fascia that runs along the ends of the rafters and closes them off, is reduced by the amount of the shave cut.

If the rafter does not continue beyond the plate and is "tail-less," as would be the case if a porch roof were to be later attached to form a continuous roof line, different methods of rafter seating are used. This involves making bobtail cuts in one fashion or another (Fig. 8-8) so that the rafter ends are flush with or slightly inset from the exterior face of the wall upon which they rest.

Where another section of roof angles off in a different direction, the framing construction gets a bit more difficult. To make an outside corner, a hip rafter must be installed, and in making an inside corner a valley rafter must be installed. These rafters run from appropriate points at the ridge to the corner locations at the plates. Hip jack rafters extend from the plate to the hip rafter, while valley jack rafters run

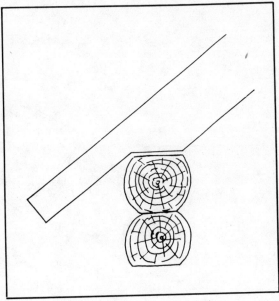

Fig. 8-7. This shave-cut rafter seats fully on a flatted plate log.

193

from the valley rafter to the ridge board. As usual, the common rafters extend clear from the ridge board to the plate wherever there are straight-through runs (Fig. 8-9). These different rafters are attached top and bottom in the same way as common rafters, with their ends

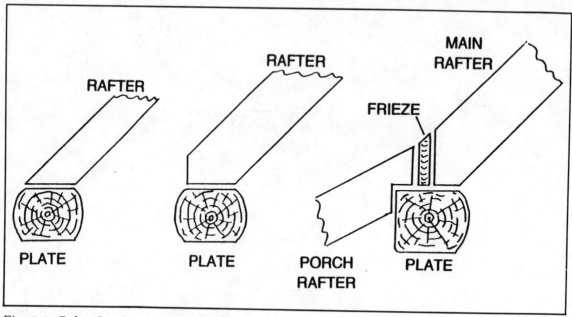

Fig. 8-8. Bobtail rafter cuts can be made in these three ways.

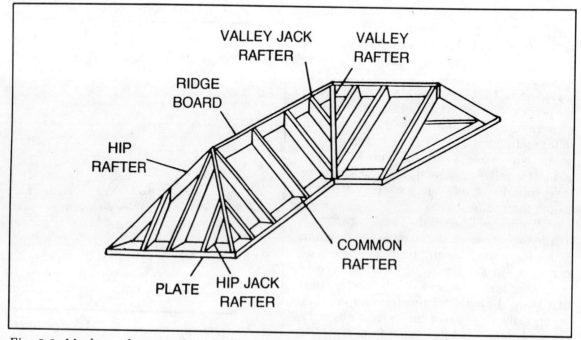

Fig. 8-9. Mockup of a typical roof frame construction shows the various component parts.

cut to whatever angles (sometimes they are compound) are necessary for a flat, tight fit.

Occasionally a roof structure is cut off short so that it extends beyond the outer surface of the end walls by an amount equal to only the thickness of a trim board or two. More often, however, a substantial overhang is desired, sometimes as great as that of the eaves. In a conventional roof frame this is accomplished by building a lookout ladder (Fig. 8-10).

To make a lookout ladder, a series of short pieces of dimension stock called lookouts are secured at right angles to the rafters. These form a ladder extending beyond the end wall of the building, providing the overhang or extended rake. Lookouts are often made from 2 × 4s which are attached at one end to the first inboard rafter, and are toe-nailed in place where they pass over the top plate of the end wall. The lookouts must be flush with the rafter tops, and the end-wall plate must be calculated to lie at the correct height. Wide overhangs might require the use of heavier stock, and ei-

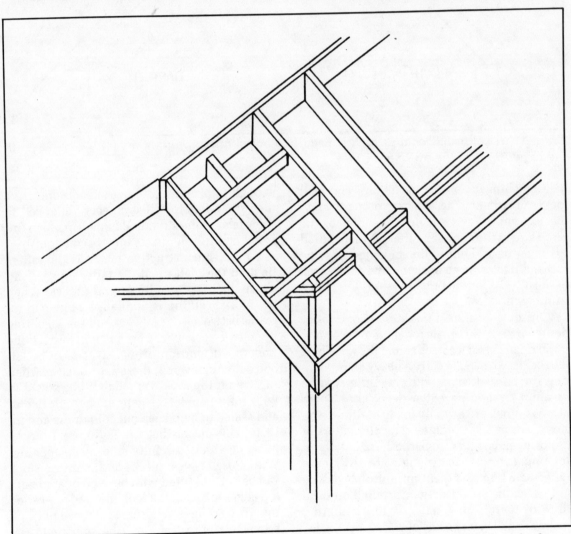

Fig. 8-10. One way to construct a lookout ladder that will provide an extended roof rake.

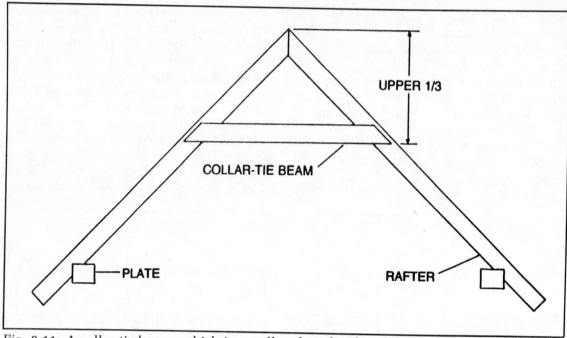

Fig. 8-11. *A collar tie beam, which is usually a board rather than an actual beam, is set in the upper third of the rafter peak.*

ther notching or shimming at the end-wall plate can be done if necessary to properly align the lookout ladder. An outside rafter of the same size as the common rafters is then nailed to the outboard ends of the lookouts. In some cases, a lighter piece of nominal 1-inch stock is substituted for the outside rafter, to act as a trim board.

In some designs it might be necessary or desirable to stiffen up the roof frame, especially if the rafters span a considerable distance or if the roof is expected to carry a heavy snow load. This can be easily done with very little expense or effort by adding collar-tie beams. These beams, which are actually made of dimension stock, are nailed to the faces of the rafters at opposite ends, and are placed horizontally in the upper third of the triangle created by the rafter pair (Fig. 8-11). In an unfinished attic 1- × -6 boards are adequate, installed on each third or fourth rafter set. In a finished attic, make the collar-tie beams of 2 × 4s or 2 × 6s, depending upon the span, and place them high

enough to provide sufficient headroom. Here they should be installed on each rafter set, to serve later as the structural framework for a finished ceiling. In effect, they become joists.

In most construction methods the rafters lie atop the plates and the rafter tops extend above the plate tops by several inches. When the roof sheathing is applied, a large gap remains between the plate top and the sheathing undersurface, between each pair of joists. If the underneath portion of the eaves is to be left open and uncovered, these gaps must be filled in. Even if the roof overhang will be boxed in with soffit panels, the gaps are best closed off and sealed to help keep out cold drafts and insects. This means that a series of frieze blocks must be fitted carefully into each opening. With closed eaves, pieces of dimension stock can be cut and fitted with beveled or angle-cut top edges to match the roof line, and toe-nailed into place (Fig. 8-12). Run a full bead of caulk around either inside or outside, or both, to seal the blocking off. Lay another bead of caulk

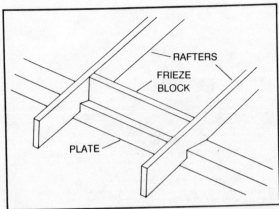

Fig. 8-12. *Frieze blocks are installed between rafters and on top of the plate to close the gaps.*

along the top surface of the blocking as the roof sheathing is laid, to seal that portion.

If the eaves are open to view, dimension-stock frieze blocks can also be used and will be just as effective, but certainly won't present the same appearance as the log wall. In this case, cut and fit short sections of log, flatted on the bottom to match the plate log and beveled off on the top to match the roof pitch.

LOG RAFTERS

A roof frame made up entirely of log rafters can be made in almost the same fashion as a dimension-stock frame. The minimum rafter diameter should be 6 inches, and larger logs must often be used. The spacing commonly chosen is either 24 or 30 inches, though in small and steeply pitched roofs this might be stretched to 36 inches. Full flatting is not essential, but cutting at least a narrow flat (2 inches or so) along the top makes for easier laying of roof sheathing. Likewise, if the underside of the rafters is to be later covered with some sort of sheathing or finish materials, a narrow flat is helpful here.

Log rafters can be installed one by one against a ridge board using the same method as with the dimension-stock roof frame, or can be erected in sets or pairs without benefit of the ridge board. Installation at the plate end is also

the same, using either the bird's-mouth notch, half-cut method, or bobtail. There is also another method that can be used, though it doesn't have the strength of the others. This involves leaving the rafter log round and cutting an angled saddle notch into the plates. This method is sometimes used with fully round logs in small buildings. Each rafter log is spiked directly to the plate log.

The other aspects of a log-rafter roof frame are also pretty much the same as for a dimension-stock frame. For an extended rake, build a lookout ladder of logs extending from the first inboard rafter across the end-wall plate to whatever distance beyond the outer wall surface is desired. The lookouts can be made from small logs or be the same size as the rafter logs or the wall logs, and spaced according to your liking. They might rest on the end-wall top, be notched in, or actually extend through the end wall. The underside of the extended rake can later be enclosed or not, and a trim board can be attached to the outer lookout ends or not—as you wish.

Collar-tie beams of saplings, poles, full logs, split logs, or dimension stock can be installed as necessary. All gaps between plate logs and the roof undersurface, whether along sidewalls or at the end walls, should be filled with frieze blocks of logs or dimension stock and sealed with caulk. For a tight fit, notch the blocking into the log rafters or lookout sides.

PURLIN ROOF

The purlin roof is a traditional old construction once widely employed but nowadays seldom seen except on log houses. The purlin roof presents an attractive appearance when left open to view from inside the building. It is also a strong and simple construction that can be put together in several different ways.

The simplest type is a small and short roof assembly using purlins only. The purlins run lengthwise of the roof and are supported by the end walls (Fig. 8-13). In most log construction they are notched into or pass through the end

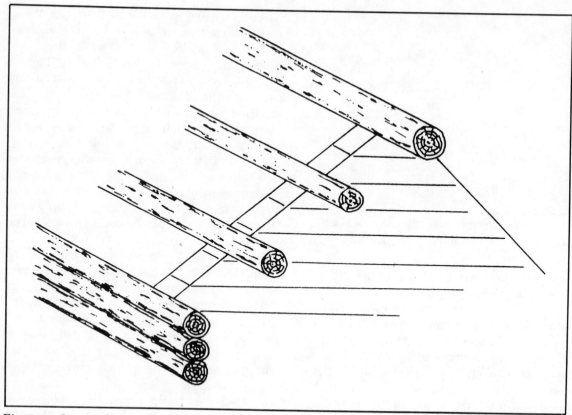

Fig. 8-13. Log purlins and ridge can be set into gable ends and projected to provide an extended roof rake.

walls to form the basis for an extended rake. They are spaced 3 or 4 feet apart up the roof slope, and in 10-inch diameter can span as much as 20 feet, longer for greater diameters. A ridge log is located at the peak, and that's all there is to the frame. The roof sheathing is applied directly to the purlin and ridge log tops. There are no plate logs as such, and the top logs of the sidewall courses are bevel-flatted to match the roof pitch. The sheathing is nailed directly to them. Boards are most often used for this purpose, running at right angles to the purlins; a double layer is sometimes laid for extra strength. End-wall logs are treated in the usual way, with their ends cut to match the roof pitch and the sheathing nailed down tight, sealed with caulk.

As the roof becomes larger and the spans

longer, some sort of support is needed for the purlins. One way of providing support is to position tie logs at right angles to the purlins and attach them to the sidewalls at ceiling height. These tie logs can be spaced approximately every 10 or 12 feet. The next step is to secure small logs from the tie beam tops directly upward to the purlin bottoms. The best method of attachment is with large mortise-and-tenon joints at each end, secured through the middle with a pin, peg, or bolt. A similar support post can be run from the tie beams to the ridge log (Fig. 8-14). This arrangement works nicely where the tie beam span is not too great, say 20 feet or less, depending upon the diameter of the tie beams.

Where the spans are greater the positions of the upright supporting logs can be shifted

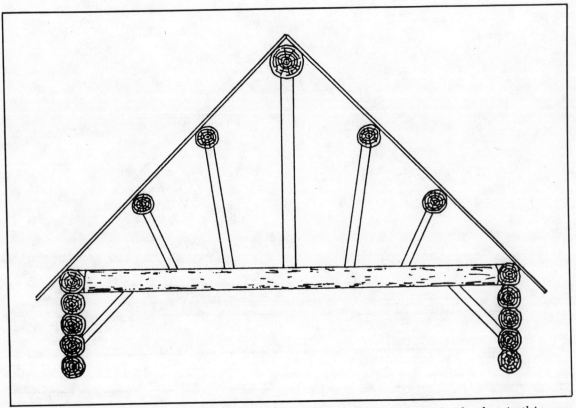

Fig. 8-14. *Side-supported tie logs hold support poles for the purlins and ridge log in this construction.*

somewhat and additional members added to form trusses. There is quite a variety of possible configurations, depending upon the number of purlins and the spans involved. One of the simplest is a large W (Fig. 8-15), where the tops of the outer arms of the W bisect the roof and the bottom ends trisect the tie beam. Another possibility is an M-truss, and the center-post truss is also widely used (Fig. 8-16). The Y-truss (Fig. 8-17) is another configuration, and the post-and-tie truss arrangement (Fig. 8-18) is effective and relatively easy to build.

Truss systems of this sort can be built with either logs or beams, and are generally installed in open-plan houses where they are a visible part of the interior design (Fig. 8-19). They can also be made of extremely large members and spaced 25 or 30 feet apart, allowing upper-level living quarters to be constructed between and around the heavy timbering. Smaller and more closely spaced trusses obviously eliminate the possibilities of having usable upper-level living space and so are relegated to cathedral ceiling spaces or unfinished attics.

Another method of setting a purlin roof involves both purlins and log rafters. This consists of first erecting a series of log rafters that are larger in diameter and spaced farther apart than ordinary common rafters would be, but installed in the same way. They can be cut to project past the plate logs if desired, resting upon the plate logs with a bird's-mouth notch, or can be cut to mate flush with the plate logs and the outside wall surface. The diameter of these logs can run from 10 inches up with a spacing of 6 or more feet, depending upon span and size, and the diameter of the purlins that will be used. The purlins are then set at right

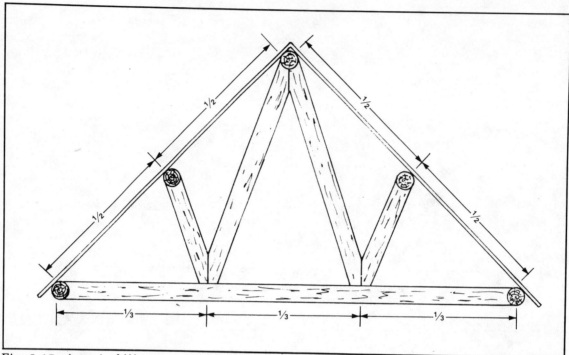

Fig. 8-15. A typical W-truss arrangement.

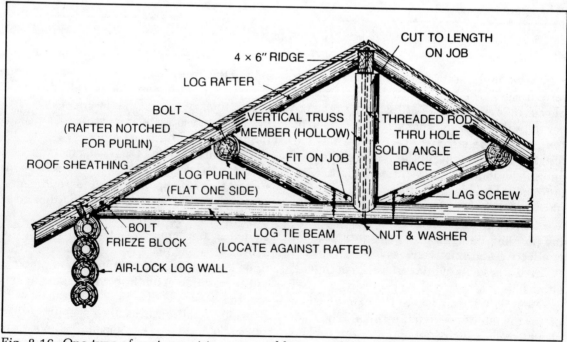

Fig. 8-16. One type of center-post truss assembly as used on wide-span buildings. (Courtesy of Air Lock Log Co., Inc.)

angles across the main rafters and lock-notched at each crossing point (Fig. 8-20). The purlins can be as small as about 5 inches in diameter if the spans are very short, but 7 to 8 inches would be considered more adequate. If the spans are long the diameter should be greater. A spacing of 3 to 4 feet is about right, and the roof sheathing can be applied directly to the purlins.

For larger roofs this system can be modi-

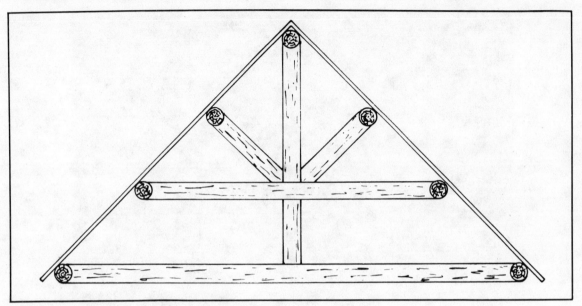

Fig. 8-17. A typical Y-truss arrangement.

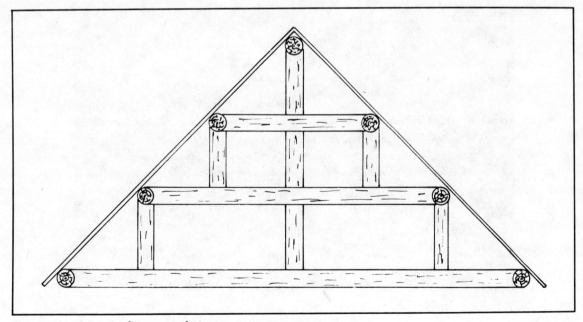

Fig. 8-18. A typical post-and-tie truss arrangement.

fied. Instead of running the main rafters out to the sidewall plates, they are shifted into a truss configuration. This involves placing one or a pair (one above the other) of tie beams from wall to wall. The main rafters are then set upon the tie beams just to the inside of the walls, making the tie beams the bottom chord of the truss. A center post is erected from the center

Fig. 8-19. *A beam truss arrangement used with a purlin log roof frame.* (Courtesy of Town and Country Cedar Homes.)

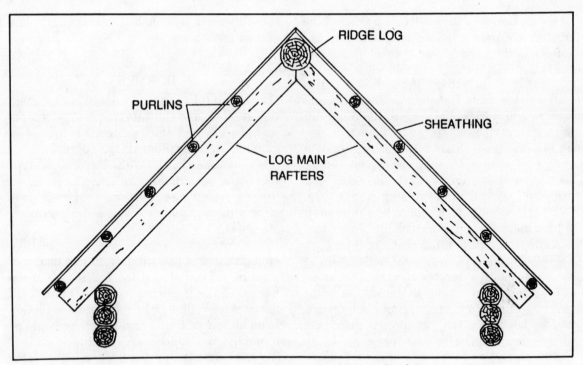

Fig. 8-20. Heavy log main rafters and ridge with smaller purlin logs.

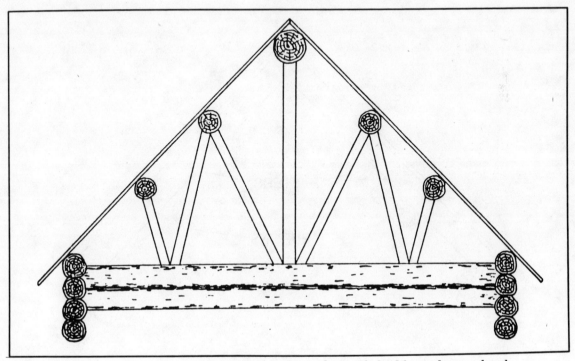

Fig. 8-21. A log purlin truss assembly with a log ridge and double tie beam chord.

of the tie beams to the peak of the rafters. The purlins are then attached lengthwise to the rafters. A ridge log is placed at the peak (Fig. 8-21).

Yet another method of building a purlin roof is to first install large purlin logs from end wall to end wall, supported or trussed or not as necessary. These are large-diameter logs, and in small roofs there might be only one on each side, with a ridge log at the peak. Rafter logs then are run from plate to ridge log, notched and spiked at crossing points (Fig. 8-22). These rafter logs should be a minimum 6-inch diameter and spaced about every 3 to 4 feet, depending upon the spans involved.

Note that any of these constructions can be strengthened in a number of ways. Diameters can be increased, spans shortened, or both; ridge logs or main rafters can doubled; trusses can be beefed up with additional members; rafter spacing can be increased or decreased, as can their size; and where purlins are the uppermost members, another full complement of

rafter logs can be attached to them as closely spaced as necessary.

DORMERS

Dormers and log houses seem to complement one another, and they are frequently incorporated in 1½- or 2-story designs having gable, gambrel, or other pitched styles of roofs. They are sometimes made with flat or shed-type roofs, and sometimes with gable roofs. Either type can originate at the main roof peak, or in steeply pitched main roofs, at some intermediate point.

A dormer can be as narrow as 3 feet, just enough to frame in a window, or in a shed-roof style might run almost the full length of the house. The main purpose of one or more small dormers is to admit light and afford ventilation in an underroof living area—such as would be found in a story-and-a-half structure—while at the same time increasing the available usable floor space and overall spaciousness to a small

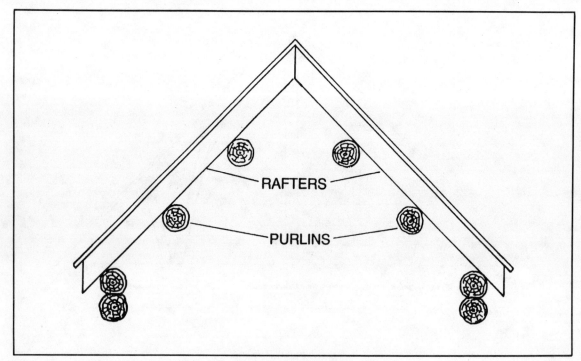

Fig. 8-22. Log purlins with log or dimension-stock rafters above.

extent. Large dormers, especially the full-length variety, perform the same functions to a much greater degree and also can expand the living quarters to virtually a full-sized second floor.

In log house construction, dormers are commonly framed with dimension stock materials, but they can also be log-framed. This is largely a matter of individual preference as to appearance, both interior and exterior. In either case, the process starts with a framed hole of appropriate size and shape in the main roof structure. This framing is carried out in the usual manner. Then the dormer itself is framed above the opening. Figure 8-23 shows typical dimension-stock dormer framing in gable-roofed style.

By eliminating the header and shortening the jack rafters, the ridge of the dormer could tie directly to the main ridge; this would move the entire assembly back up the roof. Or, the side and front studs could be made taller and the top plates extended, making a higher and longer dormer. The dormer ceiling could follow the gable roof line, or joists could be run across from plate to plate and a lower ceiling attached to them. The design is completely flexible. In a shed-roofed dormer, a series of rafters would originate at the ridge, or at the header of an opening lower down the roof, and extend to the front top plate of the dormer face.

The roof construction methods for a dormer are the same as for any other roof. To frame with logs, simply use logs or poles of appropriate diameter for the spans involved, and follow the same general principles for placement of the various structural members. To build up the walls of a dormer from logs, use the framed-out main roof opening as a starting point and build up the walls in the same fashion as the

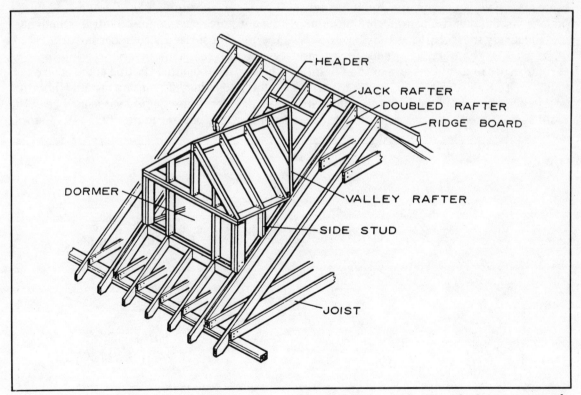

Fig. 8-23. A typical framing arrangement for a gable-roofed dormer built with dimension stock. *(Courtesy of the U.S. Department of Agriculture.)*

main walls of the structure. For both convenience and appearance, logs of smaller diameter than the main wall logs are often used for this purpose.

ROOFING

Once the roof frame is complete you can go about the task of laying the roofing. This consists of four principal elements: the sheathing, underlayment, flashing, and the weather or finish surface. There are several methods of applying each, and numerous materials that can be employed.

Sheathing

In a standard roof (as opposed to a built-up roof, which will be discussed later), the sheathing is applied first, directly to the rafters or purlins. The old method of sheathing with boards is still very much in use, and is the most practical method for one person working alone.

Relatively inexpensive 1- × -6 S3S stock is often used for the purpose of sheathing, laid at right angles to the rafters and pushed tightly together. Tongue-and-groove boards can also be used, as can wide boards, though they are more susceptible to cup warping. Regardless of the board width or kind, they should be applied with the heart side up, because cupping of flatsawn boards takes place invariably in the opposite direction (Fig. 8-24). This helps to reduce the amount of cupping and also eliminates the series of sharp ridges that would appear if the boards were laid heart side down.

In most roof constructions the boards are laid horizontally in rows up the roof. However, in roofs where the purlins are uppermost, the boards run at right angles to the purlins, in the vertical direction. This is an advantage in that full-length boards often can be used to span the roof top to bottom, eliminating joints and increasing strength and stiffness. Boards can also be applied diagonally, on either rafters or purlins, for increased structural rigidity (Fig. 8-25).

The method of applying sheathing boards tucked tightly together is called closed sheathing. Open sheathing is another method that is used in some parts of the country, often where the weather surface is composed of cedar shingles or shakes. This involves laying the first three rows of boards, starting at the eave edge, tightly together. These are usually nominal 1- × -6 stock. Subsequent boards may be of the same width but are more often 1- × -4 stock.

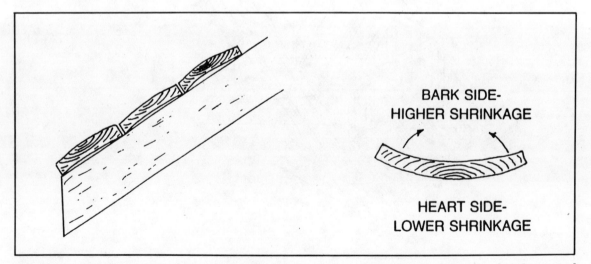

**BARK SIDE-
HIGHER SHRINKAGE**

**HEART SIDE-
LOWER SHRINKAGE**

Fig. 8-24. Flatsawn roofing boards or planks should be placed heart side up; shrinkage and cupping is less of a problem in this position.

These are laid with a gap between each board equal to the amount of shingle surface left exposed to the weather in each course (Fig. 8-26).

Closed sheathing may also be comprised of nominal 1- × -6 shiplap or tongue-and-groove boards. These fit tightly together and lock into place, forming a solid and rugged surface that is somewhat less susceptible to cupping. Also, when shrinkage occurs, cracks are less likely to open up between the boards. In the instances where the underside of the sheathing will be visible from the interior of the building and doubles as a ceiling, nominal 2- × -6 tongue-and-groove decking planks can be fitted with the best face down, just as with a decked floor. This makes an exceptionally strong roof assembly, and the planks can be applied over a frame-work of widely spaced joists or purlins without loss of strength or stiffness.

Perhaps the most widely used sheathing material nowadays is plywood. The large sheets can be laid rapidly and efficiently by a crew of workers, and an entire roof can be covered in short order. Plywood sheets are laid with the face grain at right angles to the supporting members, with all sheets offset from each other (usually by halves) so that no joints are coincidental. A 1/16-inch joint space should be left at all end joints and a 1/8-inch gap at all edge joints.

An exterior grade of plywood is generally used for the entire roof surface, but in fact an exterior grade could be used along only the eave and rake edges, with interior-grade panels

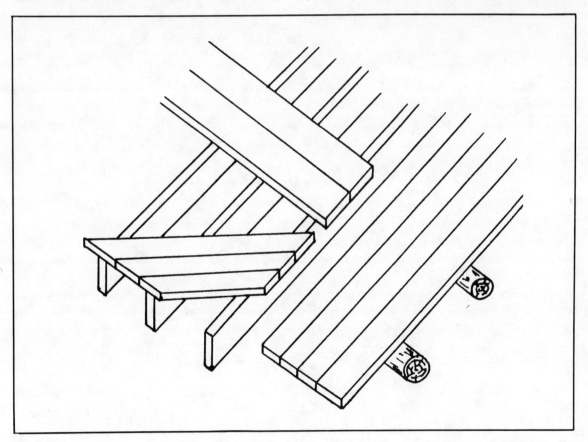

Fig. 8-25. Roofers can be laid horizontally or diagonally on rafters (left), but are laid vertically on purlins (right).

laid everywhere else. Where the rafter spacing is 16 inches or less on centers, a plywood thickness of ⅜-inch is adequate and allowable under most building codes. However, most builders prefer the ½-inch thickness. As far as minimums are concerned, that thickness is also suitable for rafters on 24-inch centers. Either ½- or ⅝-inch thicknesses can be used on rafters with 32-inch centers, and ¾-inch on 42-inch centers. For 48-inch centers, either ¾-inch or ⅞-inch plywood is suitable. Rafters spaced up to 6 feet can be handled by special 1¼-inch sheets, provided additional blocking is installed to support all free edges.

Nailing of panels that are up to ½ inch thick is done with either 6d common smooth nails or ring-shank nails. Up to a 1-inch thickness, nail with 8d nails of either type. Nails should be spaced 6 inches apart around the perimeter and 12 inches apart at intermediate supports.

Underlayment

With the sheathing all nailed down, the next step is to apply the underlayment. Roofing underlayment is a dry felt material that has been saturated with asphalt and comes in roll form. It is called roofing felt, and is designated by its weight per square (100 square feet). A number of weights are available, but those most often used for underlayment purposes are 15-pound

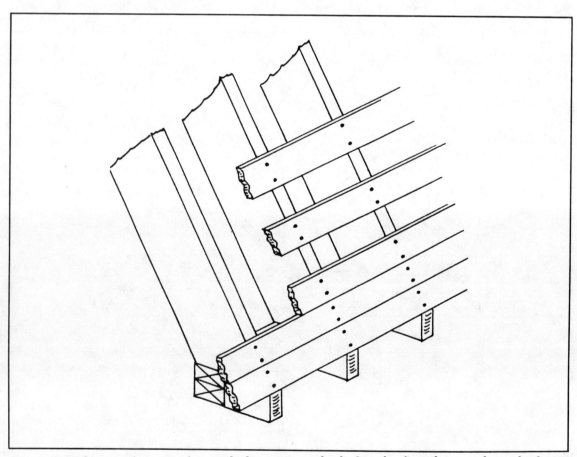

Fig. 8-26. When applying roofers with the open method, lay the first three or four planks up from the eave edge abutted together.

and 30-pound. If the roof pitch is four-in-one or more, either weight of roofing felt is applied in continuous horizontal rows, starting at the eave edge and progressing up the roof, with a 2-inch top overlap at each seam. The felt is nailed down at all edges with roofing barbs (nails) of suitable length and spaced about every 6 inches (Fig. 8-27).

If the roof pitch is less than four-in-one, ei-ther weight of roofing felt (but preferably the 30-pound) is laid up in much the same arrangement but with a greater overlap. The laying starts with a 19-inch-wide strip along the eave edge. This is followed by a full-width (36-inch) row of felt that completely covers the starter strip. Succeeding strips are laid with a 19-inch top overlap until the sheathing is fully covered (Fig. 8-28). In all cases, sidelaps should be a

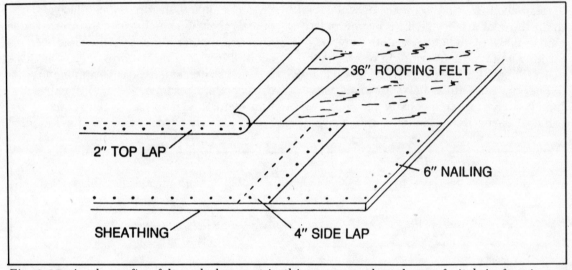

Fig. 8-27. Apply roofing felt underlayment in this manner when the roof pitch is four-in-one or steeper.

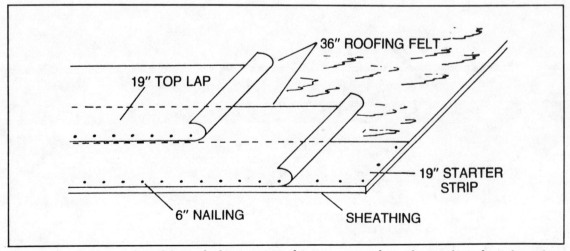

Fig. 8-28. Apply roofing felt underlayment in this manner when the roof pitch is less than four-in-one.

minimum of 4 inches wide and there is no harm whatsoever in making them a foot or more. The nailing pattern is the same as for the steeper pitches.

The next step in roof-building involves the installation of a metal drip edge along the eaves. You might find this material available at your local lumberyard, or you might have to have it made up at a sheet metal shop. Drip edge is a narrow band of metal (the width varies), about 2 or more inches of which rest upon the roof surface, with a narrower strip bent downward and outward at the eave edge, forming a lip to direct dripping water out and away (Fig. 8-29). The drip edge is aligned and nailed in place with as few short nails as will hold it safely in place. For extra insurance, you can coat the entire underside of the drip edge

that bears on the roof with roofing tar in order to seal it down firmly, and then daub each nail head with more tar.

For roof pitches of four-in-one or less, yet another layer should be added. This is sometimes called the selvedge, and consists of a strip of smooth-surface mineral roll roofing, which comes in 36-inch-wide rolls and is generally used in a 90-pound weight. Nail this strip in place along the eave edge, aligned with the outer edge of the drip edge. Place one row of nails about 6 inches apart at the up-roof edge first, and another row spaced the same but back about 8 inches from the drip edge. The same treatment, incidentally, can be applied to roofs of steeper pitches for a bit of additional protection against water and ice backup at the eaves.

Metal drip edge is also sometimes applied

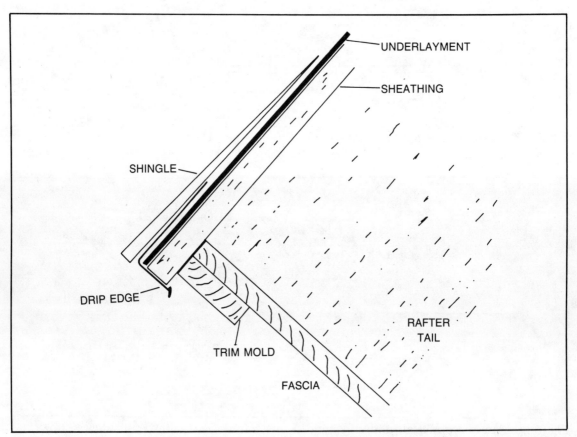

Fig. 8-29. Metal drip edge should be installed along the leading edge of the roof sheathing.

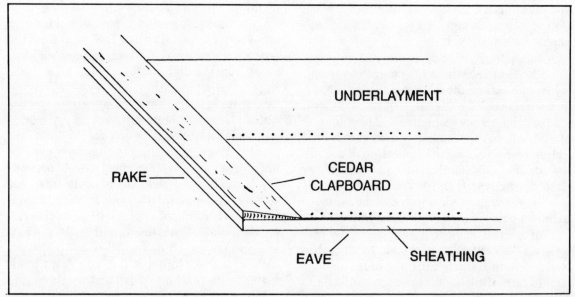

Fig. 8-30. *A clapboard installed between the underlayment and the weather surface, along the rake edge, channels runoff down to the eave.*

along the rake edges. There is another method, however, that is perhaps easier, more attractive, and less expensive. It involves nailing a standard cedar or redwood clapboard along the rake edge with the thick edge of the clapboard aligned with the roof edge and the thin edge inboard (Fig. 8-30). This diverts water from the rake edges and channels it back down the roof to drip from the eaves.

Flashing

The next consideration is flashing. Flashing is a method of completely sealing roof joints that probably would open up with time and commence to leak if only caulked or plastered over with a sealant. The material used most often is sheet metal, but in some instances a heavy asphalt-impregnated paper or felt may be laid. Some types of flashing can be installed entirely before the weather surface is put on, while others are installed concurrently as the point of application is reached. Either way, flashing details are best sorted out ahead of time.

The chief points that require flashing are valleys where downsloping roof sections join to form a natural watercourse, chimneys, pipes of any sort, vent stacks or hoods, skylights, trap doors or windows, and the junction points of dormer or other walls. Eave edges are also sometimes flashed with metal from the edge upward for 3 to 5 feet, with the weather surface beginning from 1 to 3 feet from the eave edge.

Asphalt roofing materials can be used to flash closed valleys, but all other installations where any part of the flashing is exposed to the weather should be metal or flexible membrane, such as butyl rubber or neoprene. Lead is seldom used any more but copper is, despite its cost. This is the longest-lived and most easily worked of all the flashing materials. Galvanized steel sheeting is probably the most popular, with aluminum running close behind.

Whichever metal you choose, stick with it all the way. Sheets of different metals should not be laid overlapping one another because they will quickly corrode from a process called electrostatic action. For the same reason, copper nails must be used with copper flashing, and aluminum nails with aluminum flashing. Galvanized nails can be used with zinc, galvanized steel, or lead.

Valley flashing is done one of two ways. The first is open, where the center of the valley is exposed and the edges of the weather surface are set back 2 or 3 inches or more on each side of the valley centerline. The other is closed, where the weather surfaces are butted tightly together along the centerline of the valley, or perhaps interleaved, and the valley flashing is covered and invisible.

Closed valley flashing can be applied using 90-pound mineral-surfaced roll roofing. Cut an 18-inch-wide strip and nail it lengthwise up the centerline of the valley, 9 inches to one side and 9 inches to the other. The nails should be roofing barbs on 4-inch centers and 1 inch in from the outside edges. Paint a 3-inch stripe of roofing cement down each outer edge

of this strip, and cover with a 36-inch-wide strip of the same material. Nail as before, and add a second row of nails 4 inches in from the outside edges, also on 4-inch centers but staggered from the first row (Fig. 8-31). If the flashing is applied over the underlayment, paint a 3-inch-wide strip of roofing cement under the outside edges of both strips as they are laid.

Metal flashing, whether for an open or a closed valley, is applied in the same manner but with a single layer of metal. In an open valley a single long strip of metal is fitted (or several top-lapped strips) and extends about 2 feet to either side of the centerline of the valley (Fig. 8-32). Overlaps should be about a foot and preferably 18 inches. Be sure that each overlap is a top-lap, and that you don't inadvertently make a bottom-lap that would funnel water inside the roof.

Closed valley flashing is done the same

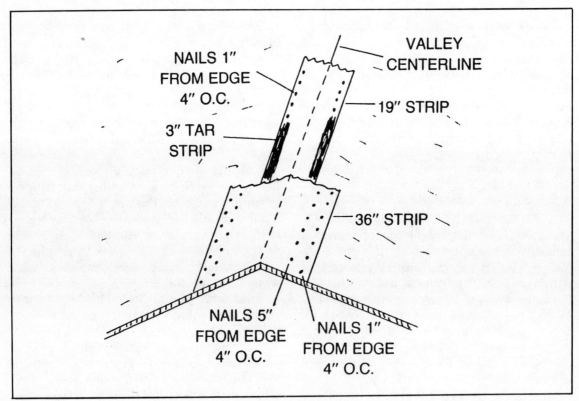

Fig. 8-31. A method of flashing a valley with roofing felt.

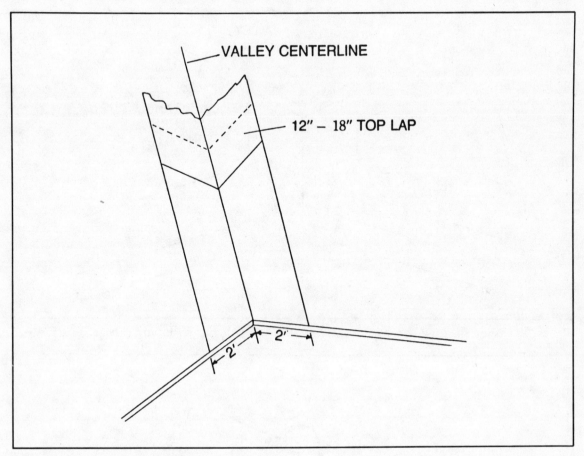

VALLEY CENTERLINE

12" – 18" TOP LAP

2'   2'

Fig. 8-32. A valley flashed with metal strips.

way for solid or sheet-type weather surfaces, but if desired can be done differently when any of the various forms of shingles are applied. Individual pieces of flashing 18 inches wide, and as long as the diagonal dimension of the shingle when cut to meet the valley centerline, are cut and bent to an appropriate V-angle to match the valley angle. These individual pieces are then interwoven with the course of shingles as they are nailed up (Fig. 8-33). The shingle nails hold the flashing in place and the material, if trimmed properly, is invisible.

Most items such as roof vents and ventilating units have their own built-in flashing bases that are interwoven with the shingles or other materials as work progresses. The object is to have the upper two-thirds or so of the flashing

plate lie beneath the weather surface, sealed in place with a layer of roofing cement, and the lower portion above the weather surface for proper water-shedding. Pipes can usually be fitted with standard flashing units called flashing sleeves or roof jacks. These consist of a lower flashing plate attached to a tall collar that fits snugly around the pipe and is sealed to it by means of a curled lead sleeve, silicone caulking, or a special expandable jacket of neoprene or a similar substance (Fig. 8-34). Round stainless or galvanized steel appliance chimneys so often used nowadays with wood stoves and fireplaces have special flashing sleeves and storm collars made to fit each chimney diameter and are adjustable for roof pitch. All of these sleeves and jacks are installed so

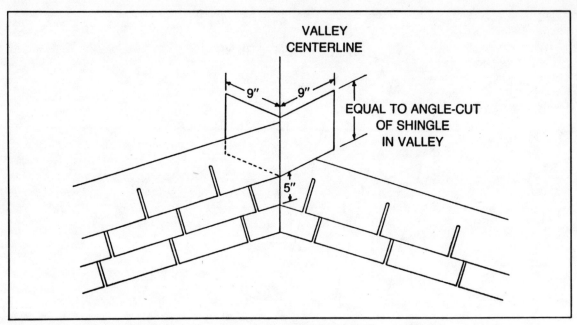

VALLEY
CENTERLINE

9"   9"

EQUAL TO ANGLE-CUT
OF SHINGLE
IN VALLEY

5"

Fig. 8-33. Valley flashing can be interwoven with the shingles as laying proceeds.

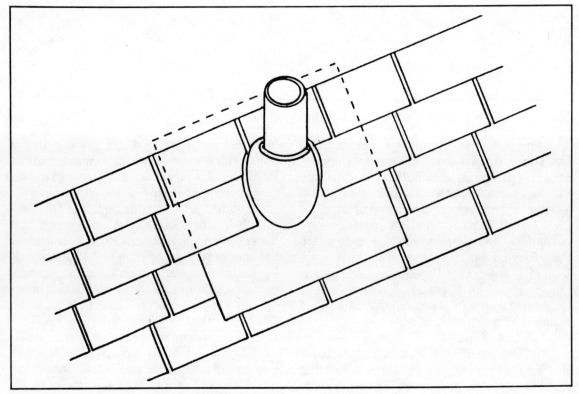

Fig. 8-34. A typical roof jack installation.

the flashing plate lies with the upper two-thirds or more below the weather surface, and the remainder above.

There are a number of methods of flashing masonry chimneys, used concurrently with the

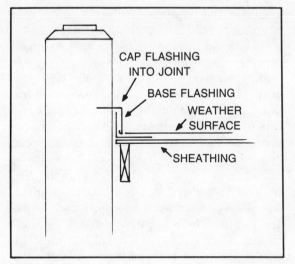

Fig. 8-35. *One method of installing chimney flashing with a slip joint to allow for settling.*

laying of the weather surface. Sometimes a special saddle or cricket is installed, and sometimes pieces of flashing are interwoven with the bricks as the chimney is made and later with the shingles as they are laid up. Waterproof roofing cement is used liberally, and a base of heavy asphalt roll roofing is sometimes installed first. As usual, the object is to shed all moisture away from the chimney joints and down over the weather surface of the roof. However, unlike a standard flashing unit as used in frame construction, a slip joint must be provided. Typically this is accomplished with a two-part system, a base flashing and a cap flashing. The two are not joined and are free to slip by one another (Fig. 8-35).

Flashing is also required where the edge of a roof meets a higher sidewall. Here individual pieces are cut and interleaved with the shingles as the courses are laid up, and attached to the sidewall sheathing before the finish siding is applied. If the weather surface is a solid material such as roll roofing, a continuous strip of flashing is installed against the roof

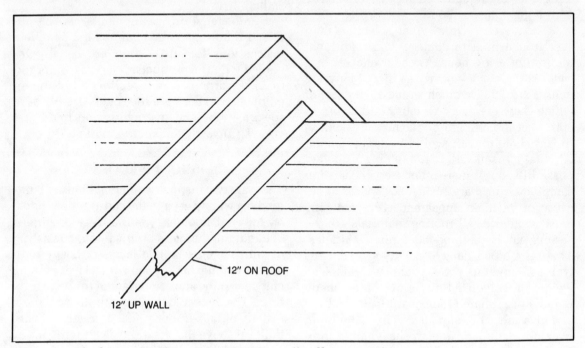

Fig. 8-36. *Flashing must be applied at all roof/wall intersections.*

surface and up against the sheathing of the sidewall (Fig. 8-36). The flashing should extend at least a foot in each direction. Dormer sides are handled in exactly the same way, and the dormer front is flashed with a continuous strip of metal laid against the roof surface and bent up against the dormer sheathing with a long wrap around the corners. The dormer front should be flashed first, with the corners sealed completely with roofing cement. The side flashing is then wrapped around the front in downward folds.

Weather Surface

After all of this preliminary work, the finish roofing or weather surface seems almost an afterthought. Don't treat it as such because it is important. The weather surface should be carefully selected to provide you with a long-lived surface that will need a minimum of maintenance and also complement the structure in the way of color, shadow-lines, pattern, and overall appearance. Pay the price and buy only top-grade, high-quality materials, preferably with a guarantee or bond.

Today you have a wider selection than ever from which to choose. The traditional roofing for a log house is cedar shakes, and cedar shingles look nearly as nice. Many log houses are fitted with sheet-metal roofing, of which there are many varieties and colors in both steel and aluminum; the newer baked-on finishes hold up very well. Single- or double-coverage mineral-surface roll roofing is another possibility, but is more often used on vacation camps than primary residences, perhaps because of its plain appearance. Probably the most popular of all roofing materials are the various kinds of three-tab asphalt shingles. There is a broad range of colors available, as well as numerous patterns and weights. The weight is calculated in terms of so many pounds per square (100 square feet), and the shingles are so designated. The 235-pound weight is a common one; the heavier the shingle, the longer it is likely to last. They are easy

to apply, especially for one person working alone.

There are several other choices, too, that are less common but well worth looking into, especially if you would like to have something a little different. Slate, for example, is still available, but requires a well-engineered roof structure to hold the weight. You might choose vinyl or aluminum shingles, which look much like three-tabs but are longer lived. Clay tile roofing, which is extremely long-lived and available in numerous colors and configurations, is staging something of a comeback and is popular in the Southwest. Like slate, it needs a rugged roof structure. One expensive but handsome and very long-lived alternative is porcelainized steel shingles. They are finished with a fused-on ceramic coating—glass, actually—and are available in several shapes and colors. There are new roofing materials coming along all the time that also merit attention, such as the composite wood fiber shingles that look like hand-riven shakes and come attached to long backing strips for ease of installation.

Preinstallation requirements can be obtained from the manufacturers, and complete instructions for installation are usually included with the products. For best results and to keep warranties valid, follow all of the requirements to the letter. Suppliers usually have specifications and instructions on hand that you can investigate before buying.

BUILT-UP ROOFS

There are two distinctly different kinds of built-up roofs widely used in the construction industry today. The older type is a weather surface of a roof that has zero or low pitch, consisting of multiple crosslapped layers of heavy roofing felt and hot tar, topped with a layer of stone chips, or some similar variant of this construction. The newer definition applies to roofs usually of four-in-one pitch or greater that are built up above the sheathing layer with one or successive layers of thermal insulating material and spacers, with the weather surface lying on top.

Because of the high value put on thermal insulation today in both cold and hot parts of the country, this latter type of roof has become most important. It is primarily used wherever the underside of the roof sheathing is open to view and is actually the finish ceiling. Or, there might be a thin finish ceiling layer applied, with logs or beams left mostly visible, which allows no room for the substantial thickness of insulation so often needed.

Of all the housing styles, log houses probably most often have roof/ceilings open to view in all or at least part of the building. Add to this the fact that very few areas in the country can get by without heating or cooling, and it becomes obvious that many log houses must have built-up roofs of one sort or another.

There are a number of ways to go about making a built-up roof, depending upon the amount of thermal insulating value needed and the type of insulation chosen. One type is actually a cross between a standard roof and a built-up roof, in that it makes use of large squares of thick, edge-matched fibrous insulating roof decking applied directly to the rafters. The underside is prefinished for the ceiling effect, or a separate finish ceiling covering can be applied. The weather surface can be applied directly to the decking in some instances, while in others nailing strips are necessary.

Most built-up roof construction, however, begins on top of the roof sheathing, which may be either boards, plank decking, or plywood. The first system discussed here starts with a layer of sheathing, which in this case becomes subsheathing, laid over the rafters or purlins. A series of dimension-stock nailers is then installed horizontally or in a grid across the roof, spaced at 24-inch intervals. They are stood on edge and the width of the nailers must be equal to or greater than the total thickness of the thermal insulation required. Roll or batt fiberglass or mineral wool insulation is bedded in the spaces, and the whole roof is covered with an-

other layer of sheathing. The remainder of the roofing materials are applied in the usual fashion (Fig. 8-37). If purlins are involved, the nailers must be run vertically.

Another method makes use of rigid thermal insulation, which is available in large sheets of various thicknesses. This material is lightweight and a little fragile, and is glued or tacked carefully to the roof sheathing. Another layer of sheathing is added over the rigid insulation and nailed through to the rafters (Fig. 8-38). The sheets should be fitted tightly together, and preferably glued with construction or other recommended adhesive along the joints. The outer edges of the insulation are protected with nailer strips laid around the perimeter of the roof. The remainder of the roofing materials are installed in the usual way.

With both of these built-up roofs, a vapor barrier should be installed over the subsheathing and under the nailers and/or insulation. The most effective material for this is thin plastic sheeting from 3 to 6 mils thick, often called construction plastic. Either the black or the transparent is fine. Note, however, that plastic sheeting is terribly slippery when dry and absolutely lethal when wet. Use extreme caution when climbing around and working on a plastic-covered pitched roof. And remember, the more slits and punctures there are in the plastic, the less effective it is as a vapor barrier. Carry a roll of duct tape right along with you, and make repairs as you spot any damage.

The top layer of sheathing in both styles of built-up roof or the insulating decking roof can be closed and solid or can be open, with the sheathing boards spaced the same distance apart as the extent of shingle that will be exposed to the weather. The sheathing boards can be nominal 1-inch stock, but 1 × 3s are generally adequate in most installations, and are the least costly.

SKYLIGHTS AND ROOF WINDOWS

There is nothing new about skylights—they have been used in houses all over the country

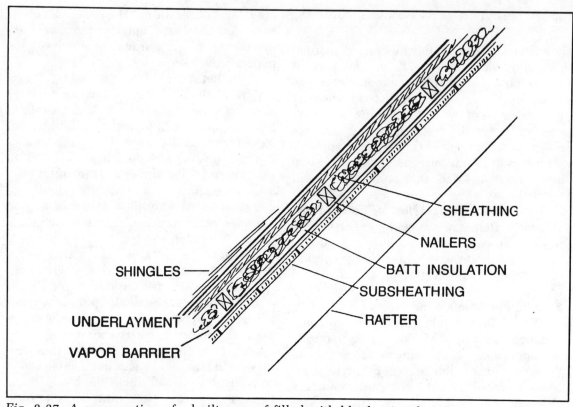

SHEATHING

NAILERS

BATT INSULATION

SUBSHEATHING

RAFTER

SHINGLES

UNDERLAYMENT

VAPOR BARRIER

Fig. 8-37. A cross-section of a built-up roof filled with blanket insulation.

for decades. But for some reason the have recently taken the house-building public by storm and have become all the rage. There are two important things to know about skylights. One is that they can dispense expensive heat to the outdoors, and conversely, gather unwanted heat in hot country. The other is that they can be potential trouble spots; if not installed exactly right, they are bound to leak sooner or later. On the other hand, properly arranged skylights can admit comforting solar heat in cold weather, and they can indeed be trouble-free if installed correctly. And, they can be most attractive and frequently serve to increase ventilation, visibility, and available light. It is worth noting, too, that there are several brands of specially built full windows that can be installed in many types of roofs, provided the pitch is not too low.

The best approach to skylights or roof windows is not to cobble up your own, but to purchase top-quality brand name units. Then follow the manufacturer's installation instructions to the letter. Better yet, let a professional do it; this is the course most likely to give you a permanent and trouble-free installation.

If you do want to make your own skylights, this is basically how it's accomplished: First, a suitable opening must be framed into the roof frame. This is done in just the same way as making an opening in a floor frame, as discussed in Chapter 5. Then a box-like sleeve must be built up around the interior of the opening, projecting a minimum of 6 inches above the roof weather surface, preferably about a foot if you live in snow country. The projecting sleeve must then be completely flashed and sealed into the roof weather surface, much like a pipe or vent is, so that leaks are virtually impossible. On a low sleeve the

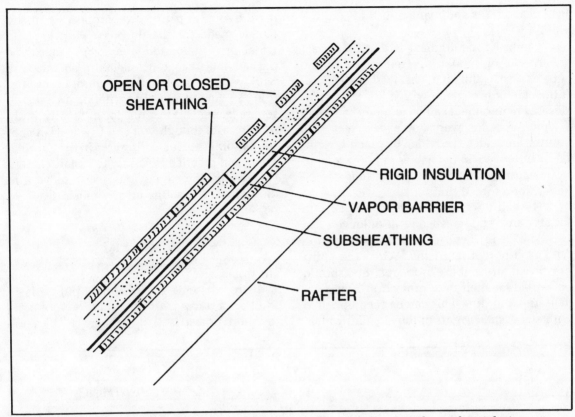

OPEN OR CLOSED SHEATHING

RIGID INSULATION

VAPOR BARRIER

SUBSHEATHING

RAFTER

Fig. 8-38. A cross-section of a built-up roof thermally protected with rigid insulation.

flashing should be wrapped completely up and over the top rim of the sleeve. On tall sleeves, run the flashing up at least halfway and cover the entire outside of the sleeve with an appropriate exterior siding material. Make liberal use of roofing cement and/or silicone or other currently recommended caulk. The skylight itself is fastened to the top of the sleeve securely and with a weathertight seal. The unit can be flat glass of one sort or another, or a plastic dome or "bubble"—check with your glass supplier for recommendations on locally available units or materials.

Various modifications can be made to a simple skylight, such as making it openable, installing double or even triple glazing to reduce heat loss, and setting in a lower pane of frosted glass to reduce the effects of direct sunlight but still admit a good quantity of diffused light. You can also use any of the several kinds of special coated glazing materials, or install a vent fan within the skylight assembly. You might also cover the bottom of the skylight well with frosted or opalescent glass or plastic, with a design painted on the upper side and lights installed above. Thus the skylight transmits light by both day and night, and also serves as an unusual accent point in the interior decor.

VENTING

Under most circumstances proper venting is a necessary part of the building construction. Ventilation in both soffit and attic areas serves to eliminate condensation in winter and also helps with cooling in the summer. Proper ventilation in an unheated attic can reduce or eliminate water backup from ice dams forming along the eaves. Ventilation is also required by

FHA regulations and many building codes as well.

The usual requirement is that there be 1 square foot of ventilating area for every 150 square feet of ceiling lying below the attic floor. If the ceiling is covered with a full vapor barrier, the requirement can be reduced by half to 1 square foot for every 300 square feet. The venting area can be provided by placing ventilators or louvers in the gables or end walls, or by installing roof vents. Exhaust fans can be added for a forced draft.

The soffit areas are sometimes open into the attic area, and screened vents or louvers can be installed in them to work in conjunction with gable or roof ventilators. Where the soffits are closed off from the attic area they should be vented for their own protection from condensation buildup. This can be accomplished with small screen vents or louvers, or by mak-

ing the soffit of perforated hardboard or metal panels made for the purpose. Plug louvers, which are tiny round louver heads made to be pushed into a 1-inch-diameter drilled hole, also work well if you install enough of them. The rule of 1 square foot of ventilation area to 150 square feet of ceiling area doesn't really apply in this case, though you can if you wish substitute soffit area for ceiling area in the formula. The usual practice is simply to install enough vents so that there is obvious free air movement through all the soffits all the time.

FINISH TRIM

The finish trim is the final step for completion of the roof assembly, and can be put on last, or all or part can be installed as the roof construction proceeds if it happens to be con-

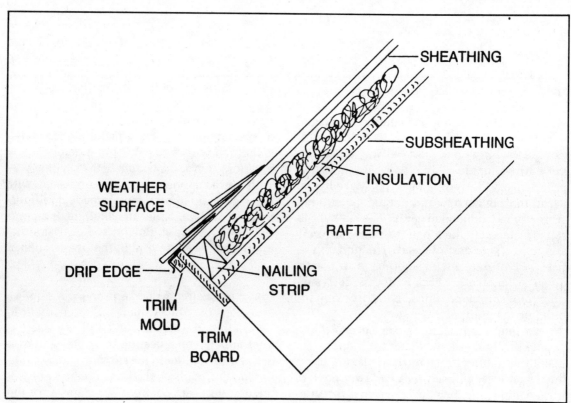

Fig. 8-39. One method of trimming out the eave edge of a built-up roof.

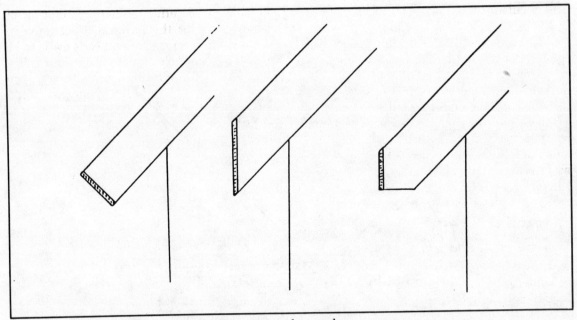

Fig. 8-40. Three popular ways of trimming rafter ends.

venient to do so. There is no point in setting up ladders or scaffolding just to install a bit of trim, if it can be done earlier.

Most of the trimwork takes place around the eaves and rakes, and the different possibilities are practically endless. The projecting rafter tails can be left completely alone with no further work done except for making sure that all the joints are fully sealed. If there is a built-up roof atop the rafters, a trim board is installed along the bottom edge to close the roof section. An additional strip of molding might be added as well at the top of the trim board and directly beneath the sheathing to dress out a slight edge projection (Fig. 8-39). The rafters remain open.

Whether the roof is built-up or not, you could also nail a fascia of 1-inch stock all the way across the faces of the rafter tails. The tails themselves can be cut at right angles, perpendicular to the ground, or with beveled bottom cuts (Fig. 8-40). The bottom of the fascia might be square, or cut in scallops or some other configuration. The underside of the rafters might be covered with soffit panels to form a com-

pletely boxed cornice. The soffit panels can be attached directly to the rafter bottoms so that the soffit pitches upward at the same angle as the roof, or the panels can run straight across and attach to a nailing strip mounted on the wall. Molding strips can be added at the wall/soffit joint, at the soffit/fascia joint, or at the fascia/roof sheathing joint (Fig. 8-41). Some of these treatments get pretty fancy and include carved bulls-eyes, ornate Swiss chalet-type ornamentation, gingerbread trim reminiscent of the Victorian era, notched-and-toothed edge trim, and a thousand other odds and ends.

The situation is basically the same at the rakes or roof ends. If there is no appreciable roof overhang, there might be only a single-thickness trim board applied along the wall at the wall/roof sheathing joint. An extended rake can be left open, and often is where log purlins protrude through the end walls. Or, the extended roof can be boxed in completely, or just faced with a trim board across the open ends. Again, you can carry out whatever decorative trimwork you like.

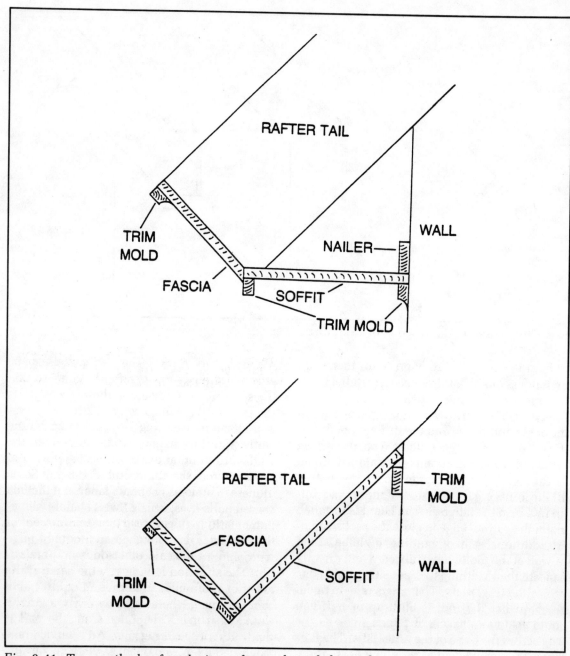

Fig. 8-41. Two methods of enclosing rafter ends and the under-eave area. There are dozens of possible trimming-out details that could be added.

9

Doors & Windows

THERE ARE SEVERAL APPROACHES TO OUTFITTING your log house with doors and windows, mostly depending upon the amount of time or the amount of cash that you want to spend. There is a tremendous variety of doors and windows commercially available from numerous manufacturers, and among them there are plenty of stock models suitable for a log house. Another possibility is to buy used units at secondhand shops, building wrecking yards, or anywhere else they might be expected to turn up. You can also build some of your own units, which isn't as difficult as it might sound. And, of course, you can use some combination of all three methods.

BUILDING BUCKS

A buck is just an empty frame, or subframe, into which a door or window unit will later be fitted, and is easy to make. The top is joined to the two sides with a simple rabbet joint (Fig.

9-1). If you wish, you can make a somewhat stronger joint by using a combined dado and rabbet, but this is not really essential. The bottom is made of the same stock (but often thicker) for window bucks, rabbet-jointed at each end but set at a 6-degree angle sloped downward to the outside for drainage. For an exterior door the bottom piece should be made of oak threshold stock. You can purchase thresholds already made up at a lumberyard, or you can fashion your own. Though oak is most commonly used, nearly any good hardwood will do. The buck sides are usually nailed directly to the threshold ends, without benefit of a joint. The threshold is set at a 12-degree angle sloping down and out.

The stock used for door buck tops and sides, and for all four of the window buck members, is open to choice. Because of the heavy, massive aspects of a log structure, thick stock seems to match up better than thin, and

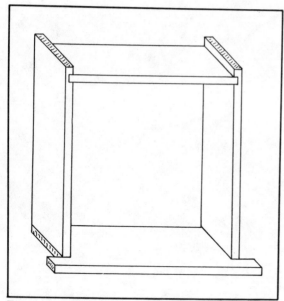

Fig. 9-1. A typical window buck assembly.

well as sash frames; that is, the glass is installed in a frame (the sash), which in turn is mounted in a larger and heavier frame consisting of head jamb, side jamb, and sill assembly. This is the way all openable windows are delivered (except for special orders and replacement sash), though fixed lights can be obtained without the jamb-and-sill frame. Likewise, prehung doors are factory assembled with the door already hinged to a frame, and sometimes with a lockset installed. These frames consist of head and side jambs and sill for exterior doors, but are minus sills on interior models. These complete units can be installed directly in the bucks and anchored permanently to them. This means that the bucks must be perfectly squared and accurately sized for the specific model of doors and windows that will be installed. Alternatively, the bucks can be slightly oversized in all directions, and the units can be fitted into place with shim wedges, aligned and secured, and the gaps closed by fitting molding or other trim all around both inside and outside.

In the second instance, the window and door bucks can be built right into the bucks, so that the bucks themselves become the head and side jambs, and sills if required. With doors, this is a matter of hinging the door to one side of the buck and installing the latch hardware on the other, then applying stop molding around the frame. Windows with glass already set in a sash frame are placed in the buck opening against a stop molding and trimmed out with a keeper molding. Or, stop strips and divider strips can be built right into the buck, panes of glass set in place, and keeper moldings applied to hold them. In this case, too, the buck becomes the jamb-and-sill assembly.

of course is stronger. Nominal 2-inch dimension stock or a width equal to the wall thickness works well. Construction-grade material is not the best to use if any part of the buck will be visible and uncovered by trimwork, unless you have some exceptionally good pieces of stock on hand. A clear, kiln-dried pine such as white or ponderosa is preferable in that case. Nail or screw the pieces together solidly and daub the joints with a waterproof glue as you assemble them.

Interior door bucks are used infrequently in most constructions, but may be indicated in log partitions as a matter of convenience. Here again, the thick stock will probably look best, but kiln-dried, high-quality nominal 1-inch stock is also satisfactory. Another possibility for either interior or exterior use is ⁵⁄₄ (five-quarter) stock, which measures an actual 1¼ inches thick and is available in various types of wood.

A buck can be used in either of two ways. First, you can install commercial or otherwise premade windows or prehung doors directly into the buck. Complete commercial window units already are fitted with outer frames as

MAKING DOORS

You can buy doors in infinite variety ranging from cheap hollow-core units to large and elaborate hand-carved types. But you can also build them yourself. There are certain types of exterior doors that are easy to make and lend themselves nicely to installation in a log house. Interior doors can be built in the same fashion, though you might prefer something a little more sophisticated, depending upon your decor. Some of the more complex doors, especially the paneled variety, require a considerable amount of skill, time, and equipment to build in a home shop. If you are a bit short on any of these, you will probably be better off buying instead of building.

Standard thicknesses for doors are 1¾ inches for exterior doors and 1⅜ inches for interior. There are numerous standard opening sizes. The most commonly used heights are 6 feet 8 inches or 7 feet for exterior, and 6 feet 8 inches for interior. Widths are 2 feet (closet); 2 feet 6 inches, 2 feet 8 inches, or 3 feet for interior doors; and 2 feet 8 inches or 3 feet for exterior doors. If you build your own doors and frames or bucks, you can alter this standard sizing to suit yourself. However, you will make life easier for yourself (and any subsequent occupants) by adopting a standard width of no less than 3 feet for all doors (except perhaps closets), whether interior or exterior.

Batten doors are the easiest to build, and can be made in a number of ways. A Z-brace style (Fig. 9-2) is a familiar one that can be used for either interior or exterior doors or storm doors. Nominal 1-inch stock will work, but for heavy, massive doors, 2- × -8 tongue-and-groove, bevel-edge decking planks are better. Cut a series of planks to proper length to match the door opening height and snug them together with pipe clamps. If you wish, you can apply waterproof glue to all the joints. Then screw and glue the Z-brace to the door back, using lengths of high-quality, kiln-dried ¾ or even 2- × -4 or 2- × -6 stock. Leave enough clearance at the outer edges of the Z-brace so that it will clear the door jambs. A similar system uses a double Z-brace, with the three cross-braces spaced down the door and the two diagonals between (Fig. 9-3). As an alternative, you could dado or rout appropriate wide grooves in the door and inlay the Z-braces, perhaps of contrasting-color hardwood.

Another type of plank door is made of three layers of nominal 1-inch tongue and groove stock. The inside and outside layers run vertically, with a middle layer set horizontally (Fig. 9-4). The whole assembly is screwed and glued together and the edges trimmed for a suitable fit. This makes an exceptionally strong door. You can also face the exterior with thin log slabs that have been squared at the edges.

An alternative method of building either style involves making the core or center layer from a piece of exterior-grade ¾-inch plywood. Cut the panel about an inch smaller all around than the door size, and apply a full filler strip of wood that matches the door faces, secured with nails and waterproof glue to protect and hide the plies. The door face planks, one or both sides, can be laid horizontally, vertically, diagonally or double-diagonally, in a single or a double V, herringbone, or whatever other patterns strike your fancy, including inlay and carvings.

Most plank doors can also be made in Dutch style, where the upper half can be opened alone or the entire door can be opened solid, or lights (panes of glass) can be installed in the upper half. Dutch doors are usually made with a rectangular outer frame and an X-brace in the center. A crosslap joint should be used at the center of the X-braces (Fig. 9-6). The horizontal meeting point of the two halves is a simple rabbet lapped down on the exterior side (Fig. 9-7). In cold climates, a deep lap with a carefully fitted length of weatherstripping cuts down drafts.

DOOR HARDWARE

Door hardware is usually composed of two or three hinges and a latch or lockset. In addition, there might be separate lock assemblies, barrel bolt, quadrant latch, and perhaps an automatic door closer or mechanical threshold weatherstripping.

Hinges for plank doors are generally

Fig. 9-2. A Z-brace plank door is easy to build.

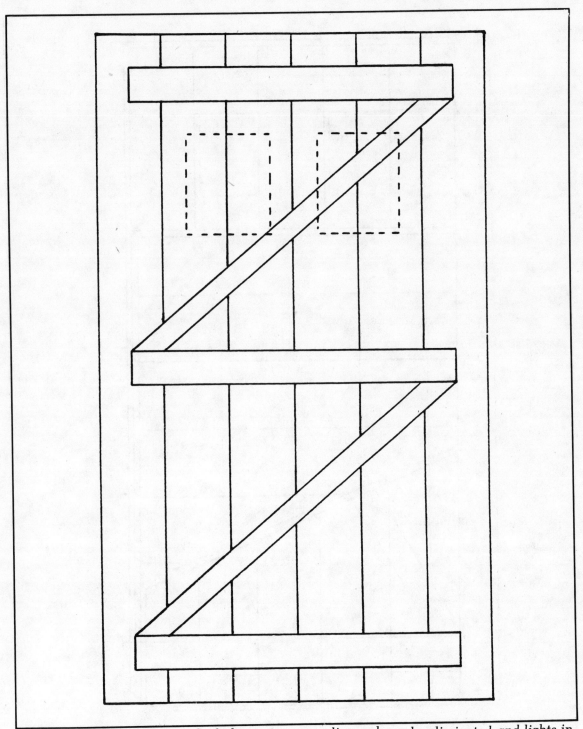

Fig. 9-3. In a double Z-brace plank door, the upper diagonal can be eliminated and lights installed.

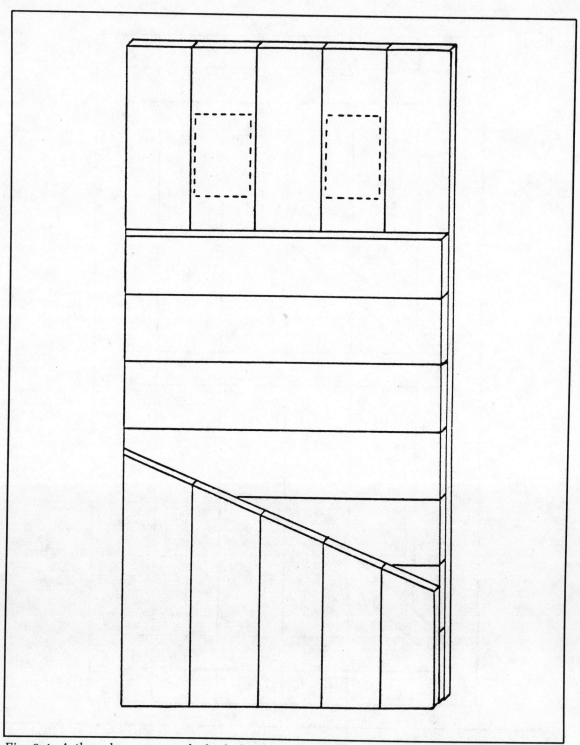

Fig. 9-4. A three-layer or cored plank door can be made with or without lights, as desired.

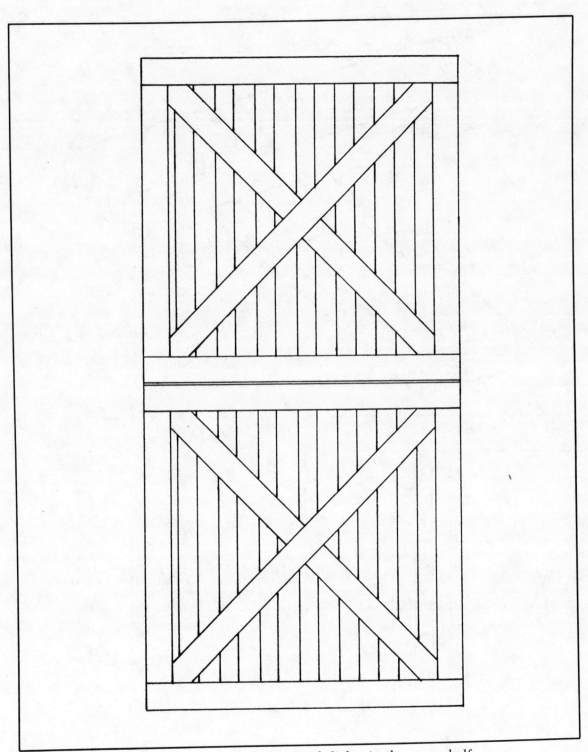

Fig. 9-5. A Dutch door can be made solid, or with lights in the upper half.

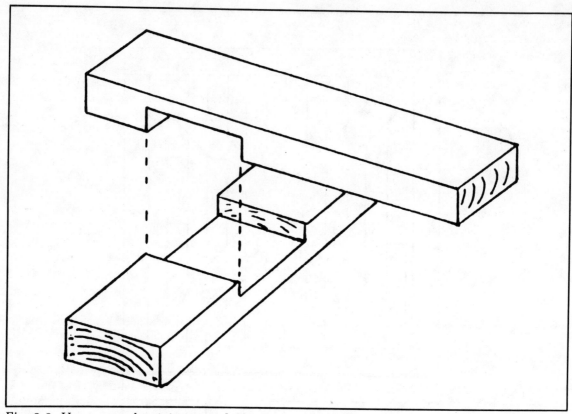

Fig. 9-6. Use a cross-lap joint at each X center in an X-braced door.

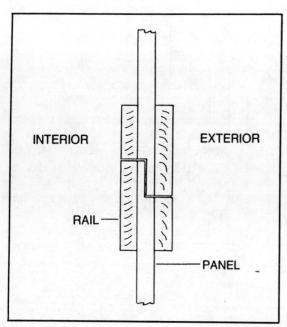

Fig. 9-7. The meeting point of the upper and lower halves of a Dutch door is fashioned in a rabbet joint.

INTERIOR

EXTERIOR

RAIL

PANEL

heavy-duty steel strap or T-hinges. These mount fully upon the surface with long, heavy screws and are attached to the side jamb and to the door face or braces. Many varieties of these hinges are available, either in plated steel or a black antiqued finish. For heavy plank doors, use large hinges of high quality.

Either plank doors or other varieties are more commonly mounted with large, stout butt hinges. Surface-mount butt hinges can be used, but most often they are installed with one leaf mortised into the door edge and the other mortised into the side jamb. The ball-bearing variety is highly recommended for all exterior doors, especially heavy ones. Very heavy doors—particularly if they are of 7-foot height and/or frequently used—are best hung on three hinges rather than the usual pair. Dutch doors must be hung with two pairs.

Latches and locksets are available in incredible profusion and a wide range of prices, combinations, and quality levels. Different types are intended for different door functions, such as exterior, interior, passageway, privacy, closet, and so on. Consult your local hardware supplier for specific details.

Perhaps the most important thing to remember about door hardware, especially locksets, is that the cheap stuff is just that, and the higher-quality and more expensive items are generally the best bet. They will last longer and perform better with minimal wear for many years. Installation varies considerably according to the particular hardware being used. However, most manufacturers supply complete instructions, often including marking templates, that are easy to follow and result in a trouble-free installation.

INSTALLING DOORS

The easiest doors to install are the prehung variety. The door is already completely framed with head and side jambs for interior doors, plus a sill for exterior doors. The hinges are set and aligned, and sometimes the lockset is installed too. All that remains for the installer to do is set the complete assembly into the rough opening or buck, shim and secure it, remove the shipping braces, and apply the trim.

Separate doors are installed by first building the door frame of side and head jambs, with a sill for exterior doors and (usually) none for interior. The frame is then installed in the buck or rough opening. Or, the buck itself sometimes serves as the door frame. The door is trimmed to fit the door frame, allowing proper clearances, and the hinges are attached to the door and then to the side jamb. After checking the door swing for smoothness and proper closing, the lockset is installed, and door stop molding is applied around the head and side jambs. The final step is to apply the trim casing.

In most types of construction the door frame is nailed solidly into the wall opening frame, with shims set in at intervals all around the jambs for proper alignment. However, in log construction this method can lead to trouble. The shrinking and settling of the logs will soon tear things apart, so other methods must be used. The outermost framework of the door, whether that be a buck or a jamb assembly, must be installed with a slip joint. Several installation methods are possible. In all cases, however, there must be a substantial gap between the head jamb and the upper log course to allow for settling. This space may be as much as 6 inches, and if correctly calculated will reduce to no more than a crack after a couple of years.

One common installation method is to provide a wide slot down the centerline of the log ends at both sides of the door opening. This slot should be about 1½ inches wide and 1¾ inches deep. The slots can be cut in the individual logs as the courses are laid up, using a saw and chisel, or can be run freehand with a chainsaw after the walls are erected. However done, it is important that the sides of the slots be square and straight and that they align properly from log to log. A 1½-inch-square strip of wood is nailed to each side jamb of the door frame (Fig. 9-8). The complete frame can be slid into place

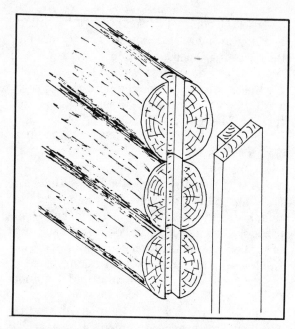

Fig. 9-8. Splined side jambs mate with dados in the log ends to form a slip joint.

into place after the walls have been erected to full door height but before the overhead log has been placed, or the frame can be set and braced and the courses built up around them. The latter system works particularly well where the frame stock is relatively thin, where foam weatherstripping is applied to the side jambs, or where a holding spline must be added to a commercial assembly that does not have provision for this kind of installation.

Another common method is just the reverse of the above, but involves more work and is applicable to frames made from nominal 2-inch stock. Here a dado is cut down the centerline of the side jambs, as deep as half the thickness of the stock. A matching series of tenons is fashioned on the log ends to fit exactly into the jamb grooves (Fig. 9-9).

A third method makes use of a spline. A groove is cut down the centerline of the log ends, with a matching groove cut down the centerline of each side jamb. A barely snug-fitting spline of hardboard or wood is then slipped into the grooves as the door assembly is set (Fig. 9-10).

No nails can be driven through the side jambs and into the logs, with one exception.

If a door frame rests upon a solid foundation, or is notched down into a sill log or beam, the bottom ends of the side jambs can be nailed in place with no ill effects. Interior door frames set in stud walls can be shimmed and nailed in place in the usual way, but if set in log walls they should be installed in the same manner as exterior doors.

Exterior door sills are best not nailed down through the surface because the fasteners will eventually rust and become unsightly, and there is the added possibility of cracking and splitting around the fasteners and subsequent moisture entrance after a time. If there is access from below, however, you might be able to secure thresholds with log wood screws driven up through other framing members from beneath and inside.

Head jambs cannot be secured because there is nothing to attach them to. The door casings or trimwork must be nailed only to the side and head jambs, and not into the log surfaces except at the very bottom, otherwise they will eventually pull away. If there are gaps along the trimwork edges, you can stuff them full of fiberglass or mineral wool insulation. After the major amount of settling has taken

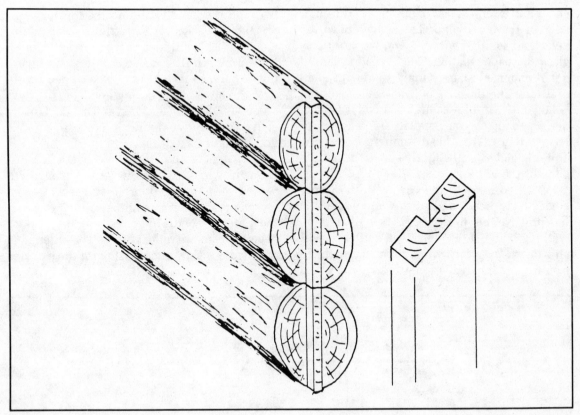

Fig. 9-9. Dadoed side jambs mate with tenoned log ends to form a slip joint in this construction.

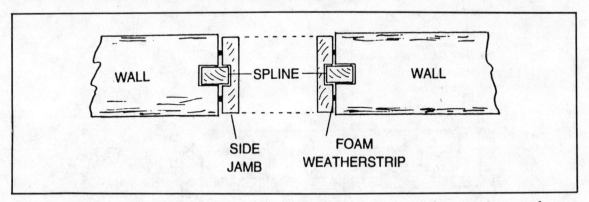

Fig. 9-10. Dadoed side jambs and matching dadoed log ends accept heavy splines to form a slip joint (sectional view from top).

place, seal exterior gaps with an elastic caulking compound.

The gap above the head jamb requires some special attention. In the case of an exterior door, a section of aluminum flashing is nailed into a kerf cut in the log above the jamb. This must be done before the log is set into position, when the job can be done easily. The flashing should be bent outward and downward to form a drip edge, and must be long enough to extend at least slightly past the outer edge of the head jamb. The space above the head jamb is filled with mineral wool or fiberglass thermal insulation. The insulation should not be crammed in, but snugly fitted with a natural loft. The flashing is bent down over the head jamb to minimize draft as much as possible, and a top casing is nailed to the upper interior edge of the head jamb to cover the opening and extend slightly above the bottom edge of the log.

Nail an exterior top casing to the upper edge of the head jamb, fitted up under the flashing. Neither piece should be nailed to the wall log (Fig. 9-11). As the wall settles, it will slip down past the window casing with no trouble, and the insulation will be compressed

between the head jamb and the top log until it is tightly packed. After settling has about finished, it is a good idea to trim off a portion of the aluminum flashing so that it doesn't hang down quite so far. Or, it can be lipped neatly over the edge of the casing and a small wood secondary drip cap attached and caulked in just above the window to aid in both appearance and moisture shedding.

Another method that works out quite satisfactorily where exterior casement trim is installed around the door, involves nailing a secondary header of nominal 1-inch stock to the underside of the log directly above the door head jamb and parallel with it. The outer edge of this piece should be flush with the extreme outer surface of the log. The space left between

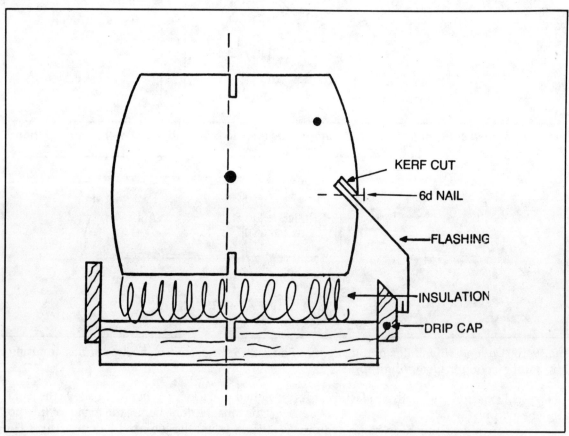

Fig. 9-11. One method of providing a flashed head space above doors and windows. (Courtesy of Vermont Log Buildings, Inc., part of Real Log Homes® .)

the log and the door head jamb is filled with insulation. The side pieces of the exterior door casing are nailed to the door frame only, not to the logs. The top door casing piece is nailed to the door head jamb (Fig. 9-12). If the door is exposed directly to the weather, a piece of flashing or a wood drip shield can be attached to the log above, keeping clearance for settling.

The installation of the door itself into its frame is not a difficult job, but does require patience and careful fitting. First, of course, the frame or jamb set has to be installed with both side jambs perfectly plumb and straight, and the head jamb perfectly level across the top. The corners must be squared to 90 degrees. Once that is done, install the trim casing on both sides of the frame. Trim the door to the size of the opening, less a clearance allowance of $\frac{1}{16}$ to $\frac{3}{32}$ inch on the lockset or latch side, $\frac{1}{32}$ to $\frac{1}{16}$ inch on the hinge side, and $\frac{1}{16}$ to $\frac{3}{32}$ inch at the top. The bottom clearance depends upon what the finish flooring will be and whether or not a threshold or weatherstripping will be installed. Exterior doors are usually trimmed to fit as closely as possible, while interior doors might clear the floor by a half inch or more.

Where butt hinges are used, they can be installed next, on the door edge. Most butt hinges can be taken apart into two halves or leaves, so the single leaves can be mounted with the barrels headed to the inside face of the door. The top hinge is usually mounted about 7 inches down from the top of the door, and the lower hinge 11 inches up from the bottom. If a third hinge is used, it is placed midway between the other two. Mortise the hinge leaf into the door edge so that the surfaces are flush, drill pilot holes, and drive the screws. Make sure that the screws are centered exactly in the hinge leaf screw holes and that the screws drive down perfectly straight. Otherwise, the hinge leaf will cock off in one direction or another by the force of the screw.

The door portion of the lockset assembly can also be installed now. Follow the manufac-turer's instructions. Standard knob height is generally considered as 38 inches above the floor, but this can be varied; logical positioning might be determined by the design of the door. Separate locks or latches are usually located a few inches below the knob, occasionally above.

The next step is to mount the remaining hinge leaves to the side jamb, exactly matched to those on the door edge. Mortise and mount them the same way as on the door, keeping the centerline of the hinges exactly lined up with the edge of the jamb. Any misalignment will result in problems like rapidly wearing hinge pins, warped doors, mounting screws pulling loose, or a binding door. Remember the top clearance, too, and set these hinge leaves to allow for it. Then the door can be hung by mating the hinge barrel segments and slipping the pins in place. Complete the lockset or latch installation by mounting the striker plate on the latch-side jamb. If all of your measurements have been correct, the door should swing freely and be well aligned within the jambs. If not, however, you will have to do a bit of trimming with a plane or some finagling with the hinge positions.

Once the door is set and aligned, the last step is to install door stop molding up both side jambs and across the head jamb. This molding prevents the door from trying to swing back through the opening. Fit the molding with miter joints at the corners, and nail it up with 1½-inch brads or 3d finish nails. The squared edge of the stop should come just shy of touching the door surface when the door is in its correct closed position, and should not interfere with the closing action.

If surface-mounted hinges are used, the situation is a bit different. Here it is easiest to install the stop molding first. It is set back from the inside edge of the door jambs, and equal to the thickness of the door plus about $\frac{1}{64}$ inch for clearance. Trim the door to fit the opening, including the operating clearances, and install the latch or lockset. Prop the door in the open-

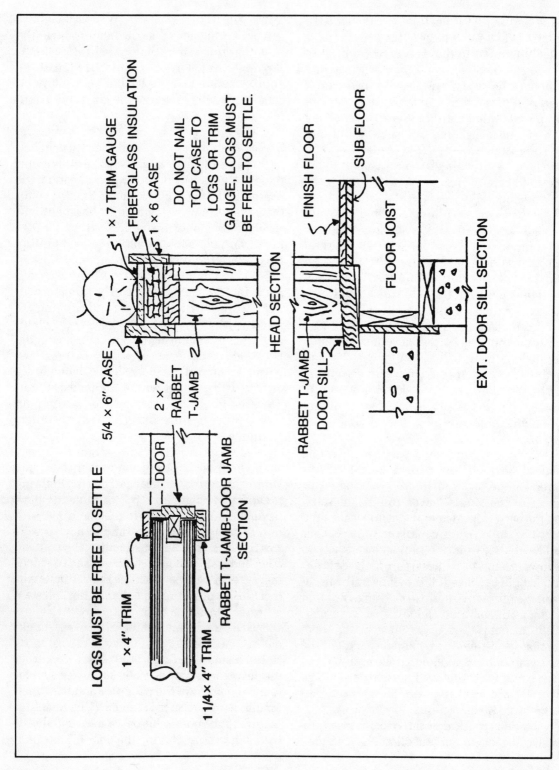

LOGS MUST BE FREE TO SETTLE

1 × 4" TRIM

1 1/4 × 4" TRIM

RABBET T-JAMB-DOOR JAMB SECTION

.DOOR

2 × 7 RABBET T-JAMB

5/4 × 6" CASE

1 × 7 TRIM GAUGE

FIBERGLASS INSULATION

1 × 6 CASE

DO NOT NAIL TOP CASE TO LOGS OR TRIM GAUGE, LOGS MUST BE FREE TO SETTLE.

HEAD SECTION

RABBET T-JAMB

DOOR SILL

FINISH FLOOR

SUB FLOOR

FLOOR JOIST

EXT. DOOR SILL SECTION

Fig. 9-12. This method of installing exterior doors provides head space and slip joints. (Courtesy of Building Logs, Inc.)

ing. It is held up off the floor with blocks and wedged in place along the sides and tops with thin shims. Position the hinges, drill pilot holes as necessary—exactly centered through the hinge mounting holes, and drive the screws home. When the shims and block are removed the door should fit and swing true, and you can complete the latch or lockset installation.

Note that some carpenters prefer to only tack the door stop molding in place so that it can easily be adjusted for clearance after the door is hung; others put a few strips of thin cardboard or doubled-over paper between the door and the stop molding to "build in" the operating clearance. This clearance between door and stop is especially important if the woodwork will later receive two or three coats of paint or varnish.

WINDOW CHOICES

The decisions you have to make in selecting windows will seem to be endless. First there is the style. One common choice for log houses is the double-hung style, where the bottom half slides upward to open and the top half slides downward. Each half of the sash can have anywhere from 1 to 12 individual panes of glass in it. Also popular is the casement style, which swings outward to open, either to the right or left. Most of these are fitted with one light. Awning windows, which swing outward and upward to open, and hopper windows, which swing outward and downward, are also widely used, usually as part of a larger combination window unit that might include fixed lights as well. Then there are the sliding windows, where one or more of the sashes slides to left or right; these are often fitted with one fixed and one movable sash. And, of course, there are fixed-light units that do not open, and various combinations of fixed and openable sash in the same unit. In addition, many commercial units are stackable, so that they can be joined to make up various combinations.

No one type is necessarily better than another, and each has advantages and disadvantages. The fixed type is the most weatherproof and easiest to seal, but of course can't be opened. The double-hung and sliding windows are hard to seal off and most prone to air infiltration, but take up no extra room when they are opened. The awning and hopper types will seal well, but sometimes have to be positioned so that when they are open they don't become a hazard for someone walking by on a deck, for instance. The hopper window will collect rain if inadvertently left open, the awning type won't. Casement windows seal well, but when open can direct a gale of wind and dust into the house. What this all comes down to is that you have to weigh the factors, then make your own choice according to what seems best for your own particular installation needs.

Framing material must be considered, too. Standard wood framing is probably still the most popular. Though somewhat prone to warping and requiring periodic maintenance, the frames are thermally efficient. They can be given a natural finish that complements log construction very well, or they can be stained or painted.

Vinyl-clad wood frames have become very popular over the past few years. This system keeps the thermal efficiency of wood while requiring no maintenance. However, the color choice is limited to brown or white, and the vinyl cannot be successfully painted or stained. Also, some vinyls might crack after a few years of weathering and baking in the hot sun. Solid vinyl is being used more these days, and it has good thermal efficiency and stability. Metal frames—mostly aluminum for residential applications—are another possibility. They are long-lived but not necessarily thermally efficient, depending upon how they are made. Some types, in fact, can freeze tightly shut (or open) in cold weather. And many people do not care for the thin, narrow sash lines and the lack of wide trim that many models have. Again, your choice must be made by weighing the pros and cons as they affect your own building situation.

Consideration must also be given to the energy efficiency of the window units. This is something that was of little concern just a few years ago; not even the manufacturers paid much attention to it. Today, that has changed. The energy efficiency of window units is comprised of two basic elements: air infiltration rates, and radiation/conduction losses. The first has to do with how well the window frame and sash is constructed and weatherstripped, and how much air can seep in (or out) through the cracks and joints. The second depends upon the thickness and type of glazing materials used in the sash, and is intentionally varied to suit different purposes and conditions. The major window manufacturers now test their products and rate them for both factors. Thus, you an compare different brands, styles, and constructions of windows according to the manufacturers' test results, weigh them against the other factors involved—such as style, size, cost, and appearance—and select the ones most suitable for your needs.

Then there is the all-important glazing to consider. Glass will most likely be your general choice, because plastics are seldom suitable for residential purposes. But what kind? There is plain window glass in single- or double-strength weights, or heavy sheet glass, the thickest of which is $7/32$ inch. Many windows are glazed with this material. You can also opt for regular float (plate) glass, or heavy float glass, ranging from $3/32$ inch thick to $7/8$ inch thick; the $1/4$-inch regular float glass is a common choice for big windows. There are various kinds of tinted or coated glass products that work to admit light but keep out radiant energy, or are reflective, or act almost as one-way mirrors. There is low-iron glass, which lets both light and solar heat in, and keeps it there. Some glazings, such as patio doors, must be safety glass. Another kind of safety glass, more like the kind your automobile windshield is made of, is now available for residential glazing. This security glass a burglar would find virtually impossible to smash in order to gain entrance. And there are various kinds of frosted, opalescent, patterned, and decorative glasses that have their uses, too.

Each of these different glasses, and there are many within each category, has its different properties. There are various colors and tints, to begin with. The closer to water-clear and the thinner the glass, the greater the amount of available light will be transmitted through it. Window glass $1/8$ inch thick, for example, has a light transmission factor of 91 percent, while that factor for $1/4$-inch float glass is 88 percent, and for $1/4$-inch gray tinted float glass only 42 percent. The percentages of solar transmission likewise vary with different kinds of glass.

To make all this more interesting, windows can be obtained with single, double, or triple layers of glazing. The space between the glazing might be air, or gas, or under vacuum, or not. The layers of glazing can be of different types and thicknesses, which leads to all sorts of combinations, and which changes all the window characteristics. But it also means that you can "engineer" your windows to suit practically any imaginable situation. The way to do this is to gather up several manufacturer's catalogs to see just what is offered, study the characteristics of the units, find out what special-order items might be available, and then tailor your selection to your needs. Above all, try to install the most energy-efficient units you can if you are building in a hot or cold climate, because the extra cost will be made up many times over in comfort, lack of problems, and fuel costs.

MAKING WINDOWS

There is no question that outfitting an entire house, especially a big one, with factory-made window units is an expensive proposition. On the other hand, making openable windows is often a difficult chore for a do-it-yourselfer, requiring experience in woodworking and a very well-equipped shop, plus lots of time. There are many kinds of windows that can really only be made in a factory, using specialized equipment as well as materials not readily available to the ordinary consumer.

There are times, however, when making one's own windows does make sense, and there are certain possibilities well within the capabilities of a do-it-yourselfer. Fixed windows can be made without much trouble, as can some openable windows. In locales where the winter weather is not very severe, or in cabins or camps that see only occasional or seasonal use, such installations serve well and are not costly. And one added benefit is that you can build windows in shapes and sizes that are not commercially available.

A single light (Fig. 9-13) can be installed as follows. First install a slip-jointed buck or frame in the rough opening, plumb on both sides, and level across top and bottom, and squared at the corners. Next, fit a rim of stop molding all around the inside of the frame at whatever distance from the front or back of the frame you want the glazing to be; this will be the exterior molding. If you want a deep-set window effect when viewed from the outside, put the molding close to the inside edge of the frame. For broad interior windowsills to hold plants or knick-knacks, place the molding close to the outside edge. The molding can be a standard pattern of your choice, a custom shape, or just squared sticks ripped out on the table saw. Mitered corners look nice, but aren't really essential; the bottom piece must be cut at an angle to match that of the window frame sill (which should slope out and down). Install these pieces with waterproof glue and finish nails. If you choose not to use glue, a thin layer of construction adhesive will work, or you can run a small bead of caulk around the outside joint.

Have a piece of glass cut just slightly smaller than the frame opening. There are several kinds of glass that could be used, such as ordinary single- or double-strength window glass (the cheapest), float glass, or tinted glass.

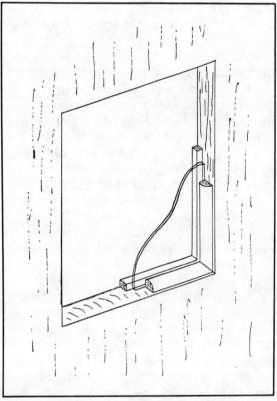

Fig. 9-13. A simple method of building a window unit with stop and trim molding set into a door or a framed opening in a wall. The glass can be caulked or glazed into place and can also be doubled, depending upon local weather conditions.

Discuss the installation with your glass supplier and follow his recommendations for which glass would work best. Your supplier might also be able to fix you up with some used float glass, which is often available as salvage from broken store-front windows.

Run a bead of glazing caulk around the inside of the stop molding and press the glass into place evenly against the molding, using sufficient pressure to flatten the caulk bead into a fairly thick film seal. Finish the job off by applying a second rim of stop molding around the inside of the glass, nailed to the window frame and also caulked in place. Don't use glue on the interior molding, because it might have to be removed at some future time for glass replacement.

A multiple-light window unit is installed in the same way, except that divider strips are built into the frame first. These strips may be the same width as the outside frame, or thinner if you wish, so long as they are sturdy enough to give plenty of support to the glazing. The divider strips can be individually installed inside the frame, or built up as a subassembly—like a grid—and then set into the frame. The latter course is sometimes easier, but much depends upon the window design and size. The individual lights are then set against stop moldings as previously discussed.

Making your own openable windows means going back to some of the arrangements that were commonly seen in houses several decades ago. By far the easiest starting point is commercial window sash units, using just the sash and glass, not a whole assembly. These can be new units that are sold by numerous manufacturers as replacement parts, or new fixed-light units without the outer frames, but a common choice is the sash from old window units that have been taken out. These are often available at building wrecking yards, second-hand shops, and auctions. Another possibility is discarded wood-frame storm windows. The key is to find sash units of a size and configuration that suits your needs and that are well made, with sturdy wood components. You can also make your own sash by assembling a frame of ¾, ⁴⁄₄, or ⁵⁄₄ stock—depending on window size—with splined and mitered corners, and inset with a sheet of glass.

Once you have the sash dimensions, then you can build bucks to suit them. There should be enough clearance on all sides to allow the window to operate; the exact amount depends on the thickness of the sash, the direction of swing, and the kind of hardware and weatherstripping used. A stop molding must be built into the buck—to the outside of the sash position for inswinging sash and to the inside of the sash position for outswinging sash (the most common arrangement).

Once the buck is installed in the rough opening in the wall, the next chore is to hinge the sash to the buck. You can set the hinges on either side, to swing the sash either in or out to right or left; at the top to swing the sash out awning-style; or at the bottom to swing the sash either in or out hopper-style. The choice is yours. Ordinary butt-type utility hinges, which are available in a range of sizes and several styles, work fine; mortise them in for a snug-fitting sash. In some instances, surface-mount hinges could be appropriate. On larger windows, full-length strips of piano hinge might be in order.

Add a knob or a small drawer pull to the window sash to operate it with, and one or two latch assemblies to keep the sash pulled tight against the stop when it is closed. Then you will have to devise some means of keeping the window in place when it is open. This depends largely on your ingenuity and what you might be able to find in the way of hardware in your area. The time-tested old arrangement for hopper windows is to attach a length of bead or small-link chain to the sash and the side jamb; the window can be let down to various positions by catching the chain on a small hook. Traditionally, awning windows were simply propped open with sticks. However, both awning and side-swinging windows can be fitted with locking supports, much like card table leg braces (which also could be used), and it is also possible to purchase replacement-type window-crank and slide-rod hardware. These items can be adapted to about any kind of window, but a better idea is to build up the window unit to suit the hardware requirements if possible, because trying to graft in the hardware after the window is all put together can lead to difficulties.

INSTALLING WINDOWS

As mentioned earlier, installing commercially

made window units in bucks is merely a matter of slipping them into place in the bucks and securing and sealing them. Some of the vinyl-clad window units are made with mounting flanges that are designed to be nailed directly to the outside surface of the walls. This will only work where the flanges can be nailed to the bucks and not to the log walls, and where exterior window casing trim can be installed to hide the flanges. A fixed or movable sash that is built up on the job site is handled as previously discussed.

In no case, however, should the side jambs of either bucks or commercial window units be anchored directly to the wall logs. The situation here is exactly the same as for door installations. Some sort of slip joint must be provided to allow for wall settling. The methods discussed earlier for doors work equally well for windows, the only difference being in the angle of the sill. The sill itself can be fastened to the log upon which it rests, the side jambs are fitted with a slip joint, and an appropriate gap is left above the head jamb. The frames of commercial window units installed directly into an opening in the logs and not into a previously fitted buck will probably have to be modified with slip rails, dados, or spline grooves on the side jambs. Caulk all seams and joints wherever possible or install foam or other weatherstripping, but in such a way as not to interfere with the slip joints. After two or three years when the settling is finally done, permanent caulking can be applied.

STORM SASHES AND DOORS

In areas where winter weather is severe, the addition of storm sash and doors helps to keep down heating costs and also reduces drafts. Various kinds of storm doors can be made in much the same way as the plank doors discussed earlier. They can be made of heavy planking, but usually are built from nominal 1-inch, tongue-and-groove stock. An alternative is to buy commercial storm doors that are either prehung or not, made of wood, alumi-

num, or steel, either single-purpose or combination storm/screen types. These doors are easy to install and are available in numerous styles for all standard door size openings. The prehung variety, however, should be attached only along the sides to the exterior door frame or casing, and not to the logs or anything that might settle. Allowance must be made for the slip joint arrangement.

The storm sash situation can be handled in any of several ways. Some homeowners prefer to install permanent double glazing, or in areas of severe winter weather, permanent triple glazing. Houses designed for solar heating often use special glazing units that are not fitted with storm sash. However, separate storm sash can be fitted over any type of window, regardless of its glazing components.

Window manufacturers usually offer separate storm sash sized exactly to their own units. Separate storm sash can also be bought for standard sizes of double-hung windows, and in the metropolitan areas there are companies that will manufacture storm windows for nearly any applications. You can also build your own units, using either wood frames and glass, or purchase any of the several kit-type options currently on the market that employ aluminum rail frames and either plastic or glass for glazing.

Though most storm sash is mounted on the exterior of the window units, some is designed to fit on the inside. Either position works equally well, provided the sash fits snugly and is well weatherstripped and sealed to reduce air infiltration.

The usual criteria for deciding whether or not to install storm sash is the cost/benefit comparison, or payout period. By calculating the heat loss through the windows themselves, then recalculating the heat loss through the same windows fitted with storm sash, you can determine how much of a reduction in heat loss can be achieved. This can then be translated into the approximate dollar savings in heating cost for an average heating season effected by the addition of storm sash. This figure divided into the total cost of the storm window installation will tell you how many years it will take to recover the cost of the windows in heating savings. From a strictly economic standpoint, sometimes the installation is worthwhile, sometimes not. Other considerations include the work involved in taking the sash down in the spring and putting it up again every fall, extra glass to keep clean, and storage for the units when not in use. Among the benefits are increased comfort because of less air infiltration, and reduction or perhaps elimination of condensation and frost on the windows. When making your initial window choices, it is good to balance these considerations against the possibilities of installing double instead of single glazing, or triple instead of double.

Insulation

10

Not many houses are built these days without at least some thermal insulation. Insulation serves to cut down heat loss during the cold winter days, and reduces heat gain during the long hot summer months. In fact, an ever-increasing number of local building codes require that new houses meet certain insulating or heat loss standards appropriate to the area. There is a side benefit to fully insulating a house, too: it cuts down noise and sound transmission.

Log houses have a special attribute, in that a certain amount of insulating value is built into the house by virtue of the materials used. This is true of any structure, but with log houses the effect is both greater and different. Thermal efficiency is sometimes touted as a selling point for log houses, and it is a valid one if not overdone. Remember, though, that this thermal insulating value applies only to the log walls of the building. All other parts of the house must be insulated in pretty much

the same way as a conventional platform-framed house, and that leaves quite a lot of insulating to be done. Another point is that the insulating value of the log walls themselves depends upon the species of wood, the moisture content of the wood, the excellence of the joint seals, the ambient temperature, and the thickness of the logs. Thermally speaking, not all log walls are created equal, by any means.

HEAT LOSS AND GAIN

Except for a few unusual periods of total temperature balance, a house is always either giving up or gaining heat. When the outside temperature is lower than the inside, the house turns into a huge radiator and loses heat to the outdoors, which must be continually replaced by internal heat generation. When the outside temperature is higher than the inside, and/or solar impact upon the structure is substantial enough, the interior of the building will gain heat, which must then be reduced by mechanical means if the temperature becomes uncomfortable.

The total heat loss of a house is measured in Btu's (British thermal unit, a unit of heat) per hour, or Btuh. It is calculated upon the basis of a certain inside temperature and a certain maximum average low outside temperature. This total indicates the capacity that the internal heating plant must have in Btuh to replace the lost heat and maintain a comfortable inside temperature. Similarly, total heat gain of a house is calculated to determine the total cooling capacity needed to maintain a given reasonable inside comfort level. Either figure can then be further calculated by means of local weather conditions to determine requirements and costs for a full average heating/cooling system.

Heat loss or heat gain is calculated by means of some formulas you can work out yourself with the aid of a heating/cooling guide. Or, you can have the job done by your heating contractor or fuel supplier.

Heat losses are figured by determining individual losses through each different kind of construction in the house, and then adding them all up. Transmission heat losses take place through ceilings or roofs, walls, windows, doors, and cold floors. Infiltration heat losses take place through normal cyclical air change within the structure; construction feature losses occur because of fireplaces, exhaust fans, or outside doors. All these losses differ according to just what kinds of materials are used and just how they are put together during construction. They are calculated on a basis of average factors determined through testing, observation, and years of practical heating experience. The actual base numbers are taken from tables compiled for the purpose.

Heat gains are estimated in much the same way but include moisture or latent heat loads, sun loads through both transparent and opaque building sections, and the presence or absence of internal sources of heat.

Obviously, then, these are the areas that must be addressed in order to minimize the heating/cooling loads. Proper insulating plays the most important part. To a lesser degree, correct caulking and sealing is important, as are proper construction practices, building siting, weather protection, sun blocking, vapor barriers, and care in keeping doors and windows closed or in providing sufficient ventilation.

HOW MUCH INSULATION?

In theory you can't have too much insulation. In practice, however, there is a point of diminishing returns beyond which added insulation is pointless. But to begin with, a house must have as much insulation as necessary to comply with local building codes. This is often expressed in terms of a thermal insulating value for a given section of the structure. For instance, one combination is to require a value of R-11 (equivalent to approximately 3½ inches of fiberglass thermal insulation) in cold floors (unheated from below), R-11 in the walls, and R-22 (approximately 6½ inches of fiberglass thermal insulation) in the ceilings or roofs. Some authorities consider the overall heat loss of a building rather than that of the several different sections. This means that the value in some areas can be beefed up in compensation for other areas, which for some reason cannot be sufficiently insulated to come up to a section standard. Whatever the situation, as long as you meet the local standards that is all that is required of you.

On the other hand, you might decide that you need more insulation than is required, in order to reduce operating costs for heating/cooling to a level that you can more easily afford, or to be more comfortable, or in order not to be wasteful. In theory, the more heavily a house is insulated the lower those costs will be. But actually, there is a cutoff point for any given house in any given location beyond which an added amount of insulation effectively neither increases comfort nor lowers operating costs, but merely increases construction costs.

The only way to discover this point is by making a series of calculations for total heat loss or gain of the structure with various combinations of insulation thicknesses, types, and costs as installed. For instance, you might choose fiberglass insulation as the type you want, and calculate the heat loss on the basis of 3½ inches in the floor and the ceiling or roof, with the log walls figured according to their own insulating value. Then make a new set of calculations based upon 6 inches of fiberglass in the roof or ceiling, and another with 12 inches, and perhaps another with thermal insulating glass instead of single glazing in the windows, one with a built-up roof incorporating rigid foam insulation, and so on. Somewhere along the line you will discover a combination of materials, installation costs, and operating costs that appears to be particularly reasonable. That point will probably be quite a bit short of the actual point of completely diminished returns.

If there are no local code requirements for insulation, you must plot your own course. You can be guided to some extent by whatever local practices are undertaken by builders in your area, but don't take this information for gospel. The insulation and the way it is installed might be right for one house but not be for another. Find out what materials are readily available to you, their costs, and their insulating values. Begin at square one and determine the basic heat loss figures for your house, then make the calculations to see what insulating arrangements might best suit your needs, and go with them.

FOUNDATION INSULATION

Under certain circumstances it is desirable to insulate around foundations. This is the case where a poured concrete slab floor is involved. This might be a slab-on-grade foundation where the slab is also the first living level. Here the perimeter insulation is installed in either of two ways. The materials most often employed are rigid sheets of expanded polystyrene or expanded polyurethane, and the minimum recommended insulating value is R-5. The rigid material is cemented with mastic to the inside of the stem wall above the footing, all around the perimeter of the foundation and extending downward from 12 to 24 inches. The concrete slab is poured on top of a vapor barrier. Alternatively, a narrow band of insulation is glued around the stem wall extending downward the full depth of the slab, and another series of sheets is laid upon a vapor barrier extending back underneath the slab to a distance of about 2 feet. The slab is then poured on top of the insulation. If desired, the rigid insulation panels can cover the entire floor area beneath the slab. (Refer to Figs. 4-27 and 4-28).

Much the same system is sometimes used where the slab floor of a full basement needs to be insulated. Here too, the rigid insulation can be installed in any of the ways described above. If the area is designed for living quarters, further insulating must be done to the basement walls. Poured concrete walls must be furred out with strips of wood nailed directly to the concrete. Insulation is then placed between the strips and a wall covering applied to the furring strips (Fig. 10-1). Sheets of rigid insulation are often used, glued right to the walls. If the furring strips are of sufficient thickness, roll or batt insulation can be stapled to them.

If the walls are made of concrete block, exactly the same system can be used, and if the blocks are hollow-core the insulation can be supplemented by pouring the cores full of a loose-fill insulation such as rock wool, vermiculite, or even sawdust. In certain applications a reflective insulation of accordian-folded aluminum foil insulation fixed between the furring strips might have sufficient insulating value to fulfill the requirements. Another method is to insulate the exterior of the foundation walls with sheets of rigid insulating board glued to the surface and extending from

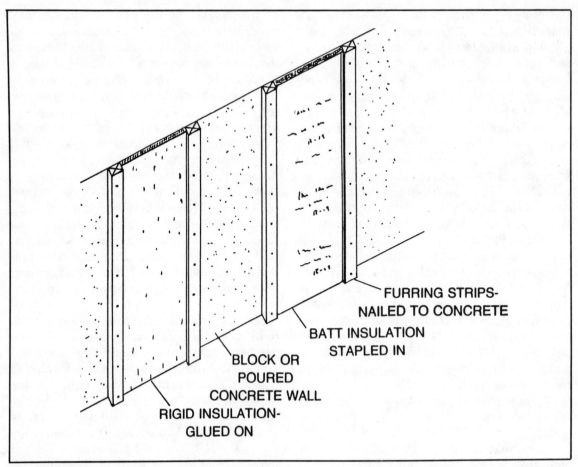

Fig. 10-1. You can insulate a masonry basement by furring out and filling the spaces with blanket or rigid insulation.

the foundation top to below frost line. The above-grade portion of the insulation can be protected with a special material made for the purpose.

A PWF system where the walls are made entirely of wood is insulated just as any other stud wall: by stapling up roll or batt insulation, blowing loose-fill insulation into the voids after the studs are covered, or by facing the studs with rigid insulation such as polyisocyanurate and then covering with plasterboard.

COLD-FLOOR INSULATION

Cold floors are those found over an unheated area such as a crawl space or garage, or over any area that is regularly heated to a lower temperature, up to within a 10-degree differential. Floors over separately heated sections that are heated to a higher temperature are best treated as ceilings, and will be discussed later. The minimum R-value for all those categories is usually considered as R-11, except that floors over open-foundation crawl spaces are best insulated to a minimum R-19. Floors separating areas that will be heated to approximately the same temperatures, plus or minus about 10 degrees, need no insulation at all unless desired for sound-damping purposes, nor should they have vapor barriers.

The usual choice for floor insulation is roll or batt in either fiberglass or mineral wool, which is available in several standard widths, thicknesses and R-values. It can also be had with foil facing, kraft paper facing, or no facing at all. This material is either stuffed or stapled into the spaces between the joists, according to the manufacturer's directions (Fig. 10-2). The facing includes the attachment flanges, and also acts as a vapor barrier. It must be placed closest to the heated area.

In many cases the insulation must be installed face-up from below, after the subfloor is laid and the building is weathertight, so there is no way to staple it in place. This means that some sort of mechanical restraint is needed to keep the material from eventually slipping down. Short pieces of wood or spring-wire (you can buy the latter for just this purpose) jammed between the joists will do the job, and so will strapping or lath nailed at intervals across the joist bottoms. Chicken wire can also be stretched out and stapled into place across the joist bottoms.

There are other insulating materials and methods that can be used, either alone or in combination with roll or batt insulation. For instance, heavy wall-to-wall carpeting installed over a thick fibrous pad has a substantial insulating value. Insulating board or low-density particleboard used as floor underlayment or subsheathing provides some degree of thermal insulation. Rigid sheet insulation can also be laid on subfloor and covered with a rigid underlayment or finish flooring, for a considerable thermal insulating value. Wood sheathing or finish flooring itself can be considered to have a value of approximately R-1 per inch of thickness.

WALL INSULATION

The thermal insulating value of R-value of log walls is built in automatically when the walls are laid up. It is part of the logs themselves. Just what that value is, assuming that the construction is tight and properly done, can be approximated by first finding the average thickness of the wall and then multiplying by the R-value for that particular species of wood. A 6-inch Northern white cedar wall, for example, would have an R-value of 8.46, which in many locales would be sufficient in itself. A 6-inch tamarack wall would have an R-value of about 5.58, still adequate in a few areas. But as a rule of thumb, you can figure that wood in general will run to a value of about R-1 per inch of thickness provided it is well dried.

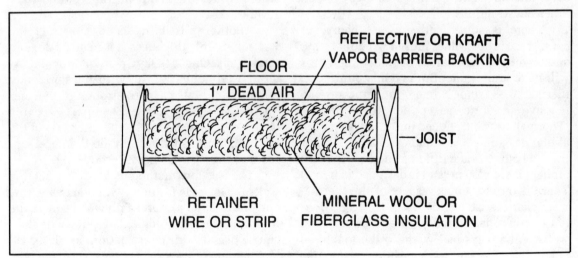

Fig. 10-2. One way to install blanket insulation in a floor frame.

Only a few of the hardwoods fall much below 0.80.

Scratch-built wall sections is made from locally felled logs could be expected to be as thin as about 4 inches on average, running in some cases to as much as 14 inches or better. This would result in thermal insulating values from R-4 well up into the teens. The latter, however, would be an exception. So in some instances—depending upon the local climatic conditions—further insulating of the log walls is not necessary. In many other instances, it is.

At this point, there is a myth that should be dispelled. You might have heard some claims that the thermal mass characteristics of log houses actually make them warmer without wall insulation than frame houses with insulation. Not so. Thermal mass performance is a very complex subject, one still being studied at length. Much simplified, it revolves around the fact that solids can absorb heat from warmer surroundings over a period of time, then release it to cooler surroundings over a period of time. Different materials do so at various rates and have varying capacities. The contention is that log walls are thick and massive, and so can absorb heat from the sun and other sources during the warm day, then release the heat slowly through the cool nights, helping to maintain even interior heating using less energy than other constructions.

There is some truth to the theory, of course; the process does indeed work that way, and in mild-climate areas of the country this will have some value. But in cold country the thermal mass factor is insignificant, even in a massive structure, as applied to log walls. (Thermal mass introduced purposely as part of a solar design—rocks, concrete, water, steel or iron, whatever—is a different matter; the factor here is significant, and is designed to be so.) There is one beneficial aspect of the thermal mass characteristic of log walls: the wood does not conduct heat rapidly. The interior of log walls will always feel warm to the touch, so you will not feel chilly when sitting next to one

(assuming a reasonably warm ambient interior temperature and a well-built wall), even on the coldest of days.

If the average R-value of a given log wall construction equals or exceeds local building code or weather condition requirements, all well and good. However, there are plenty of areas of severe winter weather where R-11 is marginal, even insufficient, in wall sections. Some building codes require that wall sections meet an R-19 average value, impossible to achieve in the traditional single-thickness log wall section in a scratch-built house. In a few areas even R-19 is not really enough. What then?

There are several possibilities. One is to make the wall sections as thick as possible using wood with the highest thermal insulating value that is available. Other parts of the house where thermal insulating materials must be installed anyway can be insulated extra heavily to achieve a very high R-value at those points. With sufficient added insulation the total heat loss of the structure can be brought into line with the local conditions or requirements. This only works, however, where local authorities recognize the "total heat loss" concept and allow compensating insulation in various sections or portions of the building, or where winter weather conditions are not very severe.

Another possibility is to construct the walls in double thickness. This can be done in three ways. One is to lay up an interior and exterior wall concurrently, with the horizontal joints of one wall staggered from the other and the logs set tight together. The thickness of the logs can be determined by the thickness of the wall section needed to provide the necessary R-value for that species of wood.

The second method is to construct the walls in stockade fashion, with one inside row and one outside row and a plywood core in the middle. Either split logs, flatted logs, or slabs can be used in this construction, as discussed in Chapter 6.

The third method involves constructing two separate walls of relatively thin stock, an inner and an outer. The logs are fully locked together in both sections, which in turn locks the sections together and closes off the wall ends. A space of whatever width is desired is left between the wall sections. This space can be left empty, and the dead air will provide a thermal insulating value of approximately R-1, regardless of the air space width. In most cases, however, the space should be filled with roll or batt fiberglass, or one of the various loose-fill insulations. With the right combination of materials, this system can result in a wall-section thermal insulation value of R-30 or even more.

With another method, the exterior of the structure has the appearance of log construction but the interior does not, though this cannot really be called a true log house. The method can be used to provide virtually any needed wall-section R-value, with the thickness of the wall section and the insulants varied to meet the requirements. The walls are essentially nothing more than standard platform-framed stud walls, put together in the usual manner with 2 × 6s or whatever is needed. Thermal insulation is installed between the studs and an interior wall covering applied in the conventional manner. The exterior is sheathed with plywood or boards and then covered with either vertical or horizontal edge-matched log slabs (refer to Fig. 6-38).

The inside surfaces of the log walls constructed of full logs, whether flatted or not, can also be further insulated. This involves building stud walls all around the interior perimeter of the house—2 × 4s are usually sufficient—and installing roll or batt insulation between the studs. The studs are then covered with an interior finish in the usual way. The stud wall sections are actually only furring strips, but the problem is that an ordinary furring job cannot be done because the strips cannot be attached solidly to the logs walls because of the settling problem. Stud-wall frames, how-ever, can be anchored at the bottom and fitted with slip joints at the top to make what might be called a semi-freestanding wall (Fig. 10-3). Problems might also be encountered at window and door openings where separate inside and outside frames, casing, and trim must be arranged so that they can slide past one another during the settling process.

In this case, though the end result of a high R-value can be achieved, it is at the expense of a considerable amount of labor and the elimination of the interior log-construction aspects. There is a possibility, though, of using the compensating-sections theory to arrive at a satisfactorily low total heat loss figure. Two or three rooms, such as the kitchen and a couple of bedrooms and baths, for instance, might be fully insulated with additional interior stud walls, while some other rooms like the dining

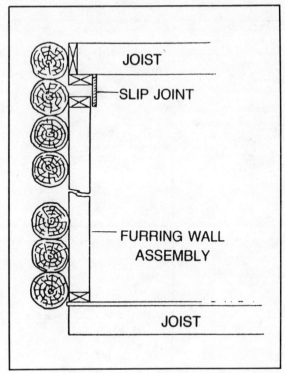

Fig. 10-3. Insulation can be installed within a furred-out interior wall assembly set against a log exterior wall.

room and living room could remain as uninsulated natural log interior.

CAP INSULATION

Cap insulation is installed above the ceilings of occupied living spaces and below unoccupied and unheated attic or roof crawl areas where the roof itself is not insulated. In many instances this insulation runs from outside wall to outside wall in all directions, and there is no insulation at all in the roof assembly. In other designs, such as a story-and-a-half house, the cap insulation might lie over only a small section of ceiling beneath the roof peak, with the lower half or two-thirds of the roof being insulated (Fig. 10-4).

Cap insulation is extremely important, and must have a high R-value and be properly installed for good results. Though heat loss from a residence is greatest on a per-square-foot basis

through windows, the largest amount of heat loss in any house is straight up (heat rises) through the cap and roof. The recommended minimum thermal insulation value is R-19. As far as overall house design, construction, and efficiency is concerned, cap insulation has some advantages, too. Unless the house is flat-roofed, a full cap is smaller than the roof area. Thus the cap will radiate a smaller amount of heat away than would the roof. Also, because the area is smaller, less insulating material and less labor are required to do the job. Cap insulation is also easier to install, sometimes by quite a bit, than roof insulation.

Probably the most commonly used material for cap insulation is fiberglass or mineral wool roll or batts. These are easily stapled directly to the joists from below, or can be stuffed into place from above in some cases, after the ceiling has been installed. Where the

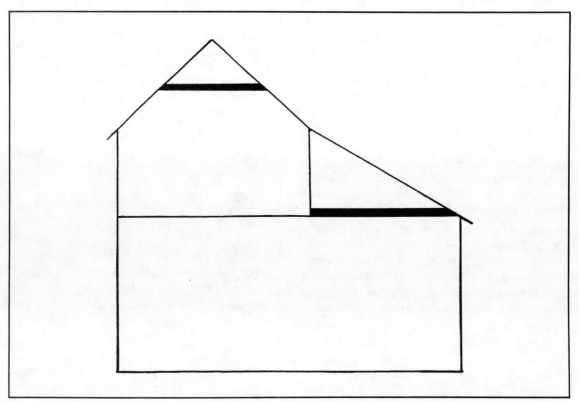

Fig. 10-4. Cap insulation is installed directly over ceilings below uninsulated roof sections.

250

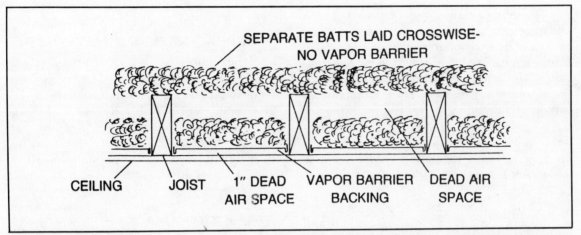

SEPARATE BATTS LAID CROSSWISE-
NO VAPOR BARRIER

CEILING   JOINT   1" DEAD   VAPOR BARRIER   DEAD AIR
                    AIR SPACE   BACKING   SPACE

Fig. 10-5. Cap insulation can be increased by laying batts across the joists. No additional vapor barrier is used.

rafter spacing is greater than 24 inches on center, nailing strips might have to be installed to which standard-width insulation can be stapled. Or, if the ceiling framework is sturdy, the material can simply be laid down and tightly pushed together at the edges. The necessary R-value can usually be achieved with a single layer of this material. However, in areas where up to R-30 or so is recommended or required, a second layer will have to be installed. The second layer should have no vapor barrier or facing attached to it, and the lengths or batts should be laid upon the first layer at right angles or with staggered parallel joints. If there happens to be an air space between the two layers, so much the better (Fig. 10-5).

Another common method of cap insulating is to install the ceiling first. One of the various loose-fill insulations can then be blown into the ceiling voids to whatever depth is necessary to achieve the desired R-value. In this case, a vapor barrier of plastic sheeting should be applied between the joists and the finish ceiling. The plastic should be sealed off around all the edges and lapped and sealed at the joints. This is actually a good idea with any cap insulation, even if faced fiberglass batts are used.

Where for one reason or another the thickness of the blanket or loose-fill insulation that can be installed in the cap is insufficient to achieve the necessary R-value, rigid insulation can be installed either alone or with a supplement of loose fill or batts. For instance, sheets of expanded polyurethane could be applied directly to the joists and then covered by plasterboard. Various combinations of expanded polystyrene, isocyanurate, mineral fiberboard, acoustic tile, and other materials might also be used. These methods do tend to be more expensive, but also provide the desired results.

ROOF INSULATION

Wherever cap insulation is not used, roof insulation must be. The material can be installed below the roof sheathing, and then covered by some sort of finish ceiling covering. This is probably the most common approach. But where the rafters or purlins are exposed to view and the undersurface of the roof is in effect the ceiling—as is the case in the cathedral ceiling design and similar open plans—insulation must be installed above the roof sheathing in a built-up roof assembly. In any case, R-19 is the recommended minimum R-value, the same as for cap insulation.

Insulating a built-up roof consists of constructing a roof assembly, as discussed in Chapter 8, and using a suitable amount and type of insulating material to achieve the necessary R-value. Insulating roof decking can be used for this purpose, as can fiberglass or mineral wool batt or roll insulation. Where cooling is the primary concern, accordian-type reflective insulation can be used in layers, separated by dead air spaces. Rigid insulation sheets are also widely used, and combinations of materials can be installed as well.

Insulating a conventional roof from the underside is not a difficult job, just tedious and hard on the arms and neck. Roll or batt blanket insulation is most often chosen because of relatively low cost and ease of installation. Rigid insulation sheets can also be used, though often at somewhat higher cost. Blanket insulation is stapled between the rafters, with nailing strips installed parallel to the rafters where the rafter spacing is greater than the widest available standard insulating material. Rigid insulation can be cut, fitted, and glued or nailed onto nailing strips attached to the rafter faces. Or it can be applied directly to the rafter edges, then covered with a finish ceiling material.

In any case, leave an airway of 1 inch or more between the insulation and the underside of the roof sheathing to provide adequate ventilation (Fig. 10-6). Install vent ports in soffits and gable ends. The net vent area should equal 1 square foot for each 900 square feet of floor area beneath the roof, for both inlet and outlet vents.

Whatever the insulating method and material employed, take special care that all joints and seams are filled and all small voids completely plugged. This, incidentally, holds true for cap insulation as well. The reason is that warm air is always on the rise, directly up to the ceiling or roof, and if there is any way for it to escape in the form of tiny air currents through cracks or thin spots, it will do so. A surprising amount of heat loss in the average house takes place in just this way.

WINDOW AND DOOR TREATMENTS

Of all the sections in the house, window glass transmits the greatest amount of heat per square foot of surface area. This is true no matter what precautions are taken, but the effects can be minimized to a certain degree. Different types of glass have different heat transmission characteristics, but for purposes of calculating residential heat loss by standard formulas, one factor is used to cover all types of clear, plain window glass. Thus, a single thickness of glass is rated at R-0.88. Double glazing, whether in one sash or a single-glazed sash and storm window combination, is figured at R-1.67. Resistance to heat transfer can be further increased by going to triple glazing, which has a value of R-2.44.

Obviously three layers of glass are considerably better than two or one, from the heat loss standpoint. But providing three layers, or even two, might not practical from other standpoints. The total amount of heat loss through all the glass area in the house might not be sufficient to warrant the considerable extra expense of additional glazing. Also, the disadvantages of multiple glazing could outweigh the advantage of saving a bit of heat.

The disadvantages of multiple glazing include additional maintenance, higher replacement cost in case of breakage, the not-unusual circumstance of double insulating glass losing its seal and clouding up on the inside. Also, each layer of glass reduces the input of light by about 10 percent and reduces visibility correspondingly. Because multiple glazing reduces the amount of heat loss to the outside, it likewise reduces the amount of heat coming into the building from sunlight, depending upon the type of glass. So whether or not there is any net loss or gain is open to question. On the other hand, multiple glazing does cut down on cold air fall from the interior glass surfaces, thus reducing cool drafts, and it is also less susceptible to moisture or frost condensation.

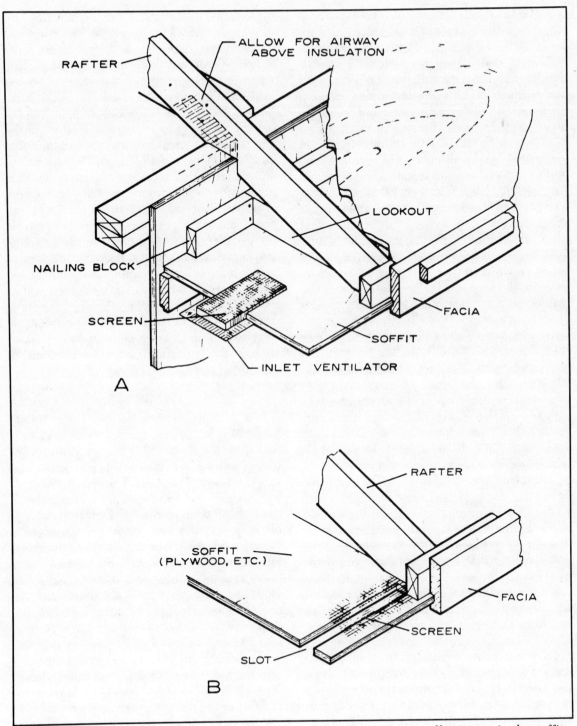

Fig. 10-6. Allow an airway between the insulation and the roof, as well as ports in the soffits, to provide adequate ventilation. (Courtesy of U.S. Department of Agriculture.)

The situation changes if you take into consideration the various specialty glazing materials now available. There is a wide variety of glass that is tinted or coated with a metallic film, as well as combinations of glass, and double glazing with a film suspended between the panes. All of these materials and combinations have differing characteristics. Furthermore, new products and combinations are being developed continuously. There are some opportunities here for installing specialized windows that have much better thermal characteristics than standard glazing, as well as other benefits. Check this out by studying the latest brochures, catalogs, and specification sheets from glass and window manufacturers.

It is worth noting that any glass areas, regardless of type, can be "insulated" from the inside, and they usually are at least to some degree. Heavy drapes, especially those that are lined with a thermally efficient material, effectively block direct heat radiation through the glass and help to reduce overall heat loss. Wood shutters do a decent job of lowering heat loss, and certain types of pull-down shades also have some effectiveness. The best arrangement, though, is to use window coverings that are made specifically to reduce heat loss through windows. These include various kinds of pull-down or pull-across fabric/insulant combinations that seal to the window casings in one way or another, interior shutters or blinds made of insulating materials, and insulating panels that are set in place on the inside as desired. Some people just cut snug-fitting pieces of rigid foil-faced insulation and set them in place every evening. Any of these practices, incidentally, work just as well in blocking sunlight out to reduce heat gain and lower cooling loads.

Exterior doors are also grouped according to factors that determine the thermal insulating value. Non metal doors over 1 inch thick and filled (cored) metal doors without windows in them are considered to have an R-value of 2.0, though some of the newer prehung, high-efficiency exterior doors might carry higher ratings, as evaluated by the manufacturer. Unfilled metal doors (hollow-cored) or nonmetal doors of less than 1 inch thickness are rated R-1. However, any door fitted with a window, whether single- or double-glazed, is calculated as though all glass at R-0.88.

Again, from a standpoint of heat loss the benefits of going to an extra-thick door or the addition of a storm door might be marginal at best. On the other hand, a thick exterior door affords an added measure of protection from the weather and is less susceptible to warping or other problems than a thin one. The addition of storm doors gives extra protection from the weather to often-expensive exterior doors, and cuts down on potential drafts, keeps rainwater or snow from creeping in under the exterior doors, and cuts down on the amount of cold air admitted to the interior when the doors are opened. All of these have some effect upon heat loss and interior comfort levels, even though the specifics might be difficult to measure.

CRACKAGE

One of the most important aspects in complete house insulation and reduction of total heat loss from the structure is preventing infiltration of cold air from the outside and coincidental exfiltration of warm air from the inside. This process goes on continuously, and occurs in all manner of strange places. Unfortunately, it often goes unnoticed. Some of the leakage paths are obvious, such as fireplace dampers, kitchen or laundry vents, and exterior doors opening and closing. Other spots are not so obvious and might go completely undetected. Air creeps in at the sill joints and travels into the wall cavities, or filters through the soffit and into the ceiling cavities, or rises in tiny jets through cracks in the floor or around the baseboards or any one of a hundred other places. While this colder air is coming in, warmer air is going out in the same way, and heat is being lost by radiation, convection, and conduction. This process is constantly aided by air pressure differentials between the inside and outside of the house that are largely caused by outside air movement: breezes or wind.

A certain amount of infiltration/exfiltration is inescapable—a completely airtight house could only be built in a laboratory as a scientific experiment. And a certain amount is not only desirable in order to keep the interior air fresh and minimize ever-present air pollutants that are found in every house, but also is essential in order to maintain a full oxygen content. For most residences a complete change of air throughout the entire structure once every 45 minutes is considered about right. Superinsulated houses are often tighter than this, and then mechanical ventilation with heat-exchanging systems must be introduced. But when there is too much infiltration, other problems arise. The first is excessive heat loss and consequently higher heating costs, and the second is drafts and air currents that reduce the comfort level of the living quarters. The same situation occurs in reverse where cooling is the primary concern. Both of these problems can be traced, at least in good measure, to sloppy construction practices and/or poorly fitted insulation. In log houses, where there are dozens of seams and joints, infiltration can be a particular difficulty.

These heat losses and cold air gains (or vice versa) can be lumped under one heading, crackage. In other words, there are just too many badly fitted and/or improperly sealed-off joints and seams, which amount to a lot of cracks in the house. The results can be amply demonstrated by an all-too-common occurrence. First assume that all the windows in a house were sloppily installed and not caulked, leaving cracks here and there around them. Then visualize this as being the equivalent of a 6- × -8-foot picture window with a $\frac{1}{16}$-inch crack all the way around it (which in itself has happened many times before). This would actually be the exact equivalent of cutting a 21-square-inch hole through a wall and leaving it open all winter. The only practical difference is that a series of small cracks all around the house might well cause an even greater heat loss than a single hole.

The remedy for this problem is simple enough. First, use good construction practices during the building of the house, fitting all the components tightly and properly together. Second, caulk and seal all obvious joints of any kind where outside air might find a way in. This is done during construction. Pay particular attention to all doors, windows, pipe openings, and other spots exposed to the outside. Third, install vapor barriers carefully, sealing off the joints and repairing any tears or punctures. Fourth, install all insulation so that the coverage is full, joints between insulating materials and framing members are tight, all cracks and voids are completely filled, and no gaps are left. Fifth, carry out maintenance procedures regularly as time goes by, sealing and caulking any new cracks or gaps that might appear as a result of settling or shrinking, while at the same time keeping an eye out for cracks that might appear in obscure spots. And last, apply adequate weatherstripping to all doors and windows, replacing or repairing it as necessary, and provide all vents with automatic-closing louvers and fireplaces or stoves with outside-combustion air sources.

VAPOR BARRIERS

A vapor barrier should always be used in conjunction with insulation in all sections of the house. This prevents the passage of moisture—always present within the house—into the building sections where it could condense and cause considerable damage, and reduce the effectiveness of the insulation itself. The vapor barrier is always placed closest to the warmer side of the building section and to the inside of the insulation.

Some types of insulation, particularly roll or batt fiberglass or mineral wool, include a vapor barrier of aluminum foil or kraft paper on one side. Some kinds of rigid insulation sheets have a foil facing on both sides. With other types of insulation, a separate vapor barrier must be installed. Many builders install a separate barrier anyway, whether the insulation has one or not, as an added measure of protection and to help reduce infiltration problems. The material most often used is construction plastic, stapled in place after the insulation has been installed but before the finish covering has been applied.

A vapor barrier should be continuous, all around the inside surfaces of the heated parts of the house, and free of slits, rips, and punctures. In effect, it is an envelope around the living quarters. A vapor barrier should always be installed between the ground and a concrete foundation slab or basement floor, and between basement walls and any finish covering applied to them. As mentioned earlier, the ground surface in a closed crawl space should also be covered. Floors and ceilings or roofs require a full barrier, as do exterior framed walls. Log walls, of course, need no protection because they are above-ground and are essentially a monolithic section—moisture will migrate through the wood without any condensation problems. The exception is log walls that are furred out and insulated on the inside, with a finish wall covering applied. In that case, a vapor barrier should be attached across the interior faces of the furring. A vapor barrier is not necessary between interior spaces that are heated to different temperatures, even if the difference is substantial.

11

Odds and Ends

THUS FAR WE HAVE CONSIDERED, FOR THE MOST part, only the construction of a basic structure, a shell. However, this constitutes only about half or less of the total work that goes into a finished house. There are a lot of important odds and ends that have to be taken care of before you can move in the furniture, and there are also a few construction features that have not yet been discussed. Much of the finish work in a log house is the same as for a conventional frame house, using identical methods, procedures, and materials. There are, however, several major areas of concern particularly applicable to log structures that deserve further investigation.

INTERIOR PARTITIONS

Interior partition walls can be built in a number of different ways. One is to construct them of logs the same size as those used for the exterior walls. They can be built right along with

the exterior walls, or left until the shell is complete. In the former case, the partition courses are built up concurrently with the wall courses, notched into place and secured in much the same way. Caulking and sealing, however, is not necessary except at exposed exterior wall joints; caulking is sometimes done just for the sake of appearance.

In the latter case, the interior wall courses are stacked and secured to one another, to the floor frame, and to the exterior walls where applicable. Joining the interior wall courses to the outside-wall logs can be accomplished in several ways. Assuming same-size logs, one way is to cut each interior log end to a curve and fit it tightly against the abutting outside wall log. Drive a lag screw through from the outside to secure each set of logs (Fig. 11-1), or toe-nail through the top of each partition log into the wall log. Also, a wide notch can be cut in the exterior wall from floor to ceiling, with the interior wall logs cut to matching tenons

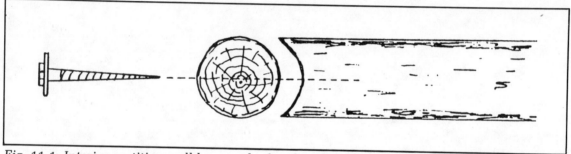

Fig. 11-1. *Interior partition wall logs can be fitted to the exterior wall logs and lagged through from the outside.*

that will fit neatly into the slot. Toe-nail each interior wall log successively from the top into the exterior wall logs to secure them in place.

Interior partition walls can be built from logs that are substantially smaller than those in the exterior courses. If laid horizontally, they are secured to one another, with the first course anchored to the floor frame. Because the rate of shrinkage will be different than that of the exterior walls, a slip joint must be provided at the ceiling level so that the main structure can settle down without buckling the partition (Fig. 11-2). Where a partition abuts exterior wall logs, the smaller logs cannot be attached to the exterior wall logs, for the same reason. A wide and deep slot can be cut from floor to ceiling in the exterior wall, to receive the interior wall log ends; these may be left full-sized or tenoned, as you wish. The slot should be carefully sized to be just big enough to allow freedom in the settling process, but not so loose that the partition wall is unstable or wobbly. The partition logs should be spiked to one another as the wall is laid up.

Log partitions that are built stockade-fashion should be fitted with a slip joint at ceiling level and should not be attached to exterior walls at any point. The settling differential will be considerable, because logs shrink much less lengthwise than they do in diameter. Again, where a partition wall abuts an exterior wall the best bet is to cut a floor-to-ceiling slot in the exterior wall logs, into which the end log of the partition can be fitted to allow just

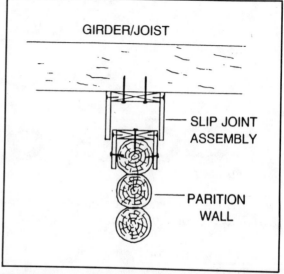

Fig. 11-2. *Interior log partition walls can be fitted into a slip joint arrangement like this one.*

enough freedom so that settling can take place without binding.

Conventional stud-wall construction for partitions can also be used with no problems in a log house, and this is often the preferred method. The partitions themselves are made in the usual fashion with 2- × -4 sole plates, studs, and top plates, covered with plasterboard or wood paneling, or both. The sole plate is nailed securely to the floor frame. The wall top must be fitted with a slip joint (as in Fig. 11-2) to allow proper settling of the structure. Where an interior partition abuts an exterior wall log, cut a floor-to-ceiling slot to accommodate the partition end. The slot should be just wide enough to admit the wall frame and the wall coverings so that the entire assembly is, in effect, mortised into the exterior wall (Fig. 11-3).

Some of the raw edges of the slot will be visible and might contrast sharply with the finished appearance of the interior partition. Should this be objectionable, you can apply a thick molding at the intersection of the walls, creating a deep shadow effect that will completely hide the rough seam. Don't anchor the partition to the exterior wall at any place except the very bottom, and attach the molding only to the partition and not to the exterior wall. The interior partition structures themselves can be joined to one another in the usual fashion, simply by nailing them together. Make sure, though, that there are no obstructions anywhere along the slip-joint arrangement that might later bind up.

FURRED WALLS

There are occasions when a log wall must be furred out—or fitted with a series of nailing strips to which another wall covering is then applied—in order to hide the logs. Such would be the case where additional insulation must be installed, as discussed in Chapter 10. A similar situation would occur where a series of pipes, wires, or heating ducts have to be installed against an outside wall but must be hidden from view. There might also be situations in which a log wall is best covered with a conventional wall covering—in a kitchen or bathroom, for example. Whatever the case, furring out a log wall is not done in quite the same manner as in conventional construction.

The usual method of furring makes use of a series of thin strips of wood, usually 1 × 2s, securely nailed to the surface being covered. But because of the settling problem, furring strips cannot be nailed to log walls, and because of the irregularity of the surfaces of many log constructions, shimming and notching a lot of individual thin strips to achieve a plane sur-

face becomes quite a chore. The solution is to use heavier, self-supporting, rigid stock such as 2 × 4s, built into a stand-alone framework just like a partition wall (Fig. 11-4).

Move the framework into position, anchor to the floor frame at the bottom, and fit with a slip joint at ceiling level. Install insulation and/or apply a wall covering to the framework as necessary. The slip joint must have sufficient clearance to admit the wall covering as well as the upper portion of the framework. If one end of the furred-out section is exposed to view, it is finished by making a return around the end with the same covering material that is used on the wall face, and a molding can then be applied from floor to ceiling at the joint between the logs and the furred-out section. Neither the molding nor any part of the furring should be rigidly attached to the log wall.

TRIMMING OUT

Trimming out is a term usually applied to the finishing-up process of installing any necessary ceiling, wall, and floor covering (floor last, usually), and then applying all the various bits and pieces of woodwork that hide the joints and seams. Putting on any applied finishes is part of the process, too. Trimwork can be prepainted or prestained, then applied. At the same time, light fixtures and switch and outlet covers are put on, any missing hardware installed, and any other missing odds and ends taken care of.

Finished ceilings are applied to the ceiling framework as discussed in Chapter 7. In a log house, wall coverings are needed only on conventional stud-type partition walls or furred-out sections as just covered. If the flooring is of the single-layer variety, all that is required is a bit of sanding and cleaning up, plus a coat or two of sealer and/or an applied finish. Underlayment and/or a finish floor covering such as hardwood, tile, sheet vinyl, or wall-to-wall carpeting may be put down as well. There is a tremendous variety of such materials, and installation is accomplished

Fig. 11-3. One method of securing paneled stud-type interior partitions is to set the ends into floor-to-ceiling grooves cut into the exterior wall logs.

simply by following the manufacturer's instructions. The only unusual aspect lies in the fact that at least in some cases the flooring material should be cut to fit closely along the exterior wall log contours, with caulking applied as necessary to ensure an airtight, draft-free fit.

Exactly how this is done depends upon just how the log structure is put together, but the object is to achieve a long-lasting joint that will not come apart and that will prevent air infiltration.

After this phase of the construction is com-

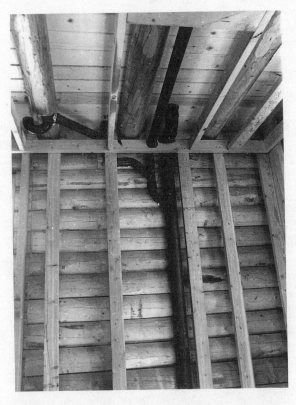

Fig. 11-4. A furred-out interior wall set against an exterior log wall, combined with a frame work for a dropped ceiling, allows room for plumbing and wiring.

plete, the various moldings and trim pieces that dress out the interior can be applied. This includes door and window casings, moldings at the ceiling/wall joints if necessary, mopboards, and shoe or base moldings. Again, most of this installation follows conventional methods, the one exception being that you must always bear in mind the settling problem.

With windows, the stool or interior sill and the apron can be solidly attached to the log wall and the window buck or frame. The casing sides, however, can be nailed only to the window frame and not to the log wall. The casing top is likewise attached to the window frame only, because the settling gap is directly behind it. The casing stock should be wide enough to completely cover the settling gap above the window. Much the same is true of door casings; attach them only to the door frames or bucks. Interior door casings on stockade log or conventional stud partitions can be attached to both door frame and partition.

Trim moldings that hide the joints between ceilings and walls must be placed and attached in such a way that subsequent settling of the structure will not peel the moldings off. They should be nailed up so that the settling sections can slide down past them, or so that they move with the settling sections. Exactly how this is done depends upon general construction methods used in the framework of the house, as well as the slip-joint arrangements.

Baseboards or mopboards installed in log houses are usually quite a bit wider than might be used in a conventional frame house. Nominal 1- × -6 or 1- × -8 stock should be satisfactory, and allows plenty of height to cover the rather large space at the floor level created by a round log. The baseboard effectively hides the rough joint where the flooring abuts the log wall, and in many cases also affords a natural runway for electrical wiring. The baseboard is nailed to the log wall at the top, and might also have to be attached to a nailing strip secured to the floor-

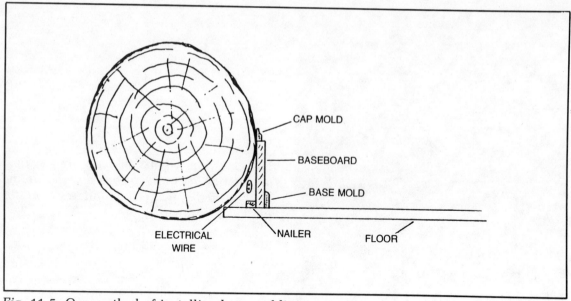

Fig. 11-5. One method of installing base molding.

ing for a stable installation. Base cap molding and/or shoe molding can be added if desired (Fig. 11-5). If the wall logs are flatted on the interior surface, any appropriate width of baseboard (or just a narrow shoe molding alone) can be nailed directly to the flat log face.

CABINETRY AND BUILT-INS

Cabinets, as might be found in a kitchen or bathroom, and built-ins, such as book shelving, window seats, storage walls, or any of a hundred other items, are just as applicable to the log style of house as any other. The installation procedures, however, are a bit different. Once again, the prime consideration is settling. For instance, kitchen wall cabinets that are attached to a log wall and butted against the ceiling will eventually drop down as the wall settles, leaving an unsightly gap at the ceiling level. To counteract this problem, space the cabinets below the ceiling to provide an extra, open top shelf so any settling will be unnoticeable. Or, add a wide face board across the top of the cabinet installation to act as a slip joint and hide the gap that is sure to develop. Cabinet fasteners should be mounted with screws

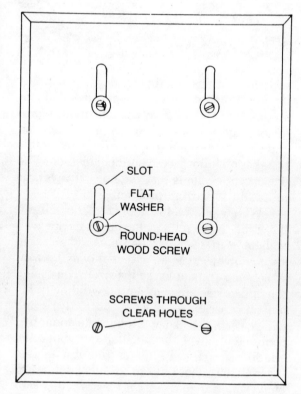

Fig. 11-6. Wall-mounted cabinets should be mounted with a slip-slot arrangement.

in slip-slots; note that the bottom fasteners are fixed (Fig. 11-6).

Kitchen base cabinets (or any other of that type, like a bathroom vanity), should be of the self-supporting, freestanding style, so they can be set in place and secured to the floor but need not be attached to a log wall at any point. If they are attached rigidly, something is eventually bound to pull apart or bind up. If base cabinets are backed up to a furred-out or conventional stud wall, however, they can be attached to the wall. Also, the space between counter tops and wall cabinets should be calculated to allow for the amount of settling that might occur. That space could diminish as much as 3 or 4 inches over a period of time, and easily put the squeeze on countertop appliances calculated to fit nicely into the standard 18-inch spacing.

Much the same situation applies to all other kinds of cabinetry or built-ins. They must be constructed and/or mounted to the building in such a way that they are unaffected by settling of the log shell. Remember, downward movement of only a fraction of an inch can break open cabinet joints or render doors and drawers inoperable. Units that are built into or installed against conventional partition walls can be anchored in normal fashion. Any units that are built into or attached to log walls—whether interior or exterior—or to or against an upper-floor frame, must be arranged to accommodate the settling drop by means of slip joints or the method of attachment, or both.

APPLIED FINISHES

Applied finishes—paints, enamels, stains, varnishes, and sealers—are employed in log structures in just the same way as in any other, with one notable exception. The log surfaces themselves should not be treated with a hard or impermeable applied finish. This is true of exterior surfaces as well as interior. The interior log surfaces should be treated before construction begins with a non-toxic clear preservative that leaves the appearance of dry wood. This surface can be left as is, but is susceptible to accumulating grime and stains as time goes on. To help alleviate this, wipe on a coat of boiled linseed oil for surface protection. This will darken the wood slightly, but also enhance its natural appearance. The treatment can be repeated every few years if necessary, but not so often that the surfaces become gummy. Another possibility, one that provides good surface protection, is an application of a neutral-colored wax of the type designed for use on raw wood. A stain-wax can also be applied to darken the color.

Log exteriors are sometimes spar-varnished or stained, or even painted. For the most part this is not a good course to follow, because the coatings always seem to produce more problems than they solve. The natural breathability (not to mention the appearance) of the logs is destroyed, and the coatings have a tendency to crack and peel away. Varnishes in particular tend to take on a shaggy, ragged appearance after a time, something that cannot be successfully corrected. The maintenance problems are continuous, and once such a finish is applied it must then be frequently reapplied to preserve the appearance. This is expensive, time-consuming, and pointless, especially since a natural log exterior will weather and last quite nicely without that kind of help.

The only treatment that a log house exterior really needs is periodic application of a log sealer/preservative. There are several brands of quality log sealers on the market that do the job nicely and can be either sprayed or brushed on. These finishes will help the log walls retain their integrity against insect and fungus attacks and keep the wood looking good without altering the natural appearance.

If you don't want to use a commercial finish, a good alternative is the traditional 50/50 mix of boiled linseed oil and turpentine, liberally applied with a brush. Or, you can use the FPL Natural Finish, developed and tested years ago by the Forest Products Laboratory (part of the U.S. Department of Agriculture, under the

Forest Service). This is a mix-it-yourself finish, which should be done outdoors using the proper precautions. The finish, for a 5-gallon batch, consists of 3 gallons of boiled linseed oil, 1 gallon of paint thinner or mineral spirits, 1 pound of paraffin wax, and ⅛ pound of zinc stearate. (The original formula also contained half a gallon of 10:1 concentrate of pentachlorophenol, but this is no longer available to the public; substitution is not recommended).

To mix the finish, pour the thinner into a metal pail. Melt the paraffin in a double boiler, and very slowly add it to the thinner, meanwhile stirring rapidly. Let this mix cool to room temperature (about 70 degrees), then put on your dust mask and add the zinc stearate. Last, add the linseed oil, and stir until all the ingredients are completely melded.

This finish can be colored and used as a stain, too. Add 1 pint of burnt sienna tinting color for a cedar color, a pint of raw umber for a light redwood color, or a pint of Indian red oxide for a dark redwood color. The first application will only last about two years or so before it weathers out. Reapply at this point, and then about every 8 to 10 years thereafter.

STAIRWAYS

The options open to you in the way of stairways are practically endless. Any of the conventional stairway designs (Fig. 11-7) work fine. The absolute minimum for a conventional stairway width is 2½ feet; 3 feet is about average, and 4 feet allows great convenience. An opening in the floor above of suitable width and a minimum length of 10 feet is required. Check local building codes for stairway details; minimum dimensions are often spelled out.

If space is tight, you might consider installing a prefabricated spiral assembly. Most of these are made of steel, and have either steel or wood treads that can be carpeted. The unit is essentially vertical and takes up less room than a conventional stairway. The bottom of the assembly bolts to the first floor and the framework extends upward into a trimmed-out rectangular hole in the floor being served. Though sizes vary, a hole about 3 to 4 feet square is common.

Most conventional stairways present a somewhat formal appearance. If an easy going rustic design is desired, to complement the overall informal and rustic appearance of a log interior, an open stairway can be built using logs for stringers and slabs or hardwood dimension stock for treads. The risers can be eliminated or not, as you wish. The length of the log stringers is calculated to hold the proper number of treads and risers (or riser spaces) to afford an easy stair angle. Treads cut from heavy slabs are attached to angle-blocks that are glued and nailed or screwed to the stringer faces. Dimension-stock treads can be similarly attached to blocks, or can be set in slots dadoed into the stringer sides (Fig. 11-8). If you prefer the appearance to be totally rustic, you can use the ancient design for second-story (especially loft) access, which consists of a series of hardwood pegs driven into a vertical post to form a rudimentary ladder. This system is easy to construct, uses little material, and takes up little space.

Whichever stairway design you opt for, the trick is to make sure that the stairway angle is neither too steep nor too shallow, and that there is a comfortable relationship between the height and the width of each step. As a general rule of thumb you can figure that the width of a tread multiplied by the height of a riser should equal approximately 70 to 75. For instance, one widely used riser/tread combination, where the total height from floor to floor is 9 feet, is a tread width of 9 inches and a riser height of 7¾ inches ($9 \times 7.75 = 69.75$), for a total run of 9 feet 9 inches. However, there is a great number of other combinations that could be used.

In any event, as with so many other items in a log building, a slip joint of some sort should be provided to compensate for settling, unless the stairway can be attached to non-settling members. This can be accomplished by

Fig. 11-7. *This is a conventional but relatively informal kind of stairway that can be built in a log house.*

leaving the top of the stairway loose and figuring in extra height at the last riser, which will diminish as time goes by. Or, the bottom of the stairway can be set upon temporary shim blocks or wedges that can be rearranged as the building settles.

STOVES AND FIREPLACES

The odds are pretty good that today, as in the past, not many log cabins or houses are built without inclusion of at least one fireplace or wood stove. There is a wide range of possibilities in either case, and what you choose is

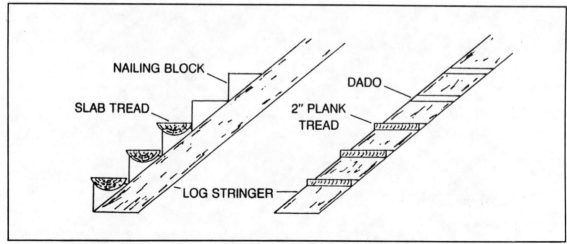

Fig. 11-8. On the left is a log-stringer stairway using log slabs for treads. The log-stringer stairway on the right uses heavy planking for treads.

largely a matter of personal preference balanced against costs, the intended use of the unit, aesthetics, building code requirements, and various other factors.

In a few areas of the country, fireplaces are no longer allowed in new houses, or are restricted to certain types, or limited to only one approved installation. In cold country it is strongly recommended that all fireplaces be equipped with dampers that will close down completely, or better yet, that they be of the newer variety that consist of a steel shell encased in the masonry, equipped with glass-front doors and special intake pipes that bring combustion air in from outdoors. This helps to minimize the tremendous heat looses attributable to conventional fireplaces.

Whichever kind, design, or style of fireplace you choose, you must consider usual installation problem: settling. Masonry fireplaces must be constructed in such a way that the structural framework can slip by the masonry as it settles, without pulling something apart. In some cases, where massive masonry construction is an integral part of the building, structural members might have to be integrated into the masonry work in such a way that settling is obviated and the building will remain intact. This usually requires some skilled de-

sign work. There is also the possibility of building the shell first and allowing most of the settling to take place before the masonry work is begun.

It is a good idea to build a masonry fireplace so that the entire mass (except for the chimney top) is enclosed within the building—even though an exposed outside construction is traditional, common, and attractive. Keeping the masonry mass inside has two advantages. The first is that the flue remains hotter and allows better and more efficient combustion with less creosote buildup, especially with a low fire. The second is the heat that builds up within the masonry mass is returned directly into the interior of the building, rather than being wasted into the outside atmosphere. This arrangement is often less expensive, too. In all cases, whether building codes are in effect or not, the fireplace is best built in conformity to the latest revision of the National Fire Protection Association's publication #211, *Chimneys, Fireplaces, and Vents.*

The installation of wood stoves is being increasingly regulated, for reasons of both safety and air pollution. This is a constantly changing situation, so before purchasing and installing a wood stove, be sure to check with local authorities for pertinent details. The matter is

266

sometimes handled by local fire departments, sometimes by building officials. You might be able to buy only certain approved models of stoves, a permit might be required for installation, and the installation might have to be made according to code and with approved materials, and inspected before being put into service.

A wood stove—whether used for occasional fires for pleasure, as a backup heating system (for a passive solar design, for example), or as the main source of heat—should be a high-quality, highly efficient, low-polluting, cast-iron type with firebrick or other refractory lining, preferably with an outside-air intake, and sized to the area to be heated. Such stoves are expensive, to be sure, but will perform very well and last a lifetime. Much has been said recently about the great advantages of stoves with catalytic combustion units in them, but actually some of the new super-stoves without such units perform better with less maintenance. Design improvements and testing are going on continually; be sure to check into all the details.

The chimneys used with wood stoves are called appliance chimneys. The best are made of double-wall stainless steel with an insulant between the walls. Some of the chimneys are triple-wall with air space between the walls, and are made of galvanized steel. Either type is designed to be held in a special support basket, mounted in the ceiling framework directly above or offset slightly from the stove. It must extend up through the roof to a height of at least 2 feet above any roof or building section within a radius of 10 feet. The section of stack from the stove to the chimney, within the living area, should be made of heavy-duty steel; these are usually painted black but sections of porcelanized piping are also available in several colors. The inexpensive blued steel smokepipe is not recommended even for this purpose, and should never be used as a chimney.

Wood stoves must be installed with great care; the fact that you think you might use it only occasionally is no excuse for making a sloppy or questionable installation. Clearances are particularly important; the specifications might change and do vary from place to place, so investigate before installing. Usually a stove (or its smokepipe) must be at least 3 feet away from a combustible wall, which includes plaster or plasterboard. However, certain kinds of noncombustible backboards can be interposed between the stove and a combustible wall, and the clearance can be reduced to as little as 12 inches, depending upon the specific material used.

All noncombustible backboards must have free air circulation all around them. A masonry or synthetic stone or ceramic tile facing built up against or glued to a combustible wall, as is so often done, does not qualify. Similarly, a stove must rest upon a suitable hearth with the firebox a certain distance from the floor, or the hearth, depending upon the design of both. The hearth must extend a certain distance beyond the stove in all directions. Clearances must also be observed as the chimney is installed; typically there must be a minimum of 2 inches between chimney walls and any combustible material. Note, however, that a few stove models are designated as zero-clearance and need no added protection. Stove manufacturers will gladly supply you with their installation recommendations; follow them and modify as necessary according to local regulations, and you will have a trouble-free installation.

The slip-joint arrangement is usually easy with a stove chimney installation. The entire chimney and the basket it rests in will gradually lower. With proper sizing, you can slide the smokepipe up inside the chimney when you install it, with a snug but free fit. Then the chimney will just lower itself around the smokepipe. If the smokepipe has a tapered end for a jam-fit into the chimney bottom, however, the smokepipe will eventually buckle and could become an instant fire hazard.

DECKS AND PORCHES

Decks or porches can easily be added to a log

house; in fact, many houses look naked without one or the other. And they can unquestionably increase the livability and convenience of the home. There are dozens of design possibilities, with decks generally being the easiest to build because there is no roof to contend with. Decks also require less material, but are completely unsheltered from the weather. Porches can be made in open style, nothing more than a roofed deck, sometimes with railings, sometimes without. They can also be partially enclosed, fully enclosed with windows or screening, depending upon the season, Some kinds of porches, in fact, can serve admirably as greenhouses, solariums, or solar collectors.

Either porches or decks can be added onto the house at any time after construction is finished, or can be built concurrently with the shell. The most useful arrangement is to have both a deck and a screened porch, the former for sunning and barbecuing, the latter for taking one's bug-free ease of a warm evening.

In most cases the component parts of a deck should be made from heavy stock, not so much for strength as for weatherability, and to preserve the appearance of solidity and massiveness of most log structures. Posts, headers, joists, and decking are best made of either redwood or stock pressure-treated with preservatives. The decking, which is often 2- × -4 or 2- × -6 stock, should be secured with decking screws rather than nails, to avoid the constant "popping" (lifting up) of nails that would otherwise occur. The deck can be left to weather naturally, or can be treated with a finish (which must then be periodically reapplied). Railings, stairs, and steps can also be made of dimension stock—again, treated stock or redwood fares best—or they can be fashioned from logs, slabs, and poles to carry out the rustic log appearance.

One easy way to make a deck frame is to secure a header to the house sill with lag screws. The header should be backed with aluminum or other flashing, curled into a joint at the top. An opposite header, properly squared

up, is secured to a sill or sill plate supported by piers or posts an appropriate distance away. End joists are installed to form a rectangle, which is filled in with joists on 24-inch or 30-inch centers, depending upon the size of the stock and decking being used. The framework is decked over and the railings and stairs added as required. If the deck is low to the ground, the front sill can be supported by stubby concrete piers poured into form tube. If the deck is high or the grade level slopes down rapidly from the house, the same short piers can be used to about a foot above grade level and the deck edge is supported by posts of whatever length is necessary (Fig. 11-9).

The deck frame might be made of logs. In that case, the log joist ends can be notched into the house sill log as the house construction begins, so that the house foundation serves as one supporting point for the deck. One drawback here is that the joints form an entry point for moisture into the sill log. This can be minimized by thoroughly caulking the joints, keeping the first run of decking back a half inch or more from the house wall to allow for air circulation. Providing a long eave or rake overhang so that roof runoff falls some distance away from the house walls will also help, and is not a bad idea even where there is no deck. Guttering can also be added for this purpose. For the outside edge of the deck, a second sill log is mounted upon appropriately spaced piers or posts, with the opposite log joist ends notched into it. The joists should be flatted and carefully leveled so that the decking will lie smooth and even.

To make a porch, all you have to do is add a roof to the deck. One way to do so is to secure a header or ledge plate to the house wall with lag screws. Posts are set across the leading edge of the deck, positioned directly over the piers, and a plate is mounted on top of them. The rafters run from the header or ledger plate to the front plate. Roof sheathing and a weather surface is laid on top of the rafters, and trim is added last.

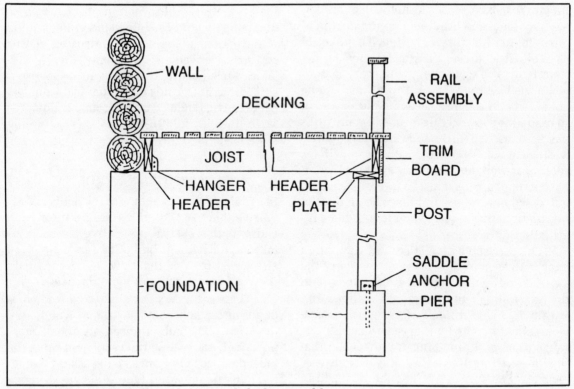

Fig. 11-9. *A cross-section of a typical deck assembly.*

On many log houses the porch roof is actually an extension of the house roof. This means that the porch framing must be done along with the house framing. If two different roof pitches are involved, the house roof rafters stop short at approximately the centerline of the house plate log. A porch plate log is erected on posts at the leading edge of the deck, and the porch roof rafters run from the house plate log to the porch plate log. The rafter logs are notched and securely spiked to make a strong, solid structure.

If the porch roof is a same-pitch continuation of the house roof, the same arrangement can be used, or full-length rafters run straight through. The whole affair must be ruggedly built, because when wind blows hard in under it, as will often happen, the entire roof assembly will want to act as a kite and sail away. Once the frame is built, the sheathing and weather surface can be laid on both the house and the porch in one continuous application. Depending upon the meeting angle of the two roofs and the type of weather surface being applied, there might be a solid, unbroken surface or there might be a flashing strip at the joint of the roofs.

UTILITIES

The general requirements for the utilities in a log house are no different than for any other kind of house. The methods of installation, however, must be handled somewhat differently. In most cases the outside walls are essentially solid, so there are no convenient voids and air spaces through which the pipes, wires, and ducts can be run. The same problems occur if some or all of the partition walls are also of log construction. In addition, many of the other structural members, such as in the floor or roof, might be large and heavy and don't lend themselves to easy notching or boring. They should be avoided wherever possible. Many log designs tend to be more open, with more components visible, than in a conventional frame house, so utility hardware and devices are not so easily hidden. All this means that the utilities systems, which include domestic water, waste disposal, electrical, heating and perhaps cooling as well, and auxiliary systems like intercoms or doorbells, must be carefully planned out ahead of time to minimize the amount of installation time required and to eliminate installation difficulties.

The easiest way to get around such problems is to keep everything you can out of the exterior log walls. Route wires, pipes, and ducting through the floors and ceilings and within hollow partition walls as much as possible, following the lines of easiest access. Arrange pipes and plumbing appliances so that they do not interfere with log walls, girders, or joists. Sometimes it is possible to build in hollow spaces hidden inside box beams that run from basement to second floor or attic, and use them as runways for pipes and wires.

Pipes and wires can often be installed as construction of the shell proceeds, thus avoiding many of the access problems that would occur if these systems were installed after shell completion. In order to do this effectively, though, the systems and the utilization points—such as electrical outlets, water and waste line connections, shutoff valves, and heating outlets—have to be well planned ahead of time. Be wary of making changes part way through an installation, because the changes might give rise to a bundle of problems later on in completing the installation. Bear in mind, too, the ever-present settling problems. Locate wires so that they won't get crushed or stretched, pipes so that they won't bend and crack or pull apart at the joints, and ducting so that it will not buckle or separate.

Most log houses contain a variety of auxiliary systems. These include such items as doorbells or chimes, integrated stereophonic sound systems, fire alarms, intrusion alarms and security systems, telephones, TV-FM aerial lead-ins, heating/cooling controls, and sensors for various kinds of mechanical troubles. All of these systems must be installed along the same lines as the utilities systems, using the same basic methods.

TERMITE CONTROL

In certain parts of the country the danger of extensive damage caused by termite infestation warrants that special preventive measures be taken as the house is built. They are simple and effective, provided that they are coupled with regular inspections and maintenance.

There are three generally recognized types of termites: subterranean, damp-wood, and dry-wood. The subterranean are much more prevalent, more difficult to spot, and cause the most damage. They are also the easiest to control. The damp-wood type is also destructive and hard to spot, but less prevalent. The dry-wood variety is much less common and confined to a much smaller geographical area. They are easy to spot and cause less damage, but are harder to control. There are virtually no places in the United States, except the very arid country and the highest elevations, that are free of termites, though the problems are worst in the damp and humid southern states.

Subterranean termites live almost entirely in the earth, especially warm and moist soil. They live on cellulose, and must have moisture to survive. They tunnel vigorously and build earthen tubes above ground to reach cellulose food supplies, like your front porch steps or the sills of your house. The damp-wood termites function in much the same way, except that they live almost entirely within damp or wet wood, and mostly stay there. The dry-wood termites, on the other hand, fly directly to wood and bore their way into it from outside, and don't need the dampness to survive. All three varieties are easiest to spot in the spring or early summer when they breed and emerge sporting new wings for their annual migration to greener pastures.

Some termite control measures can be taken during the construction of a new house. For instance, an open pier foundation affords the least opportunity for them to get a toehold, and a continuous-wall poured concrete foundation is next best. Block foundations must be solidly capped all the way around. Any cracks that appear in either type must be immediately filled and sealed off—they love to follow along masonry cracks. PWF or wood post foundations that have been pressure-treated with preservatives will not be attacked, though the termites can build tubes up them, as they can with continuous-wall foundations. Wood foundations are not recommended in any areas where termites are a serious hazard. Slab foundations afford the easiest entrance for termites, because they can come right up into the house through cracks that inevitably occur with aging.

Foundation drainage systems can be important, too, because the drier the ground is around the structure, the fewer the termites. Every effort must be made to direct ground moisture and roof run-off well away from the building. Insulation should be placed on the inside of foundation walls, rather than the outside, for two reasons. One is that the termites, while they will not eat the insulation, will burrow into it and colonize where it is warm. The other is that inside insulation allows a lesser amount of heat to escape the building into the surrounding soil, allowing a better chance to freeze them out.

As the building site is prepared, all possible bits of wood should be rooted out and cleared away from the foundation area. As construction proceeds, keep the site cleaned up and free of bits of paper and scrap wood, which they will travel to like homing pigeons. An all-too-common practice is to just bury the rubbish in utility trenches and alongside the founda-tions when the backfilling is done. Nothing could be a bigger invitation for the early onset of crumbling sills. Never bury or leave lying on the ground anything containing cellulose.

The use of wood preservatives in certain parts of the building has been mentioned previously. Those same preservatives are also effective against termites, provided the preservative is reapplied every few years. Log walls, and particularly the joint surfaces, should be liberally treated as construction goes along, and all accessible exterior surfaces should be regularly treated at intervals thereafter. Sills and any other wood members in or close to the ground—12 inches is the minimum—should be either redwood or commercially pressure-treated wood, preferably the latter. Crawl-space floors should be covered with a double layer of plastic film and be well ventilated to reduce moisture, and all the exposed wood surfaces—joists, beams, sills, or whatever—should be liberally treated with preservatives. All chases or holes where pipes or wires go through foundations or woodwork should be thoroughly sealed off with caulk or roofing compound.

For many years one method used against termite infestation has been to treat the soil around the building with pesticides. This method is still used, although there have been changes in recent years. The old chemicals were extremely toxic to termites, but also to humans, so different chemicals are coming on line, but with less effectiveness. Research continues, and procedures and chemicals are in a constant state of flux. Any of this work must now be done by trained and licensed personnel, and you can obtain details from your local exterminating or pest control company.

Another measure of termite control that used to be popular was the installation of metal termite shields between the foundation top and the sill or plate. This system has fallen into disfavor for two major reasons. First, the shielding systems often were not properly installed, and later deteriorated or were damaged and left unrepaired, which all could lead to more damage than they might have prevented. Second, the shielding system afforded the building occupants a false sense of security. The shield will not prevent termites from entering the structure. It merely forces them to tube out and over it where they can be seen. However, with regular inspections, regular maintenance, and correct installation with the proper methods and materials, termite shields do constitute another useful weapon against a tireless enemy.

Termite shields are best made of copper, about 24 gauge or better, but can also be made of galvanized iron, aluminum, or sheet zinc. Seams should be soldered, but can be overlapped substantially, caulked or tarred, and pop-riveted together. On a continuous-wall foundation place the shield directly on top of the wall, followed by sill seal and the sill or plate. The shield should cover the entire foundation top and extend outward for about 2 inches and downward at about a 45-degree angle, to the exterior for full basements and to both exterior and interior for crawl spaces. Handle piers in the same way, with the shield extending out and down on all sides. Seal all holes in the shield, such as to admit passage of anchor bolts, tightly with roofing compound or caulk.

Don't give the little bandits a toehold anywhere—if you do, they'll find it, and you can count on that!

Index

Other Bestsellers From TAB

☐ **INCREASE ITS WORTH: 101 WAYS TO MAXIMIZE THE VALUE OF YOUR HOME—Jonathan Erickson**

This book is a resource of home improvement ideas that will make your home more pleasant to live in now, and more attractive to potential buyers when you place it on the market. The author profiles the three basic types of home buyers, defines the factors that affect resale value, explains two basic methods of determining your home's resale value, devotes separate chapters to the three rooms that play the biggest role in deciding the value of a home—the kitchen, the bathroom, and the master bedroom, and makes utility systems understandable to the layman. 208 pp., 105 illus.

Paper $14.95   **Hard $23.95**
Book No. 3073

☐ **KEEP ITS WORTH: SOLVING THE MOST COMMON BUILDING PROBLEMS—Joseph V. Scaduto and Michael J. Scaduto**

his book outlines how to identify, remedy, and prevent the building problems owners are most often concerned about: wet basements, roof leaks, decay and wood-boring insects, energy maintenance, maintaining mechanical systems, and hazards. 304 pp., 271 illus.

Paper $16.95   **Hard $25.95**
Book No. 2961

☐ **DREAM HOMES: 66 PLANS TO MAKE YOUR DREAMS COME TRUE—Jerold L. Axelrod**

If you are planning on—or just dreaming of—building a new home, you will find this book completely fascinating. Compiled by a well-known architect whose home designs have been featured regularly in the syndicated "House of the Week" and *Home* magazine, this beautifully bound volume presents one of the finest collections of luxury home designs ever assembled in a single volume! 86 pp., 201 illus., 8 1/2″ × 11″, 20 pp. of full-color illus.

Paper $16.95   **Hard $29.95**
Book No. 2829

☐ **HOW TO PLAN, CONTRACT AND BUILD YOUR OWN HOME—Richard M. Scutella and Dave Heberle, Illustrations by Jay Marcinowski**

After consulting the expert information, instruction, and advice in this guide, you'll have the basic understanding of house construction that you need to get involved in all the planning and construction particulars and pre-construction choices entailed in building your home. Best of all, by learning how to make these decisions yourself, you can make choices to your advantage . . . not the builder's. 440 pp., 299 illus.

Paper $15.95   **Hard $19.95**
Book No. 2806

☐ **WOOD FRAME HOUSEBUILDING—AN ILLUSTRATED GUIDE—Bette Galman Wahlfeldt**

This comprehensive manual is an excellent resource as well as a step-by-step guide! Presents an overview of the many aspects involved in building a house—from choosing a site, materials, and a floor plan to insulating, heating, and adding the finishing touches! This book gives practical ideas and down-to-earth solutions for getting you "back to the basics" of housebuilding. 288 pp., 300 illus.

Paper $14.95   **Hard $21.95**
Book No. 3005

☐ **THE BUILDER'S EXPERIENCE—32 STEPS TO A COMPLETE LOG HOME—Gerald A. Felch**

This book relates the personal experiences of an average American family who moved to a remote piece of land and built, by hand, their own log cabin. The book describes the step-by-step approach the Felch family—with no special skills or previous home-building experience—used to build their self-designed log home. From start to finish they constructed it completely by themselves using only a minimum of tools. 60 pp., 101 illus.

Paper $10.95   **Hard $17.95**
Book No. 2935

☐ **SUNSPACES—HOME ADDITIONS FOR YEAR-ROUND NATURAL LIVING—John Mauldin, Photography by John H. Mauldin and Juan L. Espinosa**

Have you been thinking of enclosing your porch to increase your living space? Want to add a family room, but want the best use of the space for the money? Do you want information on solar energy and ideas on how you can make it work in your home? If "yes" is your answer to any of these questions, you'll want to own this fascinating guide! 256 pp., 179 illus.

Paper $14.95   **Hard $21.95**
Book No. 2816

☐ **THE BUILDING PLAN BOOK: Complete Plans for 21 Affordable Homes—Ernie Bryant**

Here, in one impressive, well-illustrated volume, are complete building plans for a total of 21 custom-designed homes offering a full range of styles and features—efficiency dwellings, ranches, capes, two-story homes, split-levels, even duplexes. It's a collection of practical, good-looking home designs that not only offer comfort, convenience, and charm but can also be built at a reasonable cost. 252 pp., 311 illus., 8 1/2″ × 11″.

Paper $14.95   **Hard $24.95**
Book No. 2714

Other Bestsellers From TAB